Off the Beaten Track
NORTHERN
FRANCE

Tony Astle • Michael Dean • Barbara Mandell
Richard Sale • Paul Scola • Christopher Turner

MOORLAND PUBLISHING

The Globe Pequot Press

Published by:
Moorland Publishing Co Ltd,
Moor Farm Road West, Ashbourne,
Derbyshire, DE6 1HD England

ISBN 0 86190 493 1 (UK)

The Globe Pequot Press,
6 Business Park Road,
PO Box 833, Old Saybrook,
Connecticut 06475-0833

ISBN 1-56440-457-9 (USA)

© Moorland Publishing Co Ltd 1994

Note on Maps

The maps for each chapter, while comprehensive, are not designed to be used as route maps, but to locate the main towns, villages and places of interest.

Cover photograph:
Azay-le-Rideau, The Loire
(International Photobank)

Black and white illustrations have been supplied as follows:

T. Astle; M. Collins; French Government Tourist Office; M. Gray; Hoseasons Holidays Abroad Ltd; B. Mandell; R. Sale; P. Scola; C. Turner.

Colour illustrations have been supplied as follows:

T. Astle (Bavoy, Felleries, La Rochepot); M. Collins (River Orne, Crèvecoeur-en-Auge, Carteret, Kaysersberg); Comité du Tourisme (St Chartier); Comité du Tourisme-Finistère (Guilvinec); M. Gray (Allouville-Bellefosse, Abbaye de la Grande Trappe, Rouffach, Colmar); Hoseasons Holidays Abroad Ltd (Rennes, Rochefort-en-Terre, Malicorne, Angers, Segré); R. Sale (Chinon, Touraine, Le Mougau); P. Tavener (Solesmes Abbey, Le Mans).

Origination by:
P & W Graphics Pte Ltd., Singapore

Printed by:
Wing King Tong Co. Ltd., Hong Kong

MPC Production Team:
Editorial: Tonya Monk
Design: Ashley Emery
Cartography: Alastair Morrison
Typesetting & Editorial
    Assistant: Christine Haines

British Library Cataloguing in Publication Data:
A catalogue record for this book is available from the British Library.

Library of Congress Cataloging-in-Publication Data
    Off the beaten track. Northern France/Tony Astle...[et al.].
        p. cm.
    Includes index.
    ISBN 1-56440-457-9
    1. France, Northern—Guidebooks.   I. Astle, Tony. II. Title: Northern France
DC601.3.044   1994
914.4'04839 — dc20
                                                    93-47308
                                                        CIP

Contents

Introduction

Western Europe is a continent of great diversity, well visited by travellers from other parts of the globe and inhabitants of its own member countries. Throughout the year and particularly during the holiday season, there is a great interchange of nationalities as one country's familiar attractions are left behind for those of another.

The sharing of cultures brings us closer in all senses to our neighbours. Yet essential differences do exist, differences which lure us abroad on our annual migrations in search of fresh sights and the discovery of unknown landscapes and people.

Countless resorts have evolved for those who simply crave sun, sea and the reassuring press of humanity. There are, too, established tourist 'sights' with which a country or region has become associated and which the manifestations of mass tourism exploit. This is by no means typical of all well known tourist attractions, but is familiar enough to act as a disincentive for those of more independent spirit who value personal discovery above prescribed experience.

It is for such travellers that this guidebook has been written. In its pages, no more than passing mention is made of the famous and the well documented. Instead, the reader is taken if not to unknown then to relatively unvisited places — literally 'off the beaten track'.

Through the specialist knowledge of the authors, visitors using this guidebook are assured of gaining insights into the country's heartland whose heritage lies untouched by the tourist industry.

From wild, scantily populated countryside whose footpaths and byways are best navigated by careful map reading, to negotiating the side streets of towns and cities, travelling 'off the beaten track' can be rather more demanding than following in the footsteps of countless thousands before you. The way may be less clear, more adventurous and individualistic, but opportunities do emerge for real discovery. With greater emphasis on exploring 'off the beaten track', the essence of Northern France is more likely to be unearthed and its true flavours relished to the full.

Tonya Monk
Series Editor

1 • Paris
Gateway to France

Some may be surprised to learn that Paris has much to offer those wishing to get off the beaten track. Surely, this great city, with its world-famous tourist sights, has managed to keep few worthwhile secrets from the enthusiastic visitor. Prepare to be surprised. Apparently, strangers to Paris stay there, on average, less than three nights and, as might be expected, spend practically all their time exploring the star attractions, often by motor coach. As most Parisian monuments and public buildings are fronted by great open spaces, it is rarely apparent that a quiet, leafy square, or a medieval street, for example, may be located a relatively short distance away.

Until the mid-nineteenth century, most of Paris comprised narrow, winding thoroughfares. True, the Grands Boulevards had already been laid out along the route of the former city wall, and the 2 mile (3km) long Avenue des Champs Elysées had existed for about two hundred years, but most churches, including Notre Dame itself, were partly hidden from view by picturesque, ancient structures, which huddled against their walls. A devastating outbreak of cholera in 1832 led to the construction of a completely new sewage system for the city and, shortly afterwards, the re-development of one-third of Paris was instigated by Napoleon III, under the direction of his planner, Baron Haussmann. Virtually all of Haussmann's work took the form of seven-storey apartment blocks, with minimal individuality, laid out along dead straight, tree-lined boulevards; architectural interest was not a prerequisite. It is the failure to identify, and avoid these 'Haussmannized' sectors which is the chief cause of some visitors' dissatisfaction with the city. The following suggestions, therefore, will keep clear of them, and introduce the reader to a Paris of human scale and architectural charm, much of it hidden away and little-known, even to the majority of Parisians.

7

Ile de la Cité and Ile St Louis

Dominated by Notre Dame, the Ile de la Cité (City Island), the historic core of Paris, suffered grievously at the hands of Haussmann, who spared little, apart from the cathedral and the major buildings that had comprised the Palais de la Cité, the residence of the medieval French kings. In the early nineteenth century, there were more than one hundred narrow, winding streets on the island and it has been estimated that around 25,000 residents lost their houses when these were demolished. Comparisons with the City of London, once similarly densely populated, but now virtually devoid of life after the office workers have departed, are inevitable.

The island is shaped like a narrow boat, and it is only at its 'prow' and 'stern' ends that vestiges of the quarter's earlier appearance have survived. The west end of the island is conveniently explored following a visit to the **Conciergerie**, where Marie-Antoinette's prison cell has survived. A short distance westward from its exit, lying off Quai de L'Horloge, Place de Dauphine is a triangular development of houses built around a small green. It was begun in 1607, immediately following the completion of the Pont Neuf, and is contemporary with the more famous Place des Vosges. When built, houses stood on all three sides, but the east range was demolished in 1874 for the new west façade of the Palais de Justice. All the buildings were originally built of rose brick with stone trims, but most have been altered. Number 14, on the north side, gives the best idea of how the Place looked when it was built. At number 25, the **Henri IV Hotel** is the only hotel on the Ile de la Cité. For many years it has been renowned for the cheapness of its rooms; facilities, however, are very basic, and there is usually a long waiting list.

The Pont Neuf crosses the island just in front of Place Dauphine and, near its centre, on **Place du Pont Neuf**, is the most popular bar on the Ile de la Cité, **Taverne Henri IV**. This closes at weekends and from mid-July to mid-August, because its patrons, the office workers and lawyers, are elsewhere. For a similar reason, its doors are always shut by 9.30pm. The liveliest period for a visit is lunchtime and early evening. Loire Valley wines are the house speciality.

In the centre of Place du Pont Neuf stands the bronze **Statue of Henri IV**. It is a nineteenth-century replacement of the original, which was melted down for cannon in 1792. Steps behind the statue descend to **Square du Vert Galant**, one of the city's most relaxing spots for a picnic on a fine day — free seats are provided. 'Vert Galant' has nothing to do with the square's green trees, but is a colloquial expression, which may be translated as old roué, and

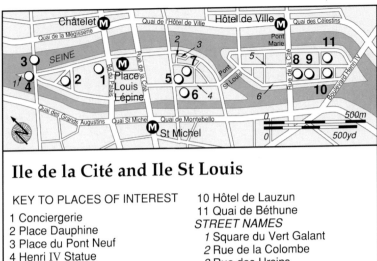

Ile de la Cité and Ile St Louis

KEY TO PLACES OF INTEREST

1 Conciergerie
2 Place Dauphine
3 Place du Pont Neuf
4 Henri IV Statue
5 Musée de Notre Dame de Paris
6 Notre Dame
7 Rue Chanoinesse
8 Berthillon
9 St Louis en l'Ile
10 Hôtel de Lauzun
11 Quai de Béthune

STREET NAMES
1 Square du Vert Galant
2 Rue de la Colombe
3 Rue des Ursins
4 Rue du Cloître Notre Dame
5 Rue St Louis en l'Ile
6 Quai d'Orléans
Ⓜ Metro Station

refers to Henri IV's liking for young ladies, even when he was advanced in years. From this square, Vedettes du Pont Neuf embark for river trips.

The eastern end of the island is easily approached from Notre Dame's north façade, skirted by **Rue du Cloître Notre Dame**. The street was laid out after the cathedral's cloister was demolished, and the houses are of little interest architecturally, however, the **Musée de Notre Dame de Paris**, at number 10, is unjustly neglected by most visitors. Roman objects found in the area are displayed, but the most impressive exhibit is the wooden screen presented to Notre Dame by Anne of Austria.

The first turning eastward, Rue Masillon, leads to the island's oldest street, **Rue Chanoinesse**, a name which commemorates its exclusive occupancy by canons until the Revolution. These houses were on the north side, with their gardens stretching down to the Seine. The south side backed the cathedral cloister. Numbers 22 and 24 are the only examples of former canon's houses to survive; both are sixteenth-century. Fortunately, the interior of number 24 has been preserved and may be inspected as it now accommodates La Lieutenance restaurant. By tradition, it was in a canon's house on the

Place de Dauphine on the Ile de la Cité

site of number 10 that Abélard stayed in 1118 when he was tutoring Héloïse, the niece of Canon Fulbert. Their romance, leading to Héloïse's pregnancy, and the emasculation of Abélard, still provides literary inspiration.

Rue de la Colombe runs northward towards the river, and displays remnants of the city's Roman wall (next to La Colombe restaurant). **Rue des Ursins**, first right, marks the earlier level of the Seine and was laid out as the first quay in Paris; its original name was Port St Landry. Ahead, it can be appreciated from Quai aux Fleurs, built on reclaimed land, how much the river level has fallen. The quay leads southward to **Pont St Louis**, the bridge that links the city's two main islands.

Happily, the **Ile St Louis** completely escaped the attentions of the wicked baron, presumably because its streets had been laid out in an acceptable grid pattern and were of reasonable width. Until 1618, in fact, there were no streets here at all; the Notre Dame chapter owned the land, and the island's prime function was to provide grazing for the canon's cows. Members of the public were not excluded, however, and it was popular with bathers, fishermen, and particularly washerwomen, who found the river breezes ideal for drying clothes. By the mid-seventeenth century, the Ile St Louis had already become a popular residential area for the aristocracy, not due to its proximity to the Ile de la Cité, but because of its easy access to the Marais, then the most fashionable residential quarter in Paris.

Although visitors may have heard of the island's charm, there are no great 'sights', and it is therefore generally given a miss, particularly when the stay in Paris is brief. Three parallel streets, two of which form quays, stretch from end to end of the island and are linked by short thoroughfares. The quays are lined by seventeenth-century mansions, all with riverside views, whilst the central street, Rue St Louis en L'Ile, serves as the island's high street. Those pressed for time are advised to concentrate on this thoroughfare and the south-facing, tree-lined quays, as the north-facing quays are not only sunless but rather spoiled by fast-flowing traffic. Pont St Louis leads directly to **Rue St Louis en l'Ile**. The only private residence of note in the first part of this shopping street is number 51, built as the Hôtel Chénizot in 1730. When the Revolution broke out, it served as the residence of Thérèse Cabarrus, Marquise de Fontenay, who was later captured at Bordeaux attempting to escape the Terror, and imprisoned. Fortunately for her, however, the charms of the Marquise had not escaped the notice of Tallien, the province's despotic ruler, who ordered her release: she became his wife. Eventually, the Marquise returned to Paris, where she gave birth to eleven children — all illegitimate.

A brief northward detour towards **Ponte Marie** (named to honour Christophe Marie, the developer of the island, not the Virgin Mary) leads to number 1 Quai de Bourbon, **Au Franc Pinot**, an old-established bar/restaurant. The bar food is very popular, with a splendid selection of smoked meats and cheeses. In the eighteenth century, this was still a private house and the owner's daughter Cécile Reynaud gained immortality by attempting to assassinate Robespierre: she failed and was guillotined.

A return to Rue St Louis en l'Ile brings the visitor to **Berthillon**, at number 31, the city's best-loved ice cream emporium. Many come to the island from afar just to sample these wonderful ices, which miraculously retain the flavour of fresh fruits and rich chocolate. On all six approach bridges, it seems that the majority of pedestrians are dreamily licking ice cream cones; it must be the island's greatest industry! Queues can be long, but the wait is amply rewarded.

The spire of **St Louis en l'Ile**, the island's only church, rises ahead on the same side of the street, curiously pierced by circular openings; its predecessor was destroyed by lightening. The church was built at a time when the parishioners were extremely wealthy, and no expense was spared on the materials employed within. Work was

Quai d'Orléans on Ile St Louis is the most popular residential area for Parisians

begun in 1664 by the royal architect Le Vau, who was responsible for designing many of the island's buildings. Particularly noteworthy are the altarpieces of Nottingham alabaster. A plaque on one of the north aisle's columns commemorates the naming of St Louis Missouri after the patron saint of the church (the French King Louis IX).

Further eastward along the street, at number 12, Philippe Le Bon invented gas lighting in 1799. The **Hôtel de Bretonvilliers** was the island's first mansion, but only its arched entrance survives, between numbers 7 and 9. The finest mansion on the Ile St Louis, the **Hôtel Lambert**, designed by Le Vau in 1642, stands on the corner at number 2. Unfortunately, it may never be visited, and even its exterior is mostly concealed. Interiors are apparently superb and include work by Le Brun and Le Sueur — perhaps one day? Voltaire, Chopin and Delacroix are known to have visited the mansion. During World War II, allied parachutists hid from the gestapo in the building's labyrinth of cellars.

At weekends between mid-April and mid-September, it is worth visiting the north side of the island specifically to enter the **Hôtel de Lauzun**, the only mansion on the Ile St Louis open to the public. This stands near the Rue Pelletier intersection, at number 17 Quai d'Anjou, and is probably another work by Le Vau. The mansion has had many famous residents, which include: Antonin Duc de Lauzun, leader of the French troops at the battle of the Boyne, Beaudelaire, Rilke, Walter Sickert and Wagner. Since 1928, the City of Paris has owned the property and it is kept in superb condition. Noteworthy externally are the gilded dolphin drainpipes, but it is the interior which is outstanding. When the mansion was built, the River Seine flooded regularly and the ground-floor rooms, therefore, are unspectacular. Most of the decor of the upper floors appears to predate the Louis XIV period, in which it was infact, executed; this applies particularly to the painted beams and frescos. The most spectacular rooms are on the second floor, where some of the finest Baroque domestic interiors in Paris are to be found. The Music Room incorporates a gilded musician's gallery and served as the venue for a reception held for Elizabeth II in 1957.

Quai de Béthune and Quai d'Orléans form the island's southern thoroughfare, and are most sought-after addresses for wealthy Parisians. The **Quai de Béthune** was originally called Quai des Balcons, because, at the instigation of Le Vau, the houses on the island overlooking the river were given balconies, then an innovation in the capital; Beaudelaire lived at number 22. Superb views of Notre Dame are obtained from the west end of **Quai d'Orléans**, framed by trees.

Montmartre

Practically all visitors to Paris visit Montmartre at some time, but few explore much of the quarter apart from Place du Tertre, where the very commercial painters operate, and the white, sugary Sacré Coeur church, which surveys the capital from its hilltop position. It is best to begin a visit at Abbesses metro station, Montmartre's most convenient approach by far, thereby avoiding a steep climb uphill.

Follow Rue Yvonne Le Tac eastward to the **Chapelle des Auxiliatrices**, the crypt of which is open Saturdays and Sundays. It is believed that this late nineteenth-century building marks the site of St Denis's martyrdom by the Romans. A church was built here over his shrine and, in its crypt, St Ignatius de Loyola and St Francis Xavier founded the Jesuit Society. Unfortunately, no trace of that church survives, it being demolished during the anti-Christian purge

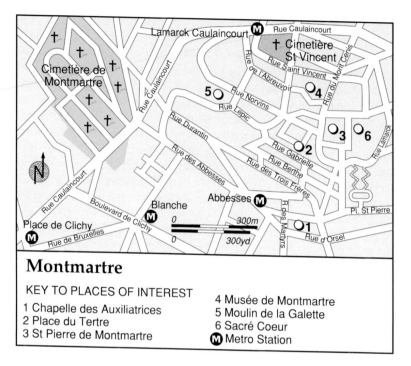

Montmartre

KEY TO PLACES OF INTEREST

1 Chapelle des Auxiliatrices
2 Place du Tertre
3 St Pierre de Montmartre

4 Musée de Montmartre
5 Moulin de la Galette
6 Sacré Coeur
Ⓜ Metro Station

of the French Revolution. Within the present chapel, a medieval carving is displayed, which depicts the saint's decapitation, together with that of his priest Rusticus and deacon Eleutheria. Also of interest are an altar and side-tables, excavated nearby, which are believed to date from the seventh century. The name Montmartre records the martyrdom of the saint on the *mont* (hill).

Continue eastward from the chapel. Immediately left, **Rue des Trois Frères** winds gradually upward. Ascend the second flight of stairs (Rue Ravignan) to **Place Emile Goudeau**, an attractive square, typical of Montmartre. Until destroyed by fire in 1970, the famous Bateau Lavoir stood at number 13, regarded by many as the birthplace of modern painting. In his studio within, Pablo Picasso completed the first Cubist work, *Les Desmoiselles d'Avignon*. Other modern masters joined Picasso in the building, which gained its name Bateau because, in a strong wind, the structure swayed like a boat; Lavoir referred to its former use as a laundry.

A short climb leads to Rue Norvins, where, at the junction with Rue des Saules and Rue St Rustique, Maurice Utrillo painted what is still the best-known view of Montmartre. It is extraordinary how little has changed. Passing through **Place du Tertre**, many visitors miss the plaque on the wall of a tourist office at number 21, which records that Louis Renault built the first fuel-driven motorcar in Montmartre, completing it on 24 December 1898 — quite a Christmas gift to the world!

Rue Norvins continues from the north side of the square to Rue du Mont Cenis and the façade of **St Pierre de Montmartre**. Due to its relatively modern exterior, this, the parish church of Montmartre, is unjustly neglected by most visitors. Its history and interior, one of the oldest in the city, are, in fact, much more interesting than that of the famous Sacré Coeur. St Pierre was built in 1143 as the church of a Benedictine nunnery, but, after the nuns left in 1680, it became the parish church; Dante is alleged to have been a parishioner. Immediately within, the two monolithic columns flanking the entrance are believed to have come from a seventh-century church, which stood just to the north. Their shafts may even be Roman, as it is known that a Roman temple had previously occupied the site of that building. The original roof of the nave collapsed in 1180, and it can be seen that the walls still lean outward (do not worry, they are now buttressed). It is interesting to compare the first three arches of the nave, which are pointed Gothic, with the fourth, which is rounded Romanesque, indicating that the church was built in two distinct stages. Surprisingly, however, both arches of the chancel are pointed, and represent the earliest examples of Gothic architecture to be found in Paris. The columns of the second arch are also believed to have come from the seventh-century church nearby. The Renaissance font, in the south chapel, is one of the oldest examples to survive in the city.

Behind St Pierre, Rue du Chevalier de la Barre passes the rear of the Sacré Coeur, from where Rue de la Bonne descends the north slope of Montmartre's hill. The view of the famous church from this point is unfamiliar to most, as it is the tower, rather than the great cupola, which dominates. From this point onwards, very few tourists will be observed. Rue St Vincent, to the left, skirts the grounds of the Musée de Montmartre (no entrance from here) and the Vigne de Montmartre, Paris's only remaining vineyard, which may be glimpsed through the railings. Wine is produced here in small quantities, and distribution is virtually restricted to selected bars in Montmartre.

At the crossing with Rue des Saules, Montmartre has retained more of its former, village aspect than elsewhere — all it lacks is a windmill! Rue St Vincent continues ahead to the **Cimetière St Vincent**, in which Maurice Utrillo, the quintessential painter of the Montmartre scene, is buried. There is, however, little of interest for visitors, and most will prefer to follow Rue des Saules southward to

Rue Cortot, where, at number 12, the **Musée de Montmartre** exhibits the quarter's ephemera, together with examples of eighteenth-century Montmartre porcelain. The house was occupied, at various times, by Utrillo, Dufy and Renoir.

On leaving the museum, return to Rue des Saules and proceed southward to **Rue Lepic**, where a restaurant, surmounted by a windmill, marks the location of the open-air dance hall, **Moulin de la Galette**, immortalised by Renoir in his late-nineteenth-century painting. Much, of course, has been rebuilt and altered. Further down Rue Lepic, at number 54, Vincent Van Gogh stayed with his brother Theo, who owned the property 1886-88, as recorded by a plaque. The next street to the right leads to the wide Rue Caulaincourt, which passes over a section of the **Cimetière de Montmartre**, where many French composers and novelists are buried (steps lead down to it from the bridge). Ahead is situated the Place de Clichy metro station.

Latin Quarter

There has never been a precise definition of the 'Latin Quarter'. The term was coined by Rabelais in the sixteenth century, and refers to the area on the left bank populated by university students, then the only Parisians to use the otherwise extinct Latin language in every-day conversation. At that time, the Sorbonne college was the most important in the university, but other colleges existed, and a large sector of the left bank was referred to as L'Université. Haussmann thrust Boulevard St Germain, Rue des Ecoles and Boulevard St Michel through the quarter, and greatly widened the existing Rue St Jacques, thus destroying most of its picturesque quality. It is these wide streets, however, that visitors tend to regard as representing the Latin Quarter, and they march along them doggedly to inspect the Panthéon, St Etienne du Mont, the Musée de Cluny and the Jardin du Luxembourg. What they generally miss, however, is the unspoilt, intimate area bounded by the river, Boulevard St Michel, Boulevard St Germain and Pont au Double, which Parisians themselves now regard as the true heart of the Latin Quarter.

St Michel metro station leads the visitor directly to **Place St Michel**, with its ornate Second Empire fountain, **Fontaine St Michel**. It was here that French students bravely fought the German army as the Allies approached Paris in August 1944. Many were killed and an inscription on the fountain commemorates their heroism.

Rue de la Huchette, which runs immediately eastward from Boulevard St Michel, was originally named Rue des Rôtisseurs,

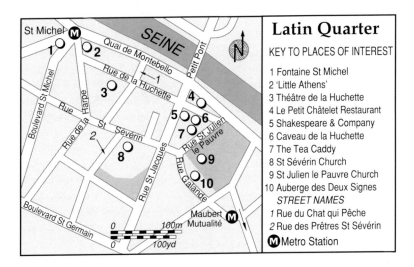

Latin Quarter

KEY TO PLACES OF INTEREST

1 Fontaine St Michel
2 'Little Athens'
3 Théâtre de la Huchette
4 Le Petit Châtelet Restaurant
5 Shakespeare & Company
6 Caveau de la Huchette
7 The Tea Caddy
8 St Sévérin Church
9 St Julien le Pauvre Church
10 Auberge des Deux Signes
    STREET NAMES
1 Rue du Chat qui Pêche
2 Rue des Prêtres St Sévérin
Ⓜ Metro Station

referring to the spit-roasting of oxen in the street during the Middle Ages; it is a strange coincidence that this tradition has been renewed within the many Greek restaurants which have earned this area the appellation **'Little Athens'**. The entry to the street was widened by Haussmann, which is why the first houses passed are nineteenth century. Fortunately, his plans to continue demolition were abandoned, and the remainder of this street is much older. **Théâtre de la Huchette**, at number 23, can only accommodate an audience of 85 and is the smallest theatre in Paris. It specializes in Ionesco's plays — always performed in French. On the opposite side of the street, number 14 dates from the seventeenth century and incorporates the monogram of its builder in the balcony's ironwork. Many of the more ancient houses of Paris are rewarding to study in detail. Look out for former street names, usually carved in stone, the earlier arrondissement number, and old trade signs. Painted on this house, between the most westerly first floor windows, a Y indicates a haberdashery.

The next street **Rue du Chat qui Pêche** leading northward, is the narrowest in Paris — just 2m (6ft) from wall to wall. It was laid out in the sixteenth century, but was then wider. Its name refers to a once prominent Fishing Cat sign on a shop. Even earlier, the street boasted a steam bath and was therefore called Rue des Etuves. The baths catered for both sexes and became virtually a brothel, thereby leading to closure in more puritanical times. Further along Rue de la Huchette, number 10 was a small hotel in 1795, and Napoléon, then a brigadier-general, lodged in one of its back rooms overlooking the Seine. His next riverside address was to be the Tuileries Palace.

The late eighteenth-century façade of an earlier house, number 4, is decorated with masks and the name á la Hure d'Or (Golden Pig's Head). **Caveau de la Huchette** (number 5) is a jazz club where 'Traditional Jazz' is the speciality. Part of the building is sixteenth century, but its cellars are alleged to have been connected with the Petit Châtelet prison nearby in the thirteenth century and provided a meeting place for the Knights Templar.

Retracing one's steps, Rue Xavier Privas, left, leads to **Rue St Sévérin**. The house with the curved corner, number 24, bears the inscription Rue Sévérin. At the Revolution, the anti-Christians insisted on the removal of 'St' from all street signs; this is a rare example to survive. Also worthy of note is the arrondissement number 18, which has since been transferred to Montmartre. Although the street is relatively narrow, it was apparently widened in 1678 and must formerly have been little more than a lane. Abbe Prevost, the author of *Manon Lascant*, the novel on which the famous opera *Manon* is based, lived at number 22. With a 2½m (8ft) wide frontage, this is one of the narrowest houses in Paris.

Return to **Rue de la Harpe**, first left. This, once the most important street in the quarter, lost two-thirds of its length when Boulevard St Michel was laid out to the south. In the tenth century, it was a Jewish ghetto, with many schools and synagogues. The present name of the thoroughfare refers to a harp-maker's premises, which once stood here displaying a large sign depicting King David playing a harp. However, the street is known to have had at least fourteen earlier names. An elegant eighteenth-century mansion, at number 35, retains in its wall the outline of a large archway through which coaches once entered. It is generally possible to view the splendid iron bannister to the courtyard's staircase.

To the north, approached via Rue de la Parcheminerie and **Rue des Prêtres St Sévérin**, lies the historic parish church of the university students, St Sévérin. The history of the church dates back to an oratory, built in the sixth century, where a pious hermit had lived, but the present building was begun in the thirteenth century. Its original main entrance, on the north side, survives, but the church is now entered from the west façade. Here, the doorway is also thirteenth century, but was brought from another church, demolished in 1839. Within St Sévérin are the only examples of fourteenth-century glass to survive in Paris; they form the upper windows of the nave's first three bays, and came from St Germain des Près. In the north aisle's third chapel, a window depicts the murder of England's Archbishop of Canterbury, Thomas à Becket, who was a student in Paris for a short time. However, the most outstanding feature of St Sévérin is the 'palm grove' vaulting at the extreme east end, behind the high altar; on request, this will be illuminated. South-west of the church, in the old graveyard, what appear to be cloisters are, in fact, ossuaries, constructed in 1500 to store the bones of dead parishioners, which could no longer be accommodated in the overcrowded graveyard.

Rue St Sévérin skirts the north side of the church, and leads eastward to **Rue St Jacques**, so-named in 1230 because it formed the commencement of the pilgrims route from Paris to the shrine of St James (Jacques) at Santiago de Compostela in Spain. This, the north end of Rue St Jacques, was widened on both sides by Haussmann, and it is only at its southern extremity that buildings of interest survive. Just before the river is reached, follow Rue de la Bûcherie and pass the small park to **Le Petit Châtelet Restaurant**, at number 39. Formerly an inn of the same name, the building dates from the early sixteenth century and its timber-framed façade is one of the most picturesque in the capital. The cellars are reputed to have been constructed in the twelfth century.

For long a Paris institution, **Shakespeare and Company** (number 37) claims to possess the largest stock of second-hand books in English on the continent; new titles are also sold. On Sundays, there are poetry readings at 8pm and, by invitation only, tea parties at 4 pm. Note the open staircase on the wall of the building next door. Only three examples survive in Paris, their use being prohibited in the seventeenth century.

Follow **Rue St Julien le Pauvre**, first right. At number 14, **The Tea Caddy**, English-style teas have been served since 1928, when the establishment was founded by Mrs Kinklin, an English governess who had served the wealthy Rothschild banking family for many years. They presented her with the premises on her retirement. Next door, number 16 dates from the fifteenth century, and is structurally built of timber, since plastered over. The entrance, carved with Justice holding the scales, was commissioned by its owner Isaac Lafémas, prefect of police under Richelieu. A three-storey basement predates the house and accommodated monks in the fourteenth century. During the Revolution it was used as a prison.

Ahead stands the delightful church of **St Julien le Pauvre**, contemporary with Notre Dame cathedral, and the oldest church built within the city walls to have survived. From Square Viviani, the

The finest views of Notre Dame are obtained from Square René Viviani

small park that fronts it, the finest views of Notre Dame are obtained; this is also a popular central Paris location for picnics. All aspects from the ancient streets around St Julien's are outstanding, and no other sector of the city matches the 'old Paris' atmosphere. Between 1208 and 1524, the church served as the assembly hall of Paris University, and it was here that rectors were elected and teachers reconfirmed the rights of students. Rioting by students, and consequent damage to the church, led to the ending of the association with the university and its members were henceforth barred from entering. The destruction was so bad that the church was forced to close: by 1651 one third of the nave had fallen into disrepair, necessitating demolition and the construction of a new west front. Eastern Christendom took over St Julien's in 1889, and since then, services have been held in Greek and Arabic. Sunday services are most appealing and all are welcome to hear the deep-pitched choral singing of the male choristers, most of whom are bearded. Roman paving slabs from Rue St Jacques are displayed beside the west façade; one is embedded in a remnant of the old city wall.

Within the church, the truncated nave and both aisles are thirteenth-century work, but the chancel was constructed 1160-80. The
arches are a mixture of rounded Romanesque and pointed Gothic,
emphasising the transitional period in which St Julien's was built.
The great wooden screen, a feature of eastern Christendom churches,
was made in 1901. Architecturally, however, the most exceptional
features of the church are the Romanesque capitals of the two chancel
columns, that on the south side being the more famous; it features
rapacious, winged harpies.

The name of **Rue Galande**, which runs south of the church,
commemorates an early thirteenth-century landowner named
Garlande. The Caveau des Oubliettes (cave of the forgotten) refers by
this name to the tradition that its cellars once formed part of the Petit
Châtelet's medieval prison. Number 65 is a sixteenth-century house
remodelled to provide apartments. Original to the façade is the
carved, garlanded head of a woman above the door. Presumably this
is a reference to the name of the street and proves that its corruption
to Galande post-dates the construction of this property. The gabled
roof is one of only thirty to survive in the capital; shortly after the
house was built such gables were prohibited by law, as rainwater
collected between them, often leaking into the ceilings below.

A voyage of discovery was made by the owner of the **Auberge des
Deux Signes**, at number 46, when he converted this former coal
merchant's premises to a restaurant. Revealed were: a huge Gothic
window with Flamboyant tracery, a remnant from the lost chapel of
St Blaise; an ancient wall; and a large thirteenth-century vaulted
room below, which is believed to have been a monks dormitory.
Attached to the wall of number 42 is a thirteenth-century carving
from the original doorway of St Julien le Pauvre. It depicts the saint
and his wife, ferrying Christ, disguised as a leper, across a river. It
may be that the bas-relief was transferred here following the partial
demolition of the nave of the church in 1651. A short distance
immediately south is the Maubert Mutualité metro station.

La Madeleine to Gare St Lazare

The rail terminal **Gare St Lazare** is situated very much in
'Haussmannland', and those leaving or approaching it on foot from
central Paris usually take Rue Tronchet or Boulevard Malesherbes,
both rather uninspired thoroughfares. However, there are two much
more attractive, almost parallel routes, both of which make the
journey seem shorter. The northern stretch of **Place de la Madeleine**,
a 'foody's' paradise, leads eastward to Rue Vignon, a street with

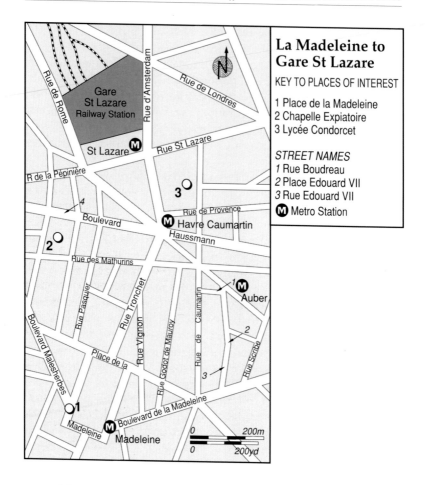

La Madeleine to Gare St Lazare

KEY TO PLACES OF INTEREST

1 Place de la Madeleine
2 Chapelle Expiatoire
3 Lycée Condorcet

STREET NAMES
1 Rue Boudreau
2 Place Edouard VII
3 Rue Edouard VII
Ⓜ Metro Station

several interesting shops. At number 21, **La Ferme St Hubert** is one of the capital's best-stocked cheese shops, with prices quite reasonable for the Madeleine area. **La Maison du Miel**, almost opposite, at number 24, is a shop where honey and honey derivatives are sold. Much of the produce comes from the beehives of the Galland family, owners since 1908, and each new season's produce is sold from late summer.

At the end of the street, only a short stretch of Rue Tronchet need be followed before turning left along Rue des Mathurins. Rue Pasquier, second right, forms the east side of **Square Louis XVI** where, in the centre, stands the **Chapelle Expiatoire**. This rather cold, neo-Classical chapel was built in 1826 by Louis XVIII, brother of the guillotined Louis XVI, in expiation of the sins of those revolutionaries who were responsible for their execution. It occupies the site of a cemetery, which was opened in 1722, attached to the convent of St Marie Madeleine. The cemetery specialised in accommodating those who had met violent deaths, as, even before the Revolution, the 133 bodies of those crushed at the fireworks display held to celebrate the wedding of Louis XVI and Marie-Antionette were interred there. Primarily, however, this was where the bodies of 1,119 victims guillotined in Place de la Concorde between August 1792 and March 1794 were buried.

A lawyer, who had been a royalist, lived in a house overlooking the cemetery, and recorded precisely where the most important burials were located. He bought the land after the cemetery was abandoned in 1797 and, following the restoration of the monarchy, was able to identify the most illustrious bodies, which included those of Louis XVI and Marie Antoinette. These were transferred to the crypt of St Denis, but most of the remainder were taken to the catacombs. After entering, via the double doors, follow the path through the garden, where stones symbolize the dead. The steps of the chapel itself are flanked by the tombs of Charlotte Corday, who assassinated Marat in his bath, and the Duc d'Orléans, cousin of the guillotined Louis XVI, who met his death in a similar way, in spite of signing the King's death warrant and proclaiming himself Philippe Egalité (Equality). Within the chapel are memorials to Marie-Antoinette and Louis XVI. The Queen is supported by a figure representing Religion, its face being a portrait of Madame Elizabeth, the Queen's sister-in-law, who was subsequently guillotined. Marie-Antoinette's last letter, written to Madame Elizabeth on the day of her execution, is inscribed below the monument.

On his memorial, Louis XVI is conducted to heaven by his confessor, in the form of an angel. Surprisingly, the King's confessor was an English Catholic, Henry Essex Edgworth. A transcript of the King's will, in which he movingly forgives his persecutors, appears at the base. Above the doorway, a carving depicts the transfer of the royal remains to St Denis Cathedral on 21 January 1815, the twenty-second anniversary of the King's execution. Steps descend to a crypt, where an altar marks the spot where Louis XVI's body had been buried. For many, this chapel, together with Marie-Antoinette's cell in the Conciergerie, is one of the most poignant reminders of the horrors of the French Revolution. How strange that it sees so few visitors.

Boulevard Haussmann runs eastward from the north side of the square, and here it is saved from the usual boredom of the nine-

This monument to Edward VII is the only statue of an Englishman in Paris

teenth-century boulevards by the two great department stores: Au Printemps and Galeries Lafayette. Au Printemps, in two blocks, is bisected by **Rue de Caumartin**, a lively, pedestrianised precinct, reminiscent of London's Carnaby Street, but with more street vendors and entertainers. It is amusingly brash, but, at its north end, one of the city's most tranquil structures calmly regards the proceedings, rather like a benign cat overseeing her mischievous kittens. Now a school, the **Lycée Condorcet**, it was built 6 years before the Revolution as a Capuchin convent, one of the last monastic structures to be erected in the capital. The splendid façade displays solidity combined with grace, which evokes Florence's Renaissance palaces. Unfortunately, the interior has been much altered.

    Rue St Lazare links the north end of the street with Gare St Lazare. Proceed southward, however, and cross Boulevard Haussmann, still following Rue de Caumartin. **Rue Boudreau**, second left, begins a succession of short streets and squares, which are a rare example of intimate city planning in the present century. Curved archways and colonnades give a neo-Baroque feel to the quarter, reminiscent of London's Sicilian Avenue, with which it is roughly contemporary. Square de l'Opéra Louis Jouvet incorporates the façade of Théâtre Athénée. From this square **Rue Edouard VII** and **Place Edouard VII**

are named to commemorate the British monarch, who spent much of his leisure time in Paris and was instrumental in forging the entente cordiale between England and France, particularly during the state visit of 1910. In the centre stands the kings equestrian statue, the only public monument to an Englishman in Paris. The sequence ends at Boulevard des Capucines, which leads south-westward to the Madeleine metro station.

L'Odéon

On both sides of Boulevard St Germain, around Place de l'Odéon, the small courtyards and narrow streets are well away from the tourist beat as, once again, there are no great 'sights' that *have* to be seen. Nevertheless, some of the city's most venerable buildings have survived in this quarter, most of them hidden away; none are in a thoroughfare of great importance.

Just west of the Odéon metro station exit, in the centre of **Place Henri Mondor**, rises the monument to the Revolutionary leader Danton, 1739-94. His house, where he was arrested on Robespierre's orders, stood precisely on the spot. George Jacques Danton is a popular subject for films, and is generally played by a handsome actor; the portly reality surprises many. The entrance to **Cour du Commerce St André** faces the statue, on the south side of the boulevard. Formerly, a wide ditch around the Paris wall passed here, on which a tennis court had been laid out. Its redevelopment began in the late eighteenth century and this picturesque courtyard was opened in 1776. At number 8, Marat published **L'Ami du Peuple**, in which he insisted that over a quarter of a million members of the ruling class should be guillotined. This fanatical demand led to his assassination by Charlotte Corday. Opposite the **Relais Odéon** brasserie was founded in 1900, and retains much of the period's Belle Epoque decor. The basement level of a circular tower in the city wall, part of the Port de Buci, has survived within the last of the terrace of houses on the east side.

The first turning right, **Cour de Rohan**, comprises a succession of spaces which once formed the internal courtyards of the fifteenth-century town house of the bishops of Rouen (corrupted to Rohan). A rural appearance prevails. and it is hard to comprehend that the bustle of the boulevards is only a few yards away. Dr Joseph-Ignace Guillotine is believed to have lived at number 9, immediately left, and experimented on sheep in this courtyard with a prototype of his beheading machine. The doctor, who was a parliamentary deputy, insisted that his invention was philanthropic, as victims would feel

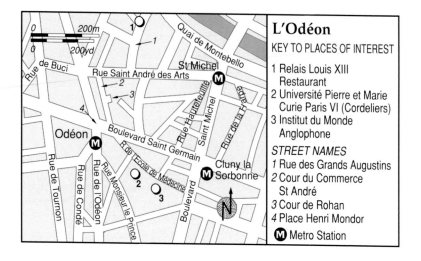

L'Odéon

KEY TO PLACES OF INTEREST

1 Relais Louis XIII
  Restaurant
2 Université Pierre et Marie
  Curie Paris VI (Cordeliers)
3 Institut du Monde
  Anglophone

STREET NAMES
1 Rue des Grands Augustins
2 Cour du Commerce
  St André
3 Cour de Rohan
4 Place Henri Mondor

Ⓜ Metro Station

only 'a slight coolness above the neck' immediately prior to their departure from this life. Nothing survives of the bishops' house, but, in the second courtyard, the creeper-covered building on the north side, left, has a Renaissance façade of brick and stone, whilst opposite stands the former residence of Diane de Poitiers, mistress of Henri II. A well and pulley survive in the third courtyard.

On returning to Cour du Commerce St André, continue northward, noting number 47, a seventeenth-century mansion, and number 45, of scant architectural interest but incorporating, on its fourth floor, the former apartment of Billand-Varenne, 'the tiger with the yellow wig', whom many believe to be guiltier than Robespierre for the sadistic excesses of the French Revolution.

Follow **Rue des Grands Augustins**, first left, to the **Relais Louis XIII Restaurant**, at number 8. Its structure, once an outbuilding, is all that survives of the Grands Augustins monastery, which, from the thirteenth century, occupied much of the quarter's riverside. Internally, exposed beams and bare stonework are genuine medieval work. Pablo Picasso lived opposite, at numbers 5-7, from 1936-1955, a period which included the German occupation of Paris. It was here that Picasso painted his famous *Guernica*, a protest against the bombing of civilians. It might have been expected that with the artist's anti-fascist views and Hitler's manic distaste for modern art, Picasso would have fled as the Germans approached the city, but he stuck it out and, apparently, suffered no persecution from the gestapo. Hitler possibly feared that an attack on a figure of such international renown would have repercussions in neutral countries, which, initially, included the USA. The mansion was remodelled in the seventeenth century, but it had been the property of Louis XII in the fifteenth century, and Francois I, the 'Renaissance King', lived here as a child. It is now the responsibility of the State, and its job includes maintaining the outstanding series of tapestries and frescos within, depicting the labours of Hercules.

Return to Rue Saint André des Arts and proceed eastward to Place St Michel. Running southward, parallel with Boulevard St Michel, **Rue Hautefeuille** possesses, at number 5, one of the city's most picturesque properties, the sixteenth-century town house of the abbots of Fécamp. Its turret, with a conical roof, is supported by an intricately carved corbel.

Rue de l'Ecole de Médecine, fourth left, retains, at number 5, the late seventeenth-century lecture hall of the College of Surgeons, now the **Institut du Monde Anglophone**. The carved portal is one of the most sumptuous in Paris. Returning westward, the **Université Pierre et Marie Curie, Paris VI**, is still known as the Cordeliers, from the Franciscan convent of that Order which stood here until the seventeenth century. Fortunately, still occupying the south-east corner of the courtyard, is a picturesque remnant of the monastery, a multipurpose block, built around 1370 in Flamboyant Gothic style. The refectory occupied the ground floor, the novices dormitory the first floor, and the attic served as a granary. No charge is made to enter the courtyard and view the exterior but, as is general in Paris, it is necessary to pay an admission charge to enter the building when exhibitions are held. The street meets Boulevard St Germain ahead, where, slightly further west, is the Odéon metro station.

North-West Marais

The Arc de Triomphe is not the only important archway in Paris. Two further examples, although not so large, are much older and, overall, of a much higher artistic standard. Both were built to commemorate the victorious Rhine campaigns of Louis XIV and are easily reached from Strasbourg St Denis metro station. The most impressive, **Porte St Denis**, was erected around 1674 as a gateway in the city wall, the route of which was soon to be followed by the Grands Boulevards. Francois Blondel based his design on the Arch of Titus in Rome, but, at 25m (81ft) high, it is very much larger. Carvings similarly followed the antique style, being inspired by sculptures in the Roman Forum. It was on this arch that Louis XIV was first publicly described, in Latin, as Ludovico Magno (Louis the Great). The south side shows the King leading his troops across the Rhine in 1672. At the base of

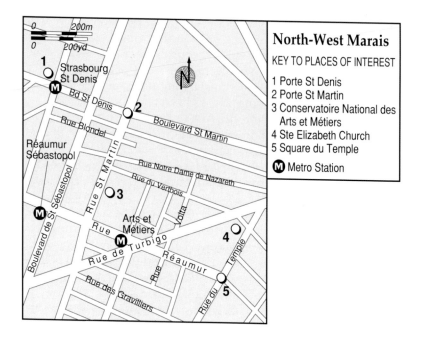

North-West Marais

KEY TO PLACES OF INTEREST

1 Porte St Denis
2 Porte St Martin
3 Conservatoire National des
   Arts et Métiers
4 Ste Elizabeth Church
5 Square du Temple

Ⓜ Metro Station

the obelisks, allegorical figures represent the conquered Netherlands and the Rhine. Above the arch, on the north side, is depicted the
capture of Maastricht in 1673.

Just south of Porte St Denis, the short Rue Blondel is a red-light
district. A few blocks eastward, **Porte St Martin** straddles Rue St
Martin. This arch is not so impressive as Porte St Denis, being 8m
(25ft) shorter, but the battle scenes are of interest, victories at Limburg
and over the German army are commemorated, and, on the south
side Besançon and the defeat of the triple alliance.

Follow Rue St Martin southward to the corner of **Rue du Vertbois**,
where the circular watch-tower was built, around 1273, as part of the
wall of the St Martin des Champs priory. Both the tower and the
adjacent **Fontaine de Vertbois**, erected in the eighteenth century,
were restored in 1886. A section of the monastery's wall has survived, best appreciated from number 72 Rue du Vertbois. The priory
buildings which remain, now form part of the **Conservatoire National des Arts et Métiers**, and are approached from number 292 Rue
St Martin. Not to be missed is the library, formerly the monastic
refectory, which is open, surprisingly, free of charge (see Further
Information). This incredibly well-preserved hall is one of the most
beautiful buildings in the High Gothic style to be found in France; the

writer Ian Nairn once described its architecture as the most thrilling in Paris. It was built in the thirteenth century, and may have been the work of the great Pierre Montreuil. Everything is light and graceful, from the slender columns, which divide the hall into aisles, to the lancet windows and cross-ribbed vaulting. Pulpits first made their appearance in monastic refectories, not churches; they were of stone and a superb example, with stiff-leaf decoration, is fixed to the east end of the north wall. Visitors are permitted to ascend its pierced staircase (no more than three at a time). A doorway in the south wall once led to the cloister, which stood between the refectory and the church; now, only the wall of the library survives from that cloister, the remainder having been demolished. Rich carving on the wall is original thirteenth-century work and, once again, in extremely fine condition.

The former church of St Martin des Champs, a short distance to the south, has been converted to a science museum. Exhibits of greatest interest are the early forms of transport displayed in the thirteenth-century nave, which just pre-dates that of St Denis Cathedral. The exterior of the chancel was built in Romanesque style, around 1130, but insensitive nineteenth-century restoration has left little original work. Also dating from the nineteenth century are the timber roof and the rather garish decoration. Where the steps descend at the end of the nave, the vaulting immediately above is the earliest cross-rib example in Paris. It is interesting to note the transition between Romanesque and Gothic within the chancel, the exuberantly-carved capitals of the columns in the former style contrasting with the pointed arches of the latter. The museum was founded during the Revolution by an engineer, who bequeathed his collection of scientific items to the state in 1783. Few monastic churches were demolished by the Revolutionaries, who preferred to use the structures for other purposes. Model trains and antique timepieces attract schoolboys, and the exhibition continues in the adjacent building.

Rue Réaumur is the next street leading eastward from Rue St Martin. At number 3 Rue Volta (second right) stands the oldest house in Paris. It is believed to have been built for the Maire (Mayor) of the St Martin des Champs district in the late thirteenth century. The exposed woodwork of the façade is little changed, but the house originally had a pointed gable, since replaced by the present sloping roof incorporating dormer windows. Return northward to Rue Réaumur and follow the street to its east end at **Square du Temple**. This square marks the site of the Knight's Templar's late twelfth-century European headquarters, where members of the Royal family

Porte St Martin, a mini Arc de Triomphe, was erected to celebrate Louis XIV's victories

were imprisoned at the Revolution. The Order had been suppressed in 1307 by Philippe le Bel, all Templars being arrested in a single day as punishment for providing refuge to fugitives from the King. Although most of the monastic complex had been demolished, its circular keep, the Tour du Temple, built in 1265, had survived, and accommodated Louis XVI and his family following their arrest in August 1792. The King was led to Place de la Concorde for execution directly from the tower five months later, but Marie-Antoinette and Madame Elizabeth, the King's sister, were transferred to the Conciergerie before meeting a similar fate. Madame Royale, the King's daughter, miraculously survived the Terror, but it is still uncertain what became of her young brother, the titular Louis XVII. Napoléon, fearing that the tower would become a rallying point for supporters of the royal dynasty, ordered its demolition in 1808. The site then became an open-air market, but acquired its present appearance in the mid-nineteenth century.

Rue du Temple runs northward from the square. At number 195, Ste Elizabeth, in Italian Baroque style, displays late sixteenth-century Flemish reliefs, some of the finest wood carving in Paris. Depicting 100 biblical scenes they were fixed against the east wall of the church in 1845. Originally, these carvings had decorated the stalls of the abbey church of St Vaast at Arras. Brass plates identify the scenes: Old Testament below, New Testament above; they will be illuminated on request. Also of interest is a painting which depicts the poignant scene of Louis XVI bidding his family farewell in The Temple on the day of his execution. It is hung in the south-east corner of the nave.

Rue du Temple continues northward to the République metro station.

Passy

The riverside sector of Passy, the capital's most westerly quarter, has retained a country atmosphere reminiscent of London's Hampstead.

From Passy metro station, steps descend, rather steeply, to Square de l'Alboni which is connected by Rue des Eaux with **Square Charles Dickens**. It is pleasant for English visitors to find their great Victorian author honoured in this way. At numbers 5-7, the **Musée du Vin** occupies the cellars of Passy Abbey, which was built in the thirteenth and fourteenth centuries; they are all that remains of the great monastic establishment. During the Middle Ages, the monks distributed wine for sale throughout Paris, which they produced from vines grown on Passy's riverside slopes. Exhibits include ancient grape presses and bottles; wine tastings are held from time to time. A limited-menu bistro is attached to the premises, and the establishment opens at mid-day except on Mondays.

From Rue Charles Dickens, right of the exit, a gateway appears to guard private property, but the path is, in fact, public and leads to Avenue Marcel Proust. Steps ascend to **Rue Raynouard**, where at, number 47, is the **Maison de Balzac** occupied by the French novelist Honoré de Balzac from 1840-47. It was here that he wrote *La Comédie Humaine*, probably his best-known work. Memorabilia displayed includes caricatures and original manuscripts. An immense bust of Balzac stands in the garden.

Continuing westward along the street, number 66 marks the site of the **Hôtel de Valentinois**, which served as the Paris residence of Benjamin Franklin who, from the mansion, negotiated with the representation of Louis XVI the alliance between France and the newly-independent American states. It is recorded that Franklin erected the first lightning conductor in Paris at the house. Unfortunately, nothing has survived of the building.

Steps, left, lead to **Rue Berton**, possibly the most bucolic of the capital's streets. Creepers adorn most of the houses, and nineteenth-century street furniture has been retained. It is worth exploring the length of this charming street before returning westward to Avenue de Lamballe. Steps immediately ahead descend to Rue du Docteur

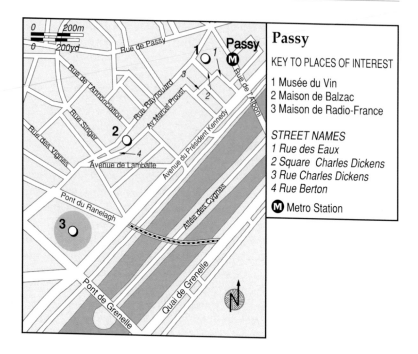

Germain See and, first right, Avenue du Président Kennedy.

After the 'villagey' streets just passed it is a surprise to come across the immense Radio-France building, built over five acres in 1963, and the country's largest single unit of construction. Guided tours are given from time to time and include a museum, which describes the progress of communications from Roman times. Vintage radio and television sets will evoke nostalgia in the over-fifties. Exhibits include the original telegram sent by Marconi in 1899, the first to cross the English Channel.

Cross Avenue Président Kennedy to the river and proceed westward. Rue Maurice Bourdet, first left, leads to **Pont de Grenelle**. From the bridge can be seen an object that might induce homesickness in all American citizens, New Yorkers in particular — a scaled-down Statue of Liberty. The statue is best approached from the bridge's ramp, which leads to the small island on which it stands. Americans resident in Paris commissioned the work, which was restored in 1986 to mark the centenary of the original; this, similarly, had been made in France to celebrate American-French amity.

Further Information
— Paris —

Museums and Other Places of Interest

Ile de la Cité
Conciergerie
1 Quai de l'Horloge
Open: June-August 9.30-6.30pm. April,
May, September 9.30-6pm. October-
March 10.00-4.30pm.

Musée de Notre Dame de Paris
10 Rue du Cloître Notre Dame
Open: at weekends and on Wednesdays 2.30-6pm.

Ile St Louis
Hôtel de Lauzun
17 Quai d'Anjou
Near the Rue Pelletier intersection
Open: mid-April to mid-September on
Saturday and Sunday. Free admission
Sunday.

Latin Quarter
St Séverin (church)
1 Rue des Prêtres
Open: Monday to Saturday 11am-
7.30pm. Also Friday and Saturday
9.30am-10.30pm. Sunday 9am-8pm.

Shakespeare and Company
37 Rue de la Bûcherie
Open: daily 12noon-12midnight,
including Christmas Day!

St Julien le Pauvre (church)
Open: daily 9am-1pm and 2.30-6pm.

La Madeleine to Gare St Lazare
Chapelle Expiatoire
Open: daily 10am-5.45pm. Closes at 6pm
October to March. Admission charge.

Montmartre
Chapelle des Auxiliatrices
11 Rue Yvonne Le Tac
Open: crypt Saturday and Sunday
9am-7pm.

Musée de Montmartre
12 Rue Cortot
Open: Tuesday to Saturday 2.30-6pm
and Sunday 11am-6pm.

North-West Marais
Conservatoire National des Arts et Métiers
292 Rue St Martin
Library open: Monday to Friday 1-
7pm, Saturday 9am-7pm, Sunday
9.30am-12noon. Closed August.

L'Odéon
*Université Pierre et Marie Curie, Paris VI
(Cordeliers)*
Open: daily 10am-7pm. Courtyard free.

Passy
Musée du Vin
5-7 Square Charles Dickens
Opens at mid-day except on Mondays.

La Maison de Balzac
47 Rue Raynouard
Open: Tuesday to Sunday 10am-5.10pm.
No admission charge on Sundays.

Maison de Radio-France
Guided tours from time to time.
Includes a museum.

2 • Pays du Nord

This flat or gently-undulating area of north-east France does not always reveal its charms at first sight. Too many visitors 'write if off' too readily: whether lured by southern sun and wine, or deterred from lingering by its undramatic scenery or relics of old, decaying industry, they either raid the supermarkets of the Channel ports and dash home with their spoils, or make use of some of the excellent roads to rush through the region as speedily as they can.

And yet the Pays du Nord is an area well worth exploring for its own sake. It has enough pleasant scenery for an enjoyable prolonged stay, not to mention a wealth of culture and history. The area of French Flanders, in the far north-east near the Belgian border, is the true *plat pays* of the Low Countries, captured with haunting sadness in the songs of Jacques Brel. Its landscape is dotted with windmills and clusters of low brick houses, studded with copses and criss-crossed with dykes; and its small towns and villages, with their brightly-painted Flemish-style buildings, and their streets lined with canals, are suggestive of Bruges or even Venice. The Boulonnais, to the west, is a stretch of chalk downland, undulating and open, which forms part of the Regional Park of the Pas de Calais. It has a coastline of fine chalk cliffs and sandy beaches called, poetically, the Opal Coast, and, inland, a landscape of rounded hills and wooded valleys reminiscent of Kent or Sussex in England.

Further south, the open agricultural land of Artois and Picardy is broken by the lush, flowery valleys of the rivers Canche, Authie and Somme. Popular with fishermen and bird-lovers, these valleys are attractive places for a restful holiday and centres for exploring the rich culture and history of the area, including many sites of armed conflict through the ages. Here, in this cock-pit of Europe, medieval battlefields jostle for attention with the vast graveyards of two World Wars. Towards the east and the Belgian border is France's largest industrial belt, centred on Lille. This is still the 'black country' of Zola's 'Germinal', of limited interest to the tourist, although many of its towns and villages are giving themselves a face-lift with the new

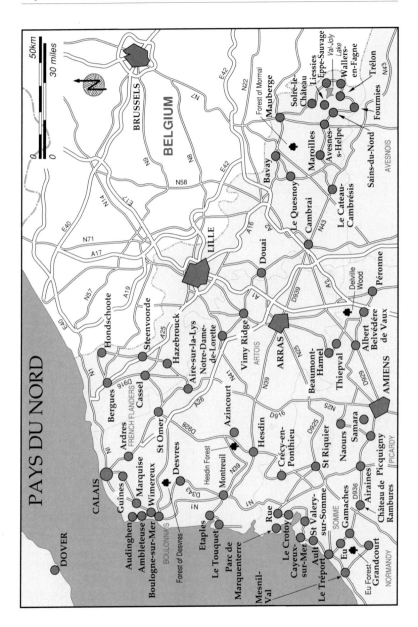

funds they are tapping in their position at the crossroads of the EEC. But south-east of Valenciennes is the Avesnois, a little-known but charming area of green fields and hedges, flowered villages, water-mills and pretty churches. Reminiscent of southern England or

Normandy, it is rich with wild flowers, lakes and woodlands, interspersed with old industrial towns and villages which offer an insight into crafts and societies that have almost disappeared.

In the Pays du Nord you are never far from reminders of the bloody history of the region. Invaders from the north and east have rampaged through this land since time began, and signs of their passage are everywhere to be found. Circuits can be made of the cities fortified by Vauban in the seventeenth century, or of the fortified churches of the Thiérache, which served the local inhabitants as places of refuge during invasions. There are grim sites of Anglo-French battles, such as Agincourt and Crécy, and happier ones where peace was made, such as Picquigny (the Hundred Years' War) and Guînes (Field of the Cloth of Gold). The fields of Flanders, Artois and Picardy are thickly-strewn with monuments and graveyards of World War I, and many other relics testify to man's inhumanity to man through the ages. The region is also rich in evidence of the region's industrial heritage, from the windmills of Flanders to the coal mines and factories of the Belgian border region.

The people of the Pays du Nord are fiercely proud of their land and sentimental about its attractions. They are in some ways a race apart from other Frenchmen, who regard them as 'honorary Belgians'. They drink beer instead of wine, have a fondness for *frites*, play darts and skittles instead of *boules*, and even keep pigeons! They cling to their folk-lore, with its numerous feast days when the famous 'Giants' appear — immense wickerwork figures representing legendary local heroes, which parade in their processions and threaten the children if they misbehave. They will eagerly tell you of the architectural splendours of the region, from the superb high Gothic cathedral at Amiens to the magnificent wide squares, lined with Flemish houses, of Arras, and the many fine belfries on their town halls. They will boast of their museums, such as the fine folk-arts and *Beaux-Arts* museums in Lille, and of their artistic traditions, such as their Flemish tapestries and paintings on wood.

The Northern table is sturdy, rich and savoury. Though fond of their *frites*, the locals prefer them as an accompaniment to rich stews such as *carbonnade flamande* (a beef stew cooked in beer), *waterzoï* (a creamy fish or chicken dish), or *lapin aux pruneaux* (rabbit stewed with prunes). Savoury tarts are popular, such as the *flamiche picarde*, a delicious leek and onion tart, the *flamiche au Maroilles*, a quiche made with the famous Avesnois cheese, or the *goyère Douaisienne*, a tart made with endives and shallots. Another rich dish is *rognons au genièvre*, kidneys cooked with gin, beer and juniper berries. A popular starter is the *ficelle picarde*, a pancake stuffed with seafood or ham and mushrooms. Fish is a speciality of the area, particularly herrings, and is often eaten pickled, or in the rich Picard fish stew called a *caudière*. Eels are popular, eaten fresh, smoked or in patés, and shellfish are widely found — mussels, shrimps, cockles and oysters. Endives and sea-fennel, or *passe-pierre*, are often eaten as vegetables.

Local cheeses, of which the best-known is Maroilles, come mainly from the lush pastures of the Avesnois or the Thiérache. They are rich, creamy and rather smelly, and sometimes pungently spiced, as in the hayrick-shaped *boulette d'Avesnes*. The chief drink is beer, brewed mainly in *brasseries* on the Belgian border near Lille and Armentières. Along with Alsace, this area is France's leading producer of beer, and a variety of types are brewed, including brown, 'white' and heavy malts. The best places to sample these are local pubs called, appropriately, *brasseries*. Beer is also widely used in cooking, as in the vegetable soup, *soupe des brasseurs*.

For the active traveller in search of outdoor pursuits, the region has much to offer. Its climate is more suited to active holidays than to lounging on a beach (though there are some fine ones on the Opal and Picardy coasts) and, though it can be hot in high summer, in other seasons rain and strong winds are not unknown. There are many miles of signed footpaths, and many horse-riding trails in the forests and along the coasts. Both sea and river fishing are popular, as are game-hunting and bird-watching. A favourite sport for the more energetic is speed-sailing and three-wheeled sail-carts on the firm sand beaches; and wind-surfing is widely practised on both sea and inland lakes. Other popular pastimes are cycling and river and canal cruising. For the motorist, even the minor roads are well surfaced, and they can quickly take you off the beaten track to explore the real France.

The Boulonnais

Visitors arriving at **Calais** should resist the temptation to join one of the motorways now encircling the city. Instead, start in the *centre ville*; and, after looking at the superb lace in the Fine Arts Museum (Musée des Beaux-Arts et de la Dentelle), the English-style Notre-Dame church and Rodin's memorial to the Burghers of Calais outside the Town Hall, take the D127 south along the canal bank to **Guînes**. This attractive road through the marshland south of Calais brings you to the edge of the Boulonnais and the regional park. This sleepy market town had its moment of glory in 1520, when two powerful kings, Henry VIII of England and François I of France, tried to outdo each other in displays of opulence while meeting here to agree a peace treaty. The meeting place, known as the 'Field of the Cloth of Gold', was just outside the town on the Ardres road, but nothing remains today to suggest the splendour of the occasion.

The forest of Guînes, to the south, is attractive walking and riding country on the edge of the downs. Its central Clearing, the 'Balloon clearing', has a marble monument known as the Blanchard Column, marking the landing place of the first man to cross the Channel in a balloon in 1786. More details of Blanchard's feat can be found in the small Emile Villez Museum in the town, and in the Cross-Channel Museum (Musée International du Transmanche) 13km (8 miles) away on the coast at **Escalles**. This depicts the 'mad adventure of the Dover Straits', telling of the many attempts to cross that treacherous stretch of water since earliest times. Between Guînes and the coast near **Landrethun-le-Nord** (10km/6 miles by the D231 and D249) is a grim reminder of World War II, especially for Londoners. The Mimoyecques Fortress was built with prisoner-of-war labour by the Germans in 1943 as a base for their V3 rockets, their new deadly weapon designed to annihilate London. It was finally destroyed by a Tallboy bomb in July 1944 after months of Allied bombardment. Today you can visit the awesome-sized fortress, 30m (98ft) under the chalk, with its 600m (1,968ft) of tunnels and its launching shafts for the rockets (guided visits with laser discs). Take a warm garment, even in summer.

Just south of here, east of Marquise, are a number of large marble quarries set in and around a complex of wooded valleys. In one of these, called the 'Happy Valley', an old quarrymen's co-operative in the village of **Hydrequent** is now a House of Marble and Geology (La Maison du Marbre et de la Géologie). This is less a museum than a series of dramatic audio-visual displays using sound and light effects: it tells of the geology, history, social life and products of the marble-quarrying industry, and of the prehistoric discoveries made in the area, including the fossilised skeleton of a large, fierce-looking amphibious reptile called a plesiosaurus. A life-sized model of this is dramatically poised in the act of seizing a hapless fish. A little further south still, in a narrow valley on the D233 east of **Wimille**, is a wonderful old water-mill, the Grisendal Mill (La Moulin de Grisendal). This is a four-storey flour-mill, still in working order, with the miller and his wife acting as guides to show you the process of flour-making and make the mill work for you. For the technically-minded, the primitive but effective mill engineering is a delight.

From here, the road west leads to the coast at the pleasantly-old-fashioned resort of **Wimereux**, while the eastward road leads up the Wimereux valley towards the extensive Forest of Boulogne, with its 13km (8 miles) of signed footpaths. The coast road north from Wimereux leads to three sites of interest to students of war. At **Ambleteuse**, sited on a rocky promontory amid the dunes, with good views of Boulogne and the English coast, is the recently-restored seventeenth-century Vauban/Mahon Fort . It has a display of old artillery in the tower, and a small museum on the sea-front. Ambleteuse also has a good World War II Museum (Musée de la Seconde Guerre Mondiale), telling the history of the war with a display of uniforms and equipment. More dramatic, 5km (3 miles) north at **Audinghen**, is a former German blockhouse or 'Todt battery' housing a Museum of the Atlantic Wall (Musée du Mur de L'Atlantique). The whole of this section of the Opal Coast is riddled with foxholes, bunkers and other fortifications from the last war — this is where Hitler thought the Allies would land, and built his defences accordingly. The blockhouse, with its structure and war equipment intact, its claustrophobic atmosphere and musty smell, evokes the feeling of war more powerfully than any normal museum.

South of Wimereux, **Boulogne-sur-Mer** has many visitors and is hardly 'off the beaten track', though its tourist industry may suffer now that the channel ferries no longer call here. It is still an attractive town and a place to visit, partly for its range of excellent sea-food restaurants to suit all pockets, and partly for its unusual museums and lovely old upper town. Its two main museums could not be more contrasting in style: in the lower town, the Nausicaà National Sea-life Centre is an ultra modern architect-designed aquarium and exhibition centre which takes you on an unforgettable underground tour of the marine world. Among its many attractions, it has a tropical coral lagoon, a diamond-shaped tuna tank, a panoramic ring-shaped shark basin, a 'tactile tank' where you can tickle skate and other fish, and an observation tank for viewing deep-sea denizens through a periscope. In contrast, the Château-Museum, impressively set inside the walls of the upper town, has a splendid collection of ancient Greek vases and other antiquities. Boulogne was the port from which Julius Caesar sailed to invade Britain, and from which Napoleon more recently planned a similar invasion — the museum contains details of this, including English cartoons ridiculing his attempt.

The quiet old walled upper town is itself a contrast with the noisy, bustling lower town, and well worth exploring before you leave Boulogne. On a hill behind the port, its medieval ramparts enclose the château, law courts, some fine old houses, narrow cobbled streets, a splendid gothic belfry, and the huge Basilica of Notre-Dame, whose enormous dome is the town's great landmark.

Leave Boulogne on the D341 and head east for Desvres. The undulating road takes you through the forest of Boulogne and skirts the forest of Desvres, the latter well worth a detour for its splendid views over the Liane valley. **Desvres** is a pottery town, with a history of the craft reaching back to the early Middle Ages; after a period of decline, it was revived in the eighteenth century and specialised in reproductions of classic styles: Delft, Moustiers, Strasbourg, Rouen and Nevers, as well as developing its own style of rustic kitchenware. Visitors are welcome at the artistic pottery works of Fourmaintraux-Dutertre, where yiu can see all the stages of production, including the hand-painting of a variety of designs (and buy good 'seconds' at knock-down prices). Then visit La Maison de la Faïence in the town, a stunning modern building constructed in huge blue and white Desvres tiles. This houses permanent and temporary exhibitions and explains, with good audio-visual aids, the origins and development of the industry, its techniques and skills. Forming a backdrop to the Centre is the 200m (656ft) high Mount Pelé, which provides pleasant walks amidst rich flora, and a fine panorama from the top.

The Picardy River Valleys

South of Desvres, the land becomes less hilly and wooded, more open and agricultural, though cut by river valleys. Take the D127 down the pretty Course valley to **Montreuil**, at the confluence of the rivers Canche and Course. This charming small town was once *sur mer* until the sea receded, leaving it impressively sited on a bluff above the river. It is completely contained within the brick ramparts built by Vauban as a defence for Louis XIV's armies; more recently, Napoleon stayed here while contemplating his invasion of England, and in World War I, Douglas Haig, commander-in-chief of the British Army, made his headquarters here. It has a lovely central square, narrow streets, an imposing seventeenth-century citadel and a grassy, wooded walk around the ramparts, with fine views of the valley below. It is also blessed with good restaurants.

West of Montreuil the Canche valley leads to the sea at Etaples, a colourful fishing port beloved of artists, and beyond to **Le Touquet-Paris-Plage**. Though hardly off the beaten track, this elegant sea and health resort is less fashionable than it was with British visitors, who virtually created it: it is now more cosmopolitan and less trendy than earlier in the century, though still smart and expensive. It consists largely of large mock-Gothic or mock-Tudor villas half-hidden in the woods, but has a stylish shopping centre, fine-arts and doll museums, and extensive sports facilities. Nearby **Etaples** has three museums, one of archaeology, one of flora and fauna, and one of the sea; and 10km (6 miles) further south, at **Merlimont**, is the large and popular Bagatelle Leisure Park (Bagatelle Parc d'Attractions), with a zoo, fun-fair, fishing lake, racing circuit and other attractions.

The Canche valley east of Montreuil becomes broad, flowery and full of small lakes renowned for fishing and fish-breeding. The D113 along its northern bank is prettier and less busy than the N39 — take this as far as Guisy, then make a detour left into the cool and tranquil Hesdin Forest, which has a 'zone of silence' in the centre (no motor vehicles or transistor radios). Emerging from this onto the D928, turn north for 10km (6 miles), then right on the D71 to **Azincourt**. This small, sleepy village has been renowned in England, cursed in France since the fateful day, 25 October 1415, when one of the bloodiest battles in history was fought here. Over 10,000 Frenchmen, many of them nobility, were slaughtered at the expense of very few English lives — one of the most ignominious defeats in French history. For many years the French chose to ignore the place, referring to it as *La Carogne* (The Slut); now it is commemorated with a monument at a nearby crossroads and a small but attractive museum (Centre Médiéval d'Azincourt) in the village square. The outline of the Agincourt battlefield is marked with flags and papier-maché figures in period costume. Returning south to Hesdin on the D123, you pass through the village of **Auchy-lès-Hesdin**, where a plaque marking the tombs of some of the French knights who fell in the battle can be seen in the abbey church (altar-table by Van Dyck).

Hesdin is a pleasant, flower-bedecked town with a wide cobbled market square, on one side of which is a town hall with a magnificently ornate seventeenth-century bay window. It has a fine belfry and, inside, a small museum (Musée Municipal) with Flemish tapestries. Leave by the D928 going south to le Boisle, a village of basketmakers, where you cross the river Authie. Turn right onto the D224 to follow the south bank of the river along the Authie Valley, a quieter, more secluded valley than the Canche. Across the river at Dompierre-sur-Authie you can see the ruins of Dommartin Abbey and, after 15km (9 miles), through a fine archway, **Valloires** Abbey (L'Abbaye et Les Jardins de Valloires) on your right. This Cistercian abbey was founded in the twelfth century and rebuilt in the eighteenth century in a harmonious blend of brick and stone. The splendid interior contains some lovely wood panelling and ironwork, while the church is rich in sculpture and ornament. The abbey gardens are well designed, with a wealth of plants.

Return to the pretty village of Argoules and turn south on the D12 and D16 to **Crécy Forest**. This, the largest forest in north Picardy, is well equipped for tourism, with marked routes for walkers, horse-riders, cyclists and motorists. Picnic places are well provided, and the keen-eyed may spot roe-deer and wild boar. On the edge of the forest is the village of **Crécy-en-Ponthieu**, again well-known to the English as the site of another famous victory, this time on 26 August 1346, when Edward III's victory over Philippe IV started the Hundred Years' War and gave England 200 years of domination over the French. On a hillock above the village is a mill-shaped observation platform, with an orientation table, giving a fine view over the wide battlefield and explaining the layout of the battle. Leaving Crécy on the D56, you will pass an old cross marking the spot where John the Blind, the old King of Bohemia, fell in battle — one of the 20,000 who died on the French side.

South of Crécy on the D12, the sleepy little town of **St Riquier** holds one of the jewels of northern-French architecture. In a square set back from the road stands a stunningly ornate flamboyant Gothic abbey church, all that remains of a once-important Benedictine monastery. The richly and delicately-carved white stone façade matches the imposing interior, which has a magnificently high and wide nave resembling that of nearby Amiens cathedral, a splendid Renaissance baptistery, seventeenth-century furnishings in the choir, and a rich treasury with mural paintings. St Riquier also has a beautiful chapel in the old hospital, a small museum of rural life (Musée Départmental) in the old abbey buildings, and a small, squat belfry in the square, quaintly housing the local Syndicat d'Initiative.

Turning north-west from St Riquier on the D32, in 26km (16 miles) you will reach **Rue**, a pleasant town near the Somme estuary. In the centre are old streets with half-timbered houses surrounding an imposing town hall with a fine fifteenth-century belfry, and nearby a small Gothic chapel of St Esprit, crumbling on the outside but with a richly-decorated interior: three finely-carved vaults to the Father, Son and Holy Spirit, and two treasury rooms, one on top of the other, with carvings of biblical scenes and a painted sculpture of the Virgin and Child. Rue was once a seaport, and is now the principal town of the Marquenterre, a broad coastal plain between the Somme and Authie estuaries. It is a wild, marshy reclaimed land of lakes and ditches, a refuge for birds and a favourite haunt of bird-watchers. At its most remote point, on the northern edge of the Somme estuary, is an Ornithological Park (Le Parc Ornithologique du Marquenterre) where in an area of 200 hectares you have a chance to view over 350 different species of wild birds in their natural setting. Two observation routes are marked out, a beginners' and a longer one among the dunes taking at least 2½ hours to walk. You should take binoculars.

The old fishing port of **Le Crotoy** looks out over the mud-flats and salt-meadows of the Somme bay towards its sister port of St Valery on the south side. To encircle the bay from here you can either take the panoramic D940, or the Somme Bay Railway, a 16km (10 mile) ride on an old train that gives you a unique view of the estuary and ends at Cayeux-sur-Mer on the coast. Much of the estuary has now silted up, and you can walk across and fish in the pools at low tide, especially for shellfish. Hunting of wild-fowl from special 'hides' is also popular. **St Valery-sur-Somme** is an attractive town in two distinct parts: the old walled upper town looks out from a bluff towards the sea, and the lower town, a colourful fishing port with a long tree-lined embankment, looks back to the estuary and river mouth. St Valery is based on an old abbey, and was the embarkation point in 1066 for William the Conqueror's invasion of England. It retains some old buildings, including two gates to the upper town, one of them named 'William Gate'. It has an interesting old church built in sandstone and flint, and a small sailors' chapel of brick and stone on a headland above the town, from where you have a fine view over the bay.

Leave St Valery by the D3 towards **Cayeux-sur-Mer**, and in 4km (2 miles) turn left for the House of Birds (La Maison de l'Oiseau). Based on a local farm, this is a museum, showplace and study centre founded by a local bird-lover and dedicated to promoting knowledge and love of bird-life. Through a series of colourful dioramas, many species of birds are shown in their natural habitat, and their origins, habits and products explained. Local wild birds are encouraged to settle by a pond behind the house and in the central courtyard. The project is still developing, and is well worth supporting. From the centre, a small side-road leads to the point of Le Hourdel, its lighthouse overlooking the mouth of the bay; and a 'white road', so-called because it is partly covered in fine white sand, runs from here through the dunes to Cayeux-sur-Mer. The road then turns inland to join the D940, and shortly a side-road turns back to the coast at **Ault**, with another wild-bird reserve in between. Neither of these seaside resorts on the Picardy coast is particularly attractive, but on entering Ault from Onival you have a fine view of the first white cliffs of the Alabaster Coast towards Le Tréport.

South of Ault is the **Bresle Valley**, which forms the boundary

The Alabaster Coast from Ault, Picardy

between Picardy and Normandy. The valley is industrial at this point, but on its southern side is some pleasant country that makes a short excursion into the Norman department of Seine-Maritime worthwhile. Cross the river on the D925 to the old town of **Eu**, which has a stylish pedestrianised centre with some good shops (excellent oysters at the fishmonger's). Eu's main attraction is its Gothic Collegiate church of Notre-Dame and St Laurent O'Toole (the Primate of Ireland who died here in the twelfth century), with its finely-proportioned interior and restored crypt full of effigies of Norman counts. Outside in the main square is a stone commemorating the fact that the future William the Conqueror married Mathilda of Flanders here in 1050. The Château belongs to the town and houses the Town Hall, public archives and the Louis-Philippe Museum (Musée Louis-Philippe), which has an extensive library and rooms decorated to the taste of the nineteenth-century 'people's monarch', who often stayed here. The College Chapel has two splendidly-sculpted seventeenth-century marble mausoleums of the Duke and Duchess of Guise.

Le Tréport, a rather drab fishing port and holiday resort 4km (2 miles) from Eu, is best appreciated from the Calvary on the chalk cliff above the town (fine views along the Alabaster Coast). From here, take the cliff-top road to **Mesnil-Val**, a much smaller and quieter resort. This and its neighbour, **Criel-sur-Mer**, have some good restaurants and camp-sites, though the beach is shingle; and the town hall at Criel is housed in the handsome sixteenth-century Briançon manor-house. Turn inland from Criel to follow the pretty chalk-banked **Yères Valley**, among typical Normandy scenery of lush fields and apple orchards, and brown-and white half-timbered granges. At **St Martin-le-Gaillard** is a thirteenth-century church with a flat-topped spire typical of the region and some quaint carved capitals inside, and a ruined feudal castle now used as a farm. Continue on the D16 as far as Grandcourt, then turn left into the **Eu Forest**. This extensive forest, famed for its beautiful beech glades, consists of three isolated massifs, with a winding road connecting them. On the south-western side near Grandcourt, a short walk from St Catherine's Post on the D149 will bring you to a good viewpoint over the peaceful Yères Valley.

A circular tour of the forest should end at Longroy, on the D49, from where you can recross the Bresle to Gamaches and back into Picardy. Take the D936 westwards and, at Le Translay, bear right on the D110 to visit the Château of **Rambures**. This striking-looking fortified medieval castle, set in a charming wooded park, is in near-perfect condition, having remained in the same family since the fifteenth century. During the Hundred Years' War it was a French enclave in the heart of territory held by the English, and its 3m (10ft)-thick brick walls withstood many a siege. The interior is sombre but impressive, with marble chimneys, good woodwork, and cellars used to shelter the villagers during invasions.

Returning to the D936 at Oisemont, continue via **Airaines**, where the twelfth-century Notre-Dame church and priory holds a Roman-esque baptismal tub with interesting sculptured figures, to **Picquigny**. This small, welcoming town, flanked by British World War I cemeteries, nestles in a particularly lush section of the Somme Valley, overlooked by an imposing ruined castle rich in history. It was here, on the island of La Trève in the middle of the Somme, that a famous peace treaty was signed on 29 August 1475 between Edward IV of England and Louis XI of France, ending the Hundred Years' War. According to the chronicler, the two kings were so suspicious of each other that they met 'like caged lions' in a specially-built hut with bars between them! The 'Peace of Picquigny' is celebrated on a stone slab in the castle. Other historic events of which the town is proud include a visit by Joan of Arc, whose *sabot* is said to have made an imprint on the cobbles at the castle gate, and a romantic meeting between Henri IV and his mistress, Gabrielle d'Estrées, on which occasion he conducted a band of violins. Though the castle (Le Château-Fort des

Sires de Picquigny) is in ruins, it is well worth a visit: its thick defensive walls, towers and arches give a strong impression of its past might; and it contains a delightful Renaissance building called the 'Sévigné Pavilion', where Madame de Sévigné stayed in the seventeenth century and described it in glowing terms to her daughter at Grignan. The thirteenth-century Collegial church of St Martin is another striking building within the castle walls.

Two kilometres (1 mile) west of Picquigny on the D3, hidden in the wooded Somme Valley, is the **Notre-Dame-du-Gard Abbey** (visits on demand ☎ 21 51 40 50: contact Gard Accueil). Founded in 1137 by the Cistercian Order, it once had Cardinal Mazarin as its abbot, but later fell into disrepair; now it has been revived as the mother house of the *Frères Auxiliaires*, a group of lay brothers who are restoring the buildings and who offer a quiet retreat with board and lodging to passing travellers. The English-speaking Brother Claude will be happy to show you round the attractive and peaceful site.

Return to Picquigny, turn left across the bridge and right at La Chaussée-Tirancourt for **Samara**. The Archéologie et Nature attraction covers 25 hectares of marshland on the north bank of the Somme, on the site of a Celtic settlement and a Roman camp. Called an 'enigma of the past, vision of the future', it combines a reconstruction of the prehistoric past with a presentation of modern flora: botanical gardens, an arboretum, pathways among the marshes and lakes. Dotted around the site are reconstructions of primitive dwellings — a hunting hut, a peat-worker's cabin, farmhouses, granaries, workshops, cellars and wells. The *pièce de résistance* is a multi-domed exhibition pavilion housing a prehistoric village, with demonstrations being held throughout the day of the life and crafts of early man. If its claims are a trifle pretentious, it provides a good day out, combining a 'living museum' with walks among lovely countryside.

Other sights of interest in the area are the châteaux of Bertangles, Long, Prouzel and Vauchelles-lès-Domart, and a number of churches, including Hangest-sur-Somme, Namps-Mesnil, Fieffes-Montrelet and Berteaucourt-les-Dames. The Somme itself is fascinating to explore, with its lakes, marshes and pretty green islets covered with market gardens, many dating from the Middle Ages. You can make a tour of some of these by boat, and panoramic views of the valley can be had at Corbie and the belvedere of Vaux, west of **Amiens**. The capital of Picardy itself is busy, modern and industrial, and not for the 'off the beaten track' visitor, that is unles you have not seen Amiens Cathedral. This is one of the architectural wonders of France, if not the world, a high-Gothic building of rare beauty and breathtaking proportions, the largest cathedral in the country and one of the purest in style. As you turn from a busy street into the cathedral square, the impact is staggering. If you do go to Amiens, you must also visit the superb Museum of Picardy (Musée de Picardie), which has a unique collection of sixteenth-century altar-paintings on wood.

Artois and Northern Picardy: The Killing Fields

The region of Artois and Picardy north of the Somme is perhaps the world's chief battlefield. In particular, the area between Amiens and Péronne in the south, and Arras and Doullens in the north, is dotted with villages whose names are all-too-familiar to students of World War I. Though souvenirs of the many battles fought here over the centuries are thick on the ground, it is as well to be selective in visiting them — the spirit can be overwhelmed by the sadness and futility of so much suffering and wasted life.

A good place to start your visit is the **Naours Caves** (Les Grottes de Naours), 16km (10 miles) north of Amiens by the N25 and D60. These are not natural grottoes but man-made, dug into the soft clay at the edge of the village by the local inhabitants as a place of refuge in time of war. Though only rediscovered in 1887, they were known about as far back as the third-century AD. The setting is charming — from the car park at the foot of a chalk cliff surrounded by woods and topped by a windmill, you climb a steep stair to a half-timbered building half-way up the cliff, through which you must go to enter the caves. Inside, the size of the operation is staggering — 26 galleries stretching for 2km (1 mile), with 300 rooms able to shelter up to 3,000 people and their livstock. There are stables, wells, open squares, food-storage rooms, a bakery with oven, a calvary and three chapels, including an odd one with three naves. The guided visit ends at the museum, which represents a typical Picard village with models of old craftsmen plying their trades: potter, blacksmith, weaver and flax-worker. Afterwards, you can climb to look at the two old wooden pivot-type windmills on the hilltop (good panoramic view over the village). There is a children's playground nearby.

From Naours the winding D60 takes you westwards towards **Albert**, a convenient centre for visiting the battlefields of the Somme. Old Albert was almost completely destroyed in that battle, but the rebuilt town is spacious and not unattractive. It has an imposing basilica with a high tower topped by a statue of the Virgin and Child, and nearby, in the town's World War II underground air-raid shelters, a Museum of the Trenches (Musée des Abris) with models depicting World War I trench warfare. Leave Albert by the D929 towards Bapaume, then turn off right at La Boisselle on the D20 to Longueval, passing many mainly British war cemeteries. Just beyond the village is **Delville Wood**, scene of one of the grimmest episodes in the Great War. Here, between 14 and 20 July 1916, the 1st South African Infantry Brigade were reduced from 3,233 to 143 men in a successful effort to hold the wood. Over this time, the Germans rained shells on them at the rate of 400 a minute, and the wood was reduced to one tree! The South African National War Memorial now stands on the spot, flanked by a cemetery of 151 graves and the beautiful Delville Wood Commemorative Museum in the form of a miniature replica of Capetown castle. This tells the ghastly story with moving visual effects. Outside the museum, in the replanted wood, you can see the one surviving tree.

Continue on the D20 to Rancourt (more British, French and German war graves) and south on the N17 to **Péronne**. This town in the middle of the battlefields has an attractive Town Hall, a smart though rebuilt centre, some of its ancient ramparts, and an exhibition on the Great War housed in its thirteenth-century castle (L'Historical de la Grande Guerre) and adjoining building. This exhibition aims to promote understanding of the war and what it meant to the people involved, by presenting a mass of evidence of the daily lives of soldiers and local civilians. The visit ends with a 'Paths of Memory' tour of local battlefields, cemeteries, trenches and memorials.

Return towards Albert on the D938 (the Vaux belvedere over the Somme and the Bronfay farm British cemetery are off to your left), then turn right on the D147 at Fricourt. At Pozières take the D73 to **Thiepval**. Here, in a space of 2km (1 mile), are three moving monuments to men who fell in World War I. The first, at Thiepval, is the British Memorial, an imposing brick and stone triumphal arch surrounded by a well-kept lawn and small wood. Visible for miles and dominating the Ancre valley, it carries the names of 73,367 British soldiers who fell in the Somme area. A little further on, to your right, is the Belfast Tower, a memorial to the dead of the Ulster division. Further on the same road, just after the hamlet of Hamel, is the **Memorial Park of Beaumont-Hamel**, perhaps the most moving and evocative of all the war monuments. In a beautiful setting, it contains the remains of trenches, with shoring, firing posts and twisted, rusty arms; and in the centre, rearing up on a 'Calvary' of large rocks, a large Caribou, memorial of the Canadian Newfoundland regiment. From the viewing platform you can view the desolate battlefield below.

Just after the village of Beaumont, take the D919 north to **Arras**.

Gallo-Roman excavations at Bavay, Pays du Nord

Wood-turning in Bois-Jolis Mill at Felleries, Pays du Nord

1,300 year-old oak at Allouville-Bellefosse, Normandy

Belfast Tower, Ulster divisions regiment memorial at Beaumont-Hamel

This town, the capital of Artois, has a dingy exterior but a glorious old centre, with its two arcaded, cobbled squares, the Grand Place and the Place des Héros, overlooked by its Gothic Town Hall and splendid belfry, surmounted by the town lion. Happily preserved from the devastations of war, this is one of the most harmonious town *ensembles* in Europe, its seventeenth-century Flemish houses with pilasters and elegant curving gables, arcaded at ground level, giving a distinctly Dutch appearance. The deep cellars under the houses were used as hiding places during the various wars. The huge Cathedral of St Vaast contains enormous statues of saints and a richly-endowed Fine Arts Museum (Musée des Beaux Arts). There is also a Fisherman's Guild building, decorated with sirens and fish, and an eighteenth-century theatre.

To the north of Arras on the Lens road is the site of one of the bloodiest World War I battles — **Vimy Ridge**. The whole of this region was the scene of particularly violent fighting both in 1915 and 1940, and the sites on the crests overlooking the town (*Les Crêtes du Sacrifice*) have been well preserved. Vimy Ridge itself has a massive memorial to the 74,000 Canadians who died in France, and below, on the wooded south slope of the ridge, original World War I trenches can still be seen. Nearby, at **Notre-Dame-de-Lorette**, is a French national cemetery and a large ossuary containing the remains of

26,000 unidentified soldiers. The ossuary houses a small museum (Musée Vivant 1914-18), and just below this desolate site, near the Cabaret Rouge cemetery outside Souchez, is an informative Museum-Diorama of the Battlefields.

East of Arras on the N50 is **Douai**, capital of the coal-mining belt and a university town. It is famous for its Gothic belfry, painted by Corot, and wickerwork Giant called *Gayant*. He is the best-known and oldest of all the northern French folk-giants, is 7½m (25ft) high and weighs 370kg, and appears on feast days with his 'family' (wife and two children) followed by a torchlight procession and firework display. Douai has some fine buildings, including an ancient Charterhouse housing a fine museum (Musée de la Chartreuse).

The Avesnois

The N43 south-east of Douai leads you towards the Avesnois, a delightful and little-known area of the Pays du Nord. The first town *en route* is **Cambrai**, the 'town of three towers' (two churches and a belfry). This was the centre of fierce fighting in 1917 and is today a busy town, known for its flax, cereals, beetroot and mint sweets. It has an old centre with houses built in white limestone, a good museum (Musée Municipal) and a Rubens in the church of St Géry. Continue via Beauvois-en-Cambresis (good restaurant) to **Le Cateau-Cambrésis**. The modern painter Matisse was born here, and a finely-staged exhibition of his paintings is housed in the former Archbishop's palace (Musée Matisse, a graceful building with pleasant gardens. Le Cateau has an old town hall with a charming bell-tower, and is the gateway to the Thièrache, a region famed for its curious fortified churches (a circuit of these can be followed by a detour of 50km/31 miles to the south-west).

Continue westwards on the D959 to Landrecies, where you skirt the vast **Mormal Forest**, the largest forest in northern France and a good centre for walks and picnics. Six kilometres (4 miles) further at **Maroilles**. Taste that famous delicious cheese at one of the farm-house factories in the village. Here take the D962 to **Avesnes-sur-Helpe**, capital of the Avesnois and a good centre for exploring the area. This was an old frontier town high on the river bank and fortified by Vauban, and some of his strong walls remain. It has a pleasantly old-fashioned air, with attractive brick-and-stone houses in the main square, an elegant Town Hall and a church with beautiful altar-pieces.

The Avesnois is a curious mixture of rich pastoral land and old, decaying industrial villages. The humid climate results in an intensely green countryside, with meadows full of wild flowers, thick hedges (a rarity in France), and many woods and lakes. Many of the villages have water-mills still working, curious oriental-style raised bandstands where the dancers can pass underneath the band, and shrines and small chapels for worship by the strongly-catholic locals. The industrial centres, none of which is particularly large, reflect patterns of work of the industrial past: each has its own specialist trade, and they are today grouped into an Ecomuseum, with branches in some of the larger villages, demonstrating the particular crafts for which the area was well-known.

For a tour of the area, leave Avesnes by the D951 to **Sains-du-Nord**. Here, in an attractive nineteenth-century house and garden, is the first of these 'theme museums': a *Maison du Bocage* or rural museum reflecting the life of the wooded countryside, with black-smith's forge, mini-farm, clog-maker's workshop and many other attractions. Continue south to **Fourmies**, where the main centre of the Fourmies-Trélon Ecomuseum is housed in an old cotton mill with a curious Romanesque chimney. This town was once an impor-tant textile centre, and the excellent museum reflects both the indus-try and the social life of the workers. There are working examples of machinery, a reconstructed old town street, and photographs and diorama of the often grim conditions of working life (the May Day international workers' holiday had its origin here, when a number of strikers were shot on that day in 1891). The museum won the *Prix Européen* in 1990. There are some marked footpaths with good views at nearby **Wignehies**.

Just north of Fourmies is **Trélon**, a glass-blowing village with an interesting Workshop-Museum of Glass (Atelier-Musée du Verre). Here you can learn about the history and process of glass-making, watch the glass-blowers at work and even have a go yourself! In **Wallers-en Fagne**, near the Belgian border, an old presbytery built in the distinctive blue stone of the region houses another section of the Ecomuseum, an exhibition of 'stone and nature in Fagne' (Maison de la Fagne et site Naturel des Monts de Baives). This explains how the blue stone is extracted from nearby quarries, dressed and used in the local architecture; it also illustrates the rich, colourful flora of the *fagnes*, or marshes, of the area. North of here, hugging the Belgian border, the road passes through **Moustier-en-Fagne**, with its charm-ing Gothic manor-house in brick and stone, to the pretty village of **Eppe-Sauvage**, at the eastern end of the Val-Joly lake. This attrac-tively-sited man-made lake has been designed and equipped as a holiday centre for the area, with sailing and wind-surfing (including

A typical farmhouse in the Avesnois

an *école de voile*), horse-riding, bathing and camping — there is a well-furnished camp-site. To the west of the lake is **Liessies**, a lovely village in the verdant Helpe-Majeure valley, whose church and abbey park form part of the Ecomuseum (Conservatoire du Patrimoine Religieux de l'Avesnois). The sixteenth-century parish church houses a beautiful collection of old statuary from the now-demolished abbey, and the park is open to the public as a conservation area for the local flora and fauna. The attractive château is now an hotel.

A pleasant run west and then north from Liessies brings you to **Felleries**, whose inhabitants have since the seventeenth century been specialists in woodwork and wood-turning. The *Bois-Jolis* or 'pretty-woods' mill in the village is a fascinating workshop-museum where you can watch the turners at work producing objects for local use, such as bobbins, shuttles and local *boules*. Three kilometres (2 miles) north at **Sars-Poteries** is a fine Glass Museum (Musée du Verre) illustrating the splendid glasswork long produced in this area, and housing an important collection of contemporary art in glass. To the north of the village is an interesting and still-working water-mill (Moulin Damotte). At **Solre-le-Château**, 5km (3 miles) west on the D962, is France's answer to the leaning tower of Pisa. The sixteenth-century Gothic parish church has a pretty bell tower which leans forward — according to local folk-lore, to see a white-clad virgin arriving to get married one day! Solre's main square is attractive, with a fine arcaded town hall with curious inscriptions above the arcades.

The north Avesnois is less attractive, though it has some features of interest. **Mauberge**, in an industrial belt, is a modern town rebuilt after war damage, though it has preserved some of its fine Vauban walls and its striking Mons Gate (1685). **Bavay**, 12km (7 miles) to the west, is the legendary capital of Gallo-Roman Belgium, and excavations have revealed the foundations of the ancient town of *Bagacum*, at the intersection of seven Roman roads. These and the small museum (Musée Archeologique et Chantier des Fouilles) holding many of the findings may be visited. The town hall has a fine belfry. Further west is **Le Quesnoy**, a sleepy citadel town hiding behind the most complete system of Vauban town walls in northern France. The walk around the walls gives pleasant views of surrounding lakes and market gardens; and at one point, in an attractive setting, is a monument to the New Zealand Rifle Brigade, who scaled the walls and freed the town in November 1918.

A good system of free motorways heading north-west allows you to by-pass the industrial belt round Lille, though both Lille and Valenciennes have strong artistic traditions and splendid fine-arts museums, well worth a detour.

French Flanders

Leave the A25 motorway at **Steenvoorde**, in the flat Flanders plain. This often-overlooked extreme north-eastern corner of France is typified by its open cultivated fields, dykes and windmills. These windmills are basically one of two types — the 'pivot' type where the whole mill revolves to face the wind, and the solid tower type with a revolving roof (apply to the local Syndicat d'Initiative or Mairie for a guided visit). Three examples can be seen just outside Steenvoorde, one to the south with a solid tower and two to the north-west of the pivot type. The small town itself, a dairy centre, is neat and pleasant, with typically Flemish painted houses with red-tiled roofs Take the D947 north, skirting the Belgian border, to **Hondschoote**, a Flemish-speaking linen-producing town with a splendid Gothic-Renaissance Town Hall and a handsome church (Eglise St Vaast et Hôtel de Ville), facing each other across a wide, flowery square. Both are worth visiting, the town hall for its fine council chamber, museum-gallery and arched cellars, and the church for its resplendent Flemish-Baroque pulpit, organ, altar and retable (altar-shelf). Hondschoote's well-restored pivot-type windmill, dated 1127, claims to be the oldest in Europe.

Take the D3 west from Hondschoote along the bank of the Lower Colme canal, with distant views of Dunkirk and the Channel coast to

*A typical pivot
Windmill at
Steenvoorde*

your right. In 11km (7 miles) is **Bergues**, a picturesque town surrounded by water and built in a circular plan within its finely-
preserved Vauban defensive walls. You enter from the north by the
Hondschoote Gate, via an elaborate system of fish-filled dykes and
bastion walls, planned by Vauban as a stout defence against invasion
and known as the 'Crown of Hondschoote'. Though badly damaged
in both World Wars, Bergues has been rebuilt in traditional style, and
today its yellow-ochre brick buildings, its canals and quays, narrow,
winding streets and wide squares are reminiscent of Bruges. Apart
from the town walls with their arched gates, the most noteworthy
buildings are the Town Hall with its fine, tall belfry, the ruins of the
ancient St-Winoc abbey, and the Mont-de-Piété, a tastefully-restored
Renaissance house dated 1630 and containing the town museum
(Musée Municipal), with some good Flemish paintings. Its founder,
Wenceslas Coeburgher, a true Renaissance man-of-many-parts,
drained the local marshes and then created the first 'calvary hills',
hence the house's name.

Leave Bergues by the Cassel Gate, heading south on the D916. Just after **Wormhout**, an attractive Flemish village with a fine avenue of chestnut trees, you pass on your left the wooden pivot-type Briarde windmill (apply to Syndicat d'Initiative or Mairie for a guided visit). Turn right up a winding hill road to **Cassel**, a charming little town perched on the only hill in the area (Mont Cassel, 175m/575ft). It has a typically Flemish long central square surrounded by old gabled houses, surrounded by narrow sloping streets and flights of steps leading up to the public garden on top of the hill. This has a wooden windmill and two observation points, one looking north and the other south, giving splendid views over the Flanders plain. The stone-built sixteenth-seventeenth-century hotel in the main square has a small museum (Musée Municipal).

South of Cassel are Hazebrouck and the pleasant Nieppe forest, and **Aire-sur-la-Lys**, a small town with an air of faded *Ancien Régime* grandeur and some impressive buildings. From here the N43 takes you back to Calais via **St Omer**, whose imposing basilica and fine waterway system are worth a visit.

Further Information
— Pays du Nord —

Museums and other Places of Interest

THE BOULONNAIS

Ambleteuse
Fort Vauban
Open: 3-7pm Saturday, Sunday, Monday July and August; March-November 3-7pm Sunday and holidays only. Groups: any time with 15 days notice.
☎ 20 54 61 54 or 21 32 61 90

Musée de la Seconde Guerre Mondiale
Open: 9.30am-7pm daily 1 April to 15 October; weekends and holidays except season. Group visits.
☎ 21 87 33 01

Audinghen
Musée du Mur de l'Atlantique
Open: daily 9am-7pm except January. Groups - 15 days notice.
☎ 21 32 97 33

Boulogne-sur-Mer
Nausicaà Centre National de la Mer
Open: 10am-8pm daily April to September; 10am-6pm Monday to Friday; 10am-7pm Saturday and Sunday October to March.
☎ 21 30 99 99 (admin)
☎ 21 30 98 98 (info)
☎ 21 30 99 89 (bookings)

Château-Musée
Open: daily 10am-6pm (10am-8pm Friday, closed Tuesday) May to September; 10am-1pm and 2-5pm except Tuesday October to April. Guided visits daily in season; group visits on demand throughout the year.
☎ 21 80 00 80

Calais
Musée des Beaux Arts et de la Dentelle
Open: 10am-12noon and 2-5.30pm daily Closed Tuesday and holidays.
☎ 21 46 62 00

Desvres
La Maison de la Faïence
Open: daily 10am-1pm and 2-6.30pm
July and August; ditto except Sunday
April to October; 2-6.30pm except
Friday November to March.
☎ 21 83 23 23

Escalles
Musée International du Transmanche
Open: 10am-12noon and 2-6pm daily.
15 October to 15 April weekends only,
same hours.
☎ 21 82 32 03

Guînes
Musée Emile Villez
Open: Sunday 3-8pm. Wednesday 2-
5pm (1 June 1 October only). At other
times by demand at Mairie.

Hydrequent (Nr Marquise)
La Maison du Marbre et de la Géologie
Open: 2.30-6.30pm daily June to
September; March-November 2.30-
6.30pm Sunday and holidays only.
Groups: guided visits by reservation.
☎ 21 83 19 10

Landrethun-le-Nord (Nr Marquise)
Forteresse de Mimoyecques
Open: daily 10am-7pm July and
August; 2-6pm Easter to 11 November;
1-hour guided visits.
☎ 21 87 10 34

Wimille (Nr Wimereux)
Le Moulin de Grisendal
Open: 3-7pm daily except Tuesday July
and August; Easter-13 September 3-
7pm Sunday and holidays only.
Groups: visits mornings by reservation, except Tuesday.
☎ 21 32 07 43

PICARDY RIVER VALLEYS
Amiens
Musée de Picardie
Open: daily 10am-12.30pm and 2-6pm
Tuesday to Sunday; closed Monday
and some holidays.
☎ 22 91 36 44

Azincourt
Centre Médiéval d'Azincourt
Open: daily 10am-9.30pm except
Wednesday; guided visits.

Cayeux-sur-Mer
La Maison de l'Oiseau
Open: daily 10am-7pm July and Aug
10am-6pm 16 Feb to 11 Nov.
☎ 22 26 93 93

Douai
Musée de la Chartreuse
Open: daily 10am-12noon and 2-5pm;
Sunday 10am-12noon and 3-6pm;
closed Tuesday and holidays.
☎ 27 87 17 82

Etaples
Musée Quentoric
Open: daily except Tuesday 10am-
12noon and 2-6pm. Closed three weeks
in September.
☎ 21 94 02 47

Maison de la Faune et de la Flore
Open: daily 9am-12noon and 2-6pm
(July and August 2-8pm). Closed
Saturday and Sunday, September to
May. Visits to Nature Reserve and
Canche bay on demand.
☎ 21 09 56 94 (Office de Tourisme)

Eu
Musée Louis-Philippe (in château)
Open: 9am-12noon and 2-6pm except
Tuesdays, 8 March to 7 November.

Hesdin
Musée Municipal
Open: daily 2-5pm Monday to Friday.
Group visits 15 days notice.
☎ 21 86 84 76

Le Touquet
Musée du Touquet
Open: 10am-12noon and 2-6pm except
Monday.
☎ 21 05 62 62

Musée des Poupées
Open: certain weekends during fêtes,
also 3-6pm during school holidays.
☎ 21 05 21 65

Merlimont
Nr Berck-sur-Mer
Bagatelle Parc d'Attractions
Open: 10am-7pm park, 10.30am-
6.30pm attractions - daily 24 April to 9
May and 29 May to 8 September;
Wednesday, Saturday, Sunday and
holidays 10-14 April, 11-29 May, 10-26
September.
☎ 21 94 60 33

Rambures
Nr Oisemont
Forteresse Féodale de Rambures
Open: daily except Wednesday 10am-
12noon and 2-6pm March to October;
2-5pm Sunday and holidays November
to February.
☎ 22 25 10 93

Samara
Archéologie et Nature
Open: from 3 March daily 9.30am-8pm;
guided visits in pavilion.
☎ 22 51 82 83

St Riquier
Abbaye Musée Départmental
Open: 10 February to 27 May daily 2-
6pm. June to September 10am-12noon
and 2-6pm. October to 11 November
10am-12noon and 2-5pm. Free entry.
☎ 22 28 81 52

St Quentin-en-Tourmont
Nr Rue
Le Parc Ornithologique du Marquenterre
Open: daily 9.30am-7pm 1 April to 11
November.
☎ 22 25 03 06

Valloires
L'Abbaye et les Jardins de Valloires
Open: daily 10am-12noon and 2-
5.30pm, 1 April to 11 November; closed
12 November to March. Guided visits.
Gardens open: daily 10am-8pm June to
August; 10am-6pm March to mid-
November.
☎ 22 29 97 55 (abbey)
☎ 22 23 53 55 (gardens)

ARTOIS AND NORTHERN PICARDY
Albert
Musée des Abris
Open: daily April to November 10am-
12noon and 2-6pm; Sunday and
holidays November; guided tours.
☎ 22 75 16 17

Arras
Musée des Beaux-Arts
Open: 10 October to 31 March 10am-
12noon and 2-5pm daily, except
Tuesday. Saturday 10am-12noon and
2-6pm. Sunday 10am-12noon and 3-
6pm. 1 April to 15 October 10am-
12noon and 2-6pm except Tuesday.
Guided visits from Office de Tourisme.
☎ 21 71 26 43.

Naours
Nr Amiens
Les Grottes de Naours
Open: daily 8.30am-12noon and 1.30-
6.30pm April to September; 11am-
12noon and 2-5pm October to March;
closed 15 November to 15 January.
☎ 22 93 71 78

Notre-Dame-de-Lorette
Nr Souchez
Musée Vivant 1914-1918
Open: daily 9am-8pm March to
November; December to February
weekends only or by reservation.
☎ 21 45 15 80

AVESNOIS
Bavay
*Musée Archeologique et Chantier des
    Fouilles*
Open: July and August 9am-12noon
and 2-6pm; April to October 9.30am-
12noon and 2-5pm; November to
March Sunday only; closed Tuesday.
☎ 27 63 13 95

Cambrai
Musée Municipal
15 Rue de l'Epée
Open: 10am-12noon and 2-5.45pm
except Monday ☎ 27 81 18 66

Felleries
*Moulin de Bois-Jolis-Musée de la
   Boissellerie*
Open: July and August daily 3-7pm;
April to November Sunday and
holidays 3-7pm.
☎ 27 59 06 71

Fourmies
*Fourmies-Trélon Ecomusée
Musée du Textile et de la Vie Sociale*
Fourmies
Open: July to September daily 9am-
6pm; March to November 9am-12noon
and 2-6pm; weekends and holidays
2.30-6.30pm.

Maison du Bocage
Sains-du-Nord
Open: March to November daily 2-
6pm; weekends and holidays 3-7pm.

*Conservatoire du Patrimoine Religieux de
   l'Avesnois*
Liessies
Guided visits by reservation.

*Maison de la Fagne et site Naturel des
   Monts de Baives*
Wallers-en-Fagne
Open: July to September weekdays 2-6pm,
weekends and holidays 2.30-6.30pm.

Atelier-Musée du Verre
Trélon
Open: April to October weekdays 2-6pm
weekends/holidays 2.30-6.30pm.
☎ 27 60 66 11 for all centres.

Le Cateau-Cambrésis
Musée Matisse
Open: daily 10am-12noon and 2-6pm
except Tuesday; Sunday 10am-12.30pm
and 2.30-6pm.
☎ 27 84 13 15

Sars-Poteries
Musée du Verre
Open: daily 3-6pm except Tuesday.
☎ 27 61 61 44

Moulin Delmotte
Open: 3-7pm daily 15 July to August.
May to September, Sunday and holidays.
☎ 27 61 60 01

FRENCH FLANDERS

Bergues
Musée Municipal
Open: daily except Tuesday 10am-
12noon and 2-5pm; closed January.
☎ 28 68 13 30

Cassel
Musée Municipal
Open: April to October daily except
Tuesday.
☎ 28 40 52 55 (Tourist Office)

Hondschoote
*Eglise Saint-Vaast, Hôtel de Ville and
   Windmill*
Guided visits available on application
to the Syndicat d'Initiative.
☎ 28 62 53 00

Tourist Information Offices

Amiens
Office de Tourisme
Rue J-Catelas
☎ 22 91 79 28

Arras
Office de Tourisme
l'Hotel de Ville
☎ 21 51 26 95

Avesnes-sur-Helpe
Syndicat d'Initiative
41 Place Géneral-Leclerc
☎ 27 57 92 40

Boulogne-sur-Mer
Office de Tourisme
Quai de la Poste
☎ 21 31 68 38

Calais
Office de Tourisme & Accueil de France
12 Boulevard Clemenceau
☎ 21 96 62 40

Lille
Office de Tourisme & Accueil de France
Palais Rihour
☎ 20 30 81 00

3 • Normandy

To a certain extent a visit to Normandy involves stepping back into history, either long past or well within living memory. On one hand there is William the Bastard, a complimentary title in those days, who was born in Falaise and died in Rouen but found time between to conquer and rule England while keeping a firm grip on his homeland as well. At the other end of the time scale there are long sandy beaches and rolling countryside over which the Allied forces swarmed in 1944, driving back the German army of occupation. Nearly everywhere you look there is evidence of these and other momentous events — magnificent churches and monasteries; fortified castles and elegant châteaux; museums filled with treasures; impressive monuments; ruined pillboxes and seemingly endless war graves, fields of white crosses set regimentally in grass as smooth and green as a billiard table.

But there is another, less militant side to Normandy where it is possible to wander through dense woodlands in splendid solitude, discover tiny villages and isolated farmsteads, rent a cottage or stay with a family in an atmosphere far removed from the popular tourist centres, often only a short drive away. Nor is there any prescribed method of travelling. Most of the lanes are wide enough for a car and, on the whole, the surfaces are good. Alternatively there is no difficulty in hiring horses and bicycles, or even a horse-drawn vehicle, be it a barouche or a caravan, while footpaths for the really energetic thread their way across the countryside, mostly signposted and covering literally hundreds of miles. Some are equipped with overnight hostels for hikers who plan their exploration on a long-term basis. The climate, by and large, is gentle, brisk but seldom freezing in winter and pleasantly hot and sunny during the summer months.

Whatever a visitor's inclinations may be, Normandy aims to satisfy them. The gourmet will discover a land not so much running with milk and honey as rich in butter, cream and cider. These ingredients find their way into a great many traditional dishes alongside such specialities as black sausages, braised tripe, salt-marsh mutton, grilled chitterlings sausages, chicken, duck and a variety of sea foods. The cheeses are famous for their flavour and variety and Calvados, the local cider-brandy, is the ideal complement to any meal. It scores over Cognac in the sense that it is drunk between courses as well as with coffee afterwards. Sports enthusiasts will find golf courses, tennis courts and swimming pools, rocks to climb, rivers and lakes for boating and fishing, beaches for bathing and windsurfing and facilities for other, less generally popular, activities such as gliding and parachute jumping. The spas cater for people who need medical treatment, are suffering from overwork or simply want to lose some extra weight while the casinos provide ample opportunities for gamblers to indulge in their favourite pastime. There are marinas for yachtsmen, often with sailing schools attached, camping sites for tents and caravans and information offices in most towns of any size which will provide details of these and other attractions available in their immediate areas.

Seine-Maritime and Eure

For visitors arriving from the north, bent on exploring the byways of Normandy, a logical place to cross the Seine, the border between the *départements* of Seine-Maritime and Eure, would be **Caudebec-en-Caux**, an attractive town overlooking the river. It is approximately 250km (156 miles) from Calais, an easy drive for motorists crossing the Channel, some 160km (100 miles) from Paris, 51km (32 miles) from Le Havre and a bare 36km (23 miles) from Rouen. Both Le Havre and Rouen are busy commercial ports, each has its own airport, good train services and facilities for hiring cars and bicycles as well as being worth visiting in their own right. Rouen, particularly, is a magical city which has been aptly described as a living museum, crammed with ancient buildings and recalling history on every side. It has a wide range of hotels, some excellent restaurants and has been a focal point for visitors since the Vikings took a liking to it more than a thousand years ago.

Caudebec-en-Caux is obviously not in the same category, nor has it a particularly historic atmosphere, especially since a disastrous fire in June 1940 destroyed many of the older buildings. A mere handful survived, including the thirteenth-century Maison des Templiers which has been skilfully restored and is now the home of a local history museum. Fortunately the fifteenth-century church of Notre-Dame, described by Henry IV as 'the most beautiful chapel in the kingdom', was virtually undamaged. It is rather austere inside with heavy pock-marked pillars from which little faces scowl down or

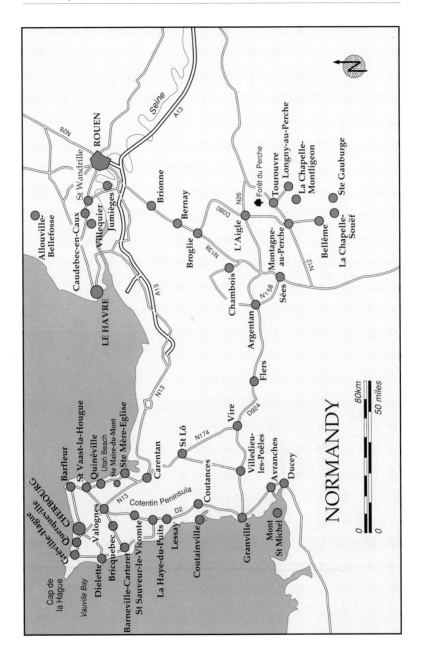

grin impishly. The beautiful stained glass windows and the ancient organ with its hundreds of decorated pewter pipes are only slightly younger. Among the candle-lit chapels on either side is one of the

Holy Sepulchre where an extremely detailed figure of Christ is watched over by seven large stone statues, the majority of them women. They came from Jumièges Abbey and have had their features restored, an operation that adds to the lifelike effect although the colour contrast in one or two cases is a trifle incongruous. When the whole church is filled with flowers the scent is almost tangible. The same applies to the Place du Marché outside where a market has been held since 1390 and where local tradesmen carry on the tradition every Saturday. The town also provides a number of up-to-date attractions like tennis, swimming and miniature golf. However it is as well to remember that a hotel room overlooking the Seine and the forest beyond can be something of a mixed blessing — it is a case of the view versus the noise from fairly constant road and river traffic.

A distinctly modern toll bridge, the Pont du Brotonne, opened in 1977, replaces the ferry which used to run from the centre of the town, a short *boules'* throw from the main waterfront hotels. But before paying up and driving across to the Brotonne Forest it would be a pity to miss some of the outstanding places of interest on the north bank in the department of Seine-Maritime. To the west is **Villequier** where the estuary and river pilots exchange places on ships making the Le Havre-Rouen run. However, it is much better known for its association with Victor Hugo, vividly recalled in the local museum which takes his name. The solidly built house overlooking the water belonged to the Valqueries whose son Charles married Hugo's daughter Léopoldine in 1843. The young couple died in a boating accident less than a year later and are buried with other members of the family in the little churchyard close by. Nobody claims that the house has been maintained exactly as it was in those days but it tends to give that impression. The beds are made, pictures and photographs hang on the walls and there are any number of personal items including letters and poems which add to the general atmosphere. The little sixteenth-century church with its original stained glass windows is also worth a visit.

The church at **Allouville-Bellefosse**, almost due north of Villequier, has quite a different claim to fame. It stands guard over the best-known tree in Normandy — a 1,300-year-old oak said to be one of the oldest in France. Two chapels, one above the other, have been built inside the hollow trunk, both of them roofed, floored and panelled in wood. Because it is getting on a bit, the tree and its main branches have been given extra support and a wooden staircase spiralling up round the outside provides access to the upper chapel. The trunk on either side of the entrance to the lower one, where the hole is not nearly so wide, has been worn to a satin finish by people edging their way in and out. There is a nature museum in an old farmhouse a short walk away and is open to anyone with time on their hands and the good fortune to find somebody there.

Two abbeys which definitely should not be missed stand some 20km (12 miles) apart to the east and south of Caudebec-en-Caux. St Wandrille Abbey is the newer by less than half a century, having been founded by a young nobleman of that name in the Fontenelle valley in AD649. It soon became established as a seat of learning and produced the first history of a Western monastery before being sacked by the Vikings. However, once these marauding Northmen had settled down and become respectable Normans, they did as much as anyone to help the monks rebuild and re-establish themselves. The new abbey took the name of its founder and, with only a slight setback during the Wars of Religion, flourished until it came to grief during the Revolution. Among its subsequent owners was the English Marquis of Stacpoole who, to his credit, built the ornamental gateway. Eventually St Wandrille reverted to its original purpose with a compliment of Benedictine monks who conduct daily mass in Gregorian Chant and welcome visitors to the services. There are also guided tours past the massive columns which are all that remain of the fourteenth-century church, and into the splendid cloister, much of it still intact. The present monastery church is a fifteenth-century tithe barn, moved in pieces in 1969 and faithfully reconstructed, its porch converted into the Chapel of the Holy Sacrament with a shrine containing the head of St Wandrille added the following year.

A choice of roads, some of them delightfully rural, lead southwards through Le Trait, which has little apart from a small church to offer, and on to the remains of **Jumièges Abbey**, considered to be one of the most outstanding ruins in France. It started life in AD604 but, like St Wandrille, crumbled at the hands of the Vikings. In the tenth century William Longsword, who was Duke of Normandy at the time, set about rebuilding it, but the vast complex was largely completed under the watchful eye of Robert Champart, a Benedictine abbot who became Archbishop of Canterbury during the reign of Edward the Confessor. A year after the Battle of Hastings William the Conqueror, on one of his periodical visits to Normandy, attended the consecration of the abbey church. From that time onwards the monks had things pretty much their own way until they were thrown out during the Revolution. Jumièges was sold off at auction to become a stone quarry and the new owner, like others of his ilk in various parts of the country, proceeded to blow it up. Fortunately it changed hands again before being razed to the ground, since which time the ruins have been treasured and preserved. Today the twin towers of the façade, soaring above the surrounding trees and enclosing stone walls, can be seen clearly from across the river. Deprived of its roof, lantern and most of the chapels it is, nevertheless, a very impressive sight. A covered passageway leads to the smaller church of St Pierre beyond which there are ruins of the twelfth-century chapter house, the cloister and a large storeroom dating from approximately the same era.

Instead of driving back to Caudebec-en-Caux it is more fun to take the car ferry which operates across the river a short distance away. It appears to run more or less when required so quite a few people stop for something to eat and drink at the restaurants on either bank before taking their place in the queue. Once across, a small road climbs up into the **Forêt de Brotonne**. It is a delightful area filled with oak, beech and pine through which there are plenty of paths but very few roads for cars, especially as some of them have chains or bars across the entrance. However, there are adequate places to park before walking through the woods over deliciously soft carpets of fallen leaves. One interesting old oak, known as the Chêne à la Cuve, has four distinct trees growing out of a single trunk slightly above ground level. It seems to exert a special fascination for children whose shouts act like a radio beacon for anyone who finds the location difficult to detect. The road running north between the main forest and the river emerges into open country to give a totally different view of the Pont de Brotonne. From one vantage point it looks rather like a giant prehistoric lizard with transparent wings snaking its way into the hills opposite. Further on the road passes a series of extremely picturesque half-timbered houses, many of them expertly restored. Some have beautiful thatched roofs along the ridge of which an occasional owner has planted a row of flowers. The idea is sometimes repeated on the top of a thatched gateway and the thick stone walls on either side.

Once in and out of the forest again and heading south there are two more trees to inspect. They are gigantic yews, said to be getting on for a thousand years old, growing in front of the little church at **La Haye-de-Routot**. Both are hollow although one would not think it from the vast canopy of leaves and branches which cast deep shadows over the graveyard. A chapel has been built inside one and an oratory in the other but, unlike the oak at Allouville-Bellefosse, there is not enough space for anyone to walk inside. The village has also preserved an old communal oven, restored the *sabot*-maker's work-

The River Orne, Normandy

Abbaye de la Grande Trappe, near Bresolettes, Normandy

shop and kept alive the festival of Ste Clare in mid-July. It is celebrated with fireworks and a bonfire which gives the participants a chance to pull out a flaming branch and so protect themselves from fire for the coming year.

Le Perche-Orne

Another area which can be surprisingly free of visitors, even at the height of the season, lies further to the south in what is known as Le Perche. It is a happy blending of forests, rivers and farmlands, dotted with ancient manor houses and an occasional abbey and is famous for its horses. Depending on time and inclination it is possible to weave one's way down through a labyrinth of country roads, discovering a host of tiny villages and interesting locations along the way, or follow one of the main routes and complete the journey in a matter of hours. The most obvious way is probably through **Brionne** with its ruined Norman castle and little fifteenth-century church and on to **Bernay**, associated with William the Conqueror through his grandmother, the Duchess Judith, who founded the local abbey in 1013. There is an interesting museum in the old abbot's lodge, the much restored original church and two other small churches of note. One contains the statue of Notre-Dame-de-la-Couture, highly revered by pilgrims who gather there on Whit Monday. Some 8km (5

The market at Tourouvre

miles) beyond Broglie a road branches off to **L'Aigle** where there is a small museum concentrating on the Battle of Normandy. It includes wax figures of the Allied leaders and recordings of their voices made at the time. From here it is a short run to **Tourouvre**, a pleasant little town with some holiday attractions, which is a good base for exploring the country round about.

Tourouvre has its own special place in history. It was from there in the seventeenth century that many of the early settlers left to found Quebec, an event graphically recalled in stained glass in the local church. A companion window depicts the official reception given to one of their descendants, Monsieur Honoré Mercier, when, as Premier Ministre de Quebec, he paid a return visit in 1891. In addition the church still has its fifteenth-century stalls and a painting from the same date *The Adoration of the Magi* incorporated into the somewhat later altarpiece. Plans are under way for a small museum nearby but in the meantime Monsieur Feugueur at the hotel opposite is a fountain of information about the area.

Nudging the northern side of the town is the **Forêt du Perche** where, at the Carrefour de l'Etoile, there is a choice of eight roads, radiating out in all directions, a relic of the days when the woods were used extensively for hunting. One leads to **Bresolettes**, with eighteen inhabitants the smallest village in the *département*, and on past ponds filled with waterlilies to the Abbaye de la Grande Trappe. It was founded in 1140 and gives the impression of having been well maintained ever since. Visitors are asked to enquire at the porter's lodge, a small door near the main entrance, where the brother on duty will arrange a show lasting about 20 minutes covering the history of the abbey and something of the life of the monks. On occasions he will sell produce from the farm as well as the pamphlets and postcards displayed in the lodge. People arriving around midday, when most doors in France are firmly shut, may be invited to attend a brief service in the abbey church which the monks, having changed into white habits, conduct in Gregorian Chant. The nearby village of **Soligny-la-Trappe** will provide an hotel, somewhere to camp, a leisure park and opportunities for bathing and fishing in addition to tennis and mini-golf. The Sentier de Grande Randonnée, designed for hikers who plan to take most of Normandy in their stride, passes the door.

Mortagne-au-Perche, the former capital of the region, is a good deal bigger but, apart from the church, comparatively little has survived from its earlier days. Beautifully manicured gardens in front of the town hall, dominated by a statue of a very small cherub

The Abbaye de la Grande Trappe, Bresolettes

on a very large horse, have a magnificent view over the undulating countryside. There are shops, hotels and restaurants, places to park a caravan and all the usual sports facilities. The whole place goes *en fête* in March with a lively Black Pudding Fair. A main road links Mortagne-au-Perche with Bellême which offers much the same in the way of attractions, some delightful old houses and a forest containing a large pool, a Roman fountain, a massive oak tree and several enticing walks.

Small, less frequented roads in the area have as much if not more to tempt the visitor than their busier counterparts. **La Chapelle-Montligeon**, although industrial, is a place of pilgrimage. Its enormous church, complete with modern stained glass windows, overshadows everything else and can be seen from top to terrace a good way off. However there is a slightly commercialised atmosphere about it, due no doubt to the fact that it is a popular holiday centre with a long list of sports and pastimes to attract the crowds. Beyond the town, on the way to La Vove Manor, is the Moulin la Vove, a delightful old mill with turbulent water which can be admired from the grass verge and a bell to be rung by passers-by who would like to inspect it more closely. The Manor itself is open from May to September. It is a typical fortified château of the type that seems to pop up out of the trees nearly everywhere you look. They are austere and businesslike, sporting watch turrets with roofs like brimless witches' hats, grim stone walls and sometimes an ancient keep or a moat for additional protection. Courboyer Manor House is another case in point with a massive round tower and a reputation for being one of the finest in the district.

La Chapelle-Souëf, beyond Bellême, introduces a touch of variety. Les Feugerets is an elegant sixteenth-century château, unfortunately not open to the public but clearly visible from the road. Shallow stone steps with balustrades sweep up to the main entrance between two elderly detached buildings and it is easy to imagine Louis XIV's son, Le Grand Dauphin, riding up them with his friends on one of his many visits. On the other hand, L'Angenardière Manor allows people to wander through the grounds, past the walls and towers that were so essential to continued ownership in medieval times. It is not far from St Cyr-la-Rosière but is even closer to **Ste Gauburge** which is unusual in that the church has been deconsecrated and is used as an exhibition hall. This is attached to a manor house of comparable age, once part of a priory but now a private home. It has been said that after the monks were driven out during the Revolution local people got quite accustomed to seeing their ghosts returning in procession to their old stamping ground. If that is true they must be mildly surprised to see a much more up-to-date building on the far side of the lawn. It houses an interesting little museum specialising in the Perche of days gone by. There are sections devoted to a dozen different occupations, showing how hemp was spun and converted into cloth and clothes, how horses were shod and how *sabots* were made. Farm implements are much in evidence alongside the equipment needed for making cider and Calvados. In a building of its own there is a schoolroom complete with desks and a blackboard, everything necessary for lessons in history, geography, maths, science and biology and there are even hooks on which little coats of the period hang in an orderly line. The museum is open every afternoon from June to October but it is not always possible to see inside the church.

Another venue for exhibitions is La Lubinière, a sixteenth-century manor which was occupied until quite recently. The fireplaces still show traces of soot and the walls of the spiral staircase to the watch tower have been painted white which, at the moment, comes off on one's clothes.

Longny-au-Perche is much more accustomed to visitors, especially in September when there is a pilgrimage to the statue of Our Lady of Mercy in the chapel dedicated to her, one of two in the town. Designated a holiday centre, it has a leisure park, a caravan site, fishing, bathing, a swimming pool, tennis courts and bicycles for hire, not to mention opportunities for long, invigorating walks.

The old cathedral town of **Sées** would probably be more convenient than Tourouvre as a base for exploring the western side of the region. To begin with it is a delight in itself, full of religious institutions, far-from-modern houses and ancient buildings largely converted to present day use. The former abbey of St Martin is a children's home and it is only possible to examine the eighteenth-century Bishop's Palace from the outside. The same applies to the old market, a large round building, open to the world, with a quantity of pillars holding up a heavy wooden roof. The most impressive sight is the cathedral, an outstanding example of Norman Gothic architecture with some splendid stained glass, a decorated high altar and a folk museum tucked away in the chapter house.

Most people make for the **Castle d'O** which lays on conducted tours in the afternoons and will sometimes show visitors round in the morning, except on Tuesdays when it is closed all day. The whole place looks as though it could have escaped from Grimm's Fairy Tales — turrets, decorated windows, moat, parklands and all. Although the oldest part is 500 years old there is no sign of the heavy fortifications that most builders considered to be obligatory in those turbulent days. On the opposite side of the road, and slightly further on, the eighteenth-century Château de Sassy is a study in contrasts. Built in the classical style but very much at home in its rural surroundings, it is known especially for its tapestries and the superb formal gardens, laid out on immaculate terraces down the side of the hill. The château stands between a group of lakes and the small town of St Christophe-le-Jajolet where pilgrims congregate twice a year — in July and October — to take part in processions and attend the Blessing of Cars. Although, like St George, St Christopher was demoted some years ago he is still regarded as the patron saint of travellers, sportsmen, airmen and motorists. A statue of him, looking rather pensive and carrying a most attractive child, stands beside open fields near the church.

High on the list of nearby places to visit is the **Haras du Pin**, home of the national stud. One look at this extremely impressive establishment is enough to explain why it is sometimes called the Versailles of Horses. Three roads, usually described as 'rides', converge on Colbert's Court, named after the statesman who founded the stud in 1665. It was planned and built some 50 years later and, although the château at the far end is not open to visitors, grooms are on duty to show people round the stables in the wings. During the season there are colourful processions of horses and horsedrawn vehicles which

The fortified Manor of Argentelles

attract large crowds while punters are catered for on the adjacent racecourse in September and October of each year. The best time to visit the Haras du Pin is between July and February when the greatest number of stallions are in residence, although there is always a nucleus of horses to be exercised or put through their paces in the grounds. They range from thoroughbreds to hacks and from Norman cobs to Percherons, a breed which is native to Le Perche.

The Percheron is said by some people to be descended from the Arab cavalry of Abd el Rahman, the Saracen leader who was defeated at Poitiers in AD732. Be that as it may, the Percherons soon became very French indeed with fresh Arab blood introduced at intervals, in fact the chevrons on the coat of arms of the Counts of the Perche are sometimes described as the hoofprints of war horses that took part in the Crusades. As time passed the breed developed along more domesticated lines, working in the fields, pulling carts and coaches and even appearing in trotting races over ploughed land in the mid-nineteenth century. At about this time trans-Atlantic breeders started to import Percherons and today they are to be found as far afield as North and South America, Scandinavia and Japan. Sadly the advent of the car and the tractor took its toll. It is only occasionally that one of these splendid horses can be seen grazing out in the open or communing with a herd of local cattle.

Chambois

From Le Pin the usual conglomeration of small roads thread their way through farmlands which seem to be largely populated by horses, past Exmes with its archaeological connections, or Champobert where the château and chapel can be seen on request during the season, to the Manor of Argentelles. It is a fairly typical fifteenth-century fortified house, softened by a flower-filled courtyard and is open on Sundays and holidays in the afternoon from mid-April to late October. Almost as eyecatching is the extremely handsome farmhouse next door.

Chambois is one place where ancient history rubs shoulders with modern war. A large stone keep dating from the twelfth century dominates the centre of the village, cheek by jowl with a stele commemorating the American, Canadian and Polish troops who joined up there in August 1944 to cut off the German retreat. At **Mont-Ormel**, a bare 10km (6 miles) to the north-east, a large monument flanked by tanks and watched over by trees and flag poles, commands an extensive view over the western landscape. An announcement carved on stone in English, French and Polish marks the site where, on 19, 20, 21 and 22 August the 1st Polish Armoured Division sealed off the Falaise-Chambois gap, bringing about the defeat of the encircled German 7th Army. It was also the end of the Battle of Normandy.

Amongst the most rewarding châteaux from the point of view of decorations and furnishings is the one at **Le-Bourg-St-Léonard**, south of Chambois and on the direct route from L'Aigle to Argentan. It stands aloof from the surrounding village behind long stretches of lawn although there is space to park outside the gates. The building is almost entirely Louis XV and consequently has all the detached elegance of the eighteenth century. It is beautifully panelled inside and has some fine tapestries setting off its rather ornate furnishings to perfection. Guided tours are arranged each morning and afternoon but it is closed on Tuesdays.

The nearest town worthy of that description is **Argentan** which was badly damaged in the war but nevertheless managed to preserve its two main churches, although both have had to be restored considerably. The larger, St Germain, is fairly elaborate but St Martin steals its thunder somewhat with ancient stained glass windows which are still intact. There are the remains of a castle with a viewing table on the tower and a Benedictine abbey where the art of lacemaking is kept alive by the nuns. Apart from an exhibition of Point d'Argentan, which was invented by their predecessors some 200 years ago, there is usually someone on hand to explain the finer details and draw attention to the difference between original specimens and modern needlepoint lace. The town's other attractions and amenities include a racecourse, riding stables, a swimming pool and a clutch of small hotels and restaurants. It is also a convenient point from which to set out for Vire and the Cotentin Peninsula.

Manche

A choice of route on this occasion is not too easy to suggest. Some motorists will opt to follow the River Orne from the small town of Putanges-Pont-Ecrepin, past the Rabodanges Dam and along the Gorges-de-St-Aubert, stopping frequently on the way. Rabodanges, for example, has a seventeenth-century castle and anyone who is prepared to walk for up to an hour can inspect the ruins of the isolated Moulin de la Jalousie and all that is left of the ancient Devil's Bridge that keeps it company. The gorges have to be seen on foot but one outstanding view can be obtained from the Roche d'Oëtre which demands less effort and includes the services of an *auberge* as well. St Roch is a sixteenth-century pilgrim chapel where penitents in traditional dress attend a special *pardon* in the second half of August. It is also conveniently close to the Château de St Sauveur, a smallish house dating from the reign of Louis XIII, filled with delightful pictures, furniture and other items from the same period. It is open at weekends and on some weekday afternoons during the season but closes in February. From here it is an easy run to Vire. Other travellers will prefer the more direct route through **Flers** which does not seem to be particularly interested in tourists as such. They are allowed to walk in the grounds of the château, attend services in the twentieth-century church and study fossils, painting and weaving in the local museum but precious little else.

Vire, inspite of being badly mauled during the war, is much more welcoming. It is proud of the pitifully few remnants of its long history — a clock tower in the main square, a rebuilt church and a small part of the keep built by England's Henry I, son of William the Conqueror. However it makes up for its lack of obvious antiquity with a modern sports stadium, a number of tennis courts, covered and open-air swimming pools and one or two perfectly respectable hotels and restaurants for travellers who decide to linger a while. A large lake meets the needs of water sports enthusiasts, trout are on hand for any fishermen who can catch them and the town is strategically placed for excursions to other places of interest thereabouts.

St Lô, only 39km (24 miles) to the north, had an even worse time in 1944. It too has been rebuilt, somewhat less attractively, supplying the old quarter with a flower garden where the ramparts used to be. The Musée des Beaux-Arts has some worthwhile tapestries, both old and new, and is housed in the Hôtel de Ville, a couple of blocks or so from the damaged church of Notre-Dame on the road leading out to the stud. Although not as regally housed as its opposite number at Le Pin the stud makes compulsive viewing for anyone interested in horses, particularly when the magnificent stallions are there in force from about the middle of July to the middle of February.

Inspite of being well inside the *département* of La Manche, St Lô is not on the Cotentin Peninsula which actually starts at Carentan. It is a town without a great deal of character although it has an imposing church which dwarfs everything else for miles around. There is a small yacht harbour, a racecourse across the marshland to the south and a national trotting school for jockeys. This probably explains why one tends to meet them in the most unlikely places, including Utah Beach.

Utah, with Omaha to the east, is where the Americans landed on D-Day. The site is marked by a former German blockhouse and a modern memorial crypt set about with a tank, an anti-aircraft gun and three landing craft all protected from onshore winds by a sand dune. The paratroops were dropped fractionally inland around the villages of **Ste Marie-du-Mont** and Ste Mère Eglise. The former possesses a delightful old church and a very informative landings museum while the latter has the distinction of being the first place in France to be liberated. The drop is commemorated in stained glass in the twelfth-century church of **Ste Mère Eglise**, while outside is the lifelike figure of a paratrooper caught up on the belfry. Across the road the Airborne Troops' Museum is filled with reminders of the first days of the invasion accompanied by an American commentary. A Douglas C 47 has a hanger to itself and a notice at the entrance to the grounds recalls Private William Tucker who joined the battle on 6 June 1944 and survived to become vice-president of one of the largest railroads in America. Other items of interest are a Roman milestone and, bridging the centuries, a symbolic milestone marked '0' — the first of hundreds which trace General Patton's lightning advance from Normandy to Metz in Alsace et Lorraine. On the outskirts of the village an ancient farmhouse has been transformed into a museum. There is all the appropriate furniture plus fittings with Madame Tussaud type figures occupied with their daily chores and a young child in a sturdy-looking playpen of the day. Everything necessary to keep the farm going is on display and it is open morning and afternoon, apart from Tuesdays, from April Fools Day to the end of September.

A road follows the coast northwards past small holiday resorts like Quinéville with its protected yacht harbour and Fontenay-sur-Mer, which is not really '*sur mer*' (by the sea) at all but has a golf course by way of compensation. Judging by the map, the road running along the coast has distinct scenic possibilities but, in reality, there are very few places where the dunes are low enough to see the water at all. For this reason it is not a bad idea to head for **Valognes** instead, if only to visit the cider museum. It is full of equipment from a less mechanised age, although some basic designs have changed very little over the years, and traces the whole process from tree to bottle. For anyone not acquainted with cider-making it is interesting to discover how the sugary soft drink is transformed into a clear liquid with intoxicating possibilities. Local people maintain that it goes well with sea food, a theory which can be tested at **St Vaast-la-Hougue**, the centre of the oyster industry. The large oyster farms at Le Vauban are open but for the uninitiated who shy away from these delicacies, either in their natural habitat or served up on a dish with lemon, there are plenty of other things to see and do.

The yacht marina at St Vaast-la-Hougue has about fifty berths for visitors with all the usual amenities and there is tennis, riding and fishing, a sandy beach and facilities for tents and caravans. Sightseers

*Ste Mère Eglise with the first of the milestones which trace
General Patton's advance across France*

can inspect the mariners' minute chapel on the far side of the harbour, venture further afield to the seventeenth-century fort at the end of a long sandspit or walk the length of the jetty to the lighthouse to admire the views. The more adventurous can trudge across to the inshore Ile de Tatihou at low water where, if they are not careful, they will be marooned when the tide comes in. Hotel accommodation is available and idle hours can be whiled away very happily outside a quayside café watching the fishermen at work.

Barfleur is another picturesque little fishing port but has the disadvantage that it dries out completely. There are at least three pleasing, if modest, small hotels, a lifeboat station and a lighthouse which is one of the tallest in the country. Like a number of other places it was popular with Normans dashing backwards and forwards to England in the eleventh and twelfth centuries and displays the seal of the *Mora*, William the Conqueror's ship, rather ostentatiously on the quay. A footpath with some most impressive views passes close by on its way round the peninsula and down as far as Avranches. The coast road along the cliffs is also spectacular in places with plenty of opportunities to stop. However, quite a few motorists who want to stretch their legs leave their cars at Fermanville and walk along the Vallée des Moulins to the viaduct. A less frequented inland road through Le Vast, with its little waterfalls, follows the River Saire through fertile country with woods on either side before joining the seemingly endless heavy traffic, thundering resolutely along the dual carriageway into Cherbourg.

To be honest, **Cherbourg** is not everybody's idea of the perfect home from home. In other words, it is a typical Channel port, noisy and down to earth with functional buildings and a general air of putting business before pleasure and not having a great deal of time for the latter. Nor is it strictly off the beaten track although it sees fewer tourists than in the days of the great Atlantic liners which put in there. However it is worth a quick visit, if only for nostalgic reasons, when one is in the immediate vicinity. Predictably the most comfortable hotel is close to the railway station and the docks while the large marina is half the town away from the Yacht Club and the beach is nothing to get excited about. Conversely it has a casino, a skating rink, a golf course on the outskirts, an airport, regular ferry services to the south of England and Ireland and plenty of trains in and out. No foreigners are allowed into the naval base but they are welcome at the Fort de Roule with its wartime museum, at the Musée des Beaux-Arts and in the greenhouses and natural history museum of the Emmanuel-Liais Park.

From Cherbourg, travelling west towards the more rugged terrain of Cap de la Hague, there are plenty of opportunities to dally on the way. For instance, **Querqueville** is a good place to pause and visit the 1,000-year-old chapel of St Germain, the oldest religious building on the peninsula. Nacqueville Château, just outside the hamlet of La Rivière, dates from the sixteenth century. Its walls and towers are half-covered in ivy, blending perfectly with the surrounding park filled with flowers, ornamental shrubs and trees. From Easter to the end of September there are guided tours on the hour every afternoon except on Tuesdays and Fridays unless it happens to be a public holiday. The Dur-Ecu Manor was built along rather more unconventional lines, due in part to the fact that it was restored 400 years ago on foundations that were laid in the ninth century.

The painter Jean Millet spent his early years in the area so the church at **Gréville-Hague** will look familiar to anyone who knows his work but no attempt has been made to restore his birthplace at Gruchy and turn it into a museum. At this point the road swings inland, making for open country that can be rather bleak when sea mists creep in over the moors, changes its mind to take a look at tiny Port Racine and carries on towards the lighthouse, isolated on its island facing Alderney across the Race. The scenery round the other side of Cap de la Hague is very similar although the twentieth century asserts itself with an all-too-obvious nuclear processing plant at Jobourg which has an information centre open in the afternoons for anyone who is interested. Those who prefer to turn their back on it have the option of a short drive to the Nez de Jobourg and a walk along the cliffs. The rewards are a small *auberge*, a lot of seabirds and exceptional views across Vauville Bay to the atomic power station at Flamanville. A few small villages along the edge of the bay have their own specialities to offer. **Biville** attracts pilgrims to the tomb of Blessed Thomas Hélye who died in 1257, about the same time as the church was built, and is a brisk 15 minutes' walk from the Calvaire des Dunes. The only port in the vicinity is **Diélette**, almost too small to be more than a bolt-hole in an emergency but it has a nice sandy beach at the entrance when the tide is out.

A gem among showpieces within easy reach is **Bricquebec**, clustered round its sixteenth-century castle with a tower that pre-dates it by some 200 years. A road runs through the heavily fortified archway into a courtyard where, surprisingly, there is a small *auberge*. By day guides shepherd their charges round a little museum in the clock tower and a restored thirteenth-century crypt, eventually pointing them in the direction of the keep. Its four storeys fell in a long time ago but there are steps, more than 150 of them, up to the viewing platform — a rewarding climb for anyone with the necessary stamina and determination. At twilight it is even more magical, silent except for the crickets and an occasional bird, filled with the atmosphere of bygone days if you ignore the promise of a good dinner wafting out through the windows of the hotel. The Abbaye de Notre-Dame-de-Grâce is a newcomer by comparison, founded in 1824 just outside the town. Women as well as men are allowed to visit the monastery, which makes a change for everyone, provided they time their visit for 3.30pm except on Sundays and holidays.

The next part of the journey still lies to the south but involves one of those 'do we head west or east?' decisions. Choose south-east and it is a short run to **St Sauveur-le-Vicomte** which is not as impressive as it sounds due mainly to wartime bombing. The castle is practically non-existent but there is an attractive little church with a statue of St James of Compostela and a museum dedicated to the life and works of Barbey d'Aurevilly who earned himself the title of Lord High Constable of Literature. Some 12km (7 miles) further on, beyond a strip of marshland, is **La Haye-du-Puits**, a perfectly ordinary little place on weekdays but quite amusing on Sunday mornings. The crowds are much in evidence, doing nothing particularly important as far as one can see, music blares out all down the main street from loudspeakers placed rather too close together for comfort and a young man roasts up to a dozen Sunday joints at the same time on a contraption, not unlike an abacus, set up on the edge of the pavement. Mont Castre makes a pleasant deviation at this point as long as time is no object. Not that there is a great deal about except ruins, which comprise a church and an old cemetery, but a pathway leads up to the remains of a Roman lookout post commanding a long distance view of the peninsula. It is so all-embracing that the site was returned to active service during the Battle of Normandy.

On the other hand, plan a trip south-west from Bricquebec and the sea is roughly 15km (9 miles) away with **Barneville-Carteret** dead ahead. This is actually three entities for the price of one. Barneville contributes an exceptionally well decorated church; the beach is popular with holidaymakers and caters for them accordingly while Carteret weighs in with a Customs Officers' Path along the headland and a colourful port with all the usual cafés and paraphernalia associated with fishermen. Visiting yachts are not encouraged, although space can usually be found for them, as it is for cars when their owners decide to catch the ferry for an excursion to the Channel Islands. Much the same can be said for **Port Bail**, further down the coast. It is not in the same league as far as water skiing and skin diving but it duplicates most of Carteret's other holiday attractions, has its own ferry to Jersey and any number of camping sites.

Whichever route is chosen, be it south-east or south-west, it will almost certainly join its opposite number at **Lessay**, famous mainly for its abbey church founded in the eleventh century. It suffered so drastically in 1944 that it had to be almost entirely rebuilt, using all the original bits and pieces that were lying about. Although it is virtually devoid of decorations inside this adds to its tremendous dignity. The high altar is so heavy and plain that it could have graced a pagan temple, an impression carried through by the stained glass windows which owe a lot to Irish Celtic manuscripts. In contrast, there is nothing dignified about the Holy Cross Fair in September which has been held more or less regularly for the past thousand years. It is a boisterous mixture of sideshows, sales of dogs and horses, local crafts, traditional dancing, *al fresco* meals and modern amusements. In other words it is a typical example of celebrations of this kind in Normandy but is rather bigger than most of them. There is an aero club in the area and an interesting castle at Pirou, well fortified and surrounded by water, which has a tapestry on the lines of the one at Bayeux depicting the conquest of southern Italy instead of William's exploits in England in 1066.

Purists maintain that Lessay marks the end of the Cotentin Peninsula. They point out that the sea would only have to rise 10m (33ft) or so, flooding the marshes and grazing lands which separate the town from Carentan, and the whole northern section would revert to being one of the Channel Islands. But the *département* of La Manche does not write off one-third of its territory so easily and officially the Côtes du Cotentin continue merrily on their way round to the border with Brittany. The seaboard is well endowed with small coastal resorts, long sandy beaches and, apart from Coutainville and Granville, is blissfully lacking in organised entertainments.

Coutainville makes up for this apparent lapse in forward planning with everything from a casino, horse racing and golf to the whole gamut of popular sports, both by land and water. Nor does it forget to provide horses, boats and bicycles for hire. In some ways the resort could be described as a recreation centre for **Coutances** which is far more restrained. It has an outstanding cathedral, as befits the religious centre of the area, a couple of small churches, beautiful public gardens and an interesting local museum. It is the kind of town that needs to be enjoyed at leisure. Apart from one up-market establishment occupying an old château with a restaurant of equal quality the hotels are in no way out of the ordinary, but then they do not charge nearly so much!

Granville is made up of a bit of all worlds and in spite of being somewhat on the beaten track is well worth seeing, especially out of season. The ancient quarter, built largely of granite, stands above and beyond the modern town. It is a fascinating place to explore with its narrow streets and grim-faced houses, the austere church of Notre-Dame and traces of English occupation in the fifteenth century and of the Germans who followed in their footsteps after exactly 500 years. A stroll round the ramparts and out to the lighthouse on the Pointe de Roc takes in a sea-water aquarium complete with minerals and shells and a museum that includes both war and fashions. Another glimpse of old Granville can be found in the waxworks museum, there is a garden that once belonged to the Dior family, better known for haute couture, a casino, golf courses and a small beach with a swimming pool. From a busy port inside the promontory excursions leave for Jersey and the Chausey Islands, somewhat closer to the mainland. Fishing boats share the Port de Plaisance with

Villedieu-les-Poêles is well-known for its copper wares

a marina that keeps up to 200 berths for visitors, protected from tides that are reputed to be the strongest in Europe. A carnival is held in winter and a *pardon* of the sea in summer with an open-air mass, displays of banners and a torchlight procession.

Villedieu-les-Poêles, inland from Granville, holds a procession every 4 years — 1987 was one of them — to honour the Knights of Jerusalem who have been associated with the town since the twelfth century. It is a custom dating back to 1655, roughly the time when local craftsmen became famous for their copper work. They are still in evidence today with a plethora of little shops spilling their wares out onto the pavements to tempt visitors in search of souvenirs. There is a bell foundry that is open on weekdays, a House of the Lacemaker and a copper museum and work shop which shows the original processes and some of the results.

Travellers who feel that their supply of abbeys is running low will find at least two more tucked away in the woods. **Hambye,** to the north, has a magnificent ruined church open to the four winds with attendant buildings that have been restored. They include the chapter house, a spacious kitchen and an upstairs dormitory besides an old refectory which is furnished and has tapestries on the walls. At

The Patton Memorial, Avranches

Lucerne Abbey, to the south-east, the decorated façade and the bell tower are original and, in spite of some lean years, the eighteenth-century organ has survived remarkably well. Visitors are welcome all day except at lunch time but the Abbot's Palace across the water is private and not on view.

A banner over the Villedieu-les-Poêles to Granville road announces the presence of a zoo, emphasised by a glass case containing a stuffed ostrich, a crane and a clutch of eggs. Some of the resident animals are very much alive while others have been dead for years.

Avranches is a town steeped in history but modern enough to close off whole areas for a cycle race. It was at the entrance to the cathedral, unfortunately destroyed during the Revolution, that England's Henry II did penance for the murder of Thomas à Becket at Canterbury. On the other side of the town a monument marks the place where General Patton paused before launching his famous offensive towards the Ardennes. The site is American territory with soil, trees and Stars and Stripes all brought over from the United States. The town museum is largely concerned with the early days of Mont-St-Michel. According to legend St Michael appeared twice to St Aubert, the Bishop of Avranches, instructing him to build a chapel on Mont Tombe. Eventually, tired of waiting, the archangel prodded the Bishop on the head with his finger, making a hole in his skull. The oratory was built in double quick time and the head of St Aubert found a resting place in the Basilica of St Gervais-St Protias surrounded by gold, silver and stone from the old cathedral.

Fishermen with a taste for salmon and solitude will doubtless make for **Ducey** on the banks of the River Sélune to the south. It is within easy reach of the Roche Qui Boit reservoirs and the Vezins lakes where any members of the family who get tired of waiting for a bite can take lessons at the local sailing school. Alternatively visitors in search of history will find a thirteenth-century château and an American cemetery and war memorial at St James before rejoining the main road at Pontorson, on the border with Brittany.

Further Information
— Normandy —

Museums and Other Places of Interest

SEINE-MARITIME AND EURE

Caudebec-en-Caux
Museum of Local History
Maison des Templiers
Open: 10am-12noon and 2.30-6pm, mid-June to mid-September. Otherwise Sat afternoons, Sun and holidays only.

Jumièges
Jumièges Abbey
Open: 9am-6pm May to September. Otherwise 10am-12noon and 2.30-5pm. Closed Tues, 1 Jan 1 May, 1 Nov, 25 Dec.

St Wandrille-Rançon
St Wandrille Abbey
Guided tours 10.30 and 11.15am, 3 and 4pm, Sundays 11.30am.

Villequier
Victor Hugo Museum
Open: 10am-12noon and 2-5pm. Extended to 7pm April to Sept. Closed Tues, Mon in winter and from Nov to end of Jan.

LE PERCHE-ORNE

L'Aigle
Open: Palm Sunday to mid-Nov 10am-12noon and 2-6.30pm. Closed Mondays.

Argentan
Benedictine Abbey — Display of Lace
2 Rue de l'Abbaye
Open: 2-4pm except Sundays and holidays.

Church of St Martin
Apply at the presbytery, 25 Rue de la Poterie

Argentelles Manor
Open: Sundays and holidays 4-7pm, mid-April to third week in October.

Bernay
Museum
Open: mid-June to mid-September 10am-12noon and 3-7pm. Otherwise 3-5pm. Closed Tuesdays, January and 25 December.

Le Bourg-St-Léonard
Château-Le-Bourg-St-Léonard
Guided tours 9am-12noon and 2-6pm. Closed Tuesdays.

Castle d'O
Guided tours 2.30-6pm. Closed Tuesdays and 5pm out of season. Morning tours on request.

Haras du Pin
Guided tours of stables 9am-12 noon and 2-6pm. Apply at the lodge.

Longny-au-Perche
Notre-Dame-de-Pitié Chapel
Church of St Martin. Apply M. le Curé, 1 Rue de l'Eglise.

Mont-Ormel
War Memorial
Near Chambois

Mortagne-au-Perche
Church of Notre-Dame
On request at town hall ☎ 33250422

Sassy Château
Open: Palm Sunday to All Saints' Day 3-6pm. Daily July and August. Saturdays and Sundays out of season.

Sées
St Latrium Cathedral
Son et Lumière in summer.

Ste Gauburge
Farm Museum
Open: 2-7pm daily June to mid-October.

La Trappe Abbey
Enquire at porter's lodge.

La Vove Manor
Open: 10am-5pm, May to October.

MANCHE
Avranches
Avranchin Museum
Open: 9am-12noon and 2-6pm Easter to end of September. Closed Tuesdays.

Botanical Gardens
Open: until 8.30pm Easter to end of September; July and August until 11pm with illuminations to mid-September.

St Gervais-St Protias Basilica
Treasure open 9am-12noon and 2-6pm. Apply sacristan in the church. Closed Sunday mornings and Mondays.

Bricquebec
Castle and Museum
Guided tours 10am-12noon and 2-6.30pm, July to mid-Sept. Closed Tuesdays and last Saturday and Sunday in July.

Champrepus Zoo
Open: 9am-7pm March to November.

Cherbourg
Emmanuel-Liais Park
Open: 8am-7.30pm during season otherwise 8.30am-5pm. Greenhouses 2-5pm except Sat, Sun and hols. Natural history museum in Liais' former home 10am-12noon and 2-5pm May to September; 2-5pm September to April, closed Sun mornings, Tues and hols.

Museum of Fine Arts
Open: 10am-12noon and 2-6pm. Closed Tuesdays and holidays.

War Museum
Open: 9am-12noon and 2-5.30pm October to March except Tuesdays.

Coutances
Cathedral, public gardens, local museum.

Flers
Château Grounds
Open: daily 7am-7pm.

Museum
Open: Easter to mid-October 2-6pm. Closed Sunday and Monday.

Granville
Aquarium near lighthouse
Open: 9am-12noon and 2-7pm Palm Sunday to mid-November.

Old Granville Museum
Next to entrance through ramparts Open: 10am-12noon and 2-6pm, April to first Sunday in October. Otherwise Wednesday afternoons and weekends. Closed holidays out of season.

Waxworks Museum
Guided tours 9.30-11.30am and 2.30-6pm mid-July to mid-September.

Gratot
Remains of Argouges Manor
Open: 9am-1pm and 2-7.30pm, closes 7pm out of season.

Hambye Abbey
Open: 10-11.30am and 2-6pm. Closed Tuesdays out of season, 25 December and throughout January.

Lucerne Abbey
Open: 9am-12noon and 2-5.45pm.

Pirou Castle
Open: 10am-12noon and 2-6pm. Closed Tuesdays September to mid-June.

Ste Mère Eglise
Airborne Troops Museum
Open 9am-12noon and 2-7pm Easter to mid-Nov. All day July and Aug. The remainder of the year weekdays on request. 10am-12noon and 2-6pm Sun and hols.

Farm Museum
Open: 10am-12noon and 2-7pm April to September. Closed Tuesdays.

St Lô
Fine Arts Museum
Open: July and August 10.30am-12noon and 2.30-5pm. Otherwise 2.30-5pm only. Closed Tuesdays and holidays.

Stud
Open: mid-July to mid-February 10-11am and 2.30-4.30pm.

St-Sauveur-le-Vicomte
Barbey d'Aurevilly Museum
Open: 10am-12noon and 3-6.30pm, Sept to June. Closed Tues. (Apply to keeper in the rest home, also in the castle).

Valognes
Hôtel de Granval-Caligny
32 Rue des Religieuses
Open: 11am and 2.30-6pm Wednesday to Saturday inclusive.

Cider Museum
Logis du Grand Quartier
Open: 10am-12noon and 2-6pm mid-June to end Sept. Closed Weds and Sun mornings, also 14 July and 15 August.

Villedieu-les-Poêles
Copper Museum
Rue Général Huard

Guided tours 9am-12noon and 2-6.30pm, June to mid-September.

Bell Foundry
Rue du Pont-Chignon.
Open: 8am-12noon and 2-6pm except Sundays and Mondays out of season.

Tourist Information Offices

L'Aigle
Place F. de Beina ☎ 33241240
Open: June to September.

Argentan
Place Marché ☎ 33671248

Avranches
Rue Général de Gaulle ☎ 33580022

Barneville-Carteret
Place Dr Auvret ☎ 33049058

Bernay
Town Hall ☎ 32433208

Caudebec-en-Caux
At the Mairie ☎ 35961112

Cherbourg
2 Quai Alexandre III
☎ 33530544 and at the railway station
May-September ☎ 33443992

Coutainville
Place 28 Juillet 1944 ☎ 33470146
Open: June to mid-September.

Flers
Place Général de Gaulle ☎ 33650675

Granville
15 Rue Georges Clemencea☎ 33500267

Mortagne-au-Perche
Place Général de Gaulle ☎ 33250422
Open: mid-June to mid-September.

St Lô
2 Rue Havin ☎ 33050209

Tourouvre
In church porch during season
☎ 33257455 *Gîtes* from Mairie de Tourouvre, 61190 Tourouvre ☎ 33257455

Valognes
Place Château ☎ 33 401155
Open: mid-May to September.

4 • Aisne

A isne, the most easterly of the three *départements* that make up the province of Picardy, is driven like a rather stocky wedge between the Ile de France and Champagne-Ardenne. Its principal town is Laon, 140km (87 miles) from Paris, 47km (29 miles) from Reims, 230km (143 miles) from Calais and 400km (248 miles) from Strasbourg on the border with Germany. It also has direct rail links with Paris, Lille, Amiens, Dijon and Calais. Every motorist travelling along the A26 from the Channel coast to join the Autoroute de l'Est, or the Autoroute du Soleil down to the Mediterranean, passes right through the *département* but only a small percentage of them ever stop to find out something more about it. This is a pity because it is pleasantly unsophisticated, historically interesting and seldom if ever crowded to capacity.

Mountains in this area are conspicuous by their absence. Their place on the gently undulating plain is taken by rivers like the Aisne and the Marne, lakes and ponds liberally stocked with fish and forests inhabited by deer, foxes and weasles who share them with several different kinds of birds. There are any number of trails blazed through the wooded areas, towpaths along the rivers and canals, cycle tracks and bridle paths, as well as facilities for visitors who would rather play tennis, swim or play golf. Dedicated sightseers will find numerous old buildings, especially in Laon, St Quentin, Soissons and Château-Thierry, a scattering of châteaux and ancient ruins and a variety of small, informative museums.

Aisne does rather well as far as accommodation is concerned. There are several hotels, although nothing very out of the ordinary in Laon, Soissons or Château-Thierry, whereas St Quentin has a comfortable establishment with a good restaurant not far from the railway station. Motorists in search of first-class, more atmospheric surroundings would probably be happier at Fère-en-Tardenois, to the south of the *département*, or in a sprinkling of other converted châteaux. In addition there are plenty of most acceptable *logis* and

85

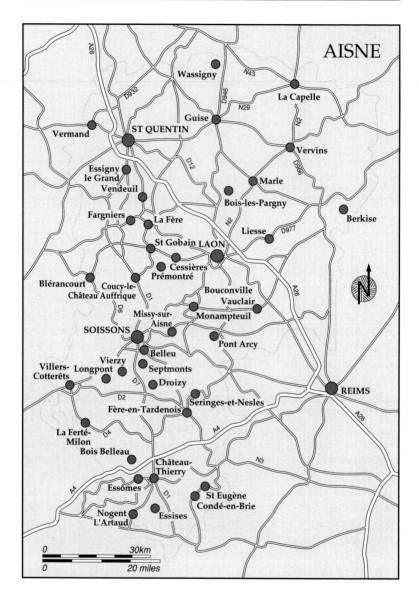

auberges as well as *gîtes*, rooms in private homes and farms and special hostels that cater for people on riding or walking holidays.

Some other examples of sports and pastimes available in Aisne are horse racing, boating and flying, either in a light aircraft or a hot-air balloon. There are also concerts and musical festivals in Laon and celebrations in honour of Jean de la Fontaine at Château-Thierry, usually based on one of his fables. It is also possible to eat well in the area, sampling dishes like Picard leek pie, *foie gras*, duck cooked with cherries, rabbit in cider, veal in a number of different guises and local fruits and cheeses. Heading the list of wines is a sparkling variety that looks like champagne, tastes like champagne but strictly speaking is not champagne for the simple reason that it is produced in Château-Thierry and at Craonelle, in Picardy, just 7km (4 miles) from the all-important provincial border. Souvenir hunters are unlikely to find anything very out-of-the-ordinary in Aisne although it is possible to buy baskets that are made locally, honey, venison pâté and, of course, sparkling wine.

At the moment the whole of Aisne could justifiably be described as off the beaten track — even the A26 autoroute goes round instead of through both Laon and St Quentin. This being so, the latter is the logical place to start exploring the *département* because it is just inside the border on the main route from Calais 134km (83 miles) away. It is an ancient town, named after St Quentin who was martyred in AD287 and whose relics soon made it a place of pilgrimage. Sadly the town was almost completely destroyed by the Germans in 1917 but it has managed to restore one or two ancient buildings, revive at least one traditional celebration and add a whole list of modern events such as an international motocross, a nautical fête and a jazz festival.

The Basilique de **St Quentin**, lying between the Place de la Basilique and the Place Winston Churchill, started life in the twelfth century but was not completed for about three hundred years. It is Gothic in character, incorporating some unusual features such as the double transept, said to be the only one in France. Two short blocks away the hôtel de ville is more flamboyantly Gothic with an obtrusive clock tower, decorative windows and a line of uniform arches creating an arcade that all but links the buildings on either side. Guided tours are arranged for visitors who are interested in its finer points, among them the Renaissance Salle des Mariages with its ornamental fireplace and the contrasting Salle du Conseil where the town council meets in decidedly Art Déco surroundings.

Apart from the town library, housed in an eighteenth-century mansion and containing some rather nice old books and manuscripts, St Quentin has two museums. The Musée d'Entomologie, in the same building as the Tourist Office, a mere stone's throw from the Place de l'Hôtel de Ville, claims that its large collection of insects, including about half a million butterflies, is the most important of its kind in Europe. Meanwhile the Musée Antoine Lécuyer, slightly further afield in a street of the same name, is devoted exclusively to art. Here the most important exhibit is a collection of more than eighty pastel drawings by the court artist Maurice-Quentin de La Tour but it also has a variety of paintings and tapestries as well as enamels, porcelain and pottery. Among St Quentin's other attractions are a nineteenth-century theatre built in the Italian style, a port de plaisance with moorings for about forty smallish craft and botanical gardens laid out along the bank of the Somme.

Sports play an important part in the life of the town, those of most interest to visitors being tennis and swimming, riding, fishing and boating, with a 9-hole golf course at Mesnil-St-Laurent a few kilometres away. In addition there is a little steam train known as the Vermandois Tourist Railway that runs on Sundays and holidays during June and early July as well as in September. For a bird's eye view of the area tourist flights are available every day except Tuesday from the Aeroclub de l'Aisne at Roupy, a small hill village on the D930 to the south-west.

There are plenty of places to visit in the neighbourhood of St-Quentin. **Vermand** on the N29 just short of Aisne's western boundary, was originally a Gallo-Roman city with prehistoric connections. Much of it has already been excavated and any number of bits and pieces discovered at the site are on display in the local archaeological museum. A museum of a very different kind has been set up in **Essigny-le-Grand**, due south of St Quentin, just off the D1. It was designed as a memorial to the French 87th Infantry Regiment who took part in World War I and contains everything from uniforms, documents and weapons to a reconstructed casemate and items recovered from the trenches after the fighting in 1914.

Anyone with children who tend to get a little restive wandering through museums could opt instead for **Vendeuil**, only slightly further away on the N44 to Laon. The main attraction of this small village on the banks of the Canal de la Sambre à l'Oise is its leisure park where the boating pool, aptly titled the Ile aux Pédalos, is encased in trees and flowers. It offers all the fun of the fair including a cable car, merry-go-rounds, swings, slides and pedalos, added to which the nearby Auberge de Vendeuil is a delightful modern *logi* with comfortable rooms, one of them adapted for disabled guests.

Vendeuil is only a short drive from **La Fère**, which appears to owe its name to a *phara*, or Merovingian farm, that once occupied the site. The town was fortified in the Middle Ages, besieged by the Huguenots in 1582 and again 13 years later by Henry IV, and eventually lost its defenses during the nineteenth century. The remains of a dam that was built to flood La Fère can still be seen in the somewhat marshy land to the south, between Beautor and Deuillet. The town has a fifteenth-century château, barracks built in 1719 on the Place de l'Esplanade, a collection of paintings in the Musée Jeanne d'Aboville and a massive statue of an artilleryman that once graced the Pont de l'Alma in Paris.

Visitors interested in the Resistance Movement in Picardy during World War II should consider a trip to the Musée Departemental de la Resistance et de la Deportation en Picardie at **Fargniers**, just next door on the outskirts of Tergnier. It is very informative, particularly about the operations carried out by the Maquis in Aisne, and has an amazingly varied collection of exhibits. They include everything from documents and photographs, items of equipment and scale models to an aircraft and even a locomotive. On the other hand, **St Gobain**, some 9km (6 miles) to the south on the D13, is far less militant. The village, surrounded by an extensive forest, had been in existence for about six hundred years when Enguerrand III chose it as the site for a new fortified castle in the thirteenth century. This barely had time to become established before Louis XI decided to knock the whole fortress down again. The ruins were left to moulder until 1692 when they were bought by the Manufacture Royale des Glaces, since when the factory has been busily engaged in producing all kinds of glass including the glazing for the Pyramid du Louvre and other ambitious projects.

The countryside to the south is well endowed with ancient buildings as well as other much more modern attractions. The eighteenth-century **Abbaye de Prémontré**, reached along the minor D14 from Septvaux, looks more like a splendid country house although it stands on the site of a monastery founded by Norbert de Xanten about nine hundred years ago. This was converted into another glass factory before being taken over by a psychiatric hospital but the chapel, part of the building and the gardens are open to visitors. **Coucy-le-Château Auffrique**, a few kilometres away, was not nearly so fortunate. It once had an enormous fortress, built on a spur overlooking the valley of the Oise and the Ailette, with a massive keep and defensive walls reinforced by at least thirty towers. Sadly the Germans blew it up in 1917, leaving nothing except an empty shell. It is possible to get some idea of what the keep and the town of Coucy looked like before the war from a scale model in the Museum Tower and items housed in the document room of the château.

In complete contrast, **Merlieux et Fouquerolles**, also on the D5 but in the opposite direction, boasts one of the first educational farms to be established in France. This Ferme Pédagogique was designed

mainly to teach children all about their environment but it also has
an enormous fish pond filled with all the different species and plants
that are common to the area and which can be inspected by sightseers
at any time of the year. The surrounding woods are ideal for walking,
especially as a *Grande Randonnée* — the GR12A — passes close by on
its way from one side of Aisne to the other. Meanwhile **Folembray**,
5km (3 miles) north-west of Coucy-le-Château, has a race track that
offers driving and piloting courses as well as using the circuit for
professional events.

Due west of Coucy-le-Château, and only 13km (8 miles) away
along the D934, the immaculate **Château de Blérancourt** is the home
of the National Museum of Franco-American Cooperation. In its
early days this seventeenth-century château, built by Salomon de
Brosse who designed the Palais de Luxembourg in Paris, played host
to such distinguished guests as Henry IV and Cardinal Richelieu.
However it was badly knocked about during the Revolution and was
in a sorry state when two American women decided to use it as the
headquarters of the American Voluntary Ambulance Corps in 1917.
Anne Morgan, the daughter of John Pierpont Morgan, and Anne
Murray Dike organised a whole range of medical and social services
behind the Allied lines until the armistice was signed the following
year in a small railway carriage parked in the woods not far away.
The return of peace did not mean the end of all the troubles caused
by years of war and Anne Morgan continued to operate from her
headquarters. In 1931 the French government showed its appreciation by giving Blérancourt its official status as a national museum.
Today it stands in beautifully manicured gardens, filled with American plants and flowers and watched over by a statue of George
Washington. Inside there are rooms devoted to the long history of
Franco-American cooperation, beginning with the American War of
Independence and including both World Wars. There is also an
extensive library, a collection of paintings and sculptures by American artists working in France and French artists in America and a
whole range of wartime exhibits including an old Ford ambulance
that once belonged to the American Field Service.

The D6, connecting Blérancourt with Soissons, 23km (14 miles)
further south, is a particularly delightful road through undulating
agricultural country and beautiful woodlands, dipping down into
small, totally unexpected valleys at infrequent intervals. **Soissons**
itself came into being some two thousand years ago and, according
to Victor Hugo, 'it saw Caesar conquer, Clovis rule and Napoléon
totter'. Things have obviously changed out of all recognition since

The National Museum of Franco-American Cooperation, Blérancourt

the city was chosen as the first capital of France after the last Roman general, Syagrius, had been defeated by Clovis in AD486. However it still has some splendid reminders of its not-quite-so-distant past. The most memorable of these is the façade of the former Abbaye de St Jean des Vignes which, apart from the sparse remains of the cloister and the reconstructed refectory, is all that is left of the medieval monastery. The nave was demolished about two hundred years ago but in some strange way this makes the façade all the more impressive. Just inside the main gate, tucked away behind the Tourist Office, is a fascinating replica of an old Merovingian house that has a surprising amount of space but practically nothing inside.

Soissons was quite severely damaged during World War I, but the cathedral had already lost much of its original stained glass when a powder magazine exploded nearby in 1815. It is not an especially admirable building from the outside, partly perhaps because it only has one tower, but the interior has several things to offer. Among them are the southern transept, left over from its twelfth-century predecessor, and the nave which was added shortly afterwards. Included in the cathedral's most noteworthy possessions are part of an ancient tapestry showing scenes from the lives of its patron saints Gervais and Protias and a handful of paintings, among them the *Adoration of the Magi* by Rubens.

A reconstructed Merovingian house at Soissons

Facing the cathedral across the Place Fernand Marquigny, the Eglise St Pierre, looking oddly well-washed and modern, is another survivor from the late twelfth century. A short walk away, on the corner of the Rue de la Congregation and the Rue de la Paix, the Ancien Abbaye de St Léger is now occupied by the Municipal Museum. The old part of the building, which includes the church, chapter house and part of the cloister, contains mostly sculptures while the rest of the items relating to archaeology, local history and fine arts are housed in the more modern section next door. Time has not dealt very kindly with the St Medard Abbey, rather out on a limb along the Rue Pepin-le-Bref on the far side of the River Aisne. It was once an important place of pilgrimage and, in fact, both Clovis's son and grandson were buried there, but now it consists mainly of the original crypt, inaugurated by Charles le Chauve in AD841 and the tower where Abélard is thought to have been imprisoned.

The hotels in Soissons are nothing much to write home about but there are at least two acceptable *logis* in the vicinity. The Millery at Ambleny is the most convenient for people who want to visit the château at Vic-sur-Aisne or simply spend their time riding, fishing, cycling or walking in the forest. Meanwhile the Hôtel de l'Abbaye at **Longpont** has an ancient Cistercian abbey practically on the doorstep. The church is in ruins but the old monastic buildings were converted into a very desirable residence during the eighteenth century and several of the furnished rooms as well as the 700-year-old cellar are open to visitors.

There are one or two places of interest in the area around Longpont, each with its own historic château. For instance, **Septmonts**, to the north-east on the banks of the River Crise, was once the summer home of the Bishops of Soissons. The fairytale keep has been expertly restored and work is going on to reconstruct the remains of the château at the far end of the fortified wall. Visitors have to walk across the grass from the entrance gate but there are places under the trees for anyone who wants to have a picnic. Due south of Septmonts, **Droizy** has an unusual claim to fame. Its 600-year-old castle belonged to Etienne Vignolles who fought alongside Joan of Arc but achieved immortality at the hands of every cardplayer when he was chosen to represent the knave of hearts. Apart from its medieval buildings the village has also preserved a typical farm from the late sixteenth century. On the other hand, **Montgobert**, on roughly the same level as Septmonts but separated from it by both the D1 and the N2, is known principally for its Musée Européen du Bois et de l'Outil. The château, once the home of Napoléon's sister Pauline Bonaparte, has now turned its attention to the history of woodwork. It recreates the conditions under which these craftsmen worked and has an extensive collection of the tools they would have used.

Villers-Cotterêts, further to the south-west, along the N2 to Paris, was the home of the Dumas family. The famous novelist Alexandre Dumas — Alexandre Dumas-Davy de la Pailleterie, to give him his full name — was born here in 1802. It is quite possible that the splendid Renaissance château helped to inspire the settings for some of his most famous novels such as *The Count of Monte Cristo*, *The Three Musketeers* and *Le Vicomte de Bragelonne*. As one would expect, the town has a very comprehensive Alexandre Dumas museum, brimming over with family memorabilia of one sort and another including documents, photographs, drawings, paintings, furniture and some not very prepossessing statues. It focuses attention on the enormous variety of works by Dumas, covering everything from romance and travel to crime and cookery, as well as on his son — also Alexandre — who wrote several novels in addition to *La Dame aux Camélias* before turning his attention to the stage.

Still with the accent on French literature, **La Ferté-Milon**, roughly 10km (6 miles) from Villers-Cotterêts along the D936, was where the seventeenth-century dramatist Jean Racine lived with his grandmother, Marie Desmoulins. Part of their old home has been set aside

Château-Thierry; the ancient gateway through which Joan of Arc led her troops in 1429

for a modest collection of documents and given the rather grand title of Musée Jean Racine, although many of the exhibits are much more concerned with the history of the town. Anyone who is interested in farming would probably feel more at home in the Musée Regional du Machinisme Agricole which claims to have one of the finest collections of old tractors in France. In addition to other agricultural machinery it has an imaginative collection of fossils and prehistoric tools and shows an unexpected interest in church clocks. Other local attractions include Louis de Orléans's fourteenth-century castle that was started but never finished, the 400-year-old Eglise de Notre-Dame and the first bridge to be built by Gustave Eiffel who went on to construct his famous tower and the framework for Bartholdi's Statue of Liberty in New York harbour.

The most southerly town of any size in Aisne is **Château-Thierry** on the D1, 96km (60 miles) from Paris in the valley of the Marne. It has a rather self-satisfied air about it, perhaps because of its many winegrowers who describe themselves as champagne houses regardless of the fact that the name should only really apply in the province next door. The town is rather short of hotels and restaurants but can provide a selection of guest houses, *gîtes*, rural inns and camp sites in the neighbourhood. Nor is it in any way overburdened with tourist attractions and leans heavily on Jean de La Fontaine for its publicity. This famous storyteller was born in a house on the street that has been called after him and which has been turned into a municipal museum. Apart from all the usual exhibits like paintings, drawings, furniture and objects d'art, it contains some personal reminders of La Fontaine such as his birth certificate and volumes of his fables illustrated by artists of the calibre of Gustave Doré.

The oldest building in Château-Thierry is an eleventh-century feudal castle that was turned into a château 200 years later but very wisely retained its ramparts and two fortified entrances to guard against any future attacks. By way of a change, beekeepers might well appreciate a conducted tour of La Ruche en Pain d'Epices where they are also invited to sample the mead and gingerbread and buy some, along with honey, to take away with them. However lovers of sparkling wine usually head for one of the many caves that are open to visitors by appointment almost every day and at set times on Sunday afternoons from March to December.

A certain amount of variety is available to anyone with plans for exploring the surrounding area. **Bois Belleau**, 16km (10 miles) north-eastwards along the D9, was captured by the 4th Brigade of the American Marines during the second Battle of the Marne in 1918. More than 2,300 men who lost their lives there are buried in the large cemetery with a memorial to all their countrymen who were killed in World War I. To the south of Château-Thierry on the D86, **Nogent l'Artaud** has an antique car museum while **Essises**, just off the D1, is concerned almost exclusively with the French campaign of 1814. It has filled its museum with weapons, documents and about a thousand little handpainted figures associated with Napoléon's war against Prussia that led to his abdication.

Continuing the arc round Château-Thierry, **Condé-en-Brie** along the D20 and not far from the border with Champagne-Ardenne, also has a collection of tiny soldiers in the elegant Château des Princes de Condé. The building dates in part from the twelfth century but was altered and refurbished on several occasions. The Grand Salon, the music room and the staircase designed by Servandoni are almost unchanged since the eighteenth century, enhanced by paintings that include works by Oudry and Watteau. If all this involves too much time and travelling, flights over the area can be arranged in a hot-air balloon from Chierry, 3km (2 miles) from Château-Thierry.

Brasles, to the north, just off the A4 autoroute, has absolutely nothing of historic importance to recommend it. Its attraction lies in the 9-hole Golf du Val Secret, an attractive course laid out in the valley with a club house, restaurant and bar. It is associated with the Golf de Champagne, an equally pleasing 18-hole course at Villers-Agron further up the motorway. The local hotel is modest and has a restaurant to match so visitors with a taste for grandeur should opt for the Château de Fère, a luxurious hostellerie standing in its own grounds on the outskirts of Fère-en-Tardenois, reached along the D967 or the D310. The château dates in part from the Renaissance and not only provides comfortable rooms, an excellent restaurant and facilities for tennis, fishing, riding and, of course, golf, but it also has its own ruined castle, reached across a splendid medieval bridge. The castle was built in the early thirteenth century by Robert de Dreux, a grandson of Louis VI. It passed into the hands of the Montmorency family and through them to the Prince de Condé. One of his descendants ran out of money and started knocking it down to sell as building material, getting rid of all the furniture and fittings at the same time. When even this failed to meet his debts everything left over was seized by his creditors and auctioned in Paris in 1793. Fortunately they could not get their hands on the old covered market that dominates the main square in Fère-en-Tardenois.

Seringes-et-Nesles, 4km (2½ miles) away along the D967, is the site of both a thirteenth-century fortified castle, which is really only of interest to students of military architecture, and a cemetery containing the graves of 6,000 American soldiers who died in World War I. From here there is not much to see in the way of scenery or elderly buildings apart from the ancient abbey church of St Yved at Braine, where the D22 joins the main road from Soissons to Reims. However, once the network of minor roads reaches the banks of the Aisne the outlook improves considerably. For instance, Pont-Arcy has a fascinating miniature railway near the canal with more than 700m (2,296ft) of tracks, along with tunnels, waterfalls, typical scenery and even cable cars. It belongs to the owner of a bar called, naturally, Au Petit Train, who shows it off to visitors every weekend.

North of Pont-Arcy, and running more or less parallel with the river, is a natural limestone crest known as the **Chemin des Dames**. In ancient times it supplied stone for the local inhabitants but during World War I their quarries were extended to provide any number of underground shelters where the soldiers lived like early cave dwellers and even adopted their habit of decorating the walls. The memorial Musée de la Caverne du Dragon, in a quarry next to the Ferme d'Hurtebise, puts on an audio-visual show with commentaries in French, English and German, and visits are arranged to some of the

Château de Crèvecoeur-en-Auge, Normandy

The quayside at Carteret, Normandy

galleries. Building on the long Bugeaud tunnel started from Craonnelle, which was completely destroyed in the fighting but somewhat later turned its attention to producing a sparkling wine that has all the properties of champagne.

From the Ferme d'Hurtebise a little scenic road leads up to the village of **Bouconville-Vauclair** with its Cistercian abbey, founded by St Bernard in 1134. It came to grief during the Revolution and for some unknown reason was bombed during World War I. Eventually volunteers decided to tidy up the ruins and have so far cleared the foundations of the abbey church, the monk's refectory and the cellar. One of the most interesting things about it is the herb garden, with hundreds of medicinal plants of every kind, created by the Révérend Père Courtois on the site of the original apothecary workshop.

Beyond these ruins the D19 takes a turn to the west and calls in at **Chamouille**, one of the oldest villages in Aisne, having been mentioned in the miracles of St Gabrien nearly 1,500 years ago. It has now been incorporated into the Parc Nautique de l'Ailette, a modern leisure complex beside a lake fringed with sand and beach umbrellas. Foremost among its many attractions are an 18-hole golf course and a 9-hole practice course along with all the usual attendant facilities. The sports school divides its attention between sailing, windsurfing and rowing and has water as well as mountain bikes for hire. There are tennis courts and a jogging course, a museum at the nature centre and facilities for bird watchers as well as riding and fishing areas set aside for anglers who have the necessary licence. The Hotel Mercure Holigolf overlooks the lake while a three-star camp site caters for the needs of holidaymakers with tents and caravans. Another less ambitious but nevertheless popular recreation centre has grown up beside the reservoir at Monampteuil a little over 10km (6 miles) away along the D19. An added attraction is that one of the finest beekeepers in the country can be found at Chavignon on the N2 quite close by. This Ateliers de l'Abielle is open every day except Tuesday and covers the whole process from harvesting pollen and breeding from selected queens to producing royal jelly and packaging the end products for sale.

Laon, the capital of Aisne, is an intriguing city, occupying a site that has been inhabited since Gallo-Roman times. In its early days the town was known as Lugdunum but changed its name in the fifth century when St Remi de Reims established the diocese of Laon. Thereafter it was favoured by the Carolingian kings, became embroiled in many local quarrels and saw its cathedral burned down and Bishop Gaudry assassinated during a citizens' revolt in 1112.

Laon; the cathedral and the former Bishops Palace

The replacement Cathedral of Notre-Dame, which dominates the plateau above the more modern town, was completed in 1235 and is an excellent example of early Gothic art. It can be reached by the convoluted Rampe d'Ardon that twists like a snake up the mountainside, a more easygoing road on the other face, or, rather unusually, by the Poma 2000, the first metro-cableway to be installed in France. At one point a turning off the Rampe d'Ardon takes a shortcut through the Pont d'Ardon, one of three fortified gateways that still lead into the ancient heart of the city. Meanwhile the road follows the line of the ramparts and eventually joins up with the Avenue Gambetta that has clambered up in company with the Poma 2000 on the opposite side.

Laon has more than eighty listed buildings but by no means all of them are regarded as tourist attractions, although they all contribute to the general atmosphere. Among the most important, apart from the cathedral, is the adjoining Bishops Palace, overlooking a large courtyard and now occupied by the law courts. Beyond the cathedral, in the Rue Georges Ermant, the original Chapelle des Templiers forms part of the Musée Archaeologique Municipal and is especially proud of the likeness of Guillaume d'Harcigny who was Charles VI's doctor. The museum also has a collection of Greek terracotta vases said to rival those in the Louvre, relics from prehistory through to the

Middle Ages and some very worthwhile pictures, notably *Le Concert* by Mathieu Le Nain.

The Eglise St Martin-au-Parvis is just on the other side of the Cuve St Vincent, a deep narrow valley that forces its way into the old city. The original abbey church was built in the twelfth century but its much younger section is now the home of the Municipal Library that contains an impressive collection of manuscripts, charts and seals as well as early printed books and documents. Beyond the church the Avenue de la République continues down one side of this thin rocky spur towards the arsenal, which has taken over St Vincent's abbey, and the Morlot battery right at the end.

The lower town with its commercial and industrial interests has a few reminders of the past such as the Bishops dovecote, or Colombier de la Grange l'Evêque, but on the whole its attractions are modern rather than antique. There is a municipal stadium with a camp site next door, and covered tennis courts have been built on the other side of the encircling N2 with a racecourse in the woods beyond. Meanwhile, a few kilometres away to the north the Aérodrome de Laon-Chambry has its own sky-diving club and an official parachute training centre. Tourist flights of varying lengths are arranged from the airfield by the Aéro-Club de Laon, but the days and times depend entirely on the weather. Laon has no hotels in the luxury bracket but La Banniere de France in the upper town is a three-star restaurant with a number of rooms for guests and the Hostellerie St Vincent on the outskirts of the town is an acceptable establishment designed on the lines of a motel.

The only place of historic interest to the east of Laon is **Liesse**, a short drive away along the D977 through Samoussy. It is frequently visited by pilgrims anxious to pay their respects to the Black Virgin in the Basilique de Notre-Dame. According to legend she was brought back to France by three crusaders who escaped from captivity in Egypt with the help of Princess Ismeria after she had been converted to Christianity. The story is illustrated in the Chapelle St-Louis and emphasised by an ex-voto left by Mary de Medici who is said to have been only one of many royal visitors to the shrine. Motorists who plan to spend a few days in the vicinity should book ahead if they are hoping to stay at the four-star Château de Barive at Sainte Preuve on a minor road to the south of the D977 that branches off just beyond Chivres-en-Laonnois.

A number of small, not at all scenic, roads head northwards across the plain with the D24 providing the shortest route to **Marle**, close to the main highway from Laon to Vervins. The town's only tourist attractions concentrate on the distant past with reproductions of Merovingian houses in its archaeological park and the Musée des Temps Barbares recalling the so-called barbaric ages in the Mill of Marle. On the opposite side of the N2, **Bois-les-Pargny** on the edge of the diminutive Forêt de Marle has a menhir called the Verzieux de Gargantua and a pink-brick château said to have been built in the reign of Louis XII but bearing the date 1611.

Vervins is a most attractive town with plenty of atmosphere regardless of its long and turbulent history. It was overrun by the Barbarians in the fifth century and again by the Normans some 400 years later. When it became the property of the Coucy family they lost no time in fortifying it with ramparts and towers, some of which survived repeated attacks during the next 600 years. Fortunately no-one paid much attention to it during the Franco-Prussian War or either of the two World Wars so it still has some very elderly buildings including the fortified church of Notre-Dame. The Musée de la Thierache, in the Place du Général de Gaulle, dabbles in everything of interest in the area from prehistoric times to the present day, not forgetting local art or popular traditions. The town's leading hotel is the Tour du Roy, a converted manor house built on the ramparts with a tower room that is rather fun and certainly unusual.

The countryside round Vervins is unexpectedly pastoral with small green hills, little streams and a many apple orchards, making a pleasant change from the rather bare plains that characterise this part of France. Although the D960 to **Guise** could certainly not be described as memorable it is worth driving the 25km (15½ miles) involved to inspect the medieval fortress which replaced a Celtic stronghold and a later Gallic settlement. The tenth century keep and its marginally younger castle were given to Claude of Lorraine by Francois I in 1527 and thereafter were strengthened and enlarged to defend an obvious invasion route to Paris. At the same time several nearby villages along the valleys of the Oise and the Serre fortified their churches and, according to one old legend, they were all linked to the castle by underground passages.

Vauban updated the defences during the reign of Louis XIV and the result proved to be most effective until the stronghold was captured by the Germans in World War I. Everything that remained after the battles of 1917 was abandoned and vandalised until the Club de Vieux Manoir was founded by Maurice Duton in 1952 with the idea of encouraging young people to help with the restoration. The venture was remarkably successful. More than 70,000 volunteers from different parts of France as well as from several other countries have taken part in the excavations and rebuilding work. In due course the club grew into a nationwide movement undertaking similar projects all over France.

The Musée Municipal Marcel Migrenne divides its attention between the Lords of Guise and two other famous personalities. They are Camille Desmoulins, the revolutionary whose cries of 'To arms' 'To Arms' inflamed the Paris crowds but who, nevertheless, ended up on the guillotine, and Jean-Baptiste André Godin, the factory owner who created an early example of a workers' co-operative with homes and other amenities attached called the Familistère. Other small museums in the vicinity are mainly concerned with wood. In **Vadencourt**, for example, the Wood Workshop Museum is filled with old tools used to make everything from clogs to cabinets, each in their own appropriate setting. The Musée Louis Cornu at **Wassigny** is a tribute to the internationally known wood carver, painter and poet and contains a cross-section of his work, while **Buironfosse**, on the N29 to the north-east, was once the home of the Sabotiers and has set up a small Musée du Sabot tracing the history of clog-making over the past 800 years.

Anyone in search of souvenirs will find a basket workshop at **Chigny**, about 13km (8 miles) east of Guise along the D462. Visitors are welcome during working hours when they can watch the articles being made and select examples to take away with them. **Le Nouvion-et-Thierache**, on the D26 north of Chigny, uses traditional methods to produce an apéritif from fruit like strawberries, raspberries and redcurrants picked in the grounds of La Chapelle Jérôme. On the other hand **La Bouteille**, 7km (4 miles) from Vervins on the D963, owes its name to a bottle factory that was established in the village in the mid-sixteenth century, but is now better known for the Vallée des Cerfs, a deer park with guided tours three times a week and delicacies like deer pâté for sale.

Beyond the Vallée des Cerfs a fairly scenic road joins the N2 at Entreaupont on the way from Vervins to **La Capelle**. The town has a church designed by the architect of the Paris Opera, a typical *logi* and plenty of opportunities for riding and walking. However its most famous attraction is a racecourse, established in 1874, where the trotting races invariably attract large crowds. **Hirson**, 15km (9 miles) from La Capelle on the N29, and about the same distance from Vervins along the D963, is a railway centre with little to interest the average tourist apart from a museum that concentrates on local history. However, people in search of a golfing holiday usually make for the Domaine du Tilleul at Landouzy-la-Ville, along a minor road to the south 7km (4 miles) away. The hotel is open all the year round, has tennis courts and an 18-hole golf course and is a good place for walking or exploring further afield. Hirson itself is practically on the border with Belgium and within easy reach of Charleville-Mézières in Champagne-Ardenne.

Further Information
— Aisne —

Museums and Other Places of Interest

Bois Belleau
American Memorial
Open: 9am-6pm mid-April to mid-Sept.
8am-5pm mid-Sept to mid-April.
☎ 23 70 62 00

Blérancourt
*Musée National de la Cooperation Franco-
   Americaine*
Open: 10am-12noon and 2-4pm. Closed
Tuesdays. ☎ 23 39 60 16

Bois-les-Pargny
Château
To visit inside the château
☎ 23 80 81 96 or 23 80 83 33

Bouconville-Vauclair
Vauclair Abbey
Open: all year round. Conducted tours
Easter to October. ☎ 23 26 70 00

La Bouteille
La Vallée des Cerfs
Open: Wednesday, Saturday and
Sunday afternoons. ☎ 23 97 49 60

Buironfosse
Musée du Sabot
Open: 2-5pm Mondays and Tuesdays.
1.30-5pm Wednesday to Saturday.
☎ 23 97 84 42

Chambry
Aéro-club
Chemin d'Aulnois
For information about flights ☎ 23 23
00 87 or enquire at the Tourist Office.

Chamouille
Parc de l'Ailette
For information ☎ 23 24 83 03
Camp Site ☎ 23 24 83 06
Golf Course. Open: 9am-12noon and 1-
7pm. Closed Tuesdays. ☎ 23 24 83 99

Château-Thierry
Castle
Enquire at the Tourist Office.
Champagne Cellars
Open: Sundays 3pm, 4pm and 5pm.
March to December, otherwise by
appointment. For information
☎ 23 69 13 10

Jean de la Fontaine Museum
Rue Jean de la Fontaine
Open: 10am-12noon and 2.30-6.30pm
July to September. 10am-12noon and 2-
6pm. April to June but closed Tuesdays. 2-5pm weekdays except Tuesdays and 10am-12noon and 2-5pm
Sundays October to March.
☎ 23 69 05 60

Ruche en Pain d'Epices
Rue du Pont
Brasles
☎ 23 69 12 63

Chavignon
Ateliers de l'Abielle
Open: 8am-7pm. Closed Tuesdays.
☎ 23 21 61 62

Chemin des Dames
Musée de la Caverne du Dragon
Open: 10.30-11.30am and 2.30-5.30pm.
Closed Tuesdays, during the winter
and February school holidays.

Condé-en-Brie
Château des Princes de Condé
Open for conducted tours 2.30, 3.30 and
4.30pm June, July and August. Sundays
and bank holidays May to September,
Easter Sunday and Monday.
☎ 23 82 42 25

Coucy-le-Château Auffrique
Château Museum and Document Room
Open: 9am-12noon and 2-6pm May to
September. 10am-12noon and 1.30-4pm
October to April. Closed Tuesdays.
☎ 23 52 71 28

Museum Tower
Open: 10am-12noon and 2-6pm July
and August. 2-6pm weekends only
September to June.

Droizy
La Tour de Droizy
Open: 2-6pm Saturdays and Sundays
May to 25 December. Please telephone
first 23 55 32 89 or 16(1) 45 20 78 04 in
Paris for guided tours.

Essigny-le-Grand
Memorial Museum
Open: daily. Closed in August.
☎ 23 63 38 16

Essises
Museum
Open: by appointment 9am-12noon
and 2-5pm for a guided tour.
☎ 23 69 88 09

Essômes-sur-Marne
Abbey church of St Ferréol
Keys at the Town Hall.
☎ 23 83 08 31

Fère-en-Tardenois
Château
Enquire at the Tourist Office
☎ 23 82 31 57

La Fère '
Musée Jeanne d'Aboville
Open: 2-6pm mid-April to mid-
October. Closed Tuesdays and 1 May.
2-5pm Wednesdays, Saturdays and

Sundays mid-October to mid-April.
Closed 25 December and 1 January.

La Ferté-Milon
Musée Jean Racine
Rue des Bouchers
Open: weekends and bank holidays.
☎ 23 96 77 77

Musée Regional du Machinisme Agricole
Open: 10am-12noon and 2-5pm Sat and
Sun. At other times by appointment.
☎ 23 96 71 79

Folembray
Driving Circuit
☎ 23 52 49 98

Guise
Castle and Fortifications
Open: 9am-12noon and 2-7pm in
summer (2-6pm in spring and otherwise 2-5pm). Closed for Christmas.
☎ 23 61 11 76

Musée Municipal Marcel Migrenne
Place de Familistère
Open: daily on request but closed Mon.

Hirson
Museum
Open: 2-5pm. ☎ 23 58 33 28

Laon
Cathedral of Notre-Dame
Open: 8.30am-7pm. Access to staircase
3.30pm Saturdays, Sundays and holidays
May to mid-October for 2-hour visit. Otherwise 3.30pm Friday to Monday inclusive
and bank holidays July and August.
☎ 23 20 28 62 (Tourist Office)

Musée Archeologique
Rue Georges Ermant
Open: 10am-12noon and 2-6pm April
to September. Closed Tuesdays. 10am-
12noon and 2-5pm October to March.
Closed 1 May, 14 July, 25 December
and 1 January. ☎ 23 20 19 87

Town Library
Abbaye St-Martin
Open: 10am-12noon and 1.30-6pm.
Tuesdays to Saturdays. Special
arrangements made for research.
☎ 23 20 19 57

Liesse
Basilique de Notre-Dame
Open: daily ☎ 23 22 20 21

Longpont
Cistercian Abbey
Open: 11.30am and 2.30-6.30pm
Saturdays, Sundays and holidays mid-
March to mid-November.
☎ 23 96 01 63

Marle
Musée des Temps Barbares
Open: 3-7pm June to September.
Closed Tuesdays. ☎ 23 24 01 33

Merlieux et Fouquerolles
Aquariums
Open: all the year round but 2-6pm Satur-
days and Sundays. Closed on holidays.

Monampteuil
Leisure centre
Open: April to September. ☎ 23 21 06 73

Montgobert
Musée Europeen du Bois et de l'Outil
Open: 2-6pm April to October. All the
year by appointment. ☎ 23 96 39 69

Nogent l'Artaud
Antique Car Museum
Open: 10am-12noon and 2-6pm April
to September. 10am-12noon and 2-5pm
October to March. Always closed on
Tuesdays. ☎ 23 70 11 10

Pont-Arcy
Miniature Railway at Au Petit Train
Open: Saturdays and Sundays.
☎ 23 24 40 39

Prémontré
Abbey of Prémontré
Visits by appointment only.
☎ 23 23 66 66

Roupy
Aéroclub de l'Aisne
Open: every day except Tuesdays.
☎ 23 62 49 00

St Gobain
Glass Factory
Place Doumer
Visits usually arranged by letter but try
telephoning 23 62 80 85

St Quentin
Basilica
Open: daily but closed for lunch.

Musée Antoine Lécuyer
Open: 10am-12noon and 2-5pm on weekdays. 10am-12noon and 2-6pm Saturdays.
2-6pm Sundays. Closed Tuesdays.
☎ 23 67 05 00

Musée d'Entomologie
Open: 2-6pm. Closed Tuesdays.
☎ 23 67 05 00

Town Library
Open: 2.30-6.30pm Tuesdays and
Thursdays. 10am-6.30pm Wednesdays.
10am-12noon and 2.30-7pm Fridays.
10am-12noon and 2-5.30pm Saturdays.
☎ 23 64 33 06

Vermandois Tourist Railway
Runs from St Quentin Sundays and
holidays June to mid-July and
September. Details available from the
Tourist Office ☎ 23 67 05 00

Septmonts
Château
Ruins open from 9am to dusk Saturdays and Sundays. Château key
available from 16 Place de la Mairie on
weekdays. Guided tours in the
afternoons, Sundays and holidays May
to mid-September. ☎ 23 74 91 28

Seringes-et-Nesles
Château
Open: daily 10am-12noon and 3-6pm.
☎ 23 82 24 53

Soissons
Cathedral of St Gervais and St Prots
Open: 8.30am-12noon and 2.30-5.30pm
on weekdays. 7.45am-12noon and
3-7pm Sundays.
☎ 23 53 17 37 or 23 59 67 73

Municipal Museum
Rue de la Congrégation
Open: 10am-12noon and 2-5pm.
Closed Tuesdays. ☎ 23 59 12 00

St Jean-des-Vignes Abbey
Open: 10am-12noon and 2-6pm June to
August. 10am-12noon and 2-5pm March
to May (except Tuesdays) and in September and October. 10am-12noon and
2-5pm Wednesdays, Saturdays and Sundays November to February.
☎ 23 53 17 57

Vadencourt
Wood Workshop Museum
Open: 10am-12noon and 2-6pm at
weekends. ☎ 23 61 10 96

Vendeuil
Leisure Park
Open: Wednesdays, Friday afternoons,
Saturdays, Sundays, public holidays
and school holidays. ☎ 23 07 82 95

Vermand
Musée Depot de Fouilles du Vermandois
Open: 9am-12noon Sundays. Otherwise
by arrangement with the Town Hall.
☎ 23 64 11 46

Vervins
Musée de la Thierache
Open: 10am-12noon and 2.30-6pm the
first Saturday of each month. Otherwise
by arrangement with the Mairie de
Vervins in the Place du Général de Gaulle.
☎ 23 98 00 30

Vic-sur-Aisne
Château
Open: Sund and hols June to September.
☎ 44 40 25 41

Villers-Cotterêts
Musée Alexandre Dumas
Open: 2.30-5pm weekdays and 2.30-
6pm Saturdays and Sundays April to
October. 2.30-4.30pm daily November
to March. Closed Tuesdays, holidays
and the last Sunday of each month.
☎ 23 96 23 30

Wassigny
Musée Louis Cornu
Open: 8am-6pm daily except Mondays.
☎ 23 60 76 26

Tourist Information Offices

Château-Thierry
Office de Tourisme
Place Hôtel de Ville
☎ 23 83 10 14

Fère-en-Tardenois
Syndicat d'Initiative Rue Moreau-Nélaton
(Closed out of season)
☎ 23 82 31 57

Laon
Office de Tourisme
Place Parvis ☎ 23 20 28 62

Soissons
Office de Tourisme
Avenue du Général Leclerc
☎ 23 53 08 27

Vervins
Office de Tourisme
Place du Général de Gaulle
Closed in the afternoons. ☎ 23 98 11 98

Villers-Cotterêts
Syndicat d'Initiative
Place Briand ☎ 23 96 30 03

5 • Champagne-Ardenne

Ardennes

Anyone who is old enough to remember World War II will probably associate Ardennes with the Allied advance on Germany in 1944. The *département* has preserved a few of its battle scars, inflicted at various times during a long and often turbulent history, but for the most part they are either impressive fortresses or relics on display in the relevant museums. These days Ardennes is essentially rural in character and positively welcomes each new invasion by holidaymakers. Among its less militant attractions are lakes with pleasant sandy beaches, leisure centres and nature parks, opportunities for fishing, riding and boating and trails blazed through forests where animals such as wild boar live in the undergrowth. One of its greatest assets is the Meuse, a wide, rather stately river that meanders between wooded hillsides whose pleasure steamers give their passengers a close-up view of everything from rocky crags and ancient hamlets to the nuclear centre at Chooz.

Geographically, Ardennes occupies the entire northern section of Champagne-Ardenne as far south as Reims, separating the *département* of Marne from Belgium. Its most important centre is Charleville-Mézières, a combination of the ancient stronghold of Mézières and the comparatively modern town of Charleville which only decided to join forces in 1966. The city has no contact with any autoroute apart from about 24km (15 miles) of the A203 to Sedan. However, it can be reached in comfort along a variety of major roads — from Reims, 83km (51 miles) to the south; St Quentin, on the route from Calais, and Paris through Reims, a total distance of 213km (132 miles). Other main roads head north into Belgium and eastwards to Lorraine-Vosges and Luxembourg.

There are no very outstanding hotels in Ardennes. Those in Charleville-Mézières are unexceptional with one comfortable establishment on the outskirts, but an excellent restaurant in Auvillers-les-Forges, near Rocroi, has quite acceptable rooms and three apart-

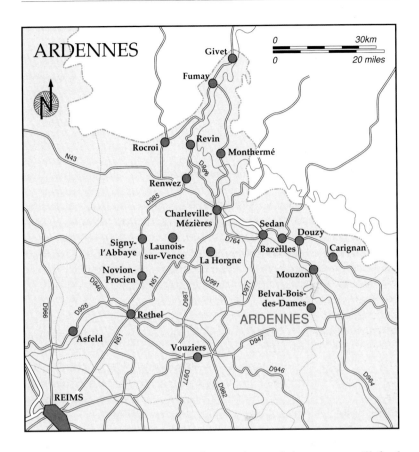

ments for guests. Anyone exploring the outlying areas will find several *logis* to choose from, an occasional auberge catering mainly for young travellers and any number of camp sites. The most up-market of these are at Givet and Bourg Fidele in the north of the *département* and both have four-star ratings which means that they are never overcrowded.

Apart from Ardennes ham the regional dishes are not particularly inspiring unless one happens to like bacon salad or white sausages followed by a fruit tart. Both pâté and cheese are produced locally but wine, eaux de vie and cider generally come from elsewhere in the province. The main festivals in Ardennes tend to be centred in and around Givet which organises its Fête de l'Eau Vive and a festival of roses in June, but switches to onions for the celebrations on 11 November. Rocroi, quite nearby, holds a Foire aux Fromages in the second half of July, roughly a fortnight after the Fêtes Nautiques at

Fumay that more or less coincides with the town's White Pudding Festival. However, the most famous of them all is the World Festival of Puppet Theatre, staged every third year in Charleville-Mézières. On the last occasion puppeteers from 37 different countries entertained more than 80,000 spectators from all over the world. The festival lasts for about 10 days and the next one is scheduled for late September 1994.

The town of **Charleville** has little of interest to attract the average sightseer with the exception of the Place Ducal, which mirrors the Place des Vosges in Paris, and the Vieux Moulin housing both the Ardenne Museum and the Musée Rimbaud, devoted to the tearaway young poet who died in 1891. **Mézières** goes one better with the remains of its ancient ramparts, including the Porte de Bourgogne and a couple of towers, and the Basilique Notre-Dame d'Espérance. The church is known for its stained glass windows and the fact that Charles IX and Elizabeth of Austria were married there in 1570.

There are quite a few places to visit around Charleville-Mézières, starting perhaps at **Renwez** on the D40 which takes leave of the N43 just 11km (7 miles) from the city. It is an unassuming little place that is mainly interested in anything to do with forestry. In addition to the Musée de la Forêt with its selection of elderly implements and illustrated descriptions, it has a sixteenth-century Gothic church. All that remains of the ruined Château de **Montcornet-en-Ardennes**, fragments of which date from the eleventh century, is within reasonable walking distance along a minor road to the east.

The D40 continues on its way, past the Lac des Vieilles Forges where boating enthusiasts, windsurfers and fishermen tend to congregate, and joins the main road to **Revin**, a much larger old town caught in a vast S-bend of the River Meuse. It is dominated by Mont Malgré Tout which has a splendid view of Revin and the meanders of the Meuse as they make their way sinuously through wooded hills and past strange rock formations down to, and well beyond, Monthermé. This little town, with its ancient houses and even older Eglise St Léger, is the starting point for excursions to any number of natural attractions in the area. Foremost among them are the Phades Waterfall in the Semoy valley, Longue Roche and the Roc de la Tour where rock climbers try out their skills at mountaineering.

The D1, which keeps company with the meanders of the Meuse, also links Revin with **Rocroi** in the other direction. It is a star-shaped town, due in no small measure to Vauban who adapted the existing ramparts when he strengthened the walls of the old village clustered round its large central Place d'Armes. The Municipal Museum, housed in the former guardroom, traces the history of the fortress with particular emphasis on the Battle of Rocroi in 1643. This was when the young Duc d'Enghien, later the Grand Condé, distinguished himself fighting against the Spanish forces led by Dom Francisco Mellos.

To the north of Revin, **Fumay** and **Haybes** are both quite ordinary waterside villages with modest hotels that cater for holidaymakers whose demands are not too sophisticated. The former has a slate museum — the Musée de l'Ardoise — and holds a White Pudding Festival at the beginning of July. Further up the N51 there is a turning off to the ruined Château de Hierges while another, a little way along on the opposite side, leads to the nuclear power station at Chooz. Other attractions in the area include the sparse remains of a Roman camp at Vireux-Molhain and a selection of caves known as the Grottes de Nichet.

The reason why this finger of land belongs to France and not to Belgium, which encloses it on three sides, can be found in the Fort de Charlemont, overlooking the frontier town of Givet. The stronghold was built in 1555 and updated by Vauban roughly a century later to such good effect that it held its ground while Napoléon was losing his. In more recent times it was used as a commando training centre but these days guided tours are arranged during the mid-summer season. Other things to see are the Tour Victoire, left over from a fourteenth-century château that belonged to the Comtes de la Marck, and the Forge Toussaint which retired from active service in 1950.

There is nothing of really outstanding interest to the south-west of Charleville-Mézières — even the former Abbaye de Sept-Fontaines, 9km (6 miles) away at Fagnon, which belonged to the de Gaulle family, is now an inn. **Signy-l'Abbaye**, a touch further along the D16, lost its monastery a long time ago. As a result it relies for attention on the Gouffre de Gibergeon, where the River Vaux makes an unexpected appearance in the middle of the town, and on several recommended walks through the forest in addition to the nearby GR12.

East of Charleville-Mézières it is quite a different story. First and foremost there is **Sedan** which manages to combine commerce and industry with history and tourism. Its most famous landmark is the vast château-fortress, generally agreed to be the most extended fortified castle in Europe. Building started in the eleventh century after which, like Little Topsy, it just grew and grew. Although Sedan has usually been engaged in wars of one kind or another, probably its most crushing defeat came in 1870 when the French defenders surrendered to the Prussians and Napoléon III, along with more than

100,000 officers and men, was taken prisoner. It was occupied by the Germans throughout World War I, only being recaptured by French and American forces just before the armistice in 1918.

A guided tour of the fortress lasts for more than an hour and takes in everything from the huge tower with its ancient timbers to the dungeons where prisoners were thrown into the underground cells and left in the dark to die. The museum has a predictable variety of exhibits but pays special attention to the Franco-Prussian War and to World War I. Sightseers who climb to the top of the ramparts are rewarded with a splendid view over the town and the surrounding countryside. Among the other local attractions are the 400-year-old Eglise St Charles on the Place d'Armes, an attractive little botanical garden facing the Place d'Alsace-Lorraine and the Tapis Point de Sedan factory on the Boulevard Gambetta. Sedan has nothing at all exceptional in the way of hotels and restaurants but there is a camp site beside the river and a port de plaisance for pleasure boats quite close by. Visitors can swim, play tennis, ride, hire a river boat for a trip along the Meuse or join one of the organised tours.

The main places of interest in the immediate vicinity of Sedan are **Bazeilles**, some 4km (2½ miles) to the south, and **Douzy**, about the same distance further along the N43. The former put up a determined struggle on 31 August and 1 September 1870 and recalls the battle in a small museum in the Maison de la Dernière Cartouche, so-called in memory of the last cartridge to be fired. Meanwhile the Sedan-Douzy airfield has a modest museum devoted to the early days of aviation.

Mouzon, about 10km (6 miles) south of Douzy on the D964, is a little village that was known to the Romans, Clovis and the archbishops of Reims and was besieged by the Spanish in 1650. The abbey church of Notre-Dame is quite impressive with its sculptured doorway, long nave and eighteenth-century organ that literally plays its part in the annual Autumn Festival. The Musée du Feutre is equally interesting, besides being somewhat unusual. It demonstrates the way in which wool is transformed into felt and illustrates its various uses with a display of all sorts of different articles made from the end products. They range from cloaks worn by nomads in the Middle East to modern decorative novelties. Finally there is a small local museum in the Porte de Bourgogne which was left standing when the defensive walls were demolished in 1671.

Still further to the east, poised on the provincial border in the valley of the Chiers, the fort of Villy-la-Ferté marked the end of the ill-fated Maginot Line. It was manned by 105 defenders when the invading German army attacked on the 15 May 1940. The fighting lasted for 4 days and everyone in the fort was either killed or fatally wounded before it was captured. A minor road connects Villy-la-Ferté with **Carignan**, which has what it describes as an Animation Centre Museum, and is only 7km (4½ miles) from Mouzon.

The southern part of the *département* contains quite a few attractions which, on the whole, are less militant than those in the north. Admittedly **Novion-Porcien**, south of Signy-l'Abbaye on the D985, maintains a Three Wars Museum devoted to military activities between 1870 and 1945, whereas Vendresse, almost on a line from Novion-Porcien to Mouzon has the remains of an ancient castle. It is the scene of a *son et lumière* in July during which the local inhabitants play their allotted parts. **Launois-sur-Vence** was a seventeenth-century staging post slightly to the north, where the D3 meets the D27. Nowadays it spends its time organising various events such as an Antique and Second Hand Dealers Market on the second Sunday of every month, except in August. From here the D27 to the east crosses the N51 for **La Horgne** which has nothing to offer apart from the Musée du Spahis inspired by the French-Algerian cavalry.

A choice of minor roads connect eventually with the secondary D991 before it passes the Lac de Bairon, a reservoir on the Canal des Ardennes. This is a largish stretch of water that has been divided into two parts. The smaller is reserved for wild life while fishing and sailing boats, canoes and windsurfers are entitled to use the rest. **Belval-Bois-des-Dame**, tucked away in the Forêt de Belval to the south-east, has an interesting Parc de Vision. It is the home of animals like deer, wild boar, bison, an occasional bear, moose and wild sheep, many of whose ancestors lived in the area anything up to 2,000 years ago. They roam about the park with its woods, ponds and open spaces in comparative freedom but there is also a short circular car track for visitors as well as footpaths and observation posts.

A minor road connects the Parc de Vision with the D947 which, in turn, crosses the River Aisne at **Vouziers**. The village is justly proud of its highly decorative Renaissance church of St Maurille and also provides a handful of small hotel-restaurants. From here a secondary road almost, but not quite, follows the route of the River Aisne and the Canal des Ardennes to **Rethel**, known for its cattle markets and white puddings as well as being the birthplace of Louis Hachette, the nineteenth-century publisher. The Eglise St Nicolas is unusual insofar as it has two naves but, like so many of its ilk, it suffered as a result of war and had to be quite extensively restored. It vies for attention with the Musée du Rethelois et du Porcien whose main interests are archaeology and folklore as well as regional and sacred art. Rethel has two quite acceptable *logis* and the added advantage of being only 38km (24 miles) from Reims along the excellent N51.

Marne

Marne, stretched right across the centre of Champagne-Ardenne, is probably the best-known *département* in the province, at least as far as holidaymakers are concerned. There are two main reasons for this. The first is Reims with its magnificent cathedral where all except six kings of France were crowned: Secondly, it is the undisputed centre of the local wine industry, using fermentation methods introduced by Dom Pérignon in the seventeenth century to create the sparkling variety known simply as champagne. Much of the countryside is smothered in vines while, below ground level, a gigantic honeycomb of caves and tunnels provides ideal conditions for producing many millions of bottles that find their way into nearly every country in the world. This is not by any means all the *département* has to offer.

Apart from Reims and Châlons-sur-Marne, the administrative centre, the towns and villages in Marne tend to be on the smallish side, with many of them concentrated in the north of the area. Cereals are grown extensively on the wide chalky plain in the middle while the Lac du Der-Chantecoq, in the far south-east, is the largest artificial lake in Europe. Travelling round is very simple, whether by car, with a bicycle, on horseback, walking or by boat on one of the canals. For motorists in a hurry there are the autoroutes — the A4 to Paris, 142km (88 miles) to the west, or eastwards to Strasbourg 346km (215 miles) away, and the A26 to Calais, a distance of 282km (175 miles), which will link up with the A5 south of Troyes and then join the Autoroute du Soleil on its way to the Mediterranean. They are augmented by several major routes and a host of secondary roads, country lanes and byways, the majority of them in good condition. Main line trains call at Reims and Châlons-sur-Marne with the added advantage of a motorail service to Reims.

Accommodation in Marne is plentiful and extremely varied. It ranges from luxury hotels in and around Reims, through three-star establishments and *logis* to modest hostelries although, as yet, there are few if any motels. Youth hostels are somewhat thin on the ground but tourists with tents or caravans can choose from a large number of camp sites, the best of them being at Châlons-sur-Marne and in the vicinity of the Lac du Der-Chantecoq. Restaurants fall into much the same categories, the most up-market providing sophisticated menus while the country inns usually concentrate on regional dishes, some-

Flower-bedecked house in Rouffach, Alsace et Lorraine

Kaysersberg, Alsace et Lorraine

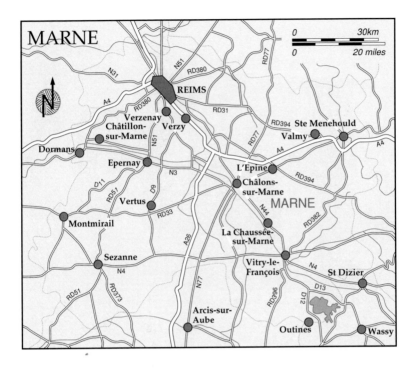

times enriched with champagne. Celebrations throughout the *département* naturally include wine festivals in addition to Châlons-sur-Marne's carnival in March and the Fête de Jeanne d'Arc at Reims in June. There are also religious events such as the summer pilgrimages to Notre-Dame de l'Epine and a time-honoured Shepherds Mass at Braux-Sainte-Cohière every Christmas.

Apart from the major role played by outdoor activities in the area, especially in the vicinity of lakes and forests, Marne has plenty of other attractions for less energetic visitors. Among them are ancient châteaux and famous battlefields, half-timbered buildings including one splendid church, historic windmills, traditional cottage industries and even a flea market at St Imoges.

Much of the history of Marne is centred on **Reims**, which by no stretch of the imagination could be described as off the beaten track. However, as most people visiting the area will probably look round the old city, a short resumé at this stage might not come amiss. In the dim and distant past the site was known as Durocorter, a formidable Gaulish stronghold belonging to a tribe called the Rèmes. They formed a useful alliance with Julius Caesar and in return the Romans promoted it to the status of the capital of Belgica Province and added

The Porte Mars (Mars Gate) in Reims, built by the Romans in AD200

several refinements of their own. These included the excellently preserved Porte Mars, said to have been the largest triumphal arch in the Roman Empire, and the Cryptoporticus, the remains of which mark the site of the original forum in the square that bears its name.

The earliest cathedral, where Clovis was baptised in AD498, was replaced by the present Cathédrale Notre-Dame in the thirteenth century, overshadowing the Basilique St Remi and its attendant abbey, which is now a museum. The former, the largest Romanesque church in northern France, was built as a shrine round St Remi's tomb. The abbey next door, on the Rue Simon, used to take care of the Holy Ampulla when it was not needed for a coronation but now deals mainly with history and archaeology.

Other churches and mansions were added quite regularly and several ancient buildings that survived a series of wars were restored and then pressed into service as administrative centres or museums. Foremost among them is the Palais du Tau, adjoining the cathedral and originally the archbishops palace, notable for its royal banqueting hall and other items associated with coronations as well as acting as a treasure house for tapestries and statues that overflowed from the cathedral. It is run a close second by the Musée St Denis which houses the Museum of Fine Arts and is much closer to the thirteenth century Eglise St Jacques just off the Rue de Vesle. Napoléon won his last victory when he recovered the city from the Russians in March 1814 but a 100 years later it was badly knocked about during World War I. The Musée-Hôtel Le Vergeur had to be virtually rebuilt to house antique furniture, documents and similar attractions whereas the former Jesuits College was adapted to include the planetarium. After Germany had been defeated for the second time in 1945 the surrender documents were signed in the map room of General Eisenhower's headquarters in the technical college, now carefully preserved with the maps still on the walls. Additional attractions are the Foujita Chapel, built in 1965 on the Rue du Champ de Mars, and the Musée de l'Automobile Française, just as far away along the Avenue Georges-Clemenceau. From here it is only a short walk to the Place du Général Gouraud, almost surrounded by champagne houses, some of which are open to visitors.

The so-called Champagne Triangle, with Reims at the top, covers a large percentage of the *département* and attracts its fair share of sightseers. However, comparatively few of them deviate from the beaten track which means that there are still a host of little places waiting to be explored. The Montagne de Reims Regional Nature Park, neatly bisected by the N51 to Epernay, is sprinkled with villages like **St Imoges**, off to the right and known for its flea market, and **Germain**, on the opposite side of the highway, whose Maison du Bucheron concentrates on the work of local woodcutters.

On the eastern edge of the forest, reached by a variety of small roads or, as far as walkers are concerned, along either of the two nearby Sentiers de Grande Randonnée, **Verzenay** is easy to identify by its windmill. This is a large, solidly built wooden construction, rather like a double story house, that stands guard over a sea of vines. As one would expect the village is famous as a wine centre but otherwise has nothing that could remotely be described as a tourist attraction. On the other hand **Verzy**, some 2km (1½ miles) to the south, opposite the Mount Sinai observatory, makes the most of a strange natural phenomenon known as the Faux de Verzy. It consists of a weird collection of gnarled and twisted beech trees which have got themselves into the most extraordinary tortured shapes, rather too fanciful for the average cartoon, although they might well have been visualised by Salvador Dali. They are surrounded by a perfectly ordinary forest which adds quite considerably to their strange appearance. The site attracts walkers and cyclists and even picnickers who are willing to carry their provisions up from the car park, a fairish distance away. Verzy itself has nothing to show for its long association with the seventh-century Abbaye St Basle which was destroyed in 1792. However, as it sits on the highest point of the Montagne de Reims, there is a pleasing view over the plateau and the city. The village is also a great place for bees and holds an annual honey market in either September or October.

Before the N51 reaches the outskirts of Epernay it is possible to pull off the road in order to admire a splendid view over the Marne valley from Champillon, which also fortunately provides parking space for cars. Alternatively, two secondary roads — the RD386 and the D1 — head off in the opposite direction for **Hautvillers** and Damery respectively. The former has the remains of a Benedictine abbey, founded in AD660 by St Nivard, although it is more frequently associated with Dom Pérignon. According to popular belief this enterprising monk was living in the monastery when he perfected the art of making champagne. It is a long process calling for quite rigid conditions but nobody seems to know how or why he discovered it in the first place. Hautvillers is a charming little village made even more attractive by a variety of eye-catching wrought-iron signs, not all of which have anything to do with wine. **Damery**, 5km (3 miles) to the east on the banks of the Marne, has a very viewable thirteenth-century church that was once attached to a priory. There is nowhere to stay but it is a good place for walking, especially along the GR14 that passes quite close by. The D1, an agreeable secondary road, continues to follow the river along to **Châtillon-sur-Marne**, built at the foot of a wooded hillside and watched over by a gigantic statue of Pope Urbain II. He was actually born in Troyes and was largely instrumental in launching the First Crusade in the eleventh century. The village is set back a little from the water's edge, whereas **Dormans** makes the most of its potential as a riverside resort. The hamlet does not bother with hotels although it has a restaurant and has built a Chapelle de la Reconnaissance in the grounds of the château to commemorate the two battles of the Marne.

Epernay vies with Reims for the unofficial title of Champagne Capital and is the home of several famous houses like Mercier, established in 1858, and Moët et Chandon which came into being in 1743 and has made Dom Pérignon an honorary member of the company. Apart from inspecting some of the cellars visitors are unlikely to find many other tourist attractions in the town. The Musée d'Epernay, housed in a rather extrovert château on the Avenue de Champagne, is foremost among those that do exist. In addition to dwelling at some length on the history of the region's most famous product it finds space for assorted archaeological discoveries including weapons, pottery and jewellery as well as a few local crafts. The château backs on to the large Jardin de l'Hôtel de Ville, designed by the Bühler brothers who laid out the Parc de la Tête d'Or in Lyon. Mercier has its own museum of wine presses while, at the far end of the Avenue de Champagne, the Jardin des Papillons is filled with exotic plants and butterflies.

The RD51 slices its way through woodlands to Montmort-Lucy, which has a very worthwhile château all set about with ramparts that is privately owned but opens its gates to visitors during the summer months. Among its most interesting neighbours is **Orbais l'Abbaye**, in the valley of the Surmelin, where there is a beautiful twelfth-century abbey church attributed to Jean d'Orbais who also worked on Reims cathedral. Meanwhile the main road presses on to **Sézanne**, a picturesque medieval town full of fascinating alleyways separating rows of ancient houses and an avenue of chestnut trees, known as the Mail des Cordeliers, marking the line of the ramparts.

The Côte des Blancs, although well known, is a rather uninterest-ing stretch of country below Epernay, covered in vines and dotted with little hamlets. It ends at **Vertus** which has an unusual old church that may have originated in the days of the Franks, but had to be restored after two different fires — one in 1167 and the other in 1940. It still has its ancient crypt, built on wooden pillars standing in an underground river that supplies St Martin's Well. Anyone planning to stay awhile will have a choice of three hotels including the Hostellerie de la Reine Blanche.

South of Vertus the D9 meets the RD33 which leads straight to **Châlons-sur-Marne**, a little over 30km (19 miles) to the east. It is a busy centre that had a nodding acquaintance with Attila the Hun, was described as the principal city in Champagne by Henri III and provided enough open country near Mourmelon for Napoléon III's entire army in 1856.

The Cathédrale St Etienne is an elegant building with some fine stained glass windows and a treasure that includes relics of St-Bernard and his friend St Malachie. The Eglise Notre-Dame-en-Vaux, a short walk away on the Place Monsiegneur Tissier, dates back to the twelfth century and is fairly austere, having lost most of its statues during the Revolution. However its adjacent cloister is regarded as a museum on account of its many and varied, intricately-carved columns. The Musée Garinet on the Rue Pasteur is worth a visit to see its representative collection of French churches and cathedrals. The city also has a handful of other churches, an interest-ing Bibliothèque and a fairly extensive park laid out during the Middle Ages but adapted at various times to suit the prevailing

The Basilique Notre-Dame de la L'Epine

fashions. One of the best ways of exploring Châlons-sur-Marne is to take a boat trip along the canals, past well-restored half-timbered houses which, along with the elderly bridges, help to preserve something of the old-world atmosphere.

Less than 7km (4½ miles) along the N3, **L'Epine** is a small village with a magnificent basilica that outshines quite a few cathedrals. It has a majestic façade complete with gargoyles representing the vices and evil spirits and houses a much-revered statue of the Virgin and a reliquary in the guise of a tabernacle said to contain a fragment of the True Cross. Pilgrims, including kings as well as commoners, have been converging on the Basilique Notre-Dame ever since the Middle Ages when it was claimed that the statue had been discovered in a burning bush. More or less opposite, an old coaching inn has been converted into a comfortable hotel with a diningroom that has an uninterrupted view of the basilica when floodlit in the evening.

Beyond L'Epine, at the point where the N3 comes within striking distance of the A4 autoroute, the village of **Valmy** was the scene of the first military victory of the Revolution. The site is marked by a large windmill, restored in 1947 and provided with four orientation tables indicating the positions of the French and Prussian armies as

Basketware in L'Epine, one of the cottage industries of Aisne and Champagne-Ardenne

battle was joined on 20 September 1792. At that time the French commander, Dumouriez, had his headquarters in the castle at **Braux-Ste-Cohière** at the far end of the D284. It is an excellent example of military, and particularly cavalry, architecture at the time of Henri IV with its vast quadrangle and protective moats. These days it recalls past history with an audio-visual programme, in addition to which it holds a traditional Champagne Shepherds Mass at Christmas every year.

Ste Menehould, just short of the provincial border with Lorraine-Vosges, is an attractive smallish town associated with two important events. In the first place, Dom Pérignon was born there in 1638. Later, as a Benedictine monk at Hautviller, he is credited with inventing and perfecting the method used for producing the sparkling wines known champagne. The second local celebrity was a stable lad called Drouet. When Louis XVI, Marie Antoinette and their family fled from Paris in June 1791 they stopped in Ste Menehould to change horses. Drouet recognised the king from a likeness he had seen on a coin and gave the alarm. The royal party was stopped soon afterwards by revolutionary guards and taken back to the capital. The town still has its quota of old houses, an up-dated thirteenth-century church and a pink and grey hôtel de ville. Anyone in search of souvenirs might find something suitable among the china and glass produced at Les Islettes, 9km (6 miles) ahead beyond the Côte de Biesme.

Motorists on their way south from Châlons-sur-Marne can follow the river and the canal down through **La Chaussée-sur-Marne**, which specialises in goats' milk cheese, and past **St Amand-sur-Fion** with its half-timbered farm buildings, to **Vitry-le-François** which was almost completely destroyed during an aerial bombardment in 1940. However it managed to resuscitate the Eglise Notre-Dame on the Place d'Armes, the nearby hôtel de ville and a triumphal arch built in honour of Louis XIV. The arch now stands in the Place Maréchal Leclerc, having been transferred from its original site to provide a more impressive entrance to the town.

Vitry-le-François has one or two quite acceptable hotels which makes it a good place from which to visit the Lac du Der-Chantecoq, generally claimed to be the largest artificial lake in Europe. It is an impressive stretch of water, linked by canal to the River Marne and largely surrounded by forests. On the northern bank Ste Marie-du-Lac is a museum-village consisting of several reconstructed buildings that are typical of the area. The eastern part of the lake belongs to the adjoining département of Haute-Marne but there is no demarcation line on the roads that skirt round the edge and then back to **Giffaumont-Champaubert** which has every intention of becoming an important holiday resort. It already has moorings for different types of craft, a pleasure boat that takes visitors for trips round the lake and the Grange aux Abeilles which can be visited by anyone who is interested in bees. There is also one modest hotel and a two-star camp site near the water.

Other attractions within easy reach of Giffaumont-Champaubert include some elderly ruins, opportunities for walking and bird watching and two half-timbered churches — at Chatillon-sur-Broue and, more particularly, at **Outines** on the D55. This is a splendid building with massive beams and stained glass windows, standing alone surrounded by trees and flowers beyond which are matching houses, one of them decorated with farm implements. From here it is a short drive up the D55 to the RD396 and back to Vitry-le-François.

Aube

The *département* of Aube, neatly tucked away below Marne in the south-eastern corner of Champagne-Ardenne, is much frequented by French holidaymakers but deserves to be better known to visitors

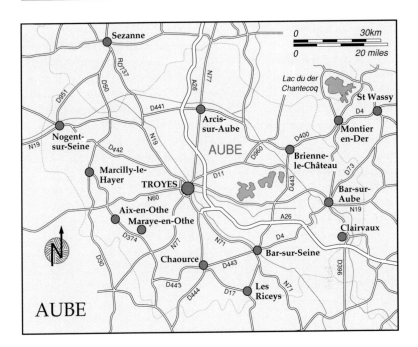

from elsewhere. It is a placid, rather unassuming area, full of lakes and forests, whose delightful little towns and villages produce anything from champagne, rosé wines and cider to cheese, ceramics, porcelain and glass. Among its many attractions are dolmens and ancient burial grounds, a plethora of photographic half-timbered buildings, the occasional château like La Motte-Tilly and little museums specialising in such unexpected subjects as antique dolls, vintage cars and Russian icons. It has close ties with famous personalities, among them St Bernard, who founded the abbey at Clairvaux; Renoir, buried with two sons in his local village churchyard; the young Napoléon who started his military career at Brienne-le-Château at the age of 9 and the lovers Héloïse and Abélade.

Aube also caters for visitors who are more interested in outdoor activities than either history or architecture. The lakes of the Forêt d'Orient, designed to regulate the flow of the Seine and the River Aube, provide ample opportunities for a wide variety of water sports. There is a bird sanctuary as well as a special animal reserve, the rivers are full of fish and the woods veined with footpaths suitable for either a gentle stroll or a long distance walk, all permanently enclosed in a large nature park. Camp sites are found nearly everywhere, the majority of them in the two-star category, in addition to which most villages of any size have their own auberge or logi.

Apart from the usual spiderweb of small back roads and country lanes linking the outlying communities, Aube has its fair share of major routes which, almost without exception, converge on Troyes, the ancient capital of Champagne. It is conveniently situated in the middle of the *département*, 162km (100 miles) from Paris on the N19, 120km (74 miles) due south of Reims and on the railway line from Paris to Basle and Zurich. As one would expect it is a splendid old town, not really off the beaten track but nevertheless an historic centre that definitely should not be missed.

The ancient quarter of **Troyes**, shaped like a champagne cork, is crammed with memorable buildings like the Basilique St Urbain, the Cathédrale St Pierre-et-St-Paul and six or seven other smaller but equally viewable churches. Among them is the Eglise St Jean where England's Henry V married Catherine of France in 1420 and became the official heir to the French throne until his death 2 years later. The Quartier St Jean, where huge crowds gathered in medieval times for the seven-week-long Midsummer Fairs, is now a preservation area. Its sixteenth-century houses have been meticulously restored, streets like the fascinating Ruelle des Chats are repaved with cobbles and some of the imposing mansions turned into museums. Among the most interesting are the Musée de la Bonneterie which is devoted to hosiery, the Hôtel de Vauluisant, the ancient Pharmacie de l'Hôtel Dieu and the Musée St Loup whose exhibits include items from the time of the Gauls, the Romans and Attila the Hun.

Troyes has plenty of hotels, the majority in the three and two-star brackets, and a selection of restaurants providing traditional dishes like *andouillettes*. These small chitterling sausages were served at a royal banquet for Louis the Stammerer in AD878, were enjoyed by Napoléon some 900 years later and even had a sonnet dedicated to them by the gourmet poet Charles Monselet. No such extravagant claims are made for other specialities like pork brawn or truffled pigs feet, although Louis XIV is said to have been very partial to the smoked lambs tongue. Aube also produces some excellent cheeses, *sauerkraut* and a sloe gin called Prunelle de Champagne as well as cider and champagne itself. Most of these products have special days set aside for them — champagne fairs in Troyes and Bar-sur-Aube, *sauerkraut* in Brienne-le-Château, cider in the Pays d'Othe and cheese in Chaource. Troyes holds a Foire au Jambon on the Thursday before Easter, Chaource has a lily-of-the-valley celebration on May Day, Brienne-le-Château diversifies with its Rassemblement Aérien at the end of July and Bar-sur-Seine is the focus of the pilgrimage of Notre-

Medieval houses can be found in the Quartier St Jean in Troyes

Dame-du-Chêne in September. However, the most spectacular of these events is probably the medieval Bernard de Clairvaux pageant, staged in the vicinity of the ancient abbey every Friday and Saturday evening during July and August.

Variety is certainly the name of the game in the area to the west of Troyes. The N19, on its way to Paris, calls at **Nogent-sur-Seine**, a pleasant little town on the border with Seine-et-Marne. It has obvious nuclear connections but prefers to draw attention to its old half-timbered buildings, among them the Henri IV Pavillon and the Turkish House, as well as to the sixteenth-century Eglise St Laurent and a small local museum. It also has a sprinkling of modest hotels and a municipal camp site, all of which come in useful for anyone who is planning to explore the surrounding countryside. While it is possible to visit the nuclear establishment, after making the necessary arrangements well in advance, two older attractions in the neighbourhood usually prove to be more popular.

The first of these is the **Château de la Motte-Tilly**, a mere 6km (4 miles) to the south-west along the D951. The sandstone exterior is fairly restrained as elderly châteaux go, but the grounds are delightful and the rooms, tastefully decorated and furnished and occupied by the Marquise de Maille before her death in 1972, are now used for concerts and exhibitions.

The ancient **Abbaye du Paraclet**, also 6km (4 miles) away but in the opposite direction via the N19 and the D442, is infinitely older and somewhat more romantic. It was founded by Pierre Abélard, the twelfth-century French scholar whose writings caused him to be branded as a heretic. However he is better known for his love of Héloïse whom he married secretly in Paris, only to be mutilated by her infuriated guardian. The couple parted but kept in touch through their famous love letters. Héloïse went into a convent, became an abbess and, some time after her death in 1164, was buried beside Abélard in the Abbaye du Paraclet. Eventually their remains were transferred to the cemetery of Père-Lachaise in Paris.

The area round **Marcilly-le-Hayer** on the CD974, south of Nogent-sur-Seine but somewhat closer to Troyes, has been occupied since very ancient times. The early inhabitants left behind a few traces of their existence, especially the Dolmen de la Pierre Couverte and the Mégalithe du Four Gaulois. **St Léger-près-Troyes** is much more up-to-date with a farm museum full of nineteenth-century tools and agricultural implements, while Montgueux has nothing to recommend it apart from the surrounding champagne vineyards and a rather nice view towards Troyes.

There are not many places of interest along the N77 apart from **Auxon** on the edge of the Forêt d'Othe, where there is a small church with a beautifully carved doorway; **Maraye-en-Othe**, to the north along the D374, which has preserved an eighteenth-century hunting lodge and an old wash-house, and **Aix-en-Othe** surrounded by apple orchards and known principally for its cider. The woods in this area are quite extensive with a variety of Grandes Randonnées interspersed with little streams and byways, making driving, riding and walking all equally enjoyable. Much the same can be said for the country on either side of the D444 that follows a more or less straight course to the south after crossing the extended A5 motorway. Almost immediately there is a side road off to Isle-Aumont which played host to a great many different newcomers down the ages. It still shows traces of the Stone Age, the ancient Celts and the Vikings who destroyed its early church but overlooked the Merovingian sarcophagi discovered later in their burial grounds. The present church has something to show for each phase of its long history including a statue of Ste Marthe and a thirteenth-century wooden crucifix.

Chaource, a little further down the D444, has an enviable reputation for making a special kind of cheese that has been appreciated by gourmets since the twelfth century. It is also known for its attractive half-timbered houses and the Eglise St Jean-Baptiste. One of its chapels is set aside for a magnificent *mise au tombeau* whose grieving women are shown in the kind of dresses worn by maid servants in the Middle Ages, while another contains a colourful wooden crèche with moveable figures. Not to be outdone **Maison-les-Chaource**, 6km (4 miles) to the south on the D34, has a pleasant *logi* and an interesting little Museum of Antique Dolls.

There are two minor roads from Maison-les-Chaource that find their way to the D17 which links Chaource with **Les Riceys**. This is, in fact, a collection of three tiny hamlets with a church apiece, a communal museum of vintage cars and the happy knack of producing fine rosé wines. It is connected to **Mussy-sur-Seine** by both a minor road and a *Grande Randonnée* — the D17 and the GR24 respectively — where there is another attractive church and a Musée de la Resistance recalling the activities of the macquis of Grancey in 1944. Beyond Mussy-sur-Seine the D117 leads off to the left from the D17 and makes for **Essoyes**, which probably would never have found its way into any tourist guide if it had not been the home of Auguste Renoir, who died in 1919. As it is, the village appears in many of his paintings, in addition to which the artist and his son Pierre and Jean are buried in the local churchyard.

For motorists heading back to Troyes the best and quickest way is along the N71 through **Bar-sur-Seine**, a pleasant smallish town with nothing really outstanding about it. However there are some rather nice old houses and the Eglise St Etienne which is worth a brief visit. The local auberges are popular with trout fishermen who, provided they have the necessary licence, can try their luck in the Ource, the Arce or the Laignes. Visitors with more sightseeing time at their disposal might well opt for a longer route back from Essoyes, taking the D70 as far as Champignol-lez-Mondeville and then branching off to **Clairvaux**. This was where St Bernard founded one of his most prestigious abbeys during the twelfth century. The present monastic buildings date from much more recent times and are now used as a detention centre. Some of them are open to view although visitors need to have some form of identification. Nothing so formal is required at **Bayel**, a touch to the north off the D396. The village is famous for its Champagne Crystal Works and arranges visits to the workshops as well as providing a shop selling some exceptionally attractive and quite unusual handmade glass.

Bar-sur-Aube is justifiably proud of its twelfth-century Eglise St Pierre, partly obscured by a wooden gallery. In the olden days

The main bridge over the River Ource at Essoyes

merchants used it as a shelter while attending the local champagne fairs, and probably still do during their modern counterpart which is held in mid-September. The first place to stop on the N19 from Bar-sur-Aube towards Brienne-le-Château is the little hamlet of **Arsonval** in order to see the Russian icons housed in its small Loukine museum. Some 2km (1 mile) further on there is a fork in the road, with the D396 pressing on northwards and a small turning off the main route at **Dolancourt**. Here a sizeable piece of land has been converted into a leisure park, crossed by the GR24. It is known as Nigloland and promises 'fun for all the family in the land of the hedgehog'.

Vendeuvre-sur-Barse, roughly 13km (8 miles) to the west, has a sixteenth-century church and a château of comparable vintage which puts on an annual *son et lumière* with a large percentage of the local population taking part. There is also a restaurant with rooms attached and a pleasant *logi* at **Mesnil-St-Père** overlooking the lake in the Parc Régional de la Forêt d'Orient. This is a small holiday resort with a beach and a sailing school, three camp sites and moorings for yachts and other craft as well as a pleasure boat that takes sightseers for trips round the lake. On the northern shore **Géraudot** also has a beach in addition to a medieval church, a modest auberge and a trio of camp sites, but needs to make a bit more progress before it

Bar-sur-Seine; the old entrance gate to the town

qualifies as a resort. The lake is largely surrounded by woods left over from the vast forest of Der that once belonged to an order of soldier-monks known as the Chevaliers de l'Orient. Part of it has been set aside as a bird sanctuary with a nearby information office in the elderly Maison du Parc that was originally the home of a well-to-do farmer. The park extends well beyond the borders of the lake and includes nearly fifty small communities, many of whom earn their living from the land.

Dienville, which has its own adjoining Lac Amance well to the north-east near the D396, is another up-and-coming resort, providing beaches and a wide variety of water sports such as windsurfing, sailing, speedboating and waterskiing. It is left to **Brienne-la-Vieille**, almost next door, to provide the park with its Ecomuseum. Known as the Musée de Charronnage, it is strategically located in the middle of the village and is full of all the different kinds of things that were used by wheel-wrights in days gone by.

To all intents and purposes the village is a suburb of **Brienne-le-Château**, which is altogether larger and more important and has never quite recovered from its association with Napoléon. He first appeared there as a 9-year-old from Corsica, calling himself Napoillonné in the Italian manner and speaking rather unconventional French. By the time he left for the military academy in Paris his progress in every respect had been excellent. Meanwhile he, for his part, had a lasting affection for Brienne. There are statues of Bonaparte in the town and the Musée Napoléon in the old academy building contains many items associated with the future emperor as well as details of some of his campaigns. Other local attractions include a very viewable thirteenth-century covered market and a rather less memorable church.

The only other places worth mentioning in the far east of the *département* are **Lentilles,** a charming little village, reached by a succession of linked cross-country roads heading northwards from the D400. Its outstanding attraction is a large half-timbered church built in the sixteenth century, whose gable, bell tower and porch are all tiled with chestnut wood. **Chavanges,** about 4km (2½ miles) further on, has some rather nice half-timbered houses and a more or less direct connection with **Rosnay-l'Hopital** on the D396. This is hardly more than a hamlet on the River Voire with some good fishing and a large twelfth-century crypt below its slightly younger Eglise Notre-Dame. Roughly 20km (12½ miles) away, on the D960 to Troyes, **Piney** is an attractive little place with a modest *logi* in the Place de la Halle which takes its name from the old covered market that dominates the square. It is a good place from which to explore the lakes and woods of the Parc Régional de la Forêt d'Orient a few kilometres to the south.

Haute-Marne

The *département* of Haute-Marne, nudging its way purposefully south-eastwards between Lorraine-Vosges and Burgundy, is an excellent choice for anyone interested in what the French call 'Le Tourisme Vert'. In other words, it offers visitors an ideal country holiday with plenty of outdoor activities but comparatively few large towns, important buildings or museums crammed with art and history. It consists mainly of undulating hills and valleys dotted with lakes and threaded through with streams and rivers. Its chequerboard of fields and pastures is peppered with small villages and shaded by forests, some of them inhabited by deer and other wild life.

The Plateau de Langres was among the first parts of the region to emerge when the seas retreated westwards some 2 million years ago. In due course it became the home of prehistoric settlers, succeeded in turn by the Celts, the Romans and other interlopers, all of whom left behind tangible proof of their presence. Thereafter the history of Haute-Marne is very similar to that of its neighbours. The area was caught up in wars and local quarrels, fortifications were built and

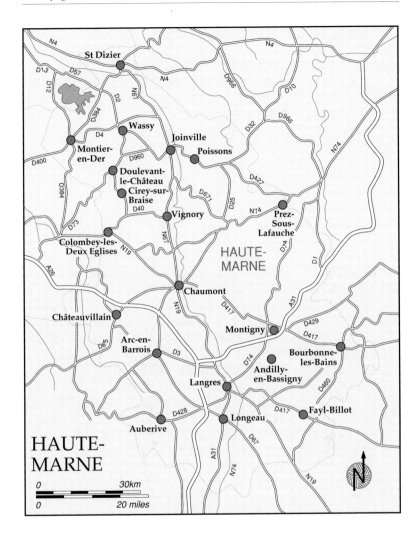

demolished and modest industries like smelting, basketmaking and the production of cheeses gradually developed. Nowadays these are woven into a varied pattern of tourist attractions, along with traditional festivals, game reserves, leisure centres and some curious natural phenomena.

The *département* is easy to get to from every direction, with a choice of autoroutes from the east, north and south and a network of main and secondary roads keeping it in touch with the rest of the region. In addition there are bridle paths, cycle routes and *Randonnées* clearly marked for people who prefer to do their exploring on foot. Visitors travelling by train can use the Paris-Basel line or book a seat on either the Metz-Dijon or the Reims-Dijon service, whichever is the more convenient. Holidaymakers in search of accommodation will find plenty of hotels, the majority of them in the two-star bracket, as well as guesthouses, *gîtes* of various descriptions and any number of camp sites, both public and private.

No great distances are involved. For example, St Dizier, in the north, is only 74km (46 miles) from Chaumont, more or less in the centre, and from there it is roughly 35km (22 miles) down to Langres which is not all that far from the southern border of the province. At the same time the River Marne and the Canal de la Marne à la Saône, accompanied first by the N67 and then by the N19, cut the area into almost equal parts from north to south. This provides an alternative way of seeing the country for anyone who has the time and inclination to hire a boat and cruise slowly and sedately towards Burgundy. Haute-Marne is also known as the Land of Springs, partly because the Aube, the Marne, the Meuse and several other less familiar rivers all begin as small streams in the region and then go their separate ways towards the North Sea, the Channel or the Mediterranean. Naturally this provides fishermen with a variety of opportunities for catching trout and grayling as well as roach, pike and perch, some of which can be found in the Marne-Saône canal.

Apart from the Lac du Der-Chantecoq, which the *département* shares with Marne, there are four quite sizeable lakes within easy reach of Langres. They are all excellent for sailing, swimming and windsurfing but only one, the Lac de la Liez to the east of Langres, adds motor boating and waterskiing to its list of other attractions. The camp sites also vary quite considerably, from the four-star Camping de la Presqu'ile de Champaubert at Braucourt, on the south-eastern shore of the Lac du Der-Chantecoq, and two in the three-star bracket near Langres and Bourbonne-les-Bains, to small rural sites that so far have no official rating.

Perhaps the most logical starting place for visitors planning to tour Haute-Marne is **St Dizier**, 370km (229 miles) from Calais and exactly half way along the N4 from Reims to Nancy. It is an industrial town with one or two comfortable hotels but very little in the way of tourist attractions. Although it was fortified in days gone by only the Holy Ghost Tower and a small section of the ramparts have survived, along with the Eglise St Martin-de-la-Noue which was built overlooking the Marne in the twelfth century but updated some 500 years later. The Municipal Museum has managed to put together an assortment of archaeological exhibits, consisting mainly of antiquated bones and the occasional Gallo-Roman sculpture, as well as some not very inspiring paintings.

St Dizier is only a short drive from the Lac du Der-Chantecoq and, as there is no sign of the border with Marne, tends to treat the whole vast expanse of water as its own. Trips by motor launch, reminiscent of the Bateau Mouche in Paris, start from Port Giffaumont and are accompanied by a guide who points out the various places of interest along the way. The most intriguing of them is the lonely Champaubert church which remained above water when the rest of the village was submerged. It is possible to walk or drive right round the lake, swim, sail, windsurf or waterski, lie on the sand or picnic under the trees.

For many people **Montier-en-Der**, some 15km (9 ½ miles) further on down the D384, is somewhat more rewarding. It has an interesting old church that was once part of the Benedictine abbey of St Pierre-St-Paul, founded in the seventh century. Very little remains of the original building because it was considerably altered by successive generations and is now mainly Gothic with some relatively modern stained glass windows. In 1820, on instructions from Napoléon, the National Stud took over part of the ancient abbey grounds adjoining the church. In due course all the necessary stables, harness rooms, coach houses and administrative offices were built and these days it holds race meetings and demonstrations while, on Thursday afternoons from September to mid-November, the stallions and much of the finery are on parade in the courtyards.

The only other places of moderate interest in the area are **Droyes** to the north-west with its museum of agricultural machinery and **Ceffonds** where Joan of Arc's father was born. The local Eglise St-Remi was practically rebuilt in the sixteenth century when it acquired a mise au tombeau and an enviable collection of stained glass windows. Meanwhile **Wassy** is an historic little town on the D4 in the opposite direction. It was here in 1562 that the followers of François de Guise surprised a group of Protestants who had gathered in the barn for a service and promptly murdered every one of them. The 'Massacre de Wassy' inflamed other Protestants throughout the country and sparked off the Wars of Religion. The town still has its twelfth-century church on the Place Notre-Dame and a two-hundred-year-old astronomical clock in the hôtel de ville.

On the other side of the N67 the most northerly attraction is the **Menhir de la Haute-Borne**, just beyond Fontaines-sur-Marne. It is a towering megalith that had been standing for about 4,000 years before it toppled over while excavations were being carried out at the base during the eighteenth century. It was roughly a hundred years before the damage was rectified and the menhir returned to its upright position. The site is within easy reach of **Joinville** whose sixteenth-century castle was built by Claude de Lorraine, the first Duc de Guise. The Château du Grand Jardin is so named because it stands in remarkably fine gardens, full of rare trees, exotic plants and shaded walks that compliment the decorative façade. Among the things to see are the requisite dungeons, a long spiral staircase, Ste-Ann's Chapel and the Musée de l'Auditoire whose main function is to show how fashions have changed down the ages. A Promenade Show is held in the park during the season, among a variety of exhibitions and concerts that can be anything from a Mozart evening to the more exuberant strains of a visiting brass band.

The village of **Poissons**, some 5km (3 miles) to the south-east along the D427, is aptly named. It is a picturesque hamlet whose rivers are full of fish, with a rather attractive little church and immediate access to Les Lacets de Melaire. These Melaire bends certainly live up to their description, corkscrewing their way for several kilometres above the valley, providing some worthwhile views and creating a circular route through the area known as La Petite Suisse.

Once back in Poissons the D16 makes a pleasant, alternative drive down to **Orquevaux** which owes its popularity to a curious ravine called Le Cul du Cerf. This is a chasm 50m (164ft) deep with steeply sloping sides carved out by the River Manoise. For part of the way it flows underground and can be followed along trails laid specially by the Office National des Forêts. Other strange quirks of nature can be seen in the so-called Zoo du Bois at nearby **Prez-sous-Lafauche** on the N74. It is really more like a museum or an art gallery with about three hundred exhibits, all consisting of branches that have grown into unusual shapes, some of them surprisingly lifelike.

Visitors who are more interested in people than in nature's curiosities would no doubt prefer to do their sightseeing to the west of Joinville. **Doulevant-le-Château** is only mildly interesting, except for anyone who plans to visit the wrought-iron and cast-iron workshops, whereas **Cirey-sur-Blaise**, on the D2 to the south, has decidedly romantic associations with Voltaire. The château belonged to the Marquise du Châtelet, his 'Divine Emilie', and he spent a lot of time there with her, writing and even designing the carving for the main door, until she decided that she preferred the poet St Lambert. A tour of the building includes the library, reception rooms hung with tapestries and the little theatre that was opened by Voltaire.

From Cirey-sur-Blaise the D2 heads south until it reaches a T-junction on the D40, which calls for one of those 'do we turn left or right?' decisions. Only 12km (7½ miles) to the left is **Vignory**, dominated by the ruins of a feudal castle that still has two towers and clings resolutely to the rocky hillside. Below it is the Eglise St Etienne, built in the eleventh century, which has a tall Roman bell tower and a splendid nave with tiers of rounded arches on either side below the exposed timber beams of the roof. Five chapels, added a century or two later, are filled with statues dating from roughly the same period.

On the other hand, by turning right on to the D40 it is only 9km (6 miles) to **Colombey-les-Deux-Eglises**, famous as the country home of Général — later President — de Gaulle. The gigantic pink granite Cross of Lorraine which he adopted as the emblem of the Free French during World War II, and which was erected as his memorial in 1972, stands out like a beacon from a hilltop close by. The family home, La Boisserie, is completely hidden by trees inside its private grounds somewhat closer to the village. It is open to the public almost every day when visitors are conducted through the library with its once-familiar desk, the dining room and the main reception room. Everywhere there are books, portraits, photographs of well-known contemporaries and souvenirs of the leader who, on one occasion, wondered aloud how it was possible to govern a country that produced more than four hundred different kinds of cheese.

The N19 connects Colombey-les-Deux-Eglise with **Chaumont** which is probably best known these days for its enormous viaduct, supported by 50 arches and stretching for 600m (1,968ft) across the valley of the Suize. The old town, poised on its rocky outcrop between the Marne and the Suize, was fortified in its youth, had a thriving textile industry in the eighteenth century and gave its name to the Treaty of Chaumont in 1814. It was this treaty that led to the signing of the Holy Alliance in Paris a year later, after the defeat of Napoléon. Alexander I of Russia, Francis II of Austria and Frederick William III of Prussia agreed ostensibly to be bound by the principles of Christianity although, in fact, they intended to perpetuate the idea of divine right, and it soon became an instrument for resisting revolutionary tendencies. Just over a hundred years later, when Europe was in the throes of World War I, Chaumont was chosen as the headquarters of the United States Expeditionary Corps when America entered the fray in 1917.

The first place to visit in the old town is undoubtedly the Basilique St Jean-Baptiste which dates in part from the thirteenth century. Although there are quite a few things to see inside, including a 400-

Chaumont; the most outstanding landmark is the viaduct, with its fifty arches spanning the valley of the Suize

year-old Tree of Jesse, its most memorable treasure is an arresting *mise au tombeau* in the Chapelle du St Sépulcre. This is slightly unusual because the ten large polychrome figures are grouped around the body of Christ which has already been placed in a shallow tomb. The Tour Hautefeuille, a short walk away along the Rue du Palais, is all that remains of the feudal castle that once belonged to the Comtes de Champagne. Its nearest neighbour is the Musée Municipal whose exhibits cover a surprisingly large field. Archaeology is well represented, there are plenty of drawings and paintings, pieces of sculpture and pearl embroidery as well as dolls and dolls houses and a collection of eighteenth and nineteenth-century cribs. The quiet streets are overlooked by a number of old houses with characteristic turrets and there is a good view from the Square Philippe Lebon which adjoins the Place Goguenheim.

Chaumont has a comfortable hotel in the Place du Général de Gaulle, near both the bus and the railway stations, and a selection of other hotels and motels scattered about the town in addition to a two-star camp site on the Rue des Tanneries, a name which recalls the days when Chaumont was famous for its gloves. There are guided tours including visits to the forest under the watchful eye of the National Forestry Commission. Bicycles are available for those who prefer to explore on their own and riding stables can be found at Choignes, on the eastern outskirts near the Canal de la Marne à la Saône.

A pleasant day's outing from Chaumont might well start at **Châteauvillain**, 21km (13 miles) to the west on the D65. It is an unassuming little place which has lost most of its old fortifications but still has some antiquated wall paintings in the Trinity Chapel, an eighteenth-century wash-house and a large 300-year-old dove-cote that is still in good working order. The deer park quite close by has several marked footpaths, the remains of some elderly quarries and a variety of trees and shrubs as well as being full of birds and animals.

Further down the D65 there is a turning off to Dancevoir beyond which the D20 heads southwards, passing reasonably close to the Cascade d'Etufs. This is one of the best-known of several petrified waterfalls in the vicinity. They are apparently caused by water with a high calcium content building up deposits that are then partly dissolved by carbonic acid, leaving behind a collection of small, natural stairways that would not look out of place in a formal garden. In this case the steps of varying heights are almost semi-circular and therefore particularly eye-catching.

From Rouvres-sur-Aube, a touch further on, a succession of minor roads make their way round the Forêt d'Arc and back up to **Arc-en-Barrois**, which has some unusual ways of drawing attention to itself. One of the strangest is La Glacière, a vast stone case in the shape of an egg in which ice off the castle pond was stored under the ground. Then there is a steam engine designed to run an old saw-mill that is put through its paces these days by an electric motor and the twelfth-century Colombier, or dovecote, of Marac with no less than fifteen hundred pigeon holes. The church in this Station Verte de Vacances, or Green Holiday Resort, has its own colourful *mise au tombeau*, the Bugnières is a large underground room at the end of an extremely long tunnel and the Château d'Arc is now a four-star hotel standing in its own park. There is also a smaller hotel and a camp site which closes out of season, all within 23km (14 miles) of Chaumont.

Nogent-en-Bassigny, on the D1 just south of the D417, has nothing quite so original although it does specialise in the production of decorative cutlery and also makes high quality surgical instruments. The town is so pleased with its achievements that it has opened not one but three museums, all devoted to the same subject. The Cutlery Museum traces the history of the industry, the employers have a permanent exhibition of their products while a private collection of more than three thousand pieces contains a variety of exhibits ranging from sheep shears to mother-of-pearl manicure sets and little dunces' caps for extinguishing candles. Strange stories are told of a dolmen in the Forêt de Marsois to the west of Nogent-en-Bassigny. It is known as either Pierre Branlante or the Devil's Stone and, according to legend, it rises up on Christmas Eve to reveal a treasure hidden underneath. Other people maintain that it changes position every hundred years or so but it is generally agreed that the stone, weighing about nine tons, could be swung round with one hand before it got either bored or dizzy and just collapsed. Opinions are even more divided about La Pierre Alot, or Water Stone, in the Lardigny forest. Some say its shallow indentation was formed by rain, others that it was designed to catch the blood during a pagan sacrifice while a few maintain that the whole dolmen marked the grave of an ancient warrior.

All the little villages hereabouts have something to offer their visitors. **Rolampont**, on the D1 below Nogent-en-Bassigny, at the point where it joins the N19, weighs in with its own petrified waterfall while **Andilly-en-Bassigny**, east of the Reservoir de Charmes, was a prosperous but nevertheless fairly typical large Gallo-Roman agricultural estate in the second-century AD. Enough of it has survived to give archaeologists a good idea of how the occupants used to live. The owners, their servants, the artisans and the farm workers all had their own quarters where they helpfully left behind enough everyday articles to make them easy to identify. However the baths are the best preserved of all the ruins with their hot and cold rooms, steam chamber, swimming pool and some fairly intricate stonework. Three hundred years later the Merovingians turned it into a cemetery but in doing so they added additional interest with the traces of a funeral pyre. A small museum has been opened on the site to take care of all the bits and pieces that have been unearthed so far. None of the other hamlets can rise to such historic heights so they content themselves with offering holidaymakers a choice of riding, fishing, swimming or sailing on one of the four lakes of the Pays de Langres.

Langres itself is a most satisfactory town with its roots buried deeply in the ancient past when it was an important settlement belonging to a tribe called the Lingons. Following the death of their chief, Neron, his successor decided that he would rather retire to an isolated cave than defend his stronghold against the Romans. The result was that the invaders moved in and built a new town of their own on the rocky spur with its views across to the Vosges mountains and the valley of the Marne. Andematunum, as they called it, was soon the meeting place for several major highways and protected by monumental arches, all except one of which have disappeared.

With the decline of the Roman Empire the stronghold was taken over by the Franks who were quite willing to leave its affairs in the hands of the bishops who had been in virtual control since the introduction of Christianity. However, because of its strategic position Langres was subjected to repeated attacks and only started to recover during the Middle Ages. The ramparts, covering a distance of more than 4km (2 miles) were extended, strengthened or rebuilt and reinforced with twelve towers and seven strategically placed and well protected entrances. These defensive walls are still virtually intact and even today there is no way in or out except through three or four or the original gateways.

Once inside these fortifications there are two good ways of getting to know the old town. Sightseers can either stroll right round along the top of the ramparts or follow the signs at ground level which lead from one historic building to another. In both cases the tour starts from the Porte des Moulins, built in 1647 to protect the southern approaches to Langres. It consists of a large archway for carriages and other vehicles with smaller ones for pedestrians on either side. It faces on to the Place des Etats-Unis and has the local Office de Tourisme for company.

Setting off along the walkway at the top of the walls where, incidentally, it is also possible to ride a bicycle, the first tower on the right is the ancient Tour St Ferjeux, followed after a fairly brisk walk by the Tour Virot and the fifteenth-century gateway named after Henri IV that was once equipped with a drawbridge. A bit further on the Faubourg-de-Sous-Murs has a splendid view over the Lac de la Liez towards the Vosges mountains but sadly the little cog railway next door has now disappeared. Turning the corner at the Tour Piquant the next port of call is the Porte Longe-Porte complete with its ancient guard-house, followed by the Tour St Jean, once the military pigeon loft, and the Tour du Petit-Saut which looks out over the valley of the Marne. Dating from the early sixteenth century it was built on an incline dictated by the hillside with a monumental staircase and five separate entrances designed so that guns could be moved in and out at different levels. Next comes the Porte de l'Hôtel de Ville and its guard-house, facing the Gallo-Roman arch that was incorporated into the ramparts some 1,800 years ago and then filled in to form a tower during the Middle Ages. Beyond the considerably altered Porte Boulière and the Porte Neuve, added in the nineteenth century, the old Tour Navarre and Tour Orval with their pill-boxes

Langres; the statue of Denis Diderot, stands in the square that was named after him

and spiral ramp were covered over in 1821 and converted into a powder magazine. Undoubtedly the most fascinating way of inspecting the ramparts is to join the Halberdier guards in their sixteenth-century uniforms as they make their rounds by torchlight, armed with passwords and traditional weapons.

The Cathédrale St Mamès, parts of which date from the twelfth century, occupies the site of the first church to be built in Langres. Unfortunately it was damaged by fire on several different occasions and the whole façade had to be replaced in the eighteenth century. The interior is quite majestic without too much decoration apart from its sculptured doorways, two elderly tapestries recalling episodes in the life of the saint and the Amoncourt chapel which contains the baptismal font. The cloister, at the end of the southern aisle, has been pressed into service as the municipal library but is worth seeing for its galleries and stone carving. The Salle du Trésor draws the attention of visitors to its three reliquaries, one of which is said to contain a slither of the True Cross, but apparently several other sacred items went missing during the Revolution and have never been seen again.

The Musée St Didier, within a longish stone's throw of the cathedral, just off the Square Henriot, is full of antiquities discovered in the neighbourhood, augmented by sculptures from the Middle Ages and the Renaissance. Meanwhile the Musée du Breuil-de-St-Germain, in an elderly mansion on the Place de Verdun, has a section allocated to some very viewable objects d'art, another devoted to the painter and engraver Claude Gillot and a third to the philosopher Denis Diderot. He was born in Langres in 1713 and is famous for both his Encyclopedia and works like *Jacques le Fataliste*. His name keeps popping up all over the place. There is the Rue Diderot which runs from the Porte des Moulins to the Place Diderot with his statue by Bartholdi in the middle, as well as his old home and the Collège Diderot just off the square, a school founded in the eighteenth century and housed in an appropriately decorative building. Other places to visit include the seventeenth-century Hopital de la Charité with its slightly younger chapel and the Eglise St Martin on the Place Jenson which started life in the thirteenth century but was added to at fairly frequent intervals. There are some most attractive old houses, the most noteworthy being a Renaissance mansion in the Rue Cardinal-Morlot, part of which is open to the public. At the same time there are more recent buildings which prevent the old quarter from giving the impression that time has passed it by completely.

Langres is not exactly overblessed with hotels and restaurants although there are a few places to stay in the old town only a few blocks away from the main attractions. Rather surprisingly it also has a camp site on the Boulevard de Lattre de Tassigny inside the walls, overlooked by the Tour d'Orval and the Tour de Navarre. At the same time visitors will find plenty of things to do in the vicinity such as riding, cycling and walking, tennis, swimming and boating of various descriptions including travelling by barge on the Canal de la Marne à la Saône. So far none of the lakes have really been developed as holiday resorts but in each case there are small villages quite close by and accommodation is available in Neuilly-l'Eveque not far from the Reservoir de Charmes and Longeau on the N74, just to the north of the Reservoir de Villegusien, while the Lac de la Liez is near enough to Langres for holidaymakers to stay in the town.

Among the places of interest to visit in the immediate vicinity is the Château du Pailly, a bare 12km (7 miles) to the southeast on the D17 below Chalindrey. It is reputed to be one of the most outstanding buildings of its kind in eastern France, dating mainly from the sixteenth century but with a keep left over from a feudal castle that once occupied the site. Visitors can judge for themselves any Sunday afternoon during the season when part of the château and the grounds are open to the public. The castle at Prangey, below Longeau and less than 2km (1 mile) along a minor road off the N74, is medieval with comparatively modern overtones. It has matching round towers, two courtyards, a grand staircase and gardens designed by Le Nôtre.

The Marne rises just south of Langres, near the grotto where Sabinus is believed to have taken refuge after refusing to defend his tribal stronghold against the Romans. From here, on the opposite side of the N74, the D428 crosses the autoroute and joins a *Grande Randonnée*, the GR7, for a short trip through the woods to **Auberive** which owes its existence to a Cistercian abbey founded by St Bernard in 1133. The sparse remains were enthusiastically restored in the eighteenth century and given an elegant wrought-iron gate designed by Jean Lamour who was responsible for the highly decorated Place Stanislas in Nancy. The hamlet has its own Parc di Vision, inhabited by wild boar and various kinds of deer, and has laid out and signposted a number of attractive footpaths through the forest.

East of Langres on the N19, **Fayl-Billot** is the centre of the basket-making industry and even has its own National Cane Weaving School. Some of the craftsmen are only too pleased to invite strangers into their workshops and it is also possible to visit the sallicetum, or willow plantation, which supplies all their raw materials. There is a permanent exhibition of articles ranging from furniture and other predictable objects to more intricate luxury items. It is a good place to look for useful souvenirs but buyers are advised to make sure that they carry the Fayl-Billot label as a guarantee of quality.

Some 4km (2 miles) east of Fayl-Billot, the secondary D460 heads almost due north for **Bourbonne-les-Bains**, an ancient town and the only thermal resort in Champagne-Ardenne. Its first visitors were the Romans who knew a good health-giving spring when they saw one, but there are hardly any Gallo-Roman remains. However there is a twelfth-century church and a 500-year-old château which provides house room for the municipal museum. The spa is well-equipped and modern and the waters are said to be particularly effective in the treatment of rheumatism, arthritis, respiratory problems and even fractures in need of special attention.

The town, nestling in a narrow valley on either side of the River Borne, has more than a dozen little hotels, the majority in the two-star bracket. For guests who are well on the road to recovery, or who have simply chosen the spa as a good place for a restful holiday, there is an indoor swimming pool and the Arboretum de Montmorency full of ornamental trees and bushes from as far afield as Asia, Africa and the Americas. Less than 3km (2 miles) to the south-west on the D26 the Parc Animalier de la Bannie is a wild life park where small herds of animals roam quite freely and a variety of birds make their homes in the aviary. From here the motorist has several convenient options, among them the D417 on the way to either Langres or Chaumont, the A31 autoroute at Montigny-le-Roi some 19km (12 miles) away, or the D460 across the provincial border into Lorraine-Vosges.

Further Information
— Champagne-Ardenne —

Museums and Other Places of Interest

ARDENNES

Bazeilles
Château
Open: mornings and afternoons.
Closed Mondays.
☎ 24 27 09 68

Maison de la Dernière Cartouche
Open: 8am-12noon and 1.30-6pm in summer. Closed Fridays. 9am-12noon and 2-5pm in winter. Closed Fridays.

Belval-Bois-des-Dame
Parc de Vision
Open: daily July and August. Wednesday, Saturday, Sunday and holidays in the afternoons February to June and September to mid-October. Special visits by arrangement.
☎ 29 70 72 81

Carignan
Municipal Museum
Open: 9am-12noon and 2-7pm Monday to Saturday. Closed the third Saturday of each month.

Charleville-Mézières
Musée Rimbaud
Open: 10am-12noon and 2-6pm. Closed Monday and some holidays.
☎ 24 33 31 64

Chooz
Nuclear Power Station
Guided tours daily except Sundays and holidays. Make arrangements 15 days in advance.
☎ 24 42 05 26

Douzy
Musée des Debuts de l'Aviation
Open: 10am-12noon and 2-6pm June to August. 2-6pm May and September. 2-6pm Saturdays, Sundays and holidays April and October. Always closed Mondays.

Forte de la Ferté
Open: afternoons July and August. Otherwise Sunday and holiday afternoons Palm Sunday to October.

Fumay
Musée de l'Ardoise
Open: daily 5-6.30pm.

Givet
Fort de Charlemont
Open: for guided tours mornings and afternoons July and August.

Grottes de Nichet
Open: for guided tours morning and afternoon April to September.
☎ 24 42 00 14

Musée de la Forge Toussaint
Open: 10am-12noon and 2-6pm mid-June to mid-September. Closed Sunday

and Monday mornings.
Tour Victoire. Same times as the Musée
de la Forge Toussaint.

La Horgne
Musée des Spahis
Open: 10am-7pm daily May to August.
10am-6pm mid-February to April and
September to mid-December Wednes-
days, Saturdays and Sundays.

Montcornet-en-Ardennes
Château
Open: afternoons July and August.
Closed Mondays. Otherwise Saturday
and Sunday afternoons Easter to All
Saints Day.
☎ 24 54 93 48

Monthermé
Eglise St Léger
Open: weekdays July and August.
Otherwise ☎ 24 53 08 74

Mouzon
Musée de la Porte Bourgogne
Open: 2.30-6.30pm Saturdays and
Sundays mid-May to August.

Musée du Feutre
Open: 10am-12noon and 2-6pm July
and August. 2-6pm daily June and
September. 2-6pm Saturdays and
Sundays April, May and October.
☎ 24 26 10 63

Novion-Porcien
Musée de la Bataille des Ardennes
Open: 9am-7pm. Closed 25 December
and 1 January.

Renwez
Musée de la Forêt
Open: 9am-12noon and 2-7pm in
summer and 2-5pm in winter. Open
throughout the day June, July and
August. Closed mid-December to mid-
January.

Rethel
Eglise St Nicolas
If closed enquire at 13 rue Carnot
☎ 24 38 41 50

Musée du Rethelois et du Porcien
Times to be advised when refurbishing
is completed.

Revin
Galerie d'art Contemporain
Open: Wednesday, Saturday and
Sunday afternoons.

Rocroi
Musée de la Bataille de Rocroi
Open: 10am-6pm Easter to September.
1.45-5.30pm October to Easter. Closed
at weekends.
☎ 24 54 24 46

Sedan
Château Fort
Open: for conducted tours daily April
to August. Otherwise 1.30-5.30pm.

Château Museum
The same hours as the fortress.

Trois Fontaines Abbey
Son et lumière 10pm every Saturday in
August.

MARNE
Braux-Ste-Cohière
*Musée Regional d'Orientation de
l'Argonne*
Open: 10am-12noon and 2-6pm.

Château
Open: mornings and afternoons July
and August. Closed Tuesdays.
☎ 26 60 83 51

Châlons-sur-Marne
Bibliothèque
Open: mornings and afternoons. Closed
Sundays, Mondays and holidays.
☎ 26 68 54 44

Cathedral Treasure
Enquire at the tourist office or at the
presbytère.

Eglise Notre-Dame-en-Vaux
Closed Sunday afternoons.

Musée du Cloître Notre-Dame-en-Vaux
Open: 10am-12noon and 2-6pm April
to September. 10am-12noon and 2-5pm

October to March. Closed Mondays
and 1 January, 1 May, 1 and 11
November and 25 December.

Musée Municipal
Open: 2-6pm daily. Closed Tuesdays.
☎ 26 68 54 44

Dormans
Musée de l'Outil Champenois
To visit ☎ 26 58 80 30
Usually open daily July to September
except Saturday mornings, Saturday af-
ternoons, Sundays and holidays May,
June and October to mid-November.

Epernay
Jardin des Papillons
Open: 10am-6pm daily May to mid-Oct.
☎ 26 55 15 33

Moët et Chandon
Open: daily for guided tours. Closed
Saturdays, Sundays and holidays
November to March.
☎ 26 54 71 11

Musée des Pressoirs
Champagne Mercier
Open: 9.30-11.30am and 2-4.45pm
Monday to Saturday. 9am-6pm
Sunday. Closed Monday to Friday
December, January and February.
☎ 26 54 75 26

Musée Municipal
Open: 10am-12noon and 2-6pm March
to November. Closed Tuesdays and
holidays and the second or third
Sunday in September.

Germain
Le Maison du Bucheron
Open: 2.30-6.30pm Saturdays, Sundays
and holidays mid-March to mid-
November.
☎ 26 59 44 44

Lac du Der Chantecoq
Boat trips leave Giffaumont-
Champaubert each afternoon from
mid-April to mid-September.

La Grange aux Abeilles
Open: afternoons July and August.
Afternoons Saturdays, Sundays and

holidays only April to June and
September. Afternoons Sundays only
in October.
☎ 26 72 61 97

Village-Musée de Ste-Marie-du-Lac
Open: afternoons July and August.
Afternoons Saturdays, Sundays and holidays April to June and in September.
☎ 26 72 36 33

Montmort-Lucy
Château
Open: for guided tours 2.30 and
4.30pm mid-July to mid-September.
2.30, 3.30, 5pm and 5.30pm Sundays
and holidays. Closed Mondays.
☎ 26 59 10 04

Orbais l'Abbaye
Eglise
If closed enquire from 1 rue Thiers
☎ 26 59 20 04

Reims
Musée du Palais du Tau
Open: 9.30am-6.30pm July and August.
9.30am-12.30pm and 2-6pm mid-March
to June and September to mid-
November. 10am-12noon and 2-5pm
Saturdays and Sundays mid-November to mid-March. Closed 1 January, 1
and 8 May,
1 and 11 November and 25 December.
☎ 26 47 49 37

Musée du Vieux Reims
Hôtel Le Vergeur
Open: 2-6pm daily except Mondays.
Closed 1 January, 1 May, 14 July,
1 November and 25 December.
☎ 26 47 20 75

Musée St Denis
Open: daily 10am-12noon and 2-6pm.
Closed Mondays, 1 January, 1 May,
14 July, 1 and 11 Nov and 25 Dec.
☎ 26 47 28 44

Musée St Remi
Open: 2-6.30pm weekdays. 2-7pm
Saturdays and Sundays. Closed on
some holidays.

Salle de Guerre
Open: mornings and afternoons March
to November. Closed Tuesdays, 1 May,
14 July, 1 and 11 November.
☎ 26 47 28 44

Ste Menehould
Musée de l'Argonne
Open: 3-6pm weekends and holidays
May to October.

Vitry-le-François
Eglise Notre-Dame
Closed Sun afternoons and some hols.

AUBE
Arsonval
Musée des Icônes Loukine
Open: 2-5pm every afternoon.

Bayel
Cristallerie
Open: 9.30am for conducted tour.
Closed Sundays and holidays and
during August.
☎ 25 92 05 02

Brienne-le-Château
Church
If closed enquire from M. le Curé, 94
rue de l'Ecole Militaire, ☎ 25 92 82 26,
or at the mairie.

Musée Napoléon
Open: 9-11.30am and 2-5pm. Closed
Tuesdays and holidays and usually
December to February.
☎ 25 92 82 41

Brienne-la-Vieille
Musée du Charronnage
Open: afternoons, May to October.
☎ 25 92 85 65

Clairvaux
Abbaye
Open for guided tours at 1.45pm and
3.30pm the first Saturday of every
month from May to October and on the
third Saturday in September.

Essoyes
Maison de la Vigne et Souvenirs de Renoir
Open: 3-6pm weekends and holidays,
Easter to All Saints Day, all day mid-
June to mid-September.

Forêt d'Orient
Maison du Parc
For information ☎ 25 41 35 57
Boat trips from Mesnil-St-Père
Each afternoon from March to mid-Sept.
☎ 25 41 21 64

Géraudot
Church
If closed enquire at 1 rue du Général-
Bertrand
☎ 25 41 24 21

Isle-Aumont
Church and site
Open: for guided tours 3pm Sundays.
Otherwise ☎ 25 41 81 94 between 9am
and 9pm.

Maison-les-Chaource
Musée des Poupées d'Antan
Open: daily 9.30am-12noon and 2-6pm.
Closed Tuesdays.

La Motte-Tilly
Open for guided tours mornings and
afternoons April to September.
Saturday and Sunday afternoons only
October and November. Closed
Tuesdays, 1 May, 1 and 11 November.
☎ 25 39 84 54

Mussy-sur-Seine
Eglise St-Pierre-ès-Liens
If closed enquire at 2 rue des Ursulines
☎ 25 38 42 89
or 37 rue Gambetta ☎ 25 38 43 33

Musée de la Resistance
Open: Saturday, Sunday and holiday
afternoons May to October.
☎ 25 38 40 10

Nogent-sur-Seine
Eglise St-Laurent
Closed Sunday afternoons.

Musée Dubois-Boucher
Open: every afternoon mid-June to mid-September. Saturday and Sunday afternoons only April to mid-June and mid-September to November.

Nuclear Centre
Open for guided tours daily. Closed Saturday afternoons, Sundays and holidays. For information and to make an appointment ☎ 25 39 32 60

La Paraclet
Abbaye
For appointment to visit ☎ 25 39 80 22

St Léger-près-Troyes
Ferme Musée Rustique
☎ 25 82 42 00

Troyes
Basilique St-Urbain
Open: daily July to mid-September. Otherwise enquire at 5 rue Charbonnet or at the Syndicat d'Initiative.

Bibliothèque
In the former Abbaye St-Loup, Rue de la Cité
Open: 10am-12noon and 2-7pm. Closed Sundays and holidays.

Cathedral Treasure
Open: every afternoon except Tuesdays mid-June to mid-October. Otherwise Saturday and Sunday afternoons from Easter to All Saints Day.
☎ 25 80 58 46

Eglise Ste-Madeleine
Open mornings and afternoons Easter to September. Otherwise enquire at the Syndicat d'Initiative.

Eglise St Jean
The same conditions that apply to the Basilica.

Eglise St Nicolas
Open: every afternoon.

Eglise St Pantaléon
Open: during July and August. Otherwise enquire at the Syndicat d'Initiative.

Eglise St Rémy
Enquire at the Syndicat d'Initiative.

Maison de l'Outil
Hotel de Mauroy
Open: 9am-12noon and 2-6pm. Closed some holidays.
☎ 25 73 28 26

Musée d'Art Moderne
Open: 11am-6pm. Closed Tues and hols.

Musée de la Bonneterie
Hôtel de Vauluisant
Open: 10am-12noon and 2-6pm. Closed Tuesdays and holidays.
☎ 25 73 49 49

Musée Historique de Troyes et de la Champagne
Hôtel de Vauluisant
Open: 10am-12noon and 2-6pm. Closed Tuesdays and holidays.
☎ 25 73 49 49

Musée St-Loup
Open: mornings and afternoons 10am-12noon and 2-6pm. Closed Tuesdays and holidays.
☎ 25 73 49 49

Pharmacie-Musée
Hôtel-Dieu
Open: 10am-12noon and 2-6pm. Closed Tuesdays and holidays.
☎ 25 73 49 49

HAUTE-MARNE

Andilly-en-Bassigny
The Gallo-Roman Remains
Open: daily from Easter to August.
☎ 28 84 00 59

Bourbonne-les-Bains
Château
Visit by arrangement 3-5pm May to September.

Chaumont
Musée Municipal
Open: every afternoon, 2-6pm. Closed Tuesdays and holidays.

Cirey-sur-Blaise
Château
Open: for guided tours in the afternoon mid-June to mid-September. Closed Tuesdays.
☎ 25 55 43 04

Colombey-les-Deux-Eglises
La Boisserie
Open: 10am-12noon and 2-5pm. Closed Tuesdays, Christmas Day and New Year's Day. ☎ 25 01 52 52

Le Memorial
Open: 9am-12noon and 2-6pm April to October. 9am-12noon and 2-4pm November to March. Closed Tuesdays, Christmas Day and New Year's Day.

Fayl-Billot
Ecole Nationale d'Osiériculture
Open: 3-5pm Wednesday and Saturday May to September.

Joinville
Château du Grand Jardin
Enquire at the tourist office while restoration is in progress.

Langres
Cathedral Treasure
Enquire at the cathedral.

Musée du Breuil-de-St-Germain
Open: 10am-12noon and 2-6pm April to September. 10am-12noon and 2-5pm October to March. Closed Tuesdays and holidays.
☎ 25 87 08 05

Musée St-Didier
Closed temporarily for rearrangement. Enquire at the tourist office.

Tours de Navarre et d'Orval
Open: for guided tours 5pm Tuesdays and Thursdays and 10.30pm Mondays during July. 3pm Sundays and holidays mid-June to mid-September.
☎ 25 87 03 32

Montier-en-Der
Haras National
Guided tours every afternoon.
☎ 25 04 22 17

Nogent-en-Bassigny
Chambre Syndicale des Industries des Metaux du Bassin Nogentais
Permanent Exhibition
Open: daily 8am-12noon and 2-6pm. Closed Sat afternoon, Sun and Mon.

Musée Coutelier
Open: 9am-12.30pm by appointment and 2-7pm Wednesday to Saturday.

Musée du Patrimoine Coutelier
Open: 2-6pm daily. Closed Mondays.

Poissons
Eglise
If closed enquire in the Place de l'Eglise.

Prez-sous-Lafauche
Zoo de Bois
Open: 2.30-6.30pm June to mid-September. Closed Mondays.
☎ 25 31 57 76

Wassy
Hôtel de Ville
Clock
Enquire at the Mairie from Monday to Friday. ☎ 25 55 31 90

Tourist Information Offices
ARDENNES

Charleville-Mézières
Bureau Municipal du Tourisme
Place Ducale ☎ 24 33 00 17

Monthermé
Office de Tourisme
Rue Etienne Dolet
Open: July to mid-September
☎ 24 53 07 46. At other times ☎ 24 53 06 50

Sedan
Office de Tourisme
At the château
Open: mid-March to mid-September.
☎ 24 27 73 73

MARNE

Châlons-sur-Marne
Office de Tourisme
Quai des Arts ☎ 26 65 17 89

Epernay
Office de Tourisme
7 Avenue de Champagne
☎ 26 55 33 00

Reims
Office de Tourisme and Accueil de France
2 rue G-de-Machault
☎ 26 47 25 69

Ste Menehould
Office de Tourisme
Place Général Leclerc
Closed mornings September to June.
☎ 26 60 85 83

Vitry-le-François
Office de Tourisme
Place Giraud ☎ 26 74 45 30

AUBE

Bar-sur-Aube
Syndicat d'Initiative
In the hôtel de ville ☎ 25 27 04 21

Troyes
Office de Tourisme and Accueil de France
Boulevard Carnot ☎ 25 73 00 36
and Quai Dampierre (Open July to mid-September) ☎ 25 73 36 88

HAUTE-MARNE

Chaumont
Office de Tourisme
Place Général de Gaulle ☎ 25 03 80 80

Joinville
Syndicat d'Initiative
Rue Briand
Open: July and August ☎ 25 94 17 90

Langres
Office de Tourisme
Square Olivier Lahalle ☎ 25 87 67 67

St-Dizier
Office de Tourisme
Pavillon du Jard ☎ 25 05 31 84

6 • Alsace et Lorraine

Despite anything the history books may say, one does not, these days, refer to Alsace-Lorraine — it is the quickest way to become thoroughly unpopular. Alsace et Lorraine or Alsace Vosges Lorraine are two acceptable alternatives. The reason is quite simple. In 1871 Alsace and a large part of Lorraine were acquired by Germany under the Treaty of Frankfurt and the new area, known as Alsace-Lorraine, was only restored to France in 1919. Both Alsace and Lorraine found themselves back in German hands in 1940, to be liberated for the second time 5 years later at the end of the war in Europe.

Even before they suffered these shared misfortunes the two had a great deal in common. They were each inhabited by the Celts, taken over by the Romans, devastated by the Huns and had their full share of war and pestilence during the Middle Ages before eventually being united with France. Their contributions to French history were many and varied. For instance, Joan of Arc was born in Lorraine, the *Battle Hymn of the Army of the Rhine*, composed in Strasbourg by Rouget de Lisle, is much better known as the *Marseillaise* and the famous Cross of Lorraine became the emblem of the Free French under General de Gaulle. Albert Schweitzer was a native of Alsace and in 1885 a small boy from the Villé area was the first to be saved by Louis Pasteur with his newly-discovered anti-rabies vaccine.

Geographically, the regions also complement each other. They lie side by side in the north-eastern corner of France, stretching from Luxembourg to Switzerland with Alsace facing Germany across the Rhine. Rivers and canals abound in the area, ranging from the Meuse and the Moselle to the Grand Canal d'Alsace which marches with the Rhine and is wider than either the Suez Canal or the Panama Canal. The Vosges mountains, although not in the same league as the Alps, have some spectacular scenic routes snaking their way up through forests of variegated pines to wooded peaks and deep blue lakes gouged out by the glaciers of a bygone age. In summer this area offers ideal conditions for walking, climbing, riding, fishing, boating and

swimming, turning its attention to winter sports when the cold weather sets in. Warm springs, particularly in the south-west, have produced a number of fashionable spas, some with a whole range of tourist attractions thrown in for good measure.

Inspite of its extensive national parks Lorraine has rather more industrial areas then its neighbour, particularly round the northern plateau in the vicinity of Metz and Nancy, leaving Alsace to concentrate on wine. Vineyards cover the hillsides from Marlenheim, west of Strasbourg, to Thann 120km (75 miles) to the south, with a special Route du Vin, duly signposted, which calls in at picturesque villages and historic towns along the way. There is also a Flower Route across the plains and, for anyone with a tendency to get lost in unfamiliar country, plaques mark the many deviations along the Road of Fortified Castles in the far north-east. Added to all this are a Green Road

with views across to the Black Forest, a mountain circuit known as
the Route des Crêtes, a Cheese Road liberally sprinkled with inns
specialising in local dishes and even a complex of little roads rejoic-
ing in the overall title of the Routes of the Fried Carp which is self-
explanatory.

There are many different ways of getting to Alsace et Lorraine.
Apart from the international airport at Strasbourg, several towns
such as Colmar, Metz, Mulhouse and Nancy are connected by air
with other parts of the country. Frequent train services run from
Paris and the Channel ports as well as from the Benelux countries,
Germany and Switzerland, with the added advantage of motorail
facilities that operate to and from Strasbourg, Nancy, Metz and
Mulhouse. France has very few long-distance buses but coach companies organise tours in and around the main centres, complement-
ing the boats that take sightseers for jaunts up and down the rivers
and round the lake at Gérardmer. Local bus services are excellent,
cars can be hired in the major centres and bicycles are available at
quite a few of the larger railway stations.

Motorists have an even wider choice. Visitors whose time is
limited might well opt for the *autoroute* from Paris through Reims to
Metz and from there either southwards, northwards or on to Strasbourg. Other alternatives would be the main route from Brussels
through Metz and Nancy to the Vosges, from Germany through
Saarbrücken or from Switzerland across the border to Mulhouse.
Major roads link all the main towns such as Epinal, St Dié, Haguenau
and Verdun while a wealth of secondary roads wander peacefully
through the countryside, providing access to any number of interesting towns and villages. There are *châteaux* and ruined castles,
churches both impressive and otherwise, museums, battlefields
with trenches from World War I and a Nazi concentration camp of
much more recent vintage for anyone whose primary interest is
history. On the sporting side every second hamlet appears to have its
own individual pathways, usually covering about 25km(15 miles),
clearly marked through fields of flowers, along the banks of mountain streams, past waterfalls or into the shade of nearby forests. Some
of the larger places run excursions up into the mountains, others
offer hunting or fishing, riding or water sports but tennis and golf are
not so easy to find. Almost without exception there is a small *auberge*
or *logis*, possibly with a modest room or two in addition to its own
selection of local dishes.

Some Alsatians insist that the reason the Romans stayed so long
was that they enjoyed the cooking. It seems a bit far-fetched but there

is no doubt that Brillat-Savarin described it as the most mouth-watering region in Europe and that *brioche* with *foie gras* became a popular hors d'oeuvres at the Russian court. Amongst a whole host of dishes which should not be missed are *baeckaoffe*, a concoction of beef, lamb and pork marinated in Reisling and cooked with onions and potatoes; *matelote de poissons*, which contains several different fish in a Reisling sauce, pheasant with grapes and sauerkraut, fried carp, venison, perch with almonds and any of the many varieties of tart, usually filled with Munster cheese, onions or fruit. Local beer is very popular and so are wines like Tokay and Gewürtztraminer. Eaux-de-vie come in well over a dozen different flavours from the familiar raspberry, pear and black cherry to more surprising things like holly. Anyone in search of souvenirs should keep an eye open for *fois gras* in earthenware pots, Vosges honey, porcelain, glass, pewter, copperware and linen and cotton materials which have been selling like hot cakes for hundreds of years.

The people of Alsace et Lorraine are great ones for *fêtes* and festivals and hardly a week goes by without someone, somewhere, celebrating something. The main centres like Strasbourg do things in style with events of the calibre of the International Music Festival in June. Flowers and folklore predominate nearly everywhere. Gérard-mer is smothered in daffodils for the Fête des Jonquilles in April, Neuf-Brisach prefers lily-of-the-valley in May, followed by Saverne with its Festival of the Rose, while Sélestat, like a number of other places, gets August off to a colourful start with a Carnival of Flowers. Regional costumes are a feature of the Fête du Mariage de l'Ami Fritz in Marlenheim, strolling fiddlers have their own day at Ribeauvillé, firework displays are a midsummer attraction in the mountains and Thann is not nearly as bloodthirsty as its Cremation of the Three Fir Trees would suggest. Both wine and beer provide ample excuses for celebrations as do such items as *sauerkraut*, *paté-en-croûte* and *quiche Lorraine*. December is marked by dozens of Christmas festivities, many of them dedicated to St Nicolas, and by the Fête de Ste Odile, who is the patron saint of Alsace and has a special mountain named after her. Myths and legends are accepted as a matter of course, whether they are miracles with religious connections and therefore much venerated or diabolical manifestations brought about by the odd giant or by witches and sorcerers, some of whom have whole towers to themselves.

Exploring Alsace et Lorraine is both easy and very enjoyable, whether you follow one of the popular routes or branch off down any of the hundreds of side turnings that can, but very seldom do, degenerate into cart tracks. Finding a hotel is just as simple except in the main tourist resorts at the height of the season. Obviously Strasbourg, home of the Council of Europe and the Court of Human Rights, has a vast number of hotels and restaurants of every description while Metz, Nancy and Mulhouse can offer much the same variety but with fewer to choose from, especially in the upper income brackets. Even quite small towns with only a modest *auberge* or two can provide high quality food at reasonable prices and will often run to rooms with private bathrooms, although swimming pools and tennis courts are the exception rather than the rule. Camping sites are a different matter. Some are fairly basic but the more up-market ones include a whole range of attractions such as tennis and volley-ball, riding, swimming, boating, windsurfing, bowls and pedalos for hire, either on the premises or in the immediate vicinity. It is even possible to find a winter site if your caravan is designed for low temperatures. It is as well to remember that the winters here can be as cold as anywhere in France apart from the Alps but spring and autumn are pleasantly invigorating and summer, give or take a short spell in August, is seldom uncomfortably hot. Tourist offices in the larger towns and main holiday resorts will often help in finding furnished accommodation but this is somewhat thinner on the ground than one might expect.

Motorists heading for Lorraine along the Paris *autoroute* cross the Meuse just south of **Verdun**, a town whose martial history goes back to Roman times. It is a fairly war-orientated area altogether. The countryside around positively bristles with forts, cemeteries, memorials and monuments pinpointing the various battlefields. Students of World War I should find it extremely interesting, particularly as the Fort de Vaux, the Fort de Douaumont, the enormous and vaguely Egyptian-looking Ossuaire de Douaumont and the Memorial Museum full of documents, uniforms, arms and equipment, are all open to visitors.

The town itself looks back a good deal further with places like the citadel, built by Vauban on the site of an ancient monastery. A twelfth-century tower is all that remains of the Abbaye de St Vanne but to one side of it, below ground level, the seemingly endless rooms and passages that originally sheltered troops in the reign of Louis XV are carefully preserved. The cathedral of Notre-Dame was rebuilt after a fire in 1048, the cloister was added a touch later to be followed in the eighteenth century by the Palais Episcopal. The Hôtel de la Princerie was a private house in the Middle Ages but is now the home of a comprehensive museum with exhibits spanning more than two thousand years. The River Meuse and its attendant canals flow through the town past a leisure park and a couple of very comfortable hotels.

A day spent touring the valley of the Meuse presents a slightly different picture depending on which direction you decide to take. To the north are such places as **Mont-devant-Sassey** where there is a nice old church, **Montmédy** whose ancient hilltop village is isolated behind ramparts enclosed in trees, and **Louppy-sur-Loison**, known for its sixteenth-century *château* which lays on guided tours each afternoon throughout the season but puts up the shutters on Mondays and during the rest of the year. To the south, almost surrounded by the Meuse and the Moselle, is the National Park of Lorraine, a delightfully wooded area full of ponds, some of which are distinctly marshy, little villages of varying attraction and the Lac de Madine complete with a holiday atmosphere and a monument to the men of the American lst Army who died there in September 1918. **St Mihiel**, on the Meuse to the west, has successfully preserved some outstanding sixteenth-century sculptures by Ligier Richier in its two ancient churches inspite of all the fighting that went on thereabouts. Opinions are divided as to which is the most emotive but the experts tend to give a slight edge to the sepulchre in the Eglise St Etienne as far as intricate workmanship is concerned.

Metz, on a direct line from Verdun, has been a city of considerable importance from the time it was founded to the present day. It has a busy airport, the main *autoroutes* go either through or round it, and commerce flourishes, as does the university established in 1972. Inspite of all this it also holds plenty of attractions for visitors as well as being a convenient centre from which to explore the surrounding area. In the first place there are something like fifty churches, starting with the impressive cathedral of St Etienne. It began life as two separate chapels back in the twelfth century, was added to every hundred years or so, given extra towers and some magnificent stained glass windows and even managed to preserve some of its treasures during the Revolution. These can be seen in the Grande Sacristie almost any afternoon except on religious holidays. Considerably smaller than the cathedral, but none the worse for that, are the church of St Pierre-aux-Nonnains, once part of a seventh-century monastery then incorporated into the fortifications and eventually returned to its original function, and the Chapelle des Templiers almost next door. They share the large, well shaded Esplanade with a much-decorated Palais de Justice and the Lac des Cygnes beyond which a footbridge crosses a narrow arm of the Moselle.

It is only a short walk from the Esplanade to the Place St-Louis, the centre of the old town with its historic houses and attractive arcades where money-changers used to carry on a thriving trade. About the same distance further on is the definitely warlike Porte des Allemands, a splendid mixture of battlements and towers guarding either end of a heavily-fortified bridge. Sorcery is the name of the game on one bank while the towers opposite look like matching pepperpots complete with witches' hats. The Museum of Art and History is another place worth visiting. The building itself is old enough to have the remains of some Roman baths in the basement from where it wends its way up through the Middle Ages to sections devoted to artisan workshops, Napoleonic uniforms, natural history and contemporary art. Opera lovers are catered for by the theatre in the Place de la Comédie, there are concerts of ancient music, the Trinitaires concentrates on jazz and there is a special centre looking into the kind of sounds we can expect to hear in years to come.

Sightseers who prefer to collect ruins by the dozen rather than one at a time should head straight on, due east, to **Sarreguemines** and the Parc Naturel Régional des Vosges du Nord. This can be done along the *autoroute*, branching off just before it makes a final spurt into Germany. A slower way is to select any of the minor roads across the countryside, avoiding industrial centres in favour of agricultural landscapes, clumps of trees, tiny lakes and ponds and villages that have no pretensions when it comes to a place in a tourist guide. Even Sarreguemines is a fairly uninteresting frontier town, or it would be but for the fact that it has a formidable reputation for producing ceramics and has set up a small museum full of pottery and china which is open daily except on Mondays and public holidays.

A reasonably fast road leads on to **Bitche** where the dour and extremely workmanlike citadel built by Vauban in 1679 overshadows everything else. It battled determinedly against invasion during the Franco-Prussian War but with no more success than the nearby Fort du Simserhof achieved 70 years later when it was one of the most important sections of the ill-fated Maginot Line. A limited number of tours of Simserhof are arranged every month, with the exception of July and August, but visitors who want to join one of them must apply in writing to the military authorities in Metz. Of course this takes time so it means planning the trip well in advance.

These days the Parc Naturel Régional des Vosges du Nord is not bothered by frontiers as such and is all of a piece with the Naturpark Pfalzerwald, its German counterpart across the border. But there is no need to venture quite so far in search of ruined *châteaux* and medieval fortifications which, more often than not, turn out to be much the same thing. The hills round about are peppered with the remains of a dozen or more, some of which have received a certain amount of attention while others consist of little apart from a few mouldering walls hidden from sight in the trees. Avid inspectors of ruins can almost castle-hop their way through, parking the car on each occasion (and remembering to lock them up — there are notices everywhere to remind visitors about this), and trudging along well-worn paths for up to half an hour or so to inspect these weathered piles of ancient stones. People who are more discerning, less energetic, or perhaps both, make their own selection beforehand and ignore all the other tempting signs along the roadside. Such a list might well include the Château de Falkenstein, founded on a hilltop in 1128. It was considerably battered during the next few centuries and eventually left to its own devices. However it is a good place to clamber about and anyone who dislikes heights can spend the time inspecting a variety of caves, both natural and man-made, in the rock below. The impressive thirteenth-century Château de Fleckenstein, hard by the German border, has been undergoing restoration work since 1968. As a result it has a small museum and a refreshment bar among its other attractions and is open from the beginning of March to the end of November. The Château de Hohenbourg, with the remains of a keep and some Renaissance sculptures, is not really in the same class but it is conveniently placed for anyone who wants to take the tiny twisting road down to Climbach and on through the Col de Pigeonnier to Wissembourg.

Wissembourg is an attractive little town that has been extremely warlike in its time, even giving its name to a battle fought near there in 1870. It has preserved some delightful old houses and a church, said to be the largest in Alsace apart from Strasbourg cathedral, whose statues had their heads cut off during the Revolution. It was built in the thirteenth century on the site of an old monastery and an even older pagan temple and, although dedicated to St Peter and St Paul, manages to find space for St Christopher as well. It is pleasant to wander round the old quarter and visit the Westercamp Museum which concerns itself with early history, furniture, traditional costumes and the Franco-Prussian War. There are a number of small hotels and restaurants in the town which are reasonably priced and the local sporting activities include hunting and fishing, a swimming pool and several country walks. During Whitsun everyone turns out for the annual festival, celebrated with songs and dances, horse shows, processions and plenty of food and wine.

An interesting route back, provided one enjoys taking the smaller, less frequented roads whenever feasible, would be through **Cleebourg**, a picturesque hamlet which owns both a vineyard and a wine cellar and **Lembach** with its almost-attendant lake and the doubtful distinction of being close to the Maginot Line. It lays on guided tours of part of the defences during July and August, even working through the lunch hour when it is necessary. Alternatively there is the Route des Villages Pittoresques linking such enchanting hamlets as **Oberseebach** and **Hunspach**. They are chock full of typical Alsation half-timbered houses some with great bridal bouquets of flowers cascading from every ledge and windowsill, gardens which are a riot of colour and even roundabouts that have been turned into floral masterpieces. Although the area is known for its traditional costumes they are rarely seen except at festivals, people going about their everyday business wear exactly the same sort of clothes as their counterparts anywhere else.

Niederbronn-les-Bains, to the south-west, is a spa, popular with local people and with historic connections. It was founded by the Romans, who made a point of installing themselves as closely as possible to any health-giving spring, but suffered badly at the hands of the Barbarians some 400 years later. After that nothing much happened until Count Philippe de Hanau took a liking to the place in the sixteenth century and set about putting the baths back into working order. They have prospered ever since, adding various attractions from time to time such as shooting, fishing, tennis, swimming, a casino and, more recently, naturism.

The Parc Naturel Régional des Vosges du Nord has something for everyone. It supports both agriculture and forestry, trains local craftsmen and tempts visitors to explore both on horseback and on foot. Numbered among its lakes is the Etang de Baerenthal, an especially good place for anyone interested in birdwatching. In addition, the local Poney [*sic*] Ranch du Dachsthal arranges riding trips into the forest, fishing is encouraged in the rivers and ponds thereabouts on payment of the usual fee and the Club Vosgien will assist hikers with all the information they need. Two municipal camping sites are provided along with bathing, picnic spots and pedalos for hire. By way of contrast one can visit the Château de Lichtenberg, considerably restored and open daily from April to October, or **Meisenthal** which has specialised in glass-making for around 200 years and has painstakingly gathered together sufficient examples to fill a small museum.

La Petite-Pierre, a fortified village further to the south-west, has a sixteenth-century castle and is very proud of its game park and hunting reserve. An added advantage is that it is only a short distance from **St Jean-les-Saverne**, known chiefly for its flowers and a round platform called L'Ecole des Sorcières where, according to legend, witches congregate at night. Apparently they move on later to a cave they have appropriated under the Chapelle St Michel which was originally intended as a sepulchre. **Saverne** itself, which straddles the Canal de la Marne au Rhin, has a splendid *château* all set about with columns, sculptures and balustrades. Its visitors have included kings and cardinals as well as army personnel who used it as a barracks for nearly 100 years. There is also an older *château* plus some attractive houses, a church and a small museum. However, for horticulturists the high spots must be the Rose Garden with its 1,300 different varieties and the Jardin Botanique just outside the town.

The usual choice between highways and byways confronts the motorist heading for Nancy. The quickest way is more or less straight and not very scenic whereas there are plenty of trees and streams, the odd lake and places to stop for an *al fresco* meal on the back roads to **Baccarat**. Here, visitors can look round the modern church and the attractive Musée du Cristal, displaying the types of glass made in the village since 1764. The next stop might well be **Lunéville** where the *château*, a modest replica of Versailles, puts on a Son et Lumière le Grand Carrousel on Friday, Saturday and Sunday evenings during the summer. Daytime attractions include a visit to the *château* where the museum has a charming collection of figurines and the Musée de la Moto et du Vélo with its fascinating display of bicycles and motorcycles built before 1939. A *château* just outside the town provides an excellent, if rather expensive, menu and may even have a room available if one thinks to book in advance. **St Nicolas-de-Port** has a very viewable church and, if you are in the market for another *château*, a guided tour through the semi-regal apartments of the Château de Fléville, on the outskirts of Nancy, takes rather less than an hour.

Of course it would be much quicker to drive straight from Metz to **Nancy**, a distance of 56km (35 miles) along the *autoroute*. Although definitely on the beaten track, especially for continental visitors, its attractions are so numerous and so varied that one would miss a great deal by simply driving past. It has just as much history as Metz but fewer churches, more museums, botanical gardens and a large park including a zoo and a sports stadium roughly 2 minutes' walk from the famous Place Stanislas. There are just as many shops, hotels and restaurants, the Ballet Theatre has a repertoire ranging from

Diaghilev to Moses Pendleton, both rock and ancient music are popular as are the traditional performances at the Opera House. Other attractions include a handful of heated swimming pools, an 18-hole golf course a short distance from the town, a racecourse, riding stables and an extensive forest where people are made extremely welcome but vehicles, on the whole, are not. With so many things to see in Nancy it is fortunate that most of them are to be found in a relatively small area in the centre of the town. The obvious place to start is the Place Stanislas which is large, ornate and positively glistens with gold paint from one end to the other. The best idea is to park the car in the nearest available space and wander round on foot past highly ornamental gates, busy fountains, statues and the eighteenth-century Hôtel de Ville. The Arc de Triomphe, built at about the same time in honour of Louis XV, is very similar to the one in Rome. It faces the old residence of the Governors of Lorraine down a wide avenue known as the Place de la Carrière which has exactly the same atmosphere. A little to one side is the Ducal Palace, an elegant building spanning several centuries and flaunting most of them to good effect. Antoine of Lorraine, looking very purposeful on a splendid charger, occupies the niche of honour over the main door while inside is an exceptionally varied and interesting museum.

At this stage it saves a great deal of energy and shoe leather if one hires a horsedrawn vehicle for a tour of the old town. It takes in churches like the Eglise et Couvent des Cordeliers, so called inspite of the fact that the cloister is all that remains of the ancient monastery, and the Porte de la Craffe which has served as both a prison and a fort. Other museums worthy of note are the School Museum founded by Emile Gallé at the turn of the century, the Musée des Beaux Arts, the Zoological Museum with its tropical aquarium and, slightly further afield, a museum devoted to the history of iron. On the face of it this hardly sounds like an outstanding holiday attraction but once inside its fascination becomes apparent. Most men gravitate to the machine section where an early narrow-gauge steam engine attracts the biggest crowds. Anyone interested in glass should make a point of touring the Daum Crystal Works in the Rue des Cristalleries between the river and the Canal de la Marne au Rhin. It is interesting to watch the experts in action, which visitors can do each weekday morning and all day Saturday as well.

Anyone with an afternoon to spare and an interest in musical instruments would find a visit to Mirecourt very rewarding, especially if it includes a slight deviation to **Sion**, known not so much for its church and small museum as for the view. There is a hotel close to the summit where cars can be parked while their owners complete the journey on foot. From here a scenic route runs along the Corniche Gaston Canel, past the monument Barrès to Vaudémont, followed by an easy run to **Mirecourt**. The town is associated with lace and embroidery but its main claim to fame lies in the manufacture of musical instruments. The initiated will recognise names like Cognier and Terrier in connection with violas and violins, Pagès for guitars and Gérome for mandolins. The local museum traces the history of this highly specialised art and it is possible to visit factories where instruments are still being made. Any members of the party who are tone deaf or simply disinterested can wander through the arcades of the seventeenth-century market place, look round the church any time except on Sunday afternoons or visit the Chapelle de la Oultre by simply asking permission from the custodian who lives almost on the premises.

If neither glass nor musical instruments appeal to you an alternative would be to drive straight from Nancy to **Toul**, 23km (14 miles) away along the *autoroute*. The road bisects the forest, passing Parc de Haye with its two museums, one devoted to aircraft and the other specialising in cars. Their opening hours have not been synchronised particularly well. The former can be visited on Saturday and Sunday afternoons from January until August whereas the latter opens on Wednesday afternoons as well but is closed from the middle of November to the beginning of March. Toul is a town with considerable military connections in addition to the church of St Gengoult with its somewhat flamboyant cloister, an ancient cathedral and several delightful houses, the whole lot almost completely surrounded by walls and water. It has nothing very inviting in the way of hotels and restaurants but one can get a bed for the night and something to eat next door as well as swimming and skating in the town.

A major road of no particular interest connects Toul with **Vaucouleurs**, the starting point of Joan of Arc's mission to save France. A small church has been built over the thirteenth-century crypt, once part of the *château* which, itself, has all but disappeared. However, the old archway through which she led her troops is still standing. Much of the excavation work was done by Henri Bataille who makes a point of showing people round, explaining the layout which is largely below ground and inviting them to inspect his private, miniscule museum. He has a very soft spot for the English who, he says, donated enough money for him to buy and restore an ancient tower in the town. The somewhat larger museum further down the hill pays tribute to Joan of Arc and also makes mention of Madame du Barry, a local girl whose subsequent achievements, although less heroic, assured her of a place in French history. As Louis XV's mistress she exercised considerable political power while he was alive but paid for it on the guillotine in December 1793.

These days, when 20km (12 miles) or so is neither here nor there, Joan of Arc would probably be regarded as another local resident. She was born in 1412 at **Domrémy-la-Pucelle**, a village which would doubtless have remained completely unknown if she had stuck to her spinning and ignored the voices she heard in the Chenu Woods. As it was, she went off to identify the Dauphin, pit her wits against the English, stand trial for heresy and witchcraft and die in the market place at Rouen, all before she was 20 years old. It is no small wonder that the family home, a typical peasant's cottage with a sloping roof, bare walls and absolutely nothing inside, received the constant attention it needed to prevent it falling down ages ago. A small museum and the village church where she was baptised are the only other places of interest apart from the basilica, built on a hillside at the edge of the Chenu Woods, decorated in part with the story of her life and consecrated in 1926, less than a decade after she was canonised in Rome.

Neufchâteau, reached by road but bypassed along a winding footpath through the woods, had early Roman connections. Fortifications were added during the Middle Ages but all trace of them was eliminated on the orders of Richelieu who made a habit of destroying anything that got in his way. Nevertheless it still has two attractive old churches and a splendid staircase in the Hôtel de Ville. It is surrounded by small villages like **Grand** with its Roman ruins, the remains of an amphitheatre and a museum full of mosaics. **Contrexéville**, on the other hand, relies entirely on its thermal baths to attract visitors, providing them with some very comfortable hotels and tennis, swimming and riding as well.

Vittel, of bottled water fame, is no distance away. It adds two 18-hole golf courses to a similar list of amenities, plus a racecourse, a flying club, a large park where one can watch polo and attend concerts during the season and a great many flowers. Folklore and traditional costumes are paraded in August for the benefit of townspeople, visitors and anyone who happens to be camping nearby. An attractive and fairly scenic road connects the spa with **Darney** which played host to part of the Czech army during World War I and later installed a Czechoslovak Museum in the town hall. An equally pleasing road skirts Vioménil within easy walking distance of the

Joan of Arc's birthplace at Domrémy-la-Pucelle

source of the Saône, passes the Valley of the Druids, edges its way round the Bouzey reservoir and ends up in the suburbs of **Epinal**.

Although not very large, Epinal is an energetic sort of place with a positive mania for collecting things. For instance, the Musée des Vosges et de l'Imagerie, which stands at one end of an island in the middle of the Moselle, has found space for bits and pieces of ancient architecture, medals and coins of comparable vintage and a host of items relating to folklore and traditions. Its picture galleries display works by Rembrandt, Brueghel and Van Loo amongst others with the same aplomb as they show off modern artists like Picasso and a clutch of local painters who are not nearly so widely known. In addition it houses the Musée International de l'Imagerie with some of the original highly coloured and distinctive drawings that were inspired by the early illustrators. Methods and treatment differed according to the nationality of the artist concerned and one English contribution shows the wreck of the *Colville*, a West Indiaman driven ashore at Weymouth during a particularly ferocious nineteenth-century storm. The collection has a serious rival in the Imagerie Pellerin Gallery, a fair distance away on the main bank of the river, which was established 200 years ago to ensure that the art form survived. Meanwhile the Parc du Château, complete with ruins and a lake, collects animals for its mini-zoo and the Parc du Cours prides itself on having gathered together a splendid selection of exotic trees and plants. Two churches, one old and one new, more or less complete the picture and there is an American cemetery 7km (4 miles) to the south with a memorial to several thousand soldiers who were killed there in the closing stages of the battle for Europe.

The roads running south from Epinal can be very busy during the season because they provide immediate access to the high spots of the Vosges. The main road from Nancy bypasses the town and follows the Moselle to **Remiremont** with its picturesque houses, old churches, eleventh-century crypt and a brace of quite entertaining museums, after which it divides its destinations between Luxeuil-les-Bains in the south-west and Mulhouse, the gateway to both Switzerland and Germany across the Rhine. There is, however, no need to follow the crowds. A variety of minor roads wend their way through the foothills to **Plombières-les-Bains** where the Romans founded a spa which has been well patronised over the centuries. If anyone had had the foresight to keep a visitors' book it would have been worth its weight in gold by now with signatures like Montaigne, Voltaire, the Empress Josephine, Cavour and Napoleon III, the last two of whom spent their time together planning the unification of France and Italy. It would be interesting to know where they all stayed. There are no likely castles in the vicinity nor any recent ruins with imperial connections. The Maison des Arcades is quite eye-catching but nothing like large enough for someone accustomed to holding court at Versailles or Fontainebleau. The baths vary considerable in age and are easily identified by the features of their founders, namely the Emperor Augustus, Napoleon Bonaparte and Napoleon III. The town is equipped for tennis and swimming, has a casino, a selection of hotels and apartments and a limited number of camping sites. Nearby attractions include the Fontaine Stanislas with its own little hotel, the Musée Hippomobile at Aillevillers-et-Lyaumont and the glass factory at La Rochère, founded in 1475 and still producing some exquisite articles. It is open to visitors every weekday afternoon, excluding public holidays, from May to September but the glassblowers and engravers are on holiday during August so only the museum and the shop are on view. There are also some very inviting woods and waterfalls at Faymont and Géhard in the opposite direction along the valley of the Roches.

The biggest and most tourist-conscious of the dozen or so mountain lakes is **Gérardmer**, a sizeable expanse of water with a town at one end. There is nothing historic about it but this does not affect its popularity in the least. On the other hand it could not, for the moment anyway, be described as an international holiday playground. It is a

The main street at Remiremont

very good place from which to explore the Vosges mountains, there is something in the sporting line to occupy every member of the family and for most of the year it has plenty of space for everyone. However, during August, when the whole of France seems to be on holiday the shores are crowded with people swimming or lying on the grass while others dash about in motor boats, water ski or proceed in a more leisurely fashion under sail. Launches are on hand for organised excursions round the lake, small craft including pedalos can be hired by visitors who prefer to do things their own way and fishermen can go off in search of solitude on payment of a daily fee. There are two covered swimming pools, tennis courts, a skating rink, bowls and a casino as well as trips up into the mountains to inspect waterfalls, valleys created by ancient glaciers and vantage points recommended for their views. Festivals are arranged at intervals throughout the year, celebrating spring with flowers, summer with fireworks and winter with the Fête of St Nicolas. Cross-country skiing takes over as soon as there is enough snow. The many ski-lifts start working full time, trails are clearly marked over a wide area and all the necessary equipment is available for hire.

Accommodation is plentiful at a predictable variety of hotels, both in the town itself and at half a dozen mini-resorts within a radius of 10km (6 miles) or less. On every side scenic drives wriggle their way round one mountain peak after another, revealing ever-more magnificent views and alternating with narrow tracks that appeal to hikers but are quite unsuitable for four wheels unless they happen to be attached to a tractor. However the main road to Colmar takes things easily as far as the Col de la Schlucht where it crosses the Route des Crêtes on its way through to Munster. The town of Munster itself is hardly worth a detour although it is a popular tourist centre and an ideal place from which to plan a walking holiday. It is also very close to Gunsbach where the house once owned by Albert Schweitzer has been turned into a museum. Anyone interested in the life of this famous doctor would find it highly illuminating because it emphasises so many different facets of his character through books and music, medicine, sermons and photographs. There are guided tours each morning and afternoon, lasting approximately half an hour. An alternative mountain road circles round, past the White Lake and the Black Lake and back to the Route des Crêtes at the Col de la Schlucht where most people stop to inspect the high altitude garden. It is open from June to the middle of October and contains hundreds of plants from all over the world that only feel at home with their heads in the clouds. Holneck, beyond it on the opposite side of the road, is one of the highest peaks with views over the Vosges, across the plain of Alsace to the Black Forest and, on a crystal clear day, even provides a glimpse of snow on the Alps. To the south Grand Ballon, the highest point in the range, boasts a hotel and a café complete with souvenirs and parking space for coaches and cars while the occupants climb up to the monument at the top.

Hereafter it is downhill most of the way with constantly changing views and, perhaps, a pause to look at the ruined Château de Freundstein or a detour to Vieil Armand with its large crypt, war cemetery and monuments to the men of both sides who died there in World War I. For all practical purposes the Route des Crêtes and its plethora of little farmhouse *auberges* ends at Uffholtz. It is virtually a suburb of Cernay, an industrial town with a history museum, a stork park and a steam train that puffs its way along the valley of the Doller to Sentheim, finds nothing much to do there and returns the way it came.

The town of **Thann**, 6km (4 miles) from Cernay, should definitely not be missed. According to legend the saintly Bishop Thiébaut, having given all his fortune to the poor, left his episcopal ring to his servant but when the unfortunate man tried to take it off the body the thumb came away as well. He hid this relic in the top of his pilgrim's staff and set off for his home in the Netherlands. One night the servant stopped to rest in a clump of fir trees, laying his staff aside and somehow damaging the home of a bumblebee. In the morning he could not get it out although the bee emerged without any trouble. At the same moment three bright lights appeared over three nearby trees. They were seen from the Château d'Engelbourg by the Countess de Ferrette who, having heard the whole story, decided to build a chapel on the site of the apparition. The news got round and a small village grew up to cater for the needs of the pilgrims who came flooding in, calling itself Thann after one of the trees. This is why three fir trees are burned at the end of June outside the church, leaving the crowds to squabble over the ashes afterwards. The *château* changed hands several times before it was eventually abandoned the resulting ruins being known, somewhat unkindly perhaps, as the Eye of the Sorceress.

The Collégiale St Thiébaut, described by some people as a church and by others as a cathedral, is generally agreed to be one of the most outstanding examples of Gothic art in Alsace. It dates from the fourteenth and fifteenth centuries and nearly everything about it is original. It possesses a whole regiment of sculptures and statues, both inside and out, including two of the saint and a beautiful Virgin of the Winegrowers whose mischievous-looking Child hides a bunch of grapes behind His back. The magnificent choir stalls have touches of humour in the form of tiny carved figures including the gossip, the bespectacled man, the scholar and the fiddler. When the doors are locked it only takes a moment to pop into the tourist office in the block opposite and explain one's predicament.

The Musée des Amis de Thann, in an old Corn Market overooking the river, is hardly 2 minutes' walk away. It not only traces the history of the town in some detail but also concerns itself with such diverse subjects as mineralogy, wine making, local art, folklore and aspects of World War I. The Witches' Tower, practically next door, is all that remains of the old fortifications but the town has a great fascination for storks which, in turn, have fascinated the people of Alsace for centuries. Riding stables and long-distance footpaths complete the list of attractions apart from a tennis court belonging to one of the *auberges*. There are very few places to stay and, apparently, no camping sites but visitors in search of a comfortable hotel have only to drive the 22km (13 miles) to Mulhouse which has plenty of accommodation and a great many things to see.

As one would expect **Mulhouse** is reasonably large and very busy. Apart from its industrial interests it has an international airport and a constant flow of road and rail traffic heading backwards and forwards between France and Germany, Switzerland, Austria and Italy. The sad fact is that so many people do pass through without ever realising how much they are missing. The town's museums attract specialists in several different fields while at the same time providing much of interest for the merely curious. Collectors and car enthusiasts spend hours in the Musée National de l'Automobile, described by one expert as the most outstanding he had ever seen. There are about ninety different makes of cars numbering some 500 vehicles in all. It was originally a private collection belonging to Hans and Fritz Schlumf, two brothers who were textile industrialists with a passion for vintage cars. They went bankrupt in 1976, and 2 years later the vehicles were scheduled as historic monuments, housed in a vast hall which was once a textile factory and opened to the public in 1982. Amongst the exhibits are 123 different Bugattis, the largest collection in the world, including the two Royales, a limousine and the incomparable Coupé Napoléon which belonged to Ettore Bugatti. Also on view are Fangio's Maserati, Charlie Chaplin's Rolls Royce and the Porsche 917 that won the Le Mans 24-hour race in 1971, along with so many others of the same calibre. Facilities are available for disabled visitors who find the walkways, covering more than a mile, rather too much of a good thing. There is also a restaurant and a playground for children which is open in the summer. When they get tired of following parents round the man-sized models they can try out one of eight little replicas, including a 1950 Ferrari F1, on a road circuit through a miniature village.

Like the Musée de l'Automobile, the Railway Museum claims to be unique and houses a collection going back about 150 years. Stephenson is represented in the foyer by the Aigle, a splendid engine that began its tour of duty in 1846. In the sheds behind are ornate carriages built for people like Napoleon III, his containing a travelling medicine chest with enough pills and potions to discourage even the most determined germ. The Fireman's Museum is just next door and there is a Musée des Beaux Arts, a Mineralogical Museum, a History Museum, a Museum of Printed Cloth with special demonstrations of the process involved and a Musée du Papier Peint crammed with machines and literally thousands of historic documents.

The town's additional attractions include stained glass windows in the church of St Etienne, the ancient chapel of the Chevaliers de St Jean-de-Jérusalem, a view from the top of the tower in the Place de l'Europe and extensive botanical gardens across the Canal du Rhône au Rhin where most children head straight for the zoo. As if all this were not enough an Ecomusée has been established at **Ungersheim**, a few kilometres north-west of Mulhouse. Some thirty-five buildings, anything up to 800 years old, have been reconstructed on a large site with space for many more. The complex is open all year round and in December St Nicolas arrives with his donkey and hot chocolate and gingerbread for the children.

This is a good place from which to join the Wine Route at **Soultz-Haut-Rhin** for the journey north. The village is practically a suburb of Guebwiller which earns its living from textiles and wine. Guebwiller has been in existence for hundreds of years during which time it has accumulated a good deal in the way of local history and folklore, now on display in the Musée de Florival opposite the church of Notre-Dame. It is also well blessed with nearby small hotels and restaurants complete with rooms and is conveniently close to the Lac de la Lauch where the fishing is said to be excellent and to woods that blanket the valley and the slopes of the Grand Ballon.

Admittedly the Route du Vin twists and turns a bit through the vineyards, sometimes joining the main roads and sometimes wandering off in search of an attractive little hamlet, but on the whole it is fairly flat. **Rouffach** is a good place to stop, partly on account of its old houses, the Witches' Tower inhabited by storks and the thirteenth-century church of Notre-Dame, the first Gothic building in the Haut-Alsace. Its favourite anecdotes recall more than a nodding acquaintance with Henry V and the fact that it once had a gallows of its very own. It was also in the direct firing line during the Allied advance in 1945. Another good reason for pausing is that there is a first rate hotel with tennis, swimming and delicious food and wine in the immediate vicinity.

Practically every village in the neighbourhood has something of interest to offer like an ancient church or a ruined *château* while **Neuf-Brisach**, to the east, rubs shoulders with the Grand Canal d'Alsace. It is worth seeing for the giant locks, hydro-electric plant and sleek bridges that carry the road onto the island, with its own camping site, and across the Rhine into Germany. The town is small and perfectly octagonal, contained in massive double ramparts built by Vauban who is the subject of a small museum at the Porte de Belfort, open every morning and afternoon except on Mondays. There are two or three modest hotels, an 18-hole golf course and a steam train that runs up to **Marckolsheim**, known chiefly for its Museum of the Maginot Line. It is open every morning and afternoon from mid-June to mid-September, thereafter only on Sundays and public holidays until it closes completely in November.

Colmar, a short distance away, is considered by many people to be the most beautiful town in Alsace. It is historic, brimming over with extremely eye-catching houses festooned with flowers, ancient buildings and enchanting little streets and alleyways. A good way to get your bearings is to join one of the guided tours arranged, sometimes on request, by the Syndicat d'Initiative. After that there is nothing to beat wandering about at a more leisurely pace, revisiting places of particular interest and discovering little gems that were missed the first time round. Fortunately most of them are to be found in a comparatively small area of the old town between the Unterlinden Museum and Little Venice on the banks of the canal.

The Musée d'Unterlinden occupies an ancient monastery and contains amongst its treasures the famous Issenheim Altarpiece painted by Mathias Grunewald in the early sixteenth century. A block or so away is an elaborate seventeenth-century house with so many sculptured heads that it really could not be called anything other than the Maison des Têtes. By way of a bonus it has a restaurant as well. Next comes the Eglise des Dominicains, built around 1500 but planned much earlier than that. It has some fine stained glass windows and Martin Schongauer's *Virgin of the Rose Bush* depicting a pensive figure dressed in scarlet against a background of matching flowers, green foliage and tiny birds with angels in attendance. St Martin's church, which is even older, is the next logical port of call to be followed by a cluster of elderly houses including the Maison Adolph dated 1350 and the Musée Bartholdi, birthplace of the sculptor whose most widely-known work is undoubtedly the Statue of Liberty.

Once in the Grand Rue historic buildings come thick and fast, everything from the Old Hospital to the ancient Customs House overlooking one of Bartholdi's fountains. Spare enough time to see the Eglise St Matthieu, the Maison Pfister, the tiny Maison au Cygne and the Ancien Corps de Garde before going on to the Tanners' Quarter. Beyond it is Little Venice where typical old houses rise from the water with more trees and flowers than can be seen in the original and, blissfully, quite free of motor boats and launches. Finally, when all these possibilities have been exhausted, there is a Natural History Museum in the Parc du Château d'Eau.

Several small hotels and some good restaurants are dotted about the old quarter with a couple of larger establishments close to the airport and to the railway station. A motel, unfortunately without a restaurant, can be found on the road to Strasbourg. Colmar believes in entertaining its guests and to this end provides swimming and

A street in the old quarter of Colmar

riding, conducted tours and excursions, paths for hikers across the plains and up into the mountains and places to pitch a tent or park a caravan.

There are two obvious points of re-entry to the Wine Route — **Turckheim** which has three ancient gates and a night watchman who does his rounds during the season and **Ammerschwir**, a once-fortified village with a Rogues' Tower. The latter is on the main road to **Kaysersberg** where there is another Albert Schweitzer museum, this time in the house where he was born. The village has changed hands several times since the Romans used it on their repeated forays up and down the Rhine but inspite of its turbulent history some antiquated buildings and much of the old world atmosphere have survived. The fifteenth-century bridge is still operational but the castle with its solid round tower is considerably the worse for wear. An interesting old church adjoins a cemetery of comparable vintage and the chapel of St Michel built in 1463. It is a delightful place to wander about, visit the little museums and possibly stay at a local hotel, which can be either up-market or on the basic side. **Kientzheim,** next door, has a lot in common in the way of buildings and atmosphere but scores an extra point for its Wine Museum.

The next place of interest is **Riquewihr** with its sixteenth-century buildings and a decorative tower-gateway called the Dolder that goes back to 1291 but has been reinforced at regular intervals since then. It is the home of the Archaeological Society Museum and vies for attention with the Musée d'Histoire des PTT d'Alsace which traces the progress of the local postal service from the days when runners set out with their version of the cleft stick. Stamp collectors and anyone with a soft spot for postcards can call in any time from April to November, leaving the rest of the party to inspect the Robbers' Tower which stays open throughout the year and has its own torture chamber.

Ribeauvillé, a little further up the Route du Vin in the foothills of the Vosges, boasts a thirteenth-century Slaughterers' Tower but is equally proud of its resident storks. It was a great place for itinerant musicians in the Middle Ages and celebrates the fact with a Festival of Strolling Fiddlers, overlaid with folklore and traditions, on the first Sunday in September. A variety of hotels and an ample supply of country walks make it a popular centre for exploring in the vicinity. The Château of St Ulrich would be a good place to start as it is only a few kilometres away so it is possible to walk there, inspect the fairly extensive ruins on their tree-covered hilltop and be back in 2 or 3 hours. Alternatively, anyone interested in mining might prefer **Ste Marie-aux-Mines** with its old silver and lead workings and a chapel used by miners in the fifteenth century. An added incentive is that the silver mine is open daily during July and August. There is a prehistoric Celtic camp outside **St Dié** which, in turn, has a cathedral and the church of Notre-Dame-de-Galilée linked by a medieval cloister, a museum and an extensive library. German tourists often head in the opposite direction to visit their war cemetery outside **Bergheim**, a village which contributes some fortifications, a fourteenth-century church and a linden tree said to be 1,000 years old.

Haut-Koenigsbourg, dominating the countryside from its perch on a mountaintop, 10km (6 miles) north of Ribeauvillé, was once a vast medieval fortress. However it was destroyed by enemy action in 1633 and left to decay for more than 250 years before being completely rebuilt. Parts of the building are still closed and the whole place is out of bounds to tourists on public holidays and all through January. A small winding road crosses the Route du Vin, tempting the motorist to visit Sélestat with its full complement of elderly buildings, a liberal sprinkling of wrought-iron work, a fine Humanistic Library and a reputation for taking more than a passing interest in flowers. It is usually crowded for the Floral Carnival in August, particularly with holidaymakers intent on spending their time out of doors. There is a large sports centre with an open-air swimming pool and motor boats on the River Ill. Facilities are available for hunting

and fishing, well clear of the marked paths that cover enough territory to satisfy all but the most determined long-distance walker.
Other amenities include a holiday village and plenty of space for
campers. In addition, nearby **Kintzheim** has an animal park, an
Eagle Reserve with demonstrations of falconry when the weather is
good and one of the best-preserved castles in the area.

Further off the wine track, with its vineyards at refreshingly short
intervals, **Villé** concentrates on local crafts and provides access to a
scenic, if occasionally tortuous, series of little roads that blaze a trail
to Struthof. It is here that guides are on hand to show people round
the well maintained but infinitely depressing Nazi concentration
camp with all its horrific reminders of death and deportation. The
tour lasts for over an hour any morning or afternoon except at
Christmas and on New Year's Day. On the other hand one can head
up through the woods to Mont Ste Odile. The lady in question is the
patron saint of Alsace and her mountain with its crowning monastery is a recognised place of pilgrimage. As so often happens the
pagans were there first, leaving behind traces of a mysterious wall
that twists about for several kilometres with no apparent rhyme or
reason for its sudden changes in direction. A festival in honour of Ste
Odile is held there on the 13 December every year with similar events
taking place in towns and villages all over Alsace.

The Route du Vin can be rejoined at **Ottrott** and Obernai, the
former having some not very outstanding buildings, a reputation for
red wine and a busy little tourist train that runs up to Rosheim and
back again. **Obernai** is very picturesque with its thirteenth-century
fortifications, dignified old houses, typical cobbles at the street inter-
sections, a corn market and an attractive market square. Apart from
the considerably up-dated Hôtel de Ville and the church of St Peter
and St Paul, there is a decorative six-bucket well dating from the
sixteenth century. It is more like a folly than a functional piece of
architecture with carved pillars holding up the roof and very new-
looking buckets filled with flowers. Visitors can ride, fish, swim, find
accommodation in the holiday villages or bring their own tents and
caravans.

Molsheim falls into roughly the same category as Obernai except
that it is slightly smaller and was once the home of Bugatti cars. Its
most outstanding feature is the 300-year-old Slaughter House, a very
respectable construction that belies its name with gables not unlike
those of the Maison des Têtes in Colmar, a double stairway up to the
main entrance on the first floor and long balconies full of plants. Its
chief function these days is to provide space for a great many local

A four-bucket well at Rosheim

wines that can be sampled on the premises, leaving room for a little museum.

Marlenheim marks the end of the Route du Vin and is an easily forgettable town although it offers opportunities for hunting and fishing, has an extremely good restaurant with rooms attached and is only a short run from Strasbourg along a fast road which turns quite suddenly into an *autoroute*.

There is really nothing you cannot do in **Strasbourg** if you put your mind to it. It is a simple matter to fly to Paris, London, Rome or Brussels, catch a train with or without your car for company, drive across the frontier into Germany almost before you have left the suburbs behind and even board a mini-train for a sightseeing tour round the city. Air trips are laid on to give visitors a bird's eye view of the capital, motor launches ply up and down the rivers and canals and, when time is no object, there is really nothing to beat a cruise along the Rhine. Evening entertainments include theatre, opera, concerts of all descriptions and an International Music Festival in June. The city is by no stretch of the imagination off the beaten track, especially since the Council of Europe and the Court of Human Rights moved in. However only a very few people who decide to explore Alsace would leave without even glancing at the capital so a brief summary of its many attractions may not come amiss. There are a great many hotels of all types and at all price levels, masses of shops and restaurants, churches, art galleries and museums. Holidaymakers can play golf and tennis, skate, ride, fish and indulge in all the usual water sports. Flying lessons are available at the local aero clubs and the Official Information Office is extremely helpful when it comes to excursions and accommodation.

The most noteworthy places of interest include the cathedral of Notre-Dame where it takes over an hour to see everything properly, the Musée du Château des Rohan with its grand apartments and a whole host of other museums. The Musée des Beaux Arts has some memorable paintings, the Museum of Decorative Arts is especially proud of its collection of ceramics and the Musée Alsacien is the place to go for anything connected with Alsace whether sophisticated or frankly rural. Other museums are devoted to history, archaeology, modern art and zoology. After this it is time to take a brisk walk. La Petite France, overlooking the canal, is extremely neat and picturesque. The Barrage Vauban is close at hand which is more than can be said for the Cour du Corbeau and its antiquated bridge where certain types of criminals were once put in iron cages and left to die. The Place Kléber, the Place Broglie and the Rue de Dôme are amongst other sights to be seen before moving out of the old town to the tree-filled Place de la Republic, the Orangerie and the Palais de l'Europe where visitors are discouraged when Parliament is in session. Whatever your personal impressions of Strasbourg may be one thing is immediately apparent — it has come a long way since the days of Julius Caesar when the fishing village of *Argentoratum* began to prosper and changed its name to *Strateburgum*, the city at the cross-roads of Europe.

Further Information
— Alsace et Lorraine —

Museums and Other Places of Interest

Baccarat
Crystal Museum
Open: morning and afternoon mid-July to mid-September except Tuesday and Sunday mornings. Otherwise afternoons but only Saturday and Sunday from May to mid-June. Closed October to April.

Cernay
Museum
Open: July and August, Wednesday and Friday afternoons only.

Colmar
Bartholdi Musée
Open: morning and afternoon throughout the season, Wednesday and Saturday only November to March.

Eglise des Dominicains
Open: daily April to mid-November

Musée d'Unterlinden
Open: April to October 9am-12noon and 2-6pm. November to March 9am-12noon and 2-5pm, closed Tuesdays. Closed 1 January, 1 May, 1 November and 25 December.

Natural History Museum
Open: July and August, 2-5pm. April, May, June, September, October and November, Wednesday, Saturday and Sunday only 2-5pm. Closed December to March.

Domrémy-la-Pucelle
Joan of Arc's Birthplace and Museum
Open: morning and afternoon, closed Tuesdays and mid-October to end of March.

Epinal
Imagerie Pellerin
Guided tours: morning and afternoon, afternoon only on Sunday and public holidays.

Musée des Vosges et de l'Imagerie
Open: morning and afternoon, closed Tuesday, 1 January, 1 May, 1 November and 25 December.

Gunsbach
Schweitzer Museum
Guided tours mornings and afternoons.

Haut-Koenigsbourg
Open: morning and afternoon, closed January and public holidays.

Kaysersberg
Albert Schweitzer Museum
Open: morning and afternoon at Easter and from May to October.

Kientzheim
Wine Museum
Open: July to September mornings and afternoons.

Eagle Reserve and Mountain of Monkeys
Open: afternoons from April to mid-September and on Wednesday, Saturday, Sunday and public holiday afternoons until mid-November.

Louppy-sur-Loison
Château
Guided tours July to September afternoons. Closed Monday and the rest of the year.

Lunéville
Château and Museum
Open: morning and afternoon except Tuesday. Son et Lumière Friday, Saturday and Sunday evenings from July to mid-September.

Musée de la Moto et du Vélo
Open: mornings and afternoons except
Monday.

Marckolsheim
Museum of the Maginot Line
Open: mid-June to mid-September
mornings and afternoons.

Metz
Cathedral of St Etienne
The crypt is open morning and afternoon, Sunday afternoon only. Closed
on religious festivals. Treasure open
afternoons except religious festivals.

Museum of Art and History
Open: morning and afternoon except
Tuesday.

Mirecourt
Museum of Stringed Instruments

Mulhouse
Automobile Museum
Open: daily 10am-6pm except Tues-
days 1 January and 25 December.

Fine Arts Museum
Open: mornings and afternoons, closed
Tuesday, Whit Monday, 14 July, 1 and
11 November, 25 and 26 December.

Museum of Printed Cloth
Open: morning and afternoon except
Tuesday and public holidays.

Museum of Printed Paper
Open: morning and afternoon except
Tuesday and public holidays.

Railway Museum and Fireman's Museum
Open: daily except 1 January, 25 and 26
December.

St Jean-de-Jérusalem Museum
Open: morning and afternoon May to
September except Tuesday, 1 May,
Whit Monday and 14 July.

Nancy
Château de Fléville
Guided tours: afternoons July and
August; Sunday and public holiday
afternoons only from April to June and
September and October.

Daum Crystal Works
Open: weekday mornings and all day
Saturday.

Ducal Palace and Museum
Open morning and afternoon except
Tuesday.

Eglise et Couvent des Cordeliers
Open: morning and afternoon, closed
Monday, Easter, Christmas and 1
January.

Fine Arts Museum
Open: morning and afternoon except
Monday morning, Tuesday and public
holidays.

Porte de la Craffe
Open: morning and afternoon, mid-
June to August. Closed Tuesday.

School Museum
Open: morning and afternoon. Closed
Tuesday, Easter, 1 January, 1 May, 14
July and Christmas.

Zoological Museum
Open: afternoons only. Closed Tuesday
except during school holidays.

Neuf-Brisach
Vauban Museum
Open: 9am-12noon and 2-5pm. Closed
Tuesday.

Obernai
Train from Ottrott to Rosheim Sunday
and public holiday afternoons leaving
at 2.30pm and 4.30pm.

Parc de Haye
Aircraft Museum
Open: January to August Saturday and
Sunday afternoon.

Car Museum
Open: March to mid-November
Wednesday, Saturday and Sunday.

Plombières-les-Bains
Spa town with ancient baths.

Pont-à-Mousson
Prémontrés Abbey
Open: mornings and afternoons.

Riquewihr
Dolder Museum
Open: morning and afternoon at Easter and July and August. Otherwise Saturday afternoon and Sunday. Closed November to June.

Postal Museum
Open: morning and afternoon April to mid-November. Closed Tuesdays except in July and August.

La Rochère
Glass Factory and Museum
Open: May to July, September and October 2.30-5.30pm. Factory closed on Sundays and holidays; museum only May to September 2.30-6pm.

St Dié
Museum
Open: mornings and afternoons. Closed Mondays and holidays.

Ste Marie-aux-Mines
Museum and Silver Mine
Open: July and August morning and afternoon.

Saverne
Château
Museum open morning and afternoon except Tuesday during July and August but Sundays and public holidays only during May, June and September.

Rose Garden
Open: morning and afternoon from mid-June to the end of September.

Jardin Botanique
Open: from June to August in the afternoon.

Sélestat
Humanistic Library
Open: morning and afternoon, closed Saturday afternoons, Sundays andpublic holidays.

Strasbourg
Archaeological Museum
Open: April to September 10am-12noon and 2-6pm; October to March 2-8pm.

Closed Tuesdays, Good Friday, Easter Sunday, Whit Sunday and 1 May.

Cathedral of Notre-Dame, including the museum
Open: daily.

Château des Rohan
Opening times as Archaeological Museum times.

Decorative Arts Museum
Opening times as above.

Fine Arts Museum
Opening times as above.

Folk Museum
Opening times as above.

Old Customs House
Open: daily 10am-12noon and 2-5pm.

Palais de l'Europe
Open: morning and afternoon except Saturday and Sunday, November to March, public holidays and when Parliament sits.

Zoological Museum
Open: Wednesday, Friday, Saturday, Sunday 2-5pm. Thursday 10am-12noon and 2-5pm.

Struthof
Nazi Concentration Camp
Guided tours: morning and afternoon. Closed 24 December and 1 January.

Thann
Collégiale St-Thiébaut
If closed enquire at the Tourist Office.

Ungersheim
Ecomusée
Open: May to August 10am-10pm. March, April, September, October 11am-6pm. January, February, November, December 11am-4pm.

Vaucouleurs
Municipal Museum
Open: mid-June to mid-September morning and afternoon. Closed Tuesday.

Little Venice, Colmar, Alsace et Lorraine

Solesmes Abbey, Pays de la Loire

Le Mougau, near Commana, Brittany

Fishing boats at Le Guilvinec, Brittany

Verdun

Citadelle
Underground fortifications open:
morning and afternoon, but closed
from mid-December to mid-January.

Hotel de la Princerie Museum
Open: morning and afternoon from
Easter to end of September. Closed on
Tuesdays.

Fort de Vaux
Open: daily from mid-February to
mid-December. Museum open mornings and afternoons except from mid-
December to mid-January.

Vieil Armand

Museum
Open: morning and afternoon, April to
October.

Vittel

Bottled water factory
Guided tours mid-April to mid-
September: morning and afternoon.
Closed Saturday, Sunday and holidays.

Wissembourg

Château de Fleckenstein
Open: daily March to November.

Westercamp Museum
Open: morning and afternoon, closed
Sunday morning, Wednesday and in
January.

Woerth

History Museum
Open: morning and afternoon from
April to October, thereafter Saturday
and Sunday only.

Tourist Information Offices

Colmar
4 Rue Unterlinden
☎ 89-41-02-29

Epinal
13 Rue de la Comédie
☎ 29-82-53-32

Gérardmer
Place Déportés
☎ 29-63-08-74

Metz
Place d'Armes
☎ 87-75-65-21
Also at the station.

Mulhouse
9 Avenue Maréchal Foch
☎ 89-45-68-31

Nancy
14 Place Stanislas
☎ 83-35-22-41

Strasbourg
Palais des Congrès
Avenue Schultzenberger
☎ 88-35-03-00
Also at the station.

St Dié
31 Rue Thiers
☎ 29-55-17-62

Verdun
Place de Nation
☎ 29-84-18-85
Open: May-mid-September.

Vittel
Rue de Verdun
☎ 29-08-42-03

Wissembourg
At the town hall
☎ 88-94-10-11

7 • Brittany

When the Saxons, heading west across Britain and pushing the native, Celtic British before them, had isolated the Celtic bands from each other, creating what were to become Wales and Cornwall, some of the British fled, in fear and despair, across the sea. They landed in an area of north-west Europe not too dissimilar from the country they had left behind and, in consequence, they called it Little Britain, later dropping the 'Little' to give Bretagne, Brittany. Some of the settlers even went as far as to call their area Cornwall. Now Cornouaille is the name of the southern part of the *département* of Finistère. With them the settlers brought their legends, of King Arthur and his knights, of Merlin and other magicians, and these old tales sat easily in the deep, mysterious woodlands that then covered the area, and are now so sadly rare.

The Celtic settlers were not, however, the first to have populated the area. Thousands of years before, a race had erected huge stones, for purposes still not clear. Brothers to those who built Stonehenge and Avebury, these megalithic peoples have left perhaps the finest legacy of their existence anywhere in the world. The chief site is Carnac with its vast avenues of stones, but the whole province is covered with magnificent sites.

When, following the megalith builders and the Celtic settlers, the Romans had come, and had then retreated to the Alps, the Franks invaded the land that now bears their name, defeating the Breton Celts at the end of the eighth century. Within fifty years the province re-established its independence, defeating the Franks in battle, declaring Brittany an independent dukedom and settling down to 600 years of fiercely defended isolation, beating back all attempts at invasion by successive waves of French and English soldiers. Only in 1514 when the Breton duchess, Anne, married not one, but two French kings — one at a time rather than together! — did Brittany finally become part of France, a union sealed by the 1532 Treaty of Vannes.

The contorted rock strata is one of the many interesting features to be found in Brittany

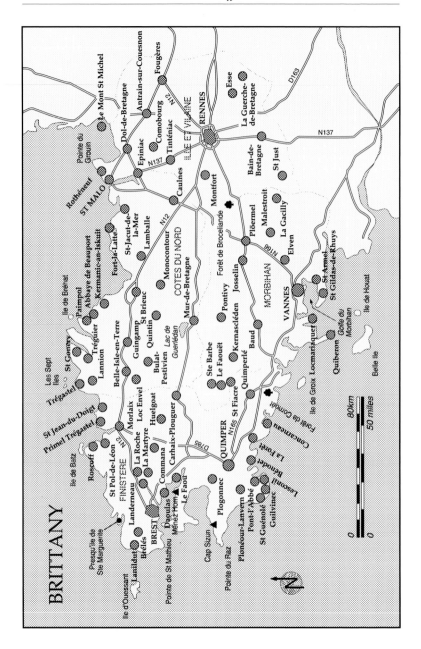

Thereafter Brittany, not surprisingly in view of the length of its coastline, became the centre of French sea power, in terms of exploration, wealth-bringing piracy and fishing, and in purely naval terms. Even today Brest is still of great importance to the French Navy.

Brittany is large, only a province of France and yet comparable in size with Denmark, Belgium or Wales. This should allow scope for considerable variation in scenery, though in fact the lack of any real highland means that inland Brittany has little diversity, large areas of agricultural land peppered with fine remnants of the ancient forest. But within this landscape there are nuggets of fine river scenery and many very pretty villages, frequently worth more than a passing interest. But Brittany also has around 1,250km (800 miles) of coastline, much of it offering magnificent seascapes.

Brittany has striven hard for its own identity. The line of castles along the eastern border of the *département* of Ille-et-Vilaine testify to this, as does the continuation of the distinctively Breton features, the *pardons*, the *crêperies*, the cider drinking — there is no genuinely Breton wine — and the language. Brittany's climate is not too dissimilar from that of south-western Britain, except, perhaps, in the *département* of Morbihan where it is both sunnier and warmer, and is not really for those who holiday purely for lazy days on hot beaches. Rather it is for the explorer, for those interested in country and village, and in history.

And just in case that sounds a little dull, where else in France do they have races for 2CVs and tractors not on land, but on the sea?

Finistère

Finistère is the first *département* of Brittany that many visitors see as they leave the Brittany Ferry at Roscoff. It is also the *département* which is the most Breton, the furthest from France. Even its name derives from its position at the extreme western end of Brittany, itself almost an island tacked onto the western end of France.This is *'Finis Terrae'*, the end of the world, and though that name is Roman, the Celts themselves had the same idea in mind when calling it *'Penn at Bed'*. Finistère has some marvellously 'soft' countryside but also has the harshest of Brittany's land, the most storm-lashed coasts, the only areas of remote, barren highland and as a rule it also has buildings to match, low and angular away from the wind and clinging to the land. The people cling too, but they to their Breton heritage, its language, folklore and costume.

It may seem a strange idea, but to most tourists using the Brittany Ferries route to **Roscoff**, the first off-the-beaten track spot is Roscoff itself. Since the ferry port is too far away from the town for a casual stroll, and now boasts a terminal building that provides all a traveller's needs, most tourists bypass the town itself, thankful either to have reached the port safely and content to wait for the boat, or happy to be in France after several hours at sea, and anxious to be away to their holiday headquarters.

Roscoff is a fine town, built around one of the fanciest church towers in the whole of Brittany, and with an array of excellent granite-built houses, dating chiefly from the sixteenth- to eighteenth-century period when the town prospered on the wealth of the corsairs. The town's fortified walls near the seafront date from the same period, a necessity in case those that were unwillingly providing the town's wealth decided to visit, to attempt to retrieve it. Near the seafront a tower and plaque commemorate the landing, in 1548, of Mary Stuart, later to become Mary, Queen of Scots. She arrived at the tender age of 5 to be engaged to the Dauphin, the heir to the French throne, who was then at the even tenderer age of 3! No plaque commemorates the arrival of another Royal Scot nearly two centuries later. Here Bonny Prince Charlie came ashore after the disastrous campaign of 1745, and the defeat at Culloden. While in the town be sure to visit the marine aquarium which holds specimens of channel fauna.

Those with more time, and an enthusiasm for ferries, can visit the **Ile de Batz** (pronounced 'Ba') a place almost never visited by the English tourist, but with a marvellous, rugged, wave-dashed north shore, and a more tranquil southern shore, quiet coves and a forgotten village. On the island a sixth-century Welsh saint, Paul (in Breton, Pol), landed, forcing a dragon to jump into the sea at the aptly named Trou du Serpent. St Pol's name is commemorated in the town, **St Pol-de-Léon** just south of Roscoff, which is also normally sped past *en route* inland or homewards. Here, be sure to visit the buildings under the two huge landmarks — the twin towers of the cathedral of St Pol and the spire of Notre-Dame-de-Kreisker. The towers are 50m (160ft) tall and top a fine Gothic building which holds the skulls of thirty-five notables from the past, as well as the skull, a finger and an arm bone of St Pol who died on the Ile de Batz at 104 years of age. By contrast the interior of the church below the 80m (260ft) spire seems almost mundane. As an aside, the headquarters of SICA the organisation that runs the famous local cauliflower and artichoke trade is in St Pol-de-Léon, its presence here starting a shipping business that at first took the vegetables to England, but grew into one whose chief cargo is now tourists.

Westward, from Roscoff to the Pointe-de-St Mathieu, is the Côte des Abers. 'Aber' here is the same as the Welsh word that preceeds Aberystwyth, for example, and means a water junction. Normally this junction is river and sea — though not, as a quick visit will show, at Abergavenny — and here the name is usually translated as the Coast of Estuaries, a series of massively incut estuaries lying all around the coast as rivers drain down from high inland Finistère. The first part of the coast is pleasant, but dull, matters improving once **Brignogan-Plage** is reached. Here there is one of the best menhirs, standing stones, in Brittany although, sadly, it has been badly served by history. The stone stands beside the road that leads from village to sea; a house has been built beside it; and a cross has been cut into, or fixed on, its top. When first erected this stone, a huge granite block nearly $9^1/_2$m (30ft) high must have been marvellously impressive. The cross on top of it — you would need to climb the stone to see if it had been chiselled or glued — is proof of the immense power the menhir had on a population well removed from its erectors. So powerful a symbol was it — in local legend this is Men-Marz, the Stone of Miracles — that there was a need to Christianise or, more likely, to de-paganise, to neutralise, its power. The house and road are sad, such a stone needs space. One interesting note is that the house is 'Ty Menhir', the same name it would have been given in Wales.

Beyond the menhir the sea is reached near a beach of sand so white that it seems unreal, set between granite blocks which offer adventure to any beachgoer with a steady head.

The first part of the Côte des Abers, or Coast of Estuaries, is also known as the Coast of Legends (Côte de Légendes), the reason being not the Celtic mythology which is so strong in Finistère, but the number of shipwrecks that took place on the razor sharp backs of rock that edge in the fjord-like estuaries. Many stories tell of shipwrecks that were assisted by false lights hung out on the shore. Aber Wrac'h is the largest and, perhaps, the finest of the estuaries. Go to the **Presqu'Ile de Ste Marguerite**, the almost-island of St Margaret. 'Almost-island' — what a very fine expression for a peninsula thinned almost to causeway size on its landward side. Ste Marguerite is ringed offshore by a half-circle of real islands, or, in their case, islets, and offers some of the very best seascapes. Further along the coast are a series of villages that were once exclusively the homes of fishermen. **Lanildut** on the Aber-Ildut is a particular favourite and nearby **Brélés** has the added interest that it is positioned at the point where, technically, the Atlantic Ocean and the English Channel meet.

La Martyre

South, and inland, is another menhir, Kerloas, the tallest in Brittany at nearly 10m (32ft), elegant, almost aloof and beautifully sited
to lend the maximum mystery to its form. South again is the **Pointe
de St Mathieu**, with one of the most evocative sites in the whole of
Brittany, the salt spray and wind-lashed remains of a Benedictine
monastery, orignally founded in the sixth century and destroyed
during the French Revolution. The founding monk was St Tanguy,
but the point, and the monastery, took St Matthew's name when a

boat, bringing the head of the Gospel writer here from Ethiopia, floundered in high seas and all on board were saved through a channel miraculously carved when the relic was held aloft. Offshore are several small islands, and the large Ile d'Ouessant, all of which form part of the French equivalent of a national park. The islands can be visited and while they are well and truly off the beaten track, the trip can only be recommended for those who like their seascapes not only wild and rugged but very, very remote.

South from Brignogan-Plage is a series of very fine small towns which should form part of anyone's itinerary. First is **Landerneau** where there is one of the last (*the* last?) bridges in Europe on which there are inhabited houses. It really is a most extraordinary slice of old history to walk over a bridge similar to those that are so often seen in old prints of London. The buildings look more modern (Pont de Rohan dates from around the start of the sixteenth century) but that cannot be helped. It is a pity that the shops and, especially, the shop fronts are not a little less intrusively modern. South from Landerneau are Daoulas and Le Faou, the former with the magnificent remains of a Romanesque abbey, the latter a pretty village with several sixteenth-century houses with slate frontages. South again be sure to visit Ménez Hom, a little way from Trégarvan, from where, the view over the River Châteaulin is quite breathtaking.

But do not hasten away from Landerneau. Further up the River Elorn which is spanned by the Pont de Rohan, be sure to visit La Roche to see the romantically overgrown remains of an old castle on a steep knoll right above the river itself. Then go inland, to visit **La Martyre.**

Since the parish close (*enclos paroissial*) is such an essentially Breton feature, it seems, at first sight, unwise to mention them in a book devoted to the more unusual aspects of the countryside. However the normal tour of closes usually takes in St Thegonnec, Guimiliau and Lampaul-Guimiliau — the Circuit de Trois Enclos — and there are others, the building of a close not being confined to the richer, merchant towns. At La Martyre the essentials of a close are all present, church, triumphal arch, ostuary and calvary, and while its constituent parts may not be as grand, as magnificent, as its better known neighbours, the village close does have both a simple dignity and a wholeness that are quite moving. Today, thankfully, the ossuary houses not the bones of the dead moved on from the graveyard when space became limited, but a small exhibition of drawings and articles on the close.

From La Martyre a very good country road leads through Sizun and past Commana to the Monts d'Arrée, the highest land in Brittany and part of the Parc Régional d'Armorique. As **Commana** is reached a road right allows a quick visit to the *allée couverte* of Le Mougau, a most beautiful megalithic burial site.

The highest point of the Monts d'Arrée is actually Ménez Kador, but what hold the eye and beg to be climbed are the rock-outcropped heights of Roc'h Trévézel. The walking here is excellent, barely beaten paths between the ferns and gorse, among granite castles. From one such granite castle, to the south of the main road, the view inland is expansive and compelling. What take the eye are the far off conical hill, just west of south, topped by a chapel to St Michael, the patron saint of mountain tops, and the white domes of the nuclear power plant of Brennilis beside the reservoir in the hollow below the high ridge. With what seems an irony of coincidence, the marshy land of this hollow, impenetrable and hostile area, was known by the Bretons as the 'Mouth of Hell'.

Off the ridge, but still within the Parc Régional d'Armorique is **Huelgoat**, a charming village — with a museum of clothes irons! — standing at the edge of one of the park's great joys, a remnant of the ancient forest which once covered much of the inland area hereabouts. Close to the town are some natural features which have been given fanciful names, the Devil's Grotto, and so on. But for all that the names are a bit out of place, the features themselves are impressive, even the steps and walkways being justifiable on the grounds that the less intrepid would also like to see the sights. Not so attractive however, is the sheer vandalism of inscribing the name 'La Roche Tremblante', on the side of a huge, 100 ton, logan rock in the forest. Logans are rare and deserve better treatment — they are delicately balanced rocks which, though huge, rock when pushed giving rise, as a result, to many legends, chief of which was that their trembling foretold the future to anyone who understood the beat.

Go beyond the obvious however, and you can be off the beaten track in an ancient forest landscape, the valley floor festooned with huge boulders, green-cased. This ancient forest is linked with the Celtic legend of Arthur. Here in this secret forest, he would apparently go to rest. The far reaches of the forest, hardly a walk from Huelgoat, more a drive to and, then just beyond, St Ambroise, envelope the early waters of the River Aulne, at this stage and for many a mile, one of the most beautiful of all Brittany's rivers. At nearby **Carhaix-Plouguer**, the church of St Trémuer has a statue of the saint holding his head in his hands, literally that is, not in despair. The story of the statue concerns Commorrus, a sixth-century count of Cornouaille who, having been warned that he would be killed by his son, murdered his first four wives as soon as they became pregnant. A fifth wife gave birth prematurely and successfully hid the child, Trémuer, but was killed when she became pregnant again. Many years later Trémuer met Commorrus, who was instantly struck by the youth's likeness to his fifth wife and cut his head off as a precaution. The saintly lad picked up his head, walked to Commorrus' castle and threw a handful of earth at it so that it collapsed and buried the murderous count.

Westward from Le Faou, over the River Châteaulin is the **Presqu'Ile de Crozon**, a bent trident-shaped piece of land, the two northern tines forming parts of a national park and offering some very fine seascapes; the best being that from **Pointe de Dinan** to the huge rock formation known, with good reason, as the Castle of the Giants; the southern tine forming a rim of the almost totally enclosed Baie de Douarnenez. On this, its northern rim, is a fine series of marine caves, huge grottoes into which it is possible to sail. Approach by means other than water is not possible for the ordinary mortal and it is best to take one of the boat trips on offer to view the caves. On a fine afternoon this is a very pleasant way to acquire a tan. On the southern rim of the bay, no visitor with an interest in ornithology should miss the seabird reserve of Cap Sizun, a noted spot for both gulls and auks, cormorants and petrels. Beyond is the mysterious Baie des Trépassés, the Bay of the Souls of the Dead. Many believe this to be a reference to the numerous shipwrecks on its jagged, enclosing arms or to the legendary transporting of the bodies of dead Druids from here to the burial island of Sein, but it is more likely to be just a misinterpretation of the very unsinister Breton name, Boe an Aon — Bay of Streams — into Boe an Anaon — Bay of Souls. However since the Pointe du Raz is France's equivalent of Land's End or John o' Groats, the bay is rarely as quiet as the grave.

Offshore here is the reputed site of *Is*, legendary drowned capital of Cornouaille, a town that was so beautiful that the capital of France was built to be as beautiful — Par-Is.

Back inland do not miss the fabulous sculpture in the church of Locronan.

South is **Quimper**, capital of Finistère and in many ways the complete Breton city. It is still small enough to explore comfortably on foot, however, and there is much that is of interest away from the main tourist highways. Perhaps the best idea is to go south of the River Odet and climb Mont Frugy, the tree-bedecked hill. From its flanks the view of the old town, dominated by the magnificent

Quimper

cathedral, is superb. For a really spectacular day and the best of all
entries into Quimper, take the Odet boat from **Bénodet**. The trip
passes trees and fields, old castles and houses, even crossing a lake
— Kerogen, where the river widens amazingly — before the twin
spires of the cathedral of St Corentin come into view.

Near Quimper, **Plonéour-Lanvern** and **Pont-l'Abbé**, are two excellent villages in which to see the traditional Breton lady's head-
piece, the *coiffe*. They are worn on Sunday mornings and, in Pont-
l'Abbé, on Thursday morning. Near Pont-l'Abbé, at **Combrit**, is an
interesting museum of mechanical music — from fairground organs
to music boxes.

As traditional as the *coiffe* is the return of the fishing boats to the
ports around the Pointe de l'Enmarch'h. At **St Guénolé**, **Guilvinec**
and **Lesconil**, for instance, the boats return at around 4.30pm each
weekday and unload to the quayside markets. Close by La Forêt-
Fouesnant, at the resort town of **Concarneau**, there is a museum to
the history of local fishing.

Going east and fast approaching the *département* of Morbihan,
one last ancient site is still to be visited, the Rochers du Diable, the
Devil's Rocks, north-east of **Quimperlé**, a strange jumble of huge
boulders beside a beautiful river, the Ellé. The rocks are named from
the legend of a Celtic saint who lived among them and chased the
devil away from the area when he came to harass him. South of

Quimperlé, the River Behan is one of Brittany's better spots for oysters. Also south is the beautiful oak and beech **Forêt de Carnoët**, a link with the legend of St Trémuer at Carhaix, because one version of the tale sites Commorrus' castle here.

Lastly in Finistère, travel north to the land lying east of Morlaix which, therefore, feels as though it should be in Côtes du Nord *département*. The village of **St Jean-du-Doigt** is named for a finger of St John the Baptist held in a reliquary in the church. It has been said many times that there are enough relics of some saints to build several bodies and so it is a claim that must be treated with caution, especially since this forgotten corner of Brittany seems such a strange repository for such a thing, and the dismemberment of the saint's body seems equally strange. Outside the church there is a fountain, itself said to be sacred,which fills a basin into which the finger is dipped at intervals. The water thus blessed is said to be a miracle cure for eyes bathed in it, the cure having given rise to an annual *pardon* of eye complaint sufferers. In addition to the finger, the church also holds some of the finest silverware of any of the province's churches.

Nearby another finger, here of hard rock, points out into the sea at **Primel-Trégastel**. This holiday village has the benefits of both a sandy beach and a rocky headland. Another fine coastal spot is the bay between the mainland and the Pointe de Barnenez. The point itself has, at its summit, perhaps the finest of all Brittany's megalithic remains, the Tumulus of Barnenez, an incredible structure of dry-stone walls, about 70m (225ft) long, 25m (80ft) wide and 8m (25ft) high covering eleven burial chambers each reached by a narrow, low passage. A site definitely not to be missed.

Morbihan

The *département* of Morbihan, or, more correctly, The Morbihan, is the only one of Brittany's *départements* to have a Breton name, that name deriving from the area's most obvious feature, the huge sea lagoon (the Gulf of Morbihan) lying to the south of Vannes, and known in Breton, as the 'Mor Bihan', the little sea. The gulf's enclosing arms almost touch, at the Pointe de Kerpenhir, south of Locmariaquer, being separated by little over half a mile of water from the headland of Port Navalo. This almost total enclosure brings to the villages along the gulf's shore a calmness not often experienced on the wild coasts of Finistère, which in turn produces a mildness of climate that is quite surprising.

In Breton history the area around Vannes, the Vannetais as it was

The Tumulus of Barnenez, the finest prehistoric site in Brittany

known, played an important role.The significant battle that ended the War of Succession and so decided who would rule Brittany, was fought at Auray, on the main river that feeds into the gulf. But many centuries before that battle the area was already important to man. Within the *département* are the finest of Brittany's megalithic sites, perhaps the finest, and certainly one of the most enigmatic, collections of prehistoric sites anywhere in the world. The megalithic alignments north of Carnac are so famous that they need no introduction, and there is little justification for their inclusion here — whatever their original purpose might have been, they are no longer off the beaten track. There is just time to mention that the stones are, not surprisingly, the source of numerous legends: that they are the soldiers of a Roman army, turned to stone for threatening a Christian saint; that they all leave their holes at midnight on Christmas Eve to drink at the River Crac'h, leaving exposed treasure that the very brave may try to retrieve; and many more. But some time should be spent exploring the area's prehistory. At Kercado is the oldest of all the monuments, and still one of the most impressive, and no visitor should miss the Grand Menhir Brisé and the Table des Marchands near **Locmariaquer**. The Grand Menhir now lies in five pieces, the victim, it is widely believed, of a lightning strike in the eighteenth century. When standing this 350 ton stone would have been 20m (65ft) tall. Just the accomplishment of its erection is astonishing, without considering why. The best current theory is that it formed a pointer for a huge observatory, erected to predict seasons and eclipses. Some say it was sighted from the Quiberon peninsula, which if true gives some idea of its size — there are 8 miles of water between here and there. The Table des Marchands is a huge dolmen, probably a burial chamber. The largest flat table stone is 6 x 4m (20 x 13ft) and is part supported by a stone that has been deliberately shaped to a cone and is covered with strange symbols. Some see crooks and a cooking pot, some see ears of corn and the sun.

But for a real treat, take the short boat trip from Larmor-Baden to the **Ile de Gavrinis** to see the decorated stones of the burial chamber there. The abstract swirls and spirals make this one of the wonders of the world. Finally, the visitor who dives might visit the next, tiny, island, **Er Iannic**, where two of the very few stone circles in Brittany are sited. One is now completely submerged, the other nearly so and diving — a snorkel will just about do if conditions are right — is fascinating.

The gulf is not all old stones however. There is fine boating here, good swimming and some beautiful views, especially from Pointe d'Arradon. For the bird watcher the area is amazing, the salt marsh margins, especially on the southern gulf shore, the **Presqu'Ile de Rhuys**, being especially renowned for summer feeding ducks, geese, spoonbills and egrets. Try the gulf reserve site of **St Armel** on the eastern shore. Alternatively go to the Rhuys pensinsula. It is rarely visited in comparison to the more famous Quiberon peninsula, yet it has seascapes that are its equal: rocky, wind-lashed coves, a sandy lee side and the marshy gulf side. Do not miss the little village of **St Gildas-de-Rhuys**, with a fine Romanesque abbey church on the site of a monastery founded by the British monk Gildas, famous as the source of many Arthurian legends.

The Quiberon peninsula cannot be recommended for the summer visitor as its single road is clogged with traffic for most weekend hours and frequently during the week as well. In winter it is a different story, and then the western edge, which takes the full brunt of Atlantic storms, is the place to experience nature in the raw. It is aptly named the Côte Sauvage, the Savage Coast. Off the peninsula is Belle-Ile, another well known spot, so go instead to the **Ile de Houat**, a smaller island to the east, a peaceful, little frequented fishing island served by boats from Port Navalo, and Quiberon. Or better, go to the **Ile de Groix**, to the west off of Lorient. The whole island, about 24sq km (some 10sq miles) is a museum to an ancient way of life, because in addition to an actual museum to the tunny fishing and sea-faring way of life of the islanders, there are two waymarked paths around the island which visit the most charming and most interesting sites.On its south-eastern tip there is also a fine seabird reserve.

Inland, Morbihan has some of the finest river scenery not only in Brittany, but also in Europe. Begin by going to the extreme west of the *département* to visit the town of **Le Faouët**, which stands besides the River Ellé, but also in the centre of a piece of quiet countryside, fields, woods and streams.The town derives its name from the Breton *faou*, a beech-tree, which is very appropriate. It is a fine place with a beautiful, huge, sixteenth-century covered market built with massive wooden legs and roof beams. Nearby are two tiny villages with excellent chapels. **Ste Barbe** has a Gothic building from the early sixteenth century, and a fountain where a floated hairpin told a girl she would be married within the year. If the hairpin sank she would not. **St Fiacre** has a fifteenth-century chapel holding what is probably the finest rood screen in Brittany, a marvellous late fifteenth-century work with fine carving including some excellent grotesques.

Eastward do not miss the equally beautiful chapel of **Kernascléden**, which has the best collection of fifteenth-century wall paintings in France. Legend has it that this chapel and that of St Fiacre were built by the same workmen, ferried by angels between the two sites so that the work was not held up. Sadly for the legend it is known that the Kernascléden chapel was completed 30 years before St Fiacre.

Just east of Kernascléden is the valley of the River Scorff, by common consent the most beautiful of all Morbihan's rivers, the stretch between Guémené-sur-Scorff and Plouay probably being the finest. It is almost impossible to choose a particular section of the river here as the best part, but a leisurely day would probably be best. Start at **Guéméne** with the remains of an old castle and a fine array of medieval buildings. **Persquen** has an interesting parish close, while **Lignol** lies in a deeply wooded section of the valley. Next is Kernascléden itself, and then comes the Forêt de Pontcallec, perhaps the most picturesque of all the wooded areas, with many views that would grace a postcard. There is a nineteenth-century *château*, viewed across a lake, and incomparable woodland views. From the tiny village of St Albaud to the Pont-Neuf, a distance of about 3km (2 miles), the forest is crossed by GR34, one of the very fine series of Grandes Randonnées, long-distance footpaths, that criss-cross the French countryside. No special knowledge is required to follow a GR, the signing being excellent and obvious, and the following of this small section can be highly recommended.

Half-timbered buildings, Rennes, Brittany

Rochefort-en-Terre, Brittany

Malicorne, Pays de la Loire

Angers - the château, Pays de la Loire

Next east is the River Blavet with, on its banks at the northern end of the *département*, **Pontivy**, once the capital of Brittany and called Napoleonville. Neither name nor status lasted a great length of time, but just long enough for the town to acquire some prosperous buildings which it has, gratefully, maintained. Napoleon's name was given as a reward for loyalty. The present, and older name is from the founding Welsh monk who had the first bridge built over the Blavet. South of Pontivy the Blavet flows delightfully through quiet countryside, less wooded than that of the Scorff Valley, but not really the worse for that.The waters of other rivers, themselves worth exploring, the Sarre, the Brandifrout and the Tarun are collected as the Blavet grows towards Hennebont. On the Tarun just a couple of miles from its confluence with the Blavet is **Baud**, a pleasant village with, just outside on the southern side of the main road to Hennebont and Lorient, an odd statue with a chequered history. It is called the *Venus of Quinipily* and has been variously ascribed to the ancient Egyptians, the Celts, the Romans and as a worthless fake of no antiquity at all. How it came here is not known, but what is known is that it was the basis of a cult in the seventeenth century that came perilously close — or so said the local churchman — to pagan idolatry. Consequently the local bishop came and supervised as the statue was thrown into the river. The locals waited until the bishop had gone away, and retrieved it for posterity.

East again the river pattern is disturbed by the high **Landes de Lanvaux**. This was once barren moorland, but it has been increasingly 'reclaimed' for farmland and forestry. The ancient nature of the landscape still shows occasionally: a piece of wild heath, an ancient menhir. In 1944, after the landings at Normandy, a genuine battle took place here between the Breton resistance fighters and a unit of French paratroopers, and the occupying Germans. The battle site, near **St Marcel**, is marked by a (well hidden) memorial.

The Landes push the south-flowing rivers east towards Redon. First is the Claie that flows by St Marcel itself, and next is the Oust which flows through **Josselin**. Josselin is famous for its castle, a marvel of Renaissance architecture, but slightly off the beaten track is the Musée de Poupées, the Doll's Museum, now established in the castle stables. The museum is formed around the collection of the Rohan family and has over 500 examples.

Downstream (the Oust is Brittany's longest river) is **Malestroit**, an old town with fine timber-framed houses, beyond which the river joins the Aff flowing from the *département* of Ille-et-Vilaine. Here is the Mortier, a river section enclosed by the Ile des Pies dam, a

The castle at Josselin

sanctuary for water birds of all kinds. The views, to chapels, rocks, wood and farmland, and the wonderful birdlife make this one of the finest spots in the whole of Brittany. The area is one of the chief centres for Breton folklore and culture, and over the marshes here the 'White Lady' floats, sometimes wreathed in mist. Those who follow her call are apparently drawn far away.

The Aff, which has joined the Oust, flows down from the Forêt de Broceliande, covered in the section on Ille-et-Vilaine, and that link with an ancient landscape has made it a centre for ancient crafts. There are numerous riverside paths through tiny hamlets of characteristic shale houses, the odd manor house or small castle. The valley is the least frequented of all, the genuine off the beaten track river, and should be savoured at length. But do go to **La Gacilly**, a fine town brimming with ancient crafts, a small industry of flower-based beauty products and, it seems, a flower-filled window box for every window.

The last valley is the Yuel that joins the Oust south of Ploërmel. **St Léry**, near the border with Ille-et-Vilaine, is a beautiful village with a fine array of old houses. Down river is the Etang au Duc, a fine lake-like expanse of the river that offers good sailing in beautiful surroundings. **Ploërmel** has near it, and appallingly badly preserved beside the dual carriageway coming in from Josselin, the Colonne des Trente. This is one of the most important of all Breton chivalric sites where, during the War of Succession, thirty knights from each side — English knights on one side — fought a duel to save greater bloodloss in their respective garrisons. The battle lasted all day despite which there was surprisingly little loss of life, the routed English losing nine men. Bad road planning means the site is little visited, though much sped past.

Throughout the Morbihan there are numerous castles, some very famous. Largoët Fortress, also known as the Towers of Elven, stands to the west of the road, the N166 from Vannes to Ploërmel and Malestroit. All that remains of the fourteenth- and fifteenth-century castle — knocked down in the late fifteenth century when the owner backed the wrong side in the fight between Brittany and France — are two huge, beautiful towers, and some low ruins. The huge, 60m (195ft), octagonal tower is a massive fourteenth-century construction, while the restored fifteenth-century round tower with pyramidal roof is more delicate. There is a real drawbridge and a fine view across a lake. It is enchanting.

Ille-et-Vilaine

This *département* is named from its principal rivers which meet at the town of Rennes, capital of both the *département* and Brittany. The Vilaine flows south to the Golfe du Morbihan while the Ille or, rather, the Ille-Rance Canal joins Rennes to the Channel near St Malo. Thus the two waters split the *département* from side to side, though the waterway does not form a barrier between Brittany and the rest of France, that barrier being further to the east. There, unlike in past centuries when Brittany strived to maintain a very real and fortified barrier with France, the boundary is fluid. France starts in a gradual way somewhere closer to Finistère, and by the time eastern Ille-et-Vilaine is reached the countryside and people are more French than Breton.

As a holiday centre Ille-et-Vilaine is blessed with few beaches, though Dinard is a very notable exception, nor is it blessed with the mild climate of Morbihan and its gulf. It makes up for this lack by an abundance of quiet countryside and pleasant, secluded villages and towns, and the marvellous line of castles along the old border between Brittany and France.

As with Roscoff in Finistère, many visitors who arrive or depart on a Brittany Ferry do not see **St Malo**, except as a hugely fortified port on the horizon. Again it is worth the time of exploration. Named after a founding Welsh monk, the present town was built on an island in the bay offshore of the original town, which had been greatly plundered by pirates. Only over the last three centuries has the island under St Malo been permanently connected to the mainland by a causeway over a widening sandbar.The town's insularity, well defended by still awesome defensive walls, built a fierce independence, the inhabitants considering themselves neither French, nor Breton, owing allegiance to no man. They were highly skilled sailors, skills they put to use in exploration — Jacques Cartier, a local man, discovered and named Canada — and in piracy, and later in legitimate trade, a trade that financed, in the seventeenth and eighteenth centuries, the array of fine granite buildings, and the excellent cathedral. There are several excellent museums in the town; the *donjon*, not the dungeon, but the keep, the English form being a misinterpretation of the French, has one to the town, while in Rue de Toulouse there is a fine Dolls' Museum.

From the town two boat trips are possible. A short trip across the bay leads to the island of Grand Bé, named from the Breton word for a tomb and, appropriately, holding the grave of the writer Châteaubriand. A longer trip follows the River Rance inland, a fine trip that can be combined with a visit to the tidal barrage power station, the world's only such station.

Near St Malo, on the road towards Rennes, is a museum of cider, a fascinating insight into that most Breton of drinks.

North-east from St Malo is a short section of the Emerald Coast, the *département*'s only piece of coastline, reaching its northern extreme at the **Pointe du Grouin,** north of Cancale, a real nose of land, poked into the English Channel. The views from it, including Mont St Michel, are excellent, and the incut cliffs of the headland are equally good for poking about in. A small offshore island is a bird sanctuary. **Cancale** itself is more popular, especially with the oyster fancier, being famous for their production.

At nearby **Rothéneuf** is a site that is not only off the beaten track but will soon be on no track at all. In the rocks above the sea here, in the early part of this century, an eccentric named Fouré spent a quarter of a century carving a group of sculptures of pirates and sea monsters. The sculptures are perhaps best described as grotesques, the work normally associated with church gargoyles, though on a grander scale.But the years have taken their toll, the endless battering by sea and wind gradually obliterating the work. Soon no trace of the sculptures will exist which, even if you would have preferred them not to have been carved in the first place, is sad.

Further south there is some fascinating country around **Dol-de-Bretagne**, not least the town itself whose cathedral is claimed by many to be the best in Brittany. It is certainly a very fine building, but some find its curiously asymmetric front less appealing than the symmetric cathedral of Quimper. Near the town is one of the few megalithic sites in this far corner of Brittany, but a very interesting one. The menhir, at **Champ-Dolent** about 1km (half a mile) south of the town, is 9m (about 30ft) high, and hugely impressive as well as huge. Legend has it that it fell to earth and is sinking slowly into the ground. When it has disappeared the world will come to an end. Strangely, the site — the Field of Grief — is named not as a consequence of this worldly egg-timer, but from a legendary battle between the armies of two brothers fought too long ago to be dated.

Also near Dol-de-Bretagne is Mont Dol — about 3km (2 miles) to the north — an odd table-topped mountain, that was a Celtic holy place and still has a summit chapel. The chapel started life as one in a chain of semaphore signalling stations from Brest to Paris, and the good visibility also offers stupendous views over the local country and, especially, over the Baie du Mont St Michel. A visit to this most magnificent site is certainly off the beaten track for Brittany — it's in Normandy! But a spectacularly different journey to it starts in Ille-de-Vilaine at **Le Vivier** on the coast north of Dol-de-Bretagne. From there a coach leaves across the sands and drives straight into the sea, where it folds up its wheel and becomes a boat for the last part of the journey.

Leaving Dol on the D795 towards Combourg the road soon passes a small village, **Epiniac**, that so typifies much of inland Brittany. It is not especially pretty or interesting, but it has a remarkable legend of women so lazy that they were forced to do their washing at night by candlelight. As a penance their ghosts do it still, so beware the small flickering lights, because if the women see you they will demand assistance with the wringing of their clothes, and anyone who wrings, rings also the bell of his own doom.

Alternatively, leave Dol on the D155 to Fougères and reach **Antrain-sur-Couesnon**, a distinguished village close to the Normandy border at the meeting point of two rivers, the Couesnon and the Loisance. It is a pleasant town, with some good fifteenth- and sixteenth-century houses set in narrow, winding lanes, a very fine twelfth-century Romanesque church and, about $1^1/_2$km (1 mile) to the south, the Château de Bonne-Fontaine.This is an elegant combination of country mansion and castle, its round towers with their conical roofs and high-set windows looking like crouched witches peering through slit eyes. The illusion is hard to maintain once the little stone chimneys breaking through the roofs have been spotted. The park alone is open to the public, no real loss as the view to the *château* is included in the park entrance fee, and the visitor can stroll through the woodland where, it is said, Brittany's famed Duchess Anne meted out justice whilst sat in the shade of an oak tree.

The *château* is more off the beaten track than the one at Fougères, though neither is it as splendid, as its more famous neighbour. One of the problems with writing about the little visited is that it can prevent the mention of the real gem. So visit **Fougères** not for the *château*, but for a couple of other delights. But see the *château* anyway!

There are two churches in Fougères, and neither should be missed. From the outside the church of St Leonard, built over many centuries from the twelfth century onwards, is a curious barn-like building, with an equally curious pagoda-like tower, but is set in a fine park in the town, close to the fourteenth-century half-timbered houses of the Place du Marchix, and is certainly worth a look. The second church, the fifteenth-century St Sulpice, is close to the castle, a slim, elegant, soaring Gothic church which contains an apparently miracle-working statue of the Virgin and Child. The statue is much older than the church, probably twelfth century, and has been much renovated since being rescued, in the fourteenth century, from the castle moat into which it had been unceremoniously thrown by heathen English soldiery. North-east of the town, around the D177 to St Hilaire du Harcouët, make time to visit the Forêt de Fougères, a beautiful, chiefly beech, wood criss-crossed by paths, with dotted menhirs and legends of Celtic Druids. An ideal spot for a picnic.

Combourg was the boyhood home of the writer Châteaubriand. Not well known in English, in France, Châteaubriand is regarded as a literary genius, though his sombre, melancholic style is not to all tastes. His home, Château Combourg, is a centre for literary pilgrimage, but is worth a visit, especially to stand in the Cat's Tower — Tour de Chat — and to contemplate what it must have been like as a young, impressionable boy, to have spent each night alone in this tower — the writer's father distributed his family all over the *château* for reasons now obscure — when it was reputedly haunted by, of all things, a previous owner's wooden leg that stamped about the corridors, pursued by a black cat.

Combourg itself is also worth a visit, if only for the view to it from across the reedy lake on its southern side, the chimneyed conical roofs of the castle rising, fairy-tale like, from the woods beside the grey-roofed houses.

South of Combourg, in **Tintiéniac**, visit the Musée de l'Outil et de Métiers, the Museum of Tools and Crafts, in an old house called the Grain Store — Le Magasin à Grains — in the Quai de la Donac. This is a delightful collection of old crafts and agricultural implements, suggesting most strongly the similarities between the agricultural peasantries of Europe who wrestled with the same seasons and the same difficulties and probably little understood, or cared for, the reason their lords occasionally threw them into combat with each other. Tinténiac itself is a fine old town with a number of interesting buildings from the twelfth to the seventeenth centuries.

Rennes, Brittany's capital, tends to be off the beaten track to those, the majority, who find the prospect of driving into a town with a population of over 200,000 people, daunting. In practice if the visitor goes in August, when, it seems, France goes on holiday, the town is quiet, the parking easy, and the very fine, old town centre worth the effort. Start at the Palais de Justice, a fine seventeenth-century building, once the site of the Parliament of Brittany, that can be visited — worthwhile for the eighteenth-century Flemish tapestries — then go along Rue Brilhac, Rue Hermine and Rue du Gueslin to the Place St Sauveur. Here go left, then right in Place du Calvaire to Rue du Chapitre. Here is the very heart of the old town, and the only part of it to have escaped a huge fire in 1720 that virtually razed the town to the ground. Go right into Rue de La Psalette for the very best of the old town, an enchanting, narrow, large-cobbled street of timber-framed houses, each different enough from the next to give a modern town planner sleepless nights, yet in truth combining to a wonderful whole rarely achieved by modern, regulated building. About half way up the street open, cautiously, a large wooden door to the right. Inside is a truly delightful courtyard.

Following the road round brings the visitor to the cathedral, a recent, late eighteenth- early nineteenth-century, building that seems a little heavy for the area. By contrast the nearby Porte Mordelaise, the last remaining part of the fifteenth-century town wall, is beautifully proportioned, tall, but elegant, even delicate, with a fine arched doorway.

South of Rennes are some fine interesting sites. The Roche-aux-Fées, near Esse is, perhaps the most beautiful megalithic site in France, a wondrous construction of over forty huge rocks, some weighing 40 tons, whose name translates as 'Fairies' Rock', since there was a legend that it was built by fairies and that it was impossible to count the stones. By tradition a boy and girl who start out in opposite directions to walk around the monument, each counting the stones, will have a happy marriage if, when they meet, their tallies differ by less than two. Modern scholarship now believes that the monument was not a tomb, though its true purpose is not known.

Old Rennes

Nearby, **La Guerche-de-Bretagne** is a fine medieval town, and an excellent centre for exploring the area of south-east Ille-et-Vilaine, much of which is quiet and little frequented. **Bain-de-Bretagne**, on the opposite side of the Roche-aux-Fées, can be used as a similar centre. It is less good as a town, though it is well sited by a lake, and just outside to the west, is the chapel of Le Coudroy containing a stone with a small hole, child's foot size, used as a healing stone for children with walking difficulties or foot ailments.

West again, at **St Just**, is the second biggest concentration of megalithic sites in Brittany — after Carnac — though the sites are not well signposted and not at all well documented. The casual visitor can just enjoy the exploration of this little visited area, while those keener to obtain information on the sites can ask the *curé* (priest) of the church of St Just, who is a mine of information.

Lastly go west of Rennes towards the border with Morbihan. At **Montfort**, visit the Ecomusée, the local history museum, if only to see a fiendish, and fiendishly clever, stone sling made from a split stick and called, for reasons obvious when you see it, *'le pied de cochon'*, the 'pig's foot'.

South-west from Montfort is the Forêt de Broceliande, an area steeped in the Arthurian legends, a wild, mysterious woodland, worth every hour spent in it. It was to here not Glastonbury, so legend says, that Joseph of Arimathea brought the Holy Grail, and the forest is still haunted by the ghosts of Arthur, Guinevere and Lancelot. Each June the Arthurian legends form the basis of a local festival. Near the village of Tréhorenteuc is the Fountain of Barenton, a holy water fountain capable of curing mental disorders, and sacred to the Druids. Here too is the Val Sans Retour, the Valley of No Return, where Morgan le Fay held Merlin prisoner, and the Perron Merlin, a flat stone which summons thunder if water from the fountain is sprinkled on it. Mention of the Druids recalls that their presence here preceded the Arthurian legends — the forest has been a place of mystery for a long time. Periodically the modern French Druids — about as genuine as those that frequent Stonehenge on Midsummer's Day, ie, not very — pull out all the site marking signposts in an effort to keep the forest's secrets. If you arrive after such a raid, the forest really is off the beaten track.

Côtes-du-Nord

As the name implies, this *département* is dominated by its coastline which, though shorter than that of Finistère, seems to exert more of an influence over the area. At one time the *département* was divided in two by a language barrier, Breton-French, along a line running almost straight, due south from St Brieuc. Today, with the pushing of the language westward, to its last stronghold in Finistère, this no longer applies. Instead there is another barrier, a north-south one dividing Armor, the land of the sea, from Argoat, the land of the forest. Even this barrier is artificial, though, the land of the forest having all but gone now, the pockets that remain being jealously, and rightly, guarded.

A quiet inlet near Ploumanach on the north Brittany coast

St Brieuc is the *département*'s capital and chief town, though it has no great merits for anyone seeking other than a modern city. There is an old quarter, though it is small, standing close to the cathedral, a building which resembles less a place of worship than a small village, all turrets and spires heaped, apparently haphazardly, on top of one another. The town is, however, a reasonable place from which to explore the fine coasts of the *département*. To the east are the Emerald Coast, shared with Ille-et-Vilaine, and the Penthièvre coast.

The Emerald Coast is beautifully named, and its delights are best sampled by choosing one of several excellent headlands which offer views to its incut bays. **Pointe du Chevet**, north of the pretty fishing village of **St Jacut-de-la-Mer** — famous not so much for its fish as a series of eleven excellent beaches in its immediate vicinity — has magnificent views, especially to the Ile des Hébihens, while Pointe de St Cast allows fine views eastward along the length of the coast itself. The village after which the headland is named, **St Cast**, is perhaps the most beautiful resort on the coast, with a backdrop of conifer forest and a foreground of sand. Less well known is the Baie de la Frênaye to the north, where sand gives way to a more rugged rock scenery, and views across to Fort-la-Latte.

Fort-la-Latte could not, in some senses, be claimed as being off the beaten track, and yet there are many who have seen pictures of it and have never visited it. It is not easy to reach, demanding a walk of around $1^1/_2$km (1 mile) but is well worth the effort. It was started in the ninth century, though what the visitor sees today is several centuries later, the archetypal castle set on a headland about 60m (200ft) above a savage sea, protected by a couple of impressive ravines.

The view from the castle is excellent and no less impressive is that from nearby **Cap Fréhel** where the cliff is higher, around 70m (230ft). On rare days the Cherbourg peninsula can be seen. The headland is a renowned seabird nesting site, but was once famous for an entirely different reason with St Malo's sailors. Once they had rounded the Cap, their wedding vows were suspended! Cap Fréhel is at one end of the Penthièvre Coast, the next fine headland of which is **Cap d'Erquy**, named after a delightful fishing village, famous for its scallops, known here as *coquilles St Jacques*. Inland a little, the Château Bien Assis is less well known than Fort-la-Latte, but is of interest for being one of the last castles built in France, sections dating from as late as the seventeenth century.

North of St Brieuc is the Côte du Goelo, with a seemingly never-ending line of very fine beaches, many with a little village attached.

Binic, close to St Brieuc, is a busy little place, and **Brehec** is a little difficult to find down some minor roads, but is beautifully set between high cliffs. Legend has it that it was here that the first settlers or refugees from Britain landed in Brittany. Inland, go to **Kermanic-an-Iskuit** where the chapel has a tremendously vibrant fifteenth-century fresco of the *Dance of Death*, skeletons being shown dancing with all classes from kings to ploughmen, to emphasise death's levelling nature.

A little north of Brehec is the Abbaye de Beauport, one of the most romantically sited abbey ruins in the whole province. On the drive north you pass a large, pleasant lake to the left, studded with rich, elegant houses. To the right, the view opens out across a green valley to the sea and then, suddenly, there is the abbey ruin. What survives is thirteenth century.

Beyond the abbey is **Paimpol**, a pleasant fishing/holiday village to the north of which, beyond Pointe de l'Arcouest is the **Ile de Bréhat** reached in a 10-minute ferry ride from the point. The island is traffic-free, a haven for trees, shrubs, flowers and birdlife. The northern coast is a fine jumble of granite boulders tinged with the pink that gives this new section of the coast its name, the Côte de Granit Rose, the pink granite coast. There is a fine old fishing village and a very worthwhile air of calm.

Over the estuary to the west of Paimpol and then north, the **Sillon de Talbert** is worth seeing, a long (3km, 2 miles) and very narrow (only 30m, 100ft) spit of shingle, that extends in a long sweep out into the sea. The spit is covered in salt-tolerant plants and is used for the collection of seaweed on a commercial basis. To the south is **Tréguier**, the town famous for its soaring 'pink' granite cathedral. If it is sunny go inside to see the coloured patterns drawn by the stained glass on the stone slab floor. Look, too, for the statue of St Yves between a rich and a poor man. This most beloved of all Breton saints and the patron saint of lawyers was asked, or so it is said, by a rich man to adjudicate on a case he had brought against a poor man, claiming that his impoverished neighbour was living by inhaling the smells from his kitchen! St Yves found in the rich man's favour ordering, in payment, the sound of a coin rattling in a tin.

North from Tréguier is one of the great delights of the area, indeed of Brittany, the little chapel with the corkscrew spire, at **St Gonery**. St Gonery, a Celtic monk, built the earliest part of the building in the eighth or ninth century. That part now contains a stone trough, not the monk's coffin, but a ballast trough from his ship, used on the voyage to hold the cooking fire. The monk's skull is also preserved

St Gonery chapel

in a glass case that sits on a sedan chair-like structure which is used to carry it in procession! But the real joy is the art work — the superb creatures carved on the roof beams so that the beams seen to come from their mouths and the equally good friezes with legendary animals carved with that great Celtic flare for savage mystery. Best of all is the frescoed ceiling of the main chapel. The paintings are of both the Old and New Testaments, the old following the Creation, Adam and Eve, and Cane and Abel. Originally the figures were nude, but at some stage this lack of propriety was catered for by the addition of robes. The New Testament scenes include an explicit Slaughter of the Innocents. The whole ceiling has a wonderful vibrancy and an uncompromising realism. It is well set off by a later, framed painting, a Deposition of moving sadness. All in all a most remarkable building.

Beyond the chapel, the shore is a chaos of fine granite boulders, at the **Pointe de Château**, but also has some good stretches of sand — a fine, unfrequented spot. Its more famous near neighbour, the Chaos Rocheaux, near Trégastel, is better, but more popular. North of it, the group of islands — Les Sept Iles — must be visited (by boat from Perros-Guirec) by all birdwatchers, being one of the most important bird sites in the whole of France. Here there are all members of the auk family, besides many gulls and petrels, and the mysterious cormorants, in undertaker's black, their wings held stiffly out as though to encircle the living. The reserve suffered badly in the wake of the *Torrey Canyon* and *Amoco Cadiz* tanker disasters, but is, thankfully, recovering.

Now go inland, south of Lannion, to the Argoat proper, where there is a small knot of castles. The ruins of Tonquédec are set in woodland in the valley of the Léguer, a beautifully evocative building, walls fully 4m (13ft) thick. A still passable circular stairway leads to the battlements and superb views. Coatfrec is even more hidden, half-lost among ivy and shrubs. It lies, almost never visited, in the same Léguer valley, but closer to Lannion. Last is Kergrist, not a medieval castle, but a later, fortified, manor. Between the castles of Coatfrec and Tonquédec is the chapel of Kerfons, a fine fifteenth-century building with a marvellously carved rood screen and some very good sixteenth-century stained glass.

Travelling south it is possible to follow the Léguer valley most of the way to **Belle-Isle-en-Terre**, a nicely situated, though curiously named town. From here almost any trip into the Argoat is worthwhile, but especially the one to **Loc-Envel**, a very pretty little village set between two fine woods, the Coat an Noz and the Coat an Hay, the Night Wood and the Day Wood. This oddity is probably Druidic in origin: twins of any kind held a special fascination for the Druids. The woods are excellent for walks and picnics, an interesting view back in time to when most of this area of Brittany really was the Argoat, the land of the forest.

An even better village, one less well known though less well sited, is **Bulat-Pestivien,** just beyond the high ridge which is a continuation of Finistère's mountain backbone. The village is a real gem, with, at its heart, a large church with a 66m (220ft) spire, the tallest in Brittany. In the vicinity there are three sacred fountains, a clear link with ancient times. Those holidaying late could attend the impressive *pardon* held here on the Sunday following 7 September.

South again, pick up the River Blavet , as picturesque here as it is in Ille-et-Vilaine. Near Kergrist it flows through the Chaos, or Gorge de Toul-Goulic, or, rather, it flows under it because for around 400m (440yd) the river is underground and can be heard thundering along below the boulder-strewn valley floor. Some of the boulders are huge, and may even have served as shelters for Stone Age man: they are also beautifully moss-covered. To the west, the Gorge du Coronc, about 3km (2 miles), north of Locarn is more off the beaten track, but not quite so spectacular. The Gorge de Toul-Goulic is passed by GR341, and this pathway now hugs the Blavet fairly close as it heads towards the Lac de Guerlédan, Brittany's largest lake, a man-made reservoir for a hydro-power station. Close to the lake, GR341 crosses

Dinan

to the River Daoulas and traverses the Gorges du Daoulas where the river has bitten deep into the rock, forming a narrow, steep gash which is alive with plant life even though it is shadowed. To the east, near **Mur-de-Bretagne**, a fine town, the Gorges de Poulancre are equally good. Also near the town there is an interesting, well signed route that hugs the water of Lac de Guerlédan around its 48km (30 mile) shoreline. That is a long way to walk with a similar — even though everchanging in aspect — view, but a section of it is very rewarding.

Northwards the two towns of **Quintin** and **Guingamp** are worth visting. The former is prettily set with remains of the old town walls, the lower part of a never completed seventeenth-century castle and some fine timber-framed houses from the sixteenth and seventeenth centuries. Guingamp is now bypassed by a good road, and so has become little frequented, but it too is a fine town, with the ruins of old fortifications and fine sixteenth-century half-timbered houses.

Eastward, **Moncontour** is another fine, but thankfully largely neglected town, and to the south Mont Bel-Air is Côtes-du-Nord's highest mountain — at 340m (1,105ft) — with a correspondingly expansive view. It is a good spot, a little spoiled by the transmitter masts, shared by a recently built chapel approached by eight beech tree-bordered walks. These, apparently, represent the rays of the sun, the site formerly being dedicated to the pagan Celtic sun-god.

North-east, beyond Lamballe, in the Forêt de la Hunaudaie, a fine spot enclosing the impressive ruins of the huge Château de la Hunaudaie. The ruins, overgrown by greenery in most romantic style, date from the fourteenth century, and prove the point that many English folly builders were trying to make, that a good, well sized ruin is a good deal more picturesque than a shiny new building.

Lastly, head south of Dinan to the area around **Caulnes**, itself a very pleasant country market town. To the east of the town is a string of very pretty villages, each well set and with its own interest. Several have the remains of old castles or fortified manor houses to add to their attractiveness. No one place stands out, so just motor quietly eastward from Caulnes, on the D25 to Guitté, passing the Châteaux de Couëlan and Beaumont. Then on across the Roplémol lake to Guenroc and St Maden, and along the D39 to Tréfumel and Le Quiou with the Château le Hac. Those interested in fossils should note that these last two villages lie close to limestone outcrops rich in fossils from the Tertiary Era.

Further Information
— Brittany —

Museums and Other Places of Interest

FINISTERE

Plogonnec
Auberge de Leurbiriou
On the road from Plogonnec to Douarnenez, 2km (1$^1/_4$ miles) from Plogonnec.

Botform en Combrit
Museum of Mechanical Music
O the road from Pont-l'Abbé to Bénodet
Open: daily 5-7pm.

MORBIHAN
Ile de Groix
Ecomuseum and Waymarked Trails
Museum
Open: daily except Monday mid-June to mid-September 10am-12.30pm and 2-5pm

Waymarked Trails
Open: daily mid-June to mid-September 9.30am-12.30pm and 3-7pm.

Josselin
Doll's Museum at Josselin Castle
Open: daily except Monday May-September 10am-12noon, 1-6pm; Wednesday, Saturday, Sunday and holidays March, April, October, early November 2-6pm.

Largoët
Fortress
(The Towers of Elven)
Open: daily March-mid-November
9am-6pm.

ILLE-ET-VILAINE

St Malo
Castle Museum
Open: daily Easter-mid-September
9am-12noon, 2-5.45pm.

Doll's Museum
Open: daily 10am-12noon, 2pm-7pm.

Antrain-sur-Couesnon
Château de Bonne-Fontaine
Park open in summer months 2pm-6pm.

Combourg
Château de Combourg
Open: daily except Tuesday, Easter-
September 2-6pm.

Tintinéac
Museum of Tools and Crafts
Open: daily except Monday July-
September 10am-12noon, 2.30-7pm.
Open on request October-June.

Montfort
Local History Museum,
Open: daily except Monday July-
September 10am-12noon, 2-6pm
Tuesday-Saturday 2-6pm Sunday;
daily except Monday and Saturday
October-June 2-6pm.

COTES-DU-NORD

Near **Matignon**
Fort-la-Latte
Open: daily June-September 10am-
12.30pm, 2.30-6.30pm.

Near **Paimpol**
Beauport Abbey
Open: all year round, 9am-12.15pm,
2-7pm. Daily.

Near **Lamballe**
Château de la Hunaudaie
Open: daily July-August 10am-1pm, 3-
7pm. Easter-June, September Sundays,
holidays only 3-7pm.

Tourist Information Offices

Finistère
Comité Départemental du Tourisme
    du Finistère
34 Rue de Douarnenez
BP 125
29104 Quimper
☎ (98) 537272

Morbihan
Comité Départemental du Tourisme
    du Morbihan
Hôtel du Département
BP400
56009 Vannes
☎ (97) 540656

Ille-et-Vilaine
Comité Départemental du Tourisme
    d'Ille-et-Vilaine
1 Rue Martenot
35000 Rennes
☎ (99) 029743

Côtes-du-Nord
Comité Départemental du Tourisme
    du Côtes-du-Nord
1 Rue Châteaubriand
BP 620
22011 St-Brieuc
☎ (96) 616670

8 • Pays de la Loire

Pays de la Loire is one of the French regions that is something of a mish-mash. It is not an historical grouping of *départements*, and in many respects the historical ties of the *départements* pull in different directions. Indeed, the area that most people think of as the 'Loire Valley' mainly lies outside the 'Pays de la Loire' area! The Loire enters Pays de la Loire just east of Saumur, working its way through Angers and Nantes to the Atlantic Ocean just beyond St Nazaire. The region, though, is one of rivers, and both Sarthe and Mayenne, the two northernmost *départements*, are named after their respective rivers. Both flow into the Loire eventually. The Loire itself is a wide and dominating river as it passes through the region, with the result that in the summer it is full of sandbanks and is distinctly uninspiring, whereas in winter it is dark and foreboding.

There is little river traffic on the Loire itself, and it is out of bounds to hired pleasure craft. However, the other rivers in the area, and especially those in the old Anjou area — the Sarthe and the Mayenne — are extremely well suited to boating. It is possible to hire cruisers from a number of places, and British boat operators have a presence here. The roads are generally very quiet, except a few of the major ones, where freight lorries speed eastwards to Paris.

Whichever way you come into the region (unless you are coming from the south), you come firstly into the influence of **Le Mans**. The A11 motorway from Paris to Rennes runs around the city outskirts, crossed by one of the main routes southwards from the Channel Ports. All too often people drive around Le Mans, and certainly avoid what looks like, on a map, a daunting city centre. However, it's not too bad, and even parking is relatively easy. The old quarter is worth devoting some time to, set alongside the huge cathedral (St Julien), and overlooking the Sarthe.

There has been quite a lot of good restoration work, and many of the old houses contain studios or trendy shops, with prices only the French could charge. The hill down to the river is quite steep, with the result that there are a number of bridges and tunnels, which add an extra dimension to the exploration. As one would expect, Le Mans has a good range of hotel accommodation, which makes it a good base for touring. If you want to visit the famous racing circuit, it is some 4.8km (3 miles) south of the city, between the N158 and D139. There is an interesting car museum there too.

Head, however, west towards Mayenne. Much of the countryside bears resemblances to Normandy, and this is inevitable as it is an area of overlap. The route passes into, in fact, a regional park — that of Normandy-Maine. This is an ideal area for walkers, especially in and around the Sillé Forest, through which the road D35 passes, at **Sillé-le-Guillaume**. Once a northern stronghold of Maine, the town now relies much on the attractions of the Sillé Forest. It has a reasonable level of basic accommodation, and good facilities for walking and riding. The GR36 and 37 long-distance footpaths pass through the town and forest, offering good opportunities for the serious walker. Unfortunately the castle is not open to the public.

It is possible to keep within the regional park boundaries after Sillé, and make a pleasant exploration north-eastwards on byroads, keeping south of Alençon. This takes you through the picturesque Alpes de Mancelle (Mancelle Alps) around St Léonard-des-Bois to the Perseigne Forest. This forest is bisected by several pretty valleys covered in forest. There are several minor roads to help exploration, but it is an area to explore on foot, following the GR22 footpath or any of many waymarked paths. From Perseigne Forest, it is possible to head back to Le Mans, or up into Normandy.

The D35 from Sillé crosses into the Mayenne *département*, and passes through some pleasant countryside before reaching Bolis. Here take the D241 through Hambers to Jublains, where there are the remains of the Roman fort of *Neodanus*. It is possible to visit some of the remains, surrounded by a thick wall with towers. The fort seems to have been as strategic an importance in Roman times as Mayenne has been since. Mayenne is only a short distance from Jublains.

Mayenne sits astride the Mayenne River, and so has been of importance throughout the ages, even in World War II, when the town was badly damaged. The castle dates originally from the eleventh century, but was rebuilt in the fifteenth. Unfortunately, it is not open to the public. The church (Notre Dame) is early Gothic, but with considerable alterations since. The river was once navigable as far as Mayenne, but lack of use and maintenance led to regular closures. Today the river is navigable only as far as Laval, further downstream, although a project is underway to restore navigation to Mayenne.

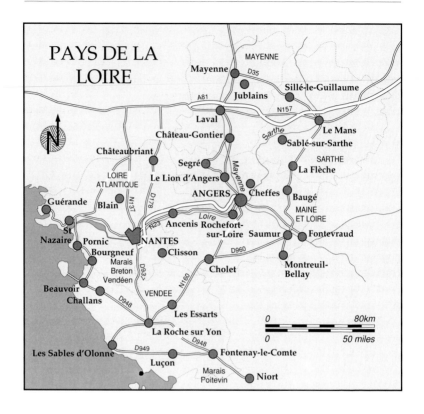

Just north of Mayenne the countryside again falls within the bounds of the Normandy-Maine Regional Park, but the bulk lies within Normandy. To the west of Mayenne is a stretch of forest, and one can make a pleasant drive by taking the N12 from Mayenne towards Fougères, but turning left into the forest just after La Meltière towards Chaillard. If one takes the D165 from Chaillard to Andouillé then the D101 to Monflours, it is possible then to turn southwards and follow a pretty route (D250/D162) along the side of the Mayenne to Laval. Alternatively, the N162 runs straight from Mayenne to Laval.

Laval sits astride the Mayenne, and is the county town for the Mayenne *département*. Laval has two *châteaux*, called appropriately enough the New Château (which now houses the Law Courts) and the Old Château. The Old Château houses a museum about the painter Henri Rousseau, who was born in the town. The old quarter has some impressive town houses and retains a medieval feel. The modern part of the town is on the opposite bank, and lacks any atmosphere. There is an interesting museum housed on a *bateau-*

lavoir (laundry boat) with various mementoes and artefacts. The quay also has a boat for trips along the river. A word of warning if you plan to stay overnight — the town is not far from the motorway, and so is popular with businessmen. It is worth booking ahead, or stopping to book something mid-afternoon, otherwise you may find everything full. And there is little else within easy striking distance.

Just south of Laval is the abbey of Port-du-Salut, founded in the thirteenth century, and renowned for its cheese. The licence was sold to a commercial company in 1959, but men (only) can visit the abbey. Following the Mayenne River downstream is possible by boat, car, or on foot, and almost the whole length to Château-Gontier is pretty. And even where the road moves away from the river, it is possible to drive down to riverside villages and hamlets, or to locks.

At Château-Gontier cross the river and take the D22 to Daon, a pretty road passing through fertile agricultural land. All the country-side around this area was home to a major Royalist uprising in 1793. Much of the west of France rose. The uprising in Maine became known as the Chouannerie, after the call signs the rebels made — that of an owl hoot (tawny owl = *chat-huant*). While the uprising in the Vendée — which we shall come to shortly — was organised, that of the Chouannerie was more along the lines of a guerrilla war with small disorganised groups. The type of countryside we are now in is known as *bocage* — small fields with plenty of hedges and woodland, and was ideal for this type of action.

After some initial success the Blancs (the 'whites' or Royalists) were relatively quickly put down by the Bleus (the 'blues' or Repub-licans), and thousands were shot or guillotined in the repression that followed. The Vendée held out somewhat longer. It is hard to imag-ine all that took place in this quiet countryside.

Across the river and about 4km (2 miles) south is Château le Plessis, a sixteenth- to eighteenth-century *château*, now a comfortable country hotel.

At Daon continue on the D22, but turn right into the heart of the countryside to Marigné, and then to **Chenillé-Changé**. This pretty village on the Mayenne has a water mill doing an impersonation of a small castle, but nice all the same. Continue to follow the river (D287) until you reach the D770. Before heading eastwards, a diver-sion is worthwhile into **Lion d'Angers**. This town is famous for its national horse stud (Haras Nationaux). Visits are possible by ad-vance arrangement. Otherwise take the D770 towards Châteauneuf, but turn off onto the D74 through Sceaux and Ecuillé to the Château du Plessis Bourré. This is a typical 'fairy-tale' *château*, in a light,

Château du Plessis Bourré

almost white, stone which is reflected in the still moat. Its relative isolation probably explains why it has survived relatively intact. The interior matches the exterior. Guided visits are available.

From the *château* head to **Cheffes**. For those who enjoy *châteaux*, or a nice hotel with a difference, the Château de Teildras is highly recommended; a sixteenth-century *château* now a 'country-house' hotel. Not the sort of place for a quick lunch! From Cheffes follow the river northwards — on either bank — to **Châteauneuf-sur-Sarthe**. Châteauneuf is a busy riverside town with simple hotel accommodation, some good restaurants, and a selection of shops.

Again follow the river, the best route being the D108 to Chemiré, then switching banks, the D159 to **Sablé-sur-Sarthe**. Sablé has some small hotels and plenty of shops but little character. Perhaps you get that impression because where you reach next is so overwhelming. From Sablé take the D138 the short drive to **Solesmes**. There is only one thing that people come to Solesmes for, and that is the abbey. Although founded in the eleventh century, the present buildings largely date from the late nineteenth and are quite austere.

However, one visits Solesmes to hear the Gregorian chant and it is possible to attend Mass and Vespers services. Solesmes is one of the places where the art of plainchant was rediscovered and restored, and so set the 'style' for others. There is a shop where you can buy records of the monks' singing as well as other items (women are allowed here!). Opposite the abbey is a good hotel, the Grand. For a good view of the abbey itself continue past the abbey, across the bridge and turn left into Port de Juigné. A left turn opposite a café takes you into a very small square beside the river. Alternatively, on crossing the bridge, bear right and continue as far as Juigné-sur-Sarthe, where you can park by an observation point. From Juigné take the D22, then a side road to Avoise. Follow the river through Parcé, which has some old houses overlooking the river and a riverside camp site. Cross banks here and follow the D8 to **Malicorne**. On entering the village, there is a pretty *château* with a moat (not open), and then a shady car park beside a mill on the river. A nice place to picnic, although there are a couple of restaurants in the village. There are several potters working here too. From Malicorne, one can head back to Le Mans, if required.

It is a short hop through the wooded countryside (D8/D12) to **La Flèche**, which is on the Loir (which, just to confuse you, is not the Loire). This important commercial town is dominated by the Prytanée Militaire. Founded as a Jesuit college by Henry IV, who spent his youth in the town, it is now a military college. The chapel (St Louis) looks relatively boring from the outside, but is dramatic inside with baroque decoration. There is limited hotel accommodation, but of a good standard. The town has a lot of woodland surrounding it, with waymarked paths, and the GR35 footpath runs just to the south, and through the town.

South of La Flèche, **Baugé**, now a small farming town surrounded by pleasant woodland, has several interesting buildings. The town hall is housed in what was the *château*; and the St Joseph *hôpital* contains its original panelled pharmacy, complete with a collection of various boxes and containers. The town's main claim to fame is housed in the Chapelle des Filles du Coeur de Marie (the Chapel of the Sisters of Mary's Heart). It is a cross, double armed, found in Constantinople in the thirteenth century and supposedly made with pieces of the True Cross. The double-armed cross became the emblem of the Dukes of Anjou (the Cross of Anjou), although the symbol is known today as the Cross of Lorraine. From Baugé it is possible to take a short drive along the Couasnon River, eastwards to Pontigné, where the church has some fine wall paintings. Slightly further east, at Noyant, walkers can pick up the GR36 footpath.

After Baugé the countryside begins to open up towards the Loire.

The water mill at Malicorne

The D938 goes to Longué, and then the N147 to Saumur. **Saumur**, of course, is a key town on the Loire, and so very much 'on' the beaten track for tourists. Its reputation — largely derived from its strategic position — is somewhat bigger than one would expect for the size of the town. There is a good level of hotel accommodation, which means that Saumur could be explored in the evening, after a day spent visiting the countryside. The castle, built of the local pale stone, looks most impressive.

Roads run along both sides of the Loire, although the south bank is by far the most attractive, and more interesting. From Saumur, one can also head south on the N147, into Poitou-Charentes, following more-or-less the valley of the Thouet. **Montreuil-Bellay**, about half-way between Saumur and Thouars, is a pleasant small town with two *châteaux* in one, and parts of the medieval town walls. Just east of Saumur is **Fontevraud**, reached on either the D145 through Fontevraud Forest or via the D947 along the Loire. The village is traditionally the meeting point of Poitou, Anjou, and Touraine. However, its main claim to fame is the great abbey, dating from the twelfth century, but partly rebuilt in the sixteenth. The Plantagenets were great patrons. The church (Notre Dame) is pure Romanesque and contains tombs of several Plantagenets, as well as monuments to Henry II (of England), Eleanor of Aquitaine, and Richard the Lionheart. The cloisters were rebuilt in the sixteenth century in a style reflecting the church, although one can see the influences of the period. The most surprising building is the kitchens, which looks like the top of a spire, with lots of chimneys sticking out. Return to Saumur either along the river or through the Forest. Alternatively, one can head eastwards along the Loire towards Chinon and Tours.

If one follows the Loire from Saumur, on the south bank, one quickly reaches **St Hilaire-St-Florent**, where much of the well-known Saumur wine is made and marketed. You can take your pick from the rows of shops all eager to sell their wares; or alternatively, see what the surrounding small farmers offer. Caves in the cliffs are known for storing wine, but they are also used for growing mushrooms, and the Mushroom Museum (Musée du Champignon) gives an insight into the industry. Before the caves were used for wine and mushrooms (and even afterwards), families made their homes in them. A detour across the countryside inland (D161 to Milly, then D69 and D177) to Rochemenier, offers the chance to visit a museum which shows what life was like for these peasant farmers. Quite different and highly recommended.

The road from St Hilaire continues through Chênehutte (which holds a Mushroom Fair in May) to **Cunault**. The church (Notre Dame) is very pretty, saved from total ruin in the nineteenth century. The carving is quite remarkable, especially inside on the capitals, which have all manner of scenes and monsters. At Gennes one can keep to the riverside road, through Le Thoureil and Juignes, to Ponts-de-Cé, or cut across country to Brissac-Quincé, which has a fine *château*, albeit a mixture of styles from medieval to seventeenth century. The *château* overlooks the large park. From Brissac it is only a short distance to Ponts-de-Cé and thence to **Angers**.

The pale stone that dominated building further back up the Loire, suddenly and dramatically gives way to a black shale in the *château* at Angers. Even when it is sunny it is difficult to drum up enthusiasm for Angers' *château*, overlooking the waters of the Maine, from which the old part of the town rises. Angers is a good touring base, with a reasonable selection of hotels. However, many of the town centre ones do not have parking facilities. The whole city can be explored on foot, with the main sights within easy reach of one another. Do not miss the quite outstanding tapestries in the *château*, dating from the fourteenth century, but almost lost in the Revolution. All good guidebooks cover the city well. A pleasant way to spend an evening

The château *at Serrant*

is to take a trip on one of the restaurant boats, operating from opposite the *château*. These provide a meal (rather expensive) and a guided trip along the river.

From Angers, it is possible to retrace one's steps to Saumur, but on the north bank of the Loire. Alternatively, one can head north to Le Lion d'Angers or Châteauneuf-sur-Sarthe. Angers was, of course, the capital of Anjou, and both west and south, the city is surrounded by the vineyards that produce the well-known Anjou *rosé* wines, although one does find sweeter wines to the south in Côteaux du Layon. It is westwards into the vineyards that the route now heads, taking the D111 to follow the Maine to its confluence with the Loire, and then crossing the Loire at Béhuard.

This arrives at **Rochefort-sur-Loire**, a pleasant village with old houses and a restored twelfth-century church. The D751 to Chalonnes is called the Corniche Angevine. It is cut into the cliffs overlooking the Loire flood plain, with some surprisingly dramatic views. Cross the Loire again at Chalonnes, and take the D961 northwards to **St Georges** (sur-Loire, it claims!) to visit the Château of **Serrant**, one of the finest in Anjou, which is just off the N23 towards Angers.

Whilst Serrant lacks the fairy-tale quality of other *châteaux* further up the Loire, it retains an elegant symmetry enhanced by the use of the dark shale and light tufa stone. It took over 100 years to build, so the style is all the more amazing in its consistency. It is possible to visit the interior (open daily, except Tuesday), which is well furnished, with some fine tapestries. From Serrant one can now return to Angers, or continue along the Loire towards Nantes.

As previously, it is possible to follow the river on the north or the south bank. The major towns and cities lie primarily on the north bank, so the main and consequently busier route (N23) follows the north side. The south bank retains a fair amount of character, and the roads are less busy and far prettier. One can cross the river at several places, so it is possible to swap sides regularly. Walkers can also follow the river, either by sticking to the roads, or by following the long distance footpath GR3 which switches from being close to the river to being further inland from time to time.

At **Ancenis** is the traditional border with Brittany, and the strategic importance of the town can be seen in its castle, although it has some sixteenth- and seventeenth-century additions. Return to, or cross to, the south bank of the Loire and continue along the D751 towards Nantes. The extent of the flood plain is quite extensive, and the river's rambling nature means that some of the area is quite marshy. After La Varenne cut inland to **Loroux-Bottereau**. The church has some superb frescoes, dating from the twelfth century, saved from a nearby chapel, including some of Charlemagne. It is now just a short hop to Nantes.

Nantes and Rennes have often been rivals as 'capital' of Brittany, although Nantes had more French influence in it than Breton, because of the Loire. Now Nantes, and its *département* of Loire-Atlantique, are in Pays de la Loire, Rennes is viewed as the 'capital', although many people in Nantes will still tell you they are Breton and proud of it. Nantes' prosperity was built on foreign trade, notably the golden triangle of slaves and sugar, and this prosperity, reflected in the private and public buildings, has to a large extent been preserved. The castle, the cathedral, and a fine selection of museums — especially the Fine Arts Museum — are well worth visiting. The city has a wide range of hotel accommodation, but as a touring base it is limited in scope, as the sights of Brittany and Vendée are just that little bit too far for comfort.

The D178 follows the Erdre River north-east out of the city, into some pleasant countryside, with evidence of ancient forest from time to time. At Corquefou it is possible to detour to Sucé, where the river broadens and there are lots of water-sports opportunities. Shortly before La Meilleraye is the Voireau Reservoir, which is a major feed for the Canal de Nantes à Brest, and the Voireau Forest. This is very much border country — between Brittany and Anjou — often fought over in late medieval times when Brittany, controlled by its dukes, sided with the English against Anjou, controlled by the French. As a result the style of building of *châteaux* in this area changes from *'château'* to castle, or at the least, fortified *châteaux* or manors. **Châteaubriant** is a good example, although the surrounding countryside can only hint at what it was like when places like the town controlled great areas of forest.

Châteaubriant is overlooked by its castle, and the changes in architectural style bear witness to its continued importance across the ages. The castle is open daily from mid-June to mid-September, except Tuesday. Of the older part all that remains are some of the ramparts, plus the huge keep. Opposite are the sixteenth-century Renaissance-style buildings built by Governor Laval which overlook some pretty gardens. East of the town are several large areas of woodland, ideal for picnicking. The D775 from Châteaubriant skirts across the northern part of the *département*, crossing the main road from Nantes to Rennes at Derval. At Guémené-Penfao, turn southwards to Blain on the D15. This goes through the Gâvre Forest — which offers many walking opportunities — to the Carrefour de la Belle Etoile. Here some ten roads and tracks meet up, so make sure you continue on the D15 down to Blain.

Blain town stands on one side of the Nantes to Brest canal, opposite the ruins of its castle (not open to the public). The canal towpath is ideal for serious walkers, and there are plenty of villages along the canal for provisions, as well as small inexpensive hotels and *gîtes d'étape*. From Blain skirt the bottom of Gâvre Forest on the D164, then turn on to the D2 across to **St Gildas**, a pretty village set in the woods with a twelfth-century church. Turn south here to Pontchâteau, which is just south of the main N165 dual carriageway that runs the length of southern Brittany. Take the D33 towards Herbignac.

A little way outside Pontchâteau is a fine calvary, called La Madeleine, with a Stations of the Cross stretching across parkland. The Calvary is the scene of regular pilgrimages, sometimes with people in traditional costume. Calvaries are relatively common in Brittany, with illustrations of the Passion either carved in the granite, or depicted with statues, beneath a crucifix. There is a good view of the surrounding countryside from a little further on. Continue along the D33 which now skirts the top of the Brière Regional Park, turning off the road to the Château de Ranrouët. This is quite an imposing castle dating from the late twelfth century and currently being restored. At Herbignac turn south to Guérande, on the D774, or on the prettier D47 and D51 which run along the western edge of the Brière.

Guérande is a quite remarkable town, retaining the complete run of city walls. Its wealth was largely built on salt from the salt pans to the south-west, but the town retains a great deal of character, especially during the summer period when cars are banned from inside the city walls (and consequently it can be fiendishly difficult to park!). It is possible to walk around the walls, which have four gates and six further towers. Alongside the tourist office there is a small museum (open April to September) in the main — St Michael's — gate, which has some interesting exhibits of local life. Inside the walls a rough grid pattern remains, with the church (St Aubin) in the centre. The church is a mixture of styles, and there is some fine stained glass.

The salt pans are just outside the town, centred upon **Saillé.** The bay where the pans are was turned into marsh by a change in sea level, and the area has been exploited since. The pans are formed by banks of soil, and the water level is controlled through a system of canals, so that only a shallow depth is left in the individual pans, or *'oeillets'*. As a result the salt from the sea water crystallises as the water evaporates. The salt is collected and left to dry out completely, before being left in huge piles at the edge of the pan. Saillé has a small museum (Maison des Paludiers, open June to September) showing artefacts and elements of the life of the salt workers. Immediately south of Saillé is the large popular resort of **La Baule**, with its superb beach and excellent facilities for all sorts of sports, including golf. There is a full range of hotels from small pensions up to the famous Hermitage, as well as self-catering villas and apartments.

The D92 from Saillé actually takes us the opposite direction, through the salt pans and then, after the small port and resort of La Turballe, along the increasingly rocky coast. There are some super views right along here. Continue through Piriac, another seaside town, along the coast road. This turns inland to go around a bay, and at St Molf head back towards Guérande. Then take the D51 to St Lyphard, and the Grande Brière Regional Park.

The Brière is a great area of marsh and bog, some 6,600 hectares (16,500 acres). Once a low forested basin, the area was flooded by the sea to create a marsh, and then the dying vegetation created peat bogs. From the Middle Ages the drainage has been improved, but the area, through whose heart no roads run, remains a haven for wildlife and waterfowl. The whole area was common land for all the local people, who until recently continued their traditional crafts of thatching, wickerwork and cutting peat. It is possible to take boat trips through the Brière from a number of places.

At **St Lyphard** it is possible to climb the church tower in July and August for a view across the Brière, as well as back towards Guérande. Continue along the D51 to Mayun, which is known for its wickerwork and baskets, then after following the D33 for about half a mile back towards Pontchâteau, turn right onto the D50. This road links the small islands that lie in the Brière. The most attractive is the Ile de Fédrun, which is just off the D50 near St Joachim. The road runs around the edge of the island. One of the thatched cottages is open to the public (open June to September), and retains a typical interior. The village holds a boat race during the local festival on 15 August.

Rejoin the D50 at the Ile de Aignac. At **Rosé** the Maison de l'Eclusier (former lock-keeper's house) which controlled the water level of the marsh, is open (June to September) with a display about the Brière. At Montoir it is possible to pick up the N171 back towards Nantes, or around St Nazaire to La Baule. Alternatively head towards the spectacular toll bridge across the Loire to the southern part of the *département*.

This modern toll bridge cuts out the long drive back to Nantes, and subsequently back again. However, if you want to head due south either way is practical. The toll bridge is a superb piece of engineering, and leads quickly into the flat countryside known as the Pays de Retz. Traditionally this has been the extreme southern part of Brittany, and it bears a number of resemblances to the Presqu'ile de Guérande, just north of the Loire. The area is today perhaps best known for the production of 'Gros Plant' wine, a dry white similar to Muscadet.

The coast is dotted with small seaside towns, many of which retain their character and life throughout the year, unlike say, St Jean de Monts. **Pornic**, just off the dual carriageway, is a case in point. A pleasant town, with a small fleet of fishing boats, it is set on the hillsides of a narrow inlet. It is best explored on foot, and there are some very pleasant walks alongside the sea (Les Corniches) and in the old part of the town. There are plenty of reasonable small hotels along this part of the coast too.

A little further down the main road is **Bourgneuf-en-Retz**, lying on the edge of a huge marshland area known as the Marais Breton-Vendéen, which extends as far south as the Vie River at St Gilles-Croix de Vie. It was once a huge bay, now drained and laid over to pasture. Unlike the Marais Poitevin further south, the image it presents is rather flat and stark, yet it does have a certain charm about it. Bourgneuf has a small, but interesting, museum of local history (open daily, except Tuesday), with exhibits of *coiffes* (lace head-dresses) and local life. The road divides here to either hug the coast, or head inland towards Machecoul (or alternatively back towards Nantes).

Whichever way is taken you cross the Marais. The drainage dykes are dotted with little huts with cranes and fishing nets. The farm-houses—known as *bourrines* —are unique to this area. The very low, single storey houses with thatched roofs are often surrounded by brown and white cows. The Marais marks the end of Brittany's traditional boundary, and the start of the Vendée. There is a change too in the architecture, and many say, in the climate. The Vendée, although it faces the Atlantic, does have a form of micro-climate with sunshine hours as good as the Riviera, and often temperatures not too far behind. Consequently, the coastal strip has seen considerable development, largely due to second homes of residents of Nantes. The result is that places like St Jean de Monts look like ghost towns for most of the year, and are impossible to get around in the height of summer! Even so, a number of towns have retained their character, and certainly inland little has changed.

Taking the coast road from Bourgneuf one reaches Beauvoir, where it is possible to make a detour to visit the island of **Noirmoutier**. For a long time Noirmoutier was only accessible at low tide, across a causeway. Today the visitor has the option of a toll bridge, but the causeway is more fun. Drivers should take note of the advice signs (in English) at Beauvoir about the tides. In spring and autumn the island has a pleasant character, especially with the blossom that abounds. As in Guérande, there are still a few salt pans active, and one can see the salt piled up alongside the pans from time to time. Part of the little museum at La Guérinière is devoted to the production of salt. After Noirmoutier the actual coastal strip is planted with forest, largely as a measure to hold the sand and dunes together. A good point to turn back inland towards Machecoul.

Machecoul, the historical 'capital' of Retz, and Challans, on the edge of the Marais, are fairly ordinary towns, with some tourist accommodation. **Challans**, though, undergoes a transformation on market day. The market is on Tuesdays, and is especially famous for its trade in ducks — get there early in the morning to sample a really good French market, full of local produce, sights, smells, and characters. Heading eastwards again, leaving the marshland area, the countryside takes on a more wooded and green flavour, and we pick up the main road heading south from Nantes to La Roche-sur-Yon (D753 then D937). Not far off this road is the Château de la Chabotterie, in fact a typical fortified manor house. (Take D18 from Les Lucs.) It was here that the leader of the Royalist uprising, Charette, was captured and imprisoned. There is an interesting museum about the uprising with uniforms and other exhibits.

La Roche-sur-Yon is the 'county' town of the Vendée, and is perhaps only remarkable for the fact that Napoleon decided to build the town from scratch, calling it, appropriately, Napoléon-Vendée. His grand design remains today, even if his name does not, except on the main square. The regional tourist office is just off the square, and the staff here are especially helpful, with plenty of information available. The town was built for strategic reasons, to control the subdued Vendée after the Royalist uprising. La Roche has, at its southern edge, an important stud farm, which it is possible to visit.

Heading north and eastwards from La Roche, one enters the heart of what is called 'La Vendée Militaire' — Military Vendée, although the area does extend outside the *département* itself. This was the location of the great Royalist uprising after the Revolution. The uprising is little known outside France, but it was an important episode in French history, as it sealed the fate of the Royalist cause.

After the execution of Louis XVI in January 1793, insurrection broke out in the area, largely as a reaction to the persecution of the clergy in what was a fiercely Catholic area; but no doubt egged on by the intervention of other European nations against France. The uprising covered much of the north-western corner of France, including Anjou where the uprising was known as the Chouannerie, but where action was dispersed. In the Vendée many of those who had fled Paris had gathered, along with the Catholic Royalist Army, so an ideal opportunity was presented which was taken. At first all went well for the Royalists, with the Army doing well at the eastern edge, while in the marshes and woodlands — the *bocage* — the tactics were of a guerilla-warfare style. The rebels adopted the symbol of the double armed cross with a heart, ironically still the symbol of Vendée today.

Within a couple of months the Republican forces (nicknamed the Blues) hit back in force, and after a major defeat at Chemillé the Royalists were pushed back, eventually into Maine and Brittany, where they fell apart in disorder. The Republican reaction followed with thousands of Royalist supporters shot or guillotined, and much of the Vendée was devastated. Even so, the uprising continued in the Vendée during 1794 and, despite a ceasefire, into 1795. The Royalists found their support diminishing, and eventually the Republicans succeeded in pacifying the whole region, having captured and executed the main leaders, notably Charette.

The countryside remains similar to how it was then, with narrow lanes, woods, and thick hedgerows, so one can get a good idea of what it was like. From La Roche head north-east along the N160 towards Cholet. **Les Essarts** has the ruins of a castle originally built in the eleventh century, rebuilt in the fifteenth and destroyed in 1794. It is open daily. Just after Les Essarts, pick up the N137 towards Nantes, but turn right on the D763 or D54 to **Clisson**, which was one of the key bases during the uprising and consequently suffered as a result. It was so well ruined that most people left.

It was rebuilt by the sculptor Lemot and architects the Cacault brothers who had returned from Italy, greatly influenced by what they had seen. As a result the town has an unexpected Mediterranean feel about it, which makes a walking tour quite enjoyable. Clisson was a border town controlled for a time by the Dukes of Brittany, so its *château* was important. The ruined *château* overlooks the Sèvre Nantaise River and is very attractive, with a moat which you cross to get in. North and west of Clisson is the main area for the production of Muscadet, a fine dry white wine, and there are plenty of opportunities for tasting and buying at shops or from individual producers.

From Clisson the road follows the Sèvre Nantaise (so-called to distinguish it from the Sèvre Niortaise in Charente-Maritime), towards Mortagne-sur-Sèvre. About 16km (10 miles) after Clisson, on the south bank of the Sèvre (follow D755 or N149 then D753) are the ruins of the Château de Tiffauges, once the home of Gilles de Rais. He was a nobleman who fought alongside Joan of Arc against the English. After Joan of Arc's death his extravagances used up all his fortune, and he turned to alchemy and devil-worship, sacrificing young children. Eventually hanged and burned, Gilles de Rais was (ironically) immortalised as Bluebeard in Perrault's fairytales. The *château* ruins cover a wide area, although the keep and one tower are the best preserved.

Mortagne-sur-Sèvre is set in a pretty location on the Sèvre River, and offers some reasonable hotel accommodation. Uranium ore was discovered close to the town, and so there are a number of mines nearby. From Mortagne head south-west on the N160 back towards La Roche. The countryside has changed significantly and is now much hillier, climbing up to Mont des Alouettes, where three windmills stand. Originally there were seven, and they were used during the Royalist uprising to send messages, different positions of the

sails representing different things. The view from the hill is spectacular, across the *bocage* countryside below, and the hills behind.

A little further on is Les Herbiers, and if one takes the D755 it is
possible to explore the hills. At **St Michel-Mont-Mercure** the church
tower can be ascended for a tremendous view — as far as the sea on
a good day. North of St Michel is the Château du Puy du Fou, which
has regular *son-et-lumière* presentations through the summer. Just
south of St Michel (about 4.8km, 3 miles, on the D26) is **Le Boupère**,
which has an interesting fortified church, which includes a guardroom on top of the tower. From Le Boupère cut across country to
Pouzauges, which is a pleasant old town, overlooked by the ruins of
another of Gilles de Rais's (Bluebeard) castles. There is another fine
view from the top of Puy Crapaud, a nearby hill, which encompasses
the whole of the Vendée.

From Pouzauges head southwards on the D752 to **Mouilleron-
en-Pareds**, birthplace of two great Frenchmen — George Clemenceau and Jean de Lattre de Tassigny. There are two museums
covering their lives in the town. Clemenceau, nicknamed 'The Tiger',
was the French Prime Minister who led them to victory in World War
I. De Lattre de Tassigny had a very distinguished military career
leading the French army, and receiving Germany's surrender for
France at the end of World War II. The road continues south towards
Fontenay-le-Comte, but turn off to Vouvant, whose church (Notre
Dame) has an exceptionally well decorated façade, more closely
allied with Poitou-Charentes.

Vouvant is at the edge of a large forest area — Le Forêt de
Mervent-Vouvant — where the river valleys have enabled dams to
be built for water reservoirs and to make electricity. It is possible to
drive through the forest, alongside the resulting lake, and there are
opportunities for boating and fishing, as well as lots of waymarked
paths. Follow the lake until you pick up the D65 to **Fontenay-le-
Comte**. Fontenay has a unique position, lying at the foot of the hills,
astride the Vendée River, reaching into the coastal plain and *bocage*
as well as the Poitevin Marshes (Marais Poitevin). The town is a good
touring base, with various hotels, and can provide a good introduction to the Vendée at the Vendée Museum, which has some very
interesting exhibits tracing the development of the region. Although
in the Vendée, and therefore the Pays de la Loire, the town has close
ties with Poitou, and was for a long time (and indeed is still regarded
as) the capital of Lower Poitou. The town reached its peak during the
Renaissance, consequently there is a considerable amount of Renaissance architecture, including in the church the Virgin's Chapel

(Chapelle de la Vierge), the Château de Terre-Neuve and many houses in the old quarter around the church. It is only a short hop into Poitou-Charentes from here, on the D745 to Parthenay, or the N148 to Niort. Immediately south of the town is the Poitevin Marsh (Marais Poitevin), divided into the 'dry' and the 'wet' marsh. It is possible to explore this area from Fontenay, but the 'wet' marsh is described in the details about Niort in the Poitou-Charentes chapter.

Now turn westwards and skirt the top of the marsh along the D949 to **Luçon**. It is, of course, possible to drive through the marsh area, as an alternative. Luçon now lies on the edge of the 'dry' marsh, but was once a sea port at the edge of the gulf that became the marsh. The city (for it has a cathedral) is best known for one of its bishops — Richelieu — who later became a cardinal and played an important role in the history of France. When he first became bishop in 1608 the city was recovering from the end of the Wars of Religion, and the cathedral and Bishop's Palace were in need of repair. Richelieu took all these problems in hand. The cathedral, dating from the twelfth century, has a mixture of styles, although the overwhelming one is Gothic. It is also possible to visit the cloisters of the Bishop's Palace, next to the cathedral.

Luçon is a good place from which to visit the 'dry', that is the chiefly drained, part of the Poitevin Marsh. The D746 southwards from Luçon quickly brings you into the marsh, which has very dark, almost black soil, and so is greatly used for growing cereal and similar crops, although there is some pasture. The D746 runs down to the sea at **L'Aiguillon-sur-Mer**. *En route* it passes the ruined Benedictine abbey of St Michel which was destroyed during the Wars of Religion. L'Aiguillon is actually set behind a line of dunes (now a bird reserve), but has everything one needs in a small seaside town. A little further along the coast is the pleasant seaside town of **La Tranche-sur-Mer**. Much of the hinterland here is used for horti-culture, especially bulbs, and La Tranche has a huge flower festival, called the 'Floralies' during March and April, with a parade of floats and other celebrations. Returning along the edge of the marsh (D747), the road passes through **Angles**. Stop to look at the church, where one of the gables carries a huge bear reputedly turned into stone by a local hermit. Take time too to visit **Moricq**, on the River Lay, just outside Angles. The fishing port here retains a large fortified watchtower. The road then turns back north to join the D949 towards Les Sables d'Olonne.

Anyone who enjoys gardens should make a point of visiting La Court d'Aron, which is on the D949 — you can't miss it. The gardens of the *château* (which can also be visited) have been transformed into a series of displays, which vary according to the time of year. It is especially beautiful in spring, and when the roses bloom. Continue on the D949 either back to Luçon, or on towards Les Sables d'Olonne.

The coast has a small number of towns, before reaching the popular town and resort of Les Sables d'Olonne. **Jard-sur-Mer** is very nice, with some hotel accommodation and a lot of villas. Next door, in **St Vincent-sur-Jard**, is the house to which Georges Clemenceau retired, and which is now a small museum. Just before Les Sables is **Talmont-St-Hilaire**, with its ruined *château* overlooking what was the port. **Les Sables d'Olonne** is a good stopping place, with a good range of hotel accommodation. The fishing port is always busy and bustling, and the area between the port and the beach, where most of the shops are, is being progressively pedestrianised. The town also has a large theatre, a casino, and all that one could need in a seaside town.

From Les Sables, one can return to La Roche-sur-Yon, and thence to Nantes, to continue into Brittany or Normandy, or eastwards up the Loire. Alternatively, one can retrace steps through Fontenay, and head into Poitou-Charentes.

Further Information
— Pays de la Loire —

Museums and Other Places of Interest

Angers
Château and Tapestries
Open: daily except holidays, 9.30am-12noon and 2-6pm.

St Maurice's Cathedral

Maison d'Adam
Rue St Aubin

Fine Arts Museum
Open: daily except Monday, 10am-12noon and 2-6pm.

Baugé
Croix d'Anjou
Chapelle des Filles du Coeur de Marie

Bourgneuf-en-Retz
Pays de Retz Museum
6 rue des Moines
Open: daily 10am-12noon, 2-5pm.

Brissac-Quincé
Château
Open: daily except Tuesday 9am-11.30am, 2-4.30pm.

Chabotterie
Château
Open: daily April-September, 10am-12noon, 2-6pm.

Châteaubriant
Château
Open: daily, except Tuesday, mid-June-mid-September, 10am-12noon, 2-7pm.

Court d'Aron
Gardens
Open: April-September, 10am-7pm.
Château interior open June-September, 10am-12noon, 2-6pm.

Les Essarts
Château ruins
Open: daily 9am-12noon, 2-6pm.

Ile de Fédrun
Chaumière Briéronne (thatched house)
Open: June-Sept, 10am-12noon, 3-7pm.

La Flèche
Prytanée Militaire

Chapel of Notre Dame des Vertus

Tetre Rouge Zoo

Fontenay-le-Comte
Notre Dame Church and Belfry

Château de Terre-Neuve
Open: June-Sept 9am-12noon, 1.30-7pm.

Vendée Museum
Opposite church
Open: Tues-Fri, 10am-12noon, 2-6pm.

Fontevraud
Abbey and Buildings
Opem: daily 9am-12noon, 2-6pm;
afternoons only October-March.

Laval
Old Château
Open: daily except Monday 9am-
12noon, 2-6pm.

Henri Rousseau Museum
Open: daily except Monday 9am-
12noon, 2-6pm.

Bateau-Lavoir Museum
Open: daily except Monday 9am-
12noon, 2-6pm.

Lion d'Angers
*National Stud (Haras Nationaux de l'Ile
   Briand)*
Advance permission is required to visit.

Montreuil-Bellay
Château
Open: July and Aug, 9am-12noon, 2-6pm.

Mouilleron-en-Pareds
Museum (Clemenceau)
Open: daily except Tuesdays and
public holidays.

Museum (de Lattre de Tassigny)
Open: daily except Tuesdays and
public holidays.

Nantes
Château
Open: daily except Tuesdays and
public holidays, 10am-12noon, 2-6pm.

Museum of Fine Art
Open: daily except Tuesday, 9am-
12noon, 2-6pm.

Local Art Museum
Open: daily except Tuesday, 9am-
12noon, 2-6pm.

Maritime Museum
Open: daily except Tuesday, 9am-
12noon, 2-6pm.

Plessis-Bourré
Château
Open: April-September, 10am-12 noon,
2-7pm, except Wednesday.

Port-du-Salut
Abbey
Open: daily 9am-6pm.

Puy-du-Fou
Château
Open: July-September 10am-12 noon,
2-6pm except Mondays. Regular *son-et-
lumière* presentations during the
season. Details from local tourist
offices, or at La Roche-sur-Yon.

La Roche-sur-Yon
The Stud (Haras)
Boulevard des Etas-Unis
Open: July-March 10am-12noon, 2-5pm.

Town Museum
Open: Tues-Fri 10am-12noon, 2-6pm.

Rosé
Maison de l'Eclusier
Exhibits about the Grande Brière
Open: daily June-September 10am-
12noon, 3-7pm.

Saillé
Maison des Paludiers
Open: June-September 2-6pm.

St Hilaire-St-Florent
Mushroom Museum
Open: March-Oct 10am-12noon, 2-6pm.

St Michel Abbey
Ruins
Open: July and August, Tuesday, Thursday, Friday, 10am-12noon, 3-5pm.

St Michel-Mont Mercure
Church Tower
Open: daily 8am-12noon, 2-5pm, except during services.

St Vincent-sur-Jard
Clemenceau's House
Open: daily except Tuesday 9am-12noon, 2-4pm.

Saumur
Château
Open: daily except Tuesday 9am-5pm.

Maison du Vin

Cavalry School Museum
Open: daily 9am-12noon, 2-6pm.

Tank Museum
Open: daily 9am-12noon, 2-6pm.

National Horse Riding School
Home of the famous Cadre Noir team.
Visits arranged by tourist office.

Serrant
Château
Open: daily April-October, except Tuesday, 9-11.30am, 2-6pm.

Solesmes Abbey
Church only open to the public.
Gregorian Chant sung at Mass (9.45am) and Vespers (5pm).

Talmont-St-Hilaire
Château
Open: March-Oct, 9am-12noon, 2-7pm.

Tiffauges
Château
Open: May-September, except Tuesday, 9am-12noon, 2-6pm.

Tourist Information Offices

Ancenis
Place du Pont
☎ 40 83 07 44
Open: daily except Sunday, 10am-12noon, 3-6pm.

Angers
Place Kennedy
☎ 41 88 69 93
Open: daily except Sunday 9.30am-12noon, 2-6pm.

Baugé
Hôtel de Ville
☎ 41 89 12 12
Open: daily except Tuesday 11am-12noon, 3-6pm.

La Baule
Place de la Victoire ☎ 40 24 34 44
Open: daily except Sunday, 9am-12noon, 2.15-6.30pm

Brissac-Quincé
Mairie ☎ 41 91 22 13
Open: daily except weekends, 10am-12noon, 3-6pm.

Challans
Rue de Lattre-de-Tassigny
☎ 51 93 19 75
Open: daily except Sunday and Monday, 9am-12noon, 2-6pm.

Châteaubriant
Rue du Château ☎ 40 81 04 53
Open: daily except Sunday, 9am-12noon, 2-6pm.

Rue Couéré
☎ 40 28 20 90

Château-Gontier
Mairie ☎ 43 07 07 10
Open: daily except Sunday, 10am-12noon, 2-6pm.

Châteauneuf-sur-Sarthe
Quai de la Sarthe
☎ 41 69 82 89
Open: daily except Sun and Mon morning, 9.30am-12.30pm, 2.30-6.30pm.

Clisson
Place Minage ☎ 40 54 02 95
Open: 9am-12noon, 2-6pm during July and August only.

Fontenay-le-Comte
Quai Poey d'Avant ☎ 51 69 44 99
Open: daily except Sunday 9am-12noon, 1.30-7pm.

Fontevraud
Hôtel de Ville ☎ 41 51 71 41
Open: daily 9.30am-12.30pm, 2-6pm.

Guérande
Tour St Michel
☎ 40 24 96 71
Open: daily June-September, 9am-12noon, 2-6pm.

Laval
Place de 11 novembre
☎ 43 53 09 39
Open: daily except Sunday, 9am-12noon, 2-6.30pm.

La Flèche
Place de Marché-au-Blé
☎ 43 94 02 53
Open: daily except weekends 9am-12noon, 1.30-5pm.

La Roche sur Yon
Galerie Bonaparte ☎ 51 36 00 85

Luçon
Place du Général Leclerc
☎ 51 56 36 52
Open: daily except Sunday, 9am-12noon, 2-6pm.

Le Mans
Place de la République
☎ 43 28 17 22
Open: daily 9am-12noon, 1.30-6pm.

Montreuil-Bellay
Mairie
☎ 41 52 33 86
Open: daily except weekends, 9am-12noon, 2-6pm.

Nantes
Place Commerce
☎ 40 47 04 51
Open: daily except Sundays, 9am-7pm.

Noirmoutier
Route du Pont ☎ 51 39 80 71
Open: daily except Sunday, 9.30am-12.30pm, 2-6pm.
Access either via the Gois causeway (see notices at Beauvoir), or via the toll bridge.

Pornic
Place Môle ☎ 40 82 04 40
Open: daily, 9am-12.30pm, 2-6pm.

Pouzauges
Mairie ☎ 51 57 01 37
Open: daily except weekends 9am-12noon, 2-6pm.

La Roche-sur-Yon
Rue Clemenceau ☎ 51 36 09 63
Open: daily except Sundays 9am-12noon, 2-6pm.

Les Sables d'Olonne
Rue du Maréchal Leclerc ☎ 51 32 03 28
Open: daily except Sunday 9.30am-12noon, 2-6.30pm.

Sablé-sur-Sarthe
Place Elize
☎ 43 95 00 60
Open: daily except Sunday 9am-12noon, 2-6pm.

Saumur
Rue Beaurepaire
☎ 41 51 03 06
Open: daily except Sunday 9.15am-12.30pm, 4-6pm.

La Tranche-sur-Mer
Place de la Liberté
☎ 51 30 33 96
Open: daily except Sunday 9am-12noon, 2-6pm.

9 • Touraine-Blésois-Orléanais

The French region of Centre-Val de Loire covers six *départements*.
In this chapter and the one that follows we narrow down that
region to two distinct areas, ignoring the *département* of Eure-et-Loir,
which is removed from the Loire, and adding the *département* of
Allier which actually forms the most northerly part of the regions
that form the Massif Centrale. At first sight this exclusion of Eure-et-
Loir is a strange omission, but the second river is the Loir, not the
Loire, and the country around Chartres, though beautiful, is different in character to the land of the châteaux to the south. In this chapter
we visit the country of the Châteaux of the Loire, following the river
through the *départements* of Indre-et-Loire, Loir-et-Cher, Loiret areas
normally named for the major cities of Tours, Blois and Orléans.

The region covered by the two chapters is about the same size as
Switzerland, making exploration no short journey. It seems strange
then that the region has recently decided to publish maps for the
cyclist, with day circuits and longer, linear routes between them. But
though large, Centre-Val de Loire is a very flat region and the bicycle
is a good means of exploring, especially for those wanting to get close
to the important wildlife areas of the Sologne and the Brenne, or just
wanting to be off-the-beaten-track. With little traffic on the minor
roads and the joys of riding through countryside in which fields of
poppies are separated by fields of cornflowers, cycling is an ideal
way to get about. For those who do not wish to travel with their own
cycles, the local Tourist Information Office will have details on cycle
hire.

Touraine: The Département Of Indre-et-Loire

Although its position, where Cher meets the Loire, has meant that
Tours has always been an important place, particularly when those
rivers were important trade routes, the prosperity of the city is
largely based on its having been a pilgrimage centre in medieval
times. The story is told of Martin, a Roman officer in the fourth
century, who cut his cloak in two so that he could give half to a

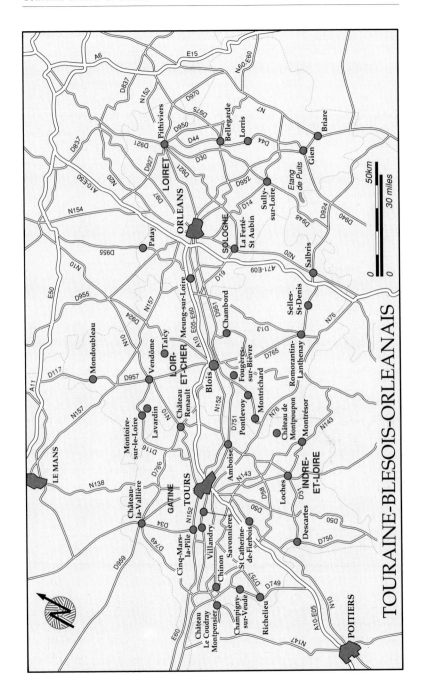

shivering beggar. That night Martin dreamt he saw Christ in the half-cloak: he became a Christian, founding the first monastery in France and becoming Bishop of Tours in AD372. He died in Candes in November AD397, and as his body was being rowed up the Loire back to Tours the trees burst into leaf, flowers bloomed and birds sang. As a result of this miracle the French have a St Martin's Summer rather than the English Indian Summer when warm, sunny weather arrives in early Autumn. Years after Martin's death, Clovis, leader of the Franks and a recent convert to Christianity, came to Tours to visit St Martin's tomb. As Frankish power grew so did the importance of Tours as a centre for pilgrimage and meditation. Gregory of Tours, elected bishop in AD573, made the city of centre for learning, and miracles recorded at St Martin's tomb made it a centre for healing.

Most visitors to the city assume that St Martin's tomb is in the magnificent cathedral, but it is not. A church was raised over the tomb in AD471, and this was replaced by another in the eleventh century. That church was partially destroyed by the Huguenots and eventually pulled down. Only in 1886 was a new church raised over the tomb. By then, however, only St Martin's arm remained in the tomb, his body — or what remained of it — having been desecrated by the Hugeunots in 1562. The new church, the basilica of St Martin, lies about 1km (½ mile) to the west of the cathedral in the Place de Châteauneuf. Opposite the new church is the Charlemagne Tower, built during the reign of Charlemagne and part of the older church. The tower partially collapsed in 1928, but has ben faithfully restored.

Although Tours is now a light industrial city, it is well-known to visitors to the Loire Valley, the cathedral and major museums being the chief attractions. But there are odd corners that are quiet and worthwhile. One, close to St Martin's basilica, is the Musée de Gemmail with an exhibition of contemporary stained-glass art housed in the nineteenth-century Hôtel Raimbualt an a twelfth-century subterranean chapel.

From the museum it is a short step to Rue Colbert which can be followed towards the cathedral. Number 41, a half-timbered house has a sign announcing *A la pucelle armée*, the armed maiden. This is reputedly the house of the armourer who made Joan of Arc's armour. Whether that story is true or not, the house is certainly an attractive one. The remainder of Rue Colbert is also very attractive, the street having some excellent restaurants. If you are trying one you must sample rillettes, fat pork cooked with salt, then minced. Rillettes can also be made from rabbit (*rillettes de lapin*) and goose (*rillettes d'oie*), and is a Tours speciality. *Quiche Tourangelle* is a *rillettes* quiche. Other items on the Rue Colbert menus that might be worth sampling are *porc aux pruneaux*, pork with prunes, and a fricasse of chicken in a white wine sauce with mushrooms and onions.

Leaving Rue Colbert along Rue Nationale the visitor can reach the Jardin de Beaune Semblançay by going through an archway near number 28. The courtyard is all that remains of a magnificent Renaissance mansion and chapel and includes a superb fountain constructed of white marble. The animals on the vase at the top are ermine, the emblems of Anne of Brittany. The mansion was built by Jacque de Beaune, Finance Minister under François I, who was hanged for treason.

Finally, and in keeping with the sadness of the courtyard, travel westward, across the city, to reach the suburb of La Riche and the Plessis-lès Tours Château. The château was built by Louis XI and it was here he died in 1483. Little now remains, and that is in brick, an odd material for a royal château, but what has survived includes the room in which the king died. Louis was a strange man, one who loved hunting but who made enemies easier than friends, and towards the end of his life was obsessed with the fear that he was being hunted. The château was ringed by iron fences topped with spikes and the grounds were patrolled by soldiers, armed with crossbows, who had orders to shoot intruders on sight. The king changed his valets frequently and sometimes disguised himself so he could wanter the château in secret listening to conversations, certain that people were plotting against him.

West of Tours is **Savonnières**, a village whose name is said to derive from the flowers *Sapanaria Offiinalis*, the delicate, pink flowered soapwort. The flowers, which still grow locally, were harvested by the Romans and used as soap. Presumably the Romans did not try to raise a lather from the water flowing in the caves at the western end of the village — on the D7 to Villondry — that water being very hard. The hardness, caused by calcium salts in solution, has created the *Grottes Petrifiantes*, where objects placed beneath cascading water-falls becomes encased in a layer of limestone so that they are turned to stone before the visitor's eyes. The caves have excellent stalactites and stalagmites, a collection of prehistoric animals and wine tasting.

The Loire leaves the *département* close to the **Avoine-Chinon** Nuclear Power Station. That might seem an odd choice for a holiday visit, but such a visit is instructive. The French see nuclear power in a quite different way than, say, the British, extolling the expertise of French engineers. A museum to the industry has been set up in the first reactor's building, with information on the later, still operating, station. The audio and display board information is in English as well as French.

A more conventional museum can be visited at **Chinon**, where the Musée Animé du Vin et de la Tonnellerie uses life-sized automatons to explain the process of wine and barrel making. This fascinating museum, which includes a collection of old equipment, is housed, appropriately enough, in an old wine cellar. The cellar is in Rue Voltaire one of the prettiest streets in a very pretty town, a town that is well worth a visit and a leisurely exploration on foot. Most visitors will want to visit the château. It offers a superb view of the old town, and its Great Hall was the scene of Joan of Arc's first audience with the Dauphin. Charles hid among the 300 courtiers in the hall, one of whom was dressed in his robes, but Joan went straight to him. Many saw this as proof of her sainthood, but there is a story that her recognition of the Dauphin was because she was of Royal descent having been fostered to Domrémy peasants because of the inconvenience of her birth. North of the château are the Clos de l'Echo vineyards, their name deriving from a local echo that was exploited by Chinon menfolk to the embarrassment of their womenfolk.

From Chinon a steam train runs southward, passing through **Champigny-sur-Veude** where the chapel is worth visiting, to reach Richelieu. The chapel served the now long-gone château and has some of the finest Renaissance stained glass windows in the Loire valley. The subject matter adds to the interest, including portraits of members of the Bourbon-Montpensier family as well as the more usual religious themes. **Richelieu** is named for Cardinal Richelieu who was responsible for the loss of Champigny château—he bought it, then pulled it down in order to use the stone to build the town he named for himself. Richelieu (born Armand du Plessis in 1585) created a model village, fully walled and entered through an elaborate gate, built on a grid plan. It is still a fine place, and a perfect example of seventeenth-century French architecture. The Musée de l'Hôtel de Ville, housed as the name implies in the Town Hall, deals with Richelieu and the village, and there is a fine statue of the Cardinal in the equally splendid Parc du Château.

To the east of Richelieu lies another village which shares its name with a famous Frenchman. Descartes was originally called La Haye, but changed its name in deference to René Descartes, born here in 1590, who become one of the greatest of all philosophers. His statement 'I think, therefore I am' has been much abused, but is still the only philosophical statement recognised by most laymen. There is a museum to the philosopher in the house in which he was born.

The Clock Tower at Amboise

Staying south of Chinon the visitor can journey to a little known château, a building that is less architecturally splendid, or as well furnished, as, the great châteaux of Chambord, Chenonceau, Cheverny and Azay-le-Rideau, but still very interesting. **Le Coudray-Montpensier** lies south of Seuilly and is unusual in being circular rather than the more conventional rectangle. The château was built in the fourteenth/fifteenth centuries by the Duke of Anjou, the name reflecting later ownership by Louis de Bourbon, the Montpensier family being a branch of the Bourbons. Today the château is a centre for handicapped children, only the surrounding parkland being open to the public.

Going east from Tours the visitor reaches **Amboise**, famous for its château, but interesting for the exhibition devoted to Leonardo da Vinci at the Manoir Clos-Lucé where the great man spent his last days. Leonardo was brought to Amboise by François I after the king had failed to persuade *The Last Supper* off its Milanese refectory wall. Leonardo came in 1516, arriving by donkey and bringing, among other works, the *Mona Lisa* which he hung in his studio on the first floor. Although Leonardo planned several engineering and architectural works in the Loire Valley, nothing specific has ever been identified as an Amboise work. Chiefly, it seems, Leonardo built extravagant models for the delight of the court. Leonardo died here in 1519, aged 67. Today the basement of Close-Lucé houses a collection of models made from Leonardo's drawings. The models include a helicopter and a parachute.

To the south of Amboise the visitor on the D31/N76 passes the glorious château of Chenonceau, once the home of Diane de Poitiers, mistress of Henri II. When Henri was killed in a tournament, Diane was thrown out of the château which, understandably, she adored, by Catherine de Medici, the king's vengeful wife. Continuing south the visitor passes **Montpoupon**, a château that combines a thirteenth-century castle with a fifteenth-century mansion. In the château both the kitchen and the laundry have been restored to their original form, and there is a small museum of hunting.

South of Montpoupon is **Montrésor** named for the treasure once thought to lie below the hillside. The village claims to be the most beautiful in France, and with its old houses and the delightful view of it across the River Indrois, it has a point. Close to the village is **Loches**, one of the best preserved of all small medieval French towns. The walk around the ramparts is a delight. From Loches, Tours is regained along the N143, though a westward detour to **Ste Catherine-de-Fierbois** is worthwhile to see the church, dedicated to the saint who was one of Joan of Arc's 'voices', close to which Joan found the rusting sword that she carried during her battles.

North of Tours, between the Loire and the Loir, is the **Gâtine**, an area whose name means devastated. Once this land was covered by forest, but this was hacked down to leave a windblown sandy soil that makes poor farming land. It is a neglected area, having none of the great châteaux and pretty villages of southern Touraine, but is excellent country for the walker, and does have one or two gems. To the west is **Cinq-Mars-la-Pile** named for one of France's least understood monuments, a tower that is 5m (16½ft) square and 30m (nearly 100ft) high and is topped by four pyramids. It is believed to be Gallo-Roman from the second century AD, but no-one can define its purpose. To the north of Tours is Château-le-Vallière, where the old Gâtine woodlands of oak and pine re-appear. Here there are forests to enjoy, heathland to explore and the Étang du Val Joyeux — Happy Valley Lake! — where the visitor can swim or enjoy a full range of water-sports.

Finally, we head east from **Château-la-Vallière**, taking the D766 to **Château Renault**, an old leather working town whose traditions are explored in a fine museum housed in an old tannery.

Blésois: The Département Of Loir-et-Cher

Blois, the city for which this area of the Loire valley is named, is only half the size of either Orléans and Tours, making it more 'manageable' for the visitor. But the site, on the northern bank of the river, is steep so that walks are for the keen (or the fit), and car parking can be a trial. Historically the town was the centre of a powerful duchy, the Counts of Blois numbering Stephen, King of England, among their heirs, and Blois being a royal city for many years in the fifteenth century. Louis XII was born here in 1462 and lived here with his wife, Anne of Brittany. The highlight of a trip to Blois is the château, a magnificent building which includes, in François I's external spiral staircase, one of the great architectural features of the Loire. But there are other, less well-populated, places in Blois. The Jardin du Roi, King's Garden, to the north-west of the château, though small is very elegant and offers superb views, both of the château and of Anne of Brittany's Pavilion. The Pavilion, built when Louis XII and Anne lived in Blois, is a fine building now occupied by the town's Tourist Information Office.

Elsewhere, it is best just to wander the steep streets of medieval houses. Inevitably such wanderings reach the Denis Papin Steps. Papin was born in Chitenay, near Blois, in 1647, but because of his Huguenot parentage he left the city to work in England and Germany. He was something of a polymath, being a trained doctor but an engineer by inclination. In England he invented an early form of pressure cooker and experimented with steam power some 100 years before James Watt. In Germany he built the world's first steam driven boat, but when this was tested on the River Weser the local fishermen, fearful of their livelihoods, destroyed it. A heartbroken Papin returned to England where he died in poverty. Now the city of his birth has honoured him with steps, a road name and a statue. The somewhat fanciful named Maison Denis Papin — a very beautiful house that spans the road — can be found near the city's cathedral. Close by is the Maison des Acrobates, a fifteenth-century house with a half-timbered façade on which are carved medieval acrobats and jugglers. The cathedral, dedicated to St Louis, stands on the site of an old church dedicated to St Soulaine, a Frankish monk. The story is told that due to a misunderstanding of the name, the church was a pilgrimage centre in medieval times. The misunderstanding was over St Soulaine and *Se Soûler* (to get drunk) the pilgrims being alcoholics seeking salvation from the demon drink!

South-eastwards from Blois are the châteaux of Cheverny and Chambord, two more highspots of a trip to the Loire valley. **Chambord**

The magnificent external spiral staircase of the Château François I in Blois

can also be visited by those going off-the-beaten-track as the château stands in a magnificent park that can be explored on foot. At several points hides have been constructed and from these the visitor can watch for deer, wild boar or the local bird life.

South of another fine château, that of Chaumont-sur-Loire is the village of **Montrichard**. Montrichard is a good place to see troglo-dyte houses, the name given to dwellings dug out of the soft limestone rock through which the Loire and its tributaries have carved a passage. Occasionally, entire villages were created by quarrying, chimneys having been built from finished blocks of stone. In places some of the houses are still inhabited, but between Montrichard and the neighbouring village of Bourré the old houses have been turned into wine cellar and mushroom 'farms'. The wine is chiefly sparkling made by what is known as the champagne method. Presumably to actually call Touraine sparkling wines 'cham-pagne' would be an infringement of copyright or *appellation*. As an aside, one of the best wines, Monmousseeau's *Cuvée JM93*, is so called because the company was founded by J.M. Monmousseau who lived to be 93 and claimed never to have drunk anything else!

Not surprisingly, in view of the mushroom caves, many of the restaurants of Montrichard include dishes seasoned with mush-rooms. The best restaurants, and the best of the old village, are to be found close to the beautiful, half-timbered Maison Ave Maria which now houses the Tourist Information Office. The best view of the town is from the old castle, of which only the keep and a section of wall remains. The castle can be approached along Rue de la Brèche, named for the breach in the walls created when French soldiers dug under them during Philippe-Auguste's siege of Richard Coeur de Lion. The French soldiers tunnelled under the walls, supporting their tunnel with wooden props which they then set alight. The collapse of the tunnel brought the wall down.

East of Montrichard, in the country that lies south of Blois, between Montrichard and Romorantin-Lanthenay, there are a number of excellent places to visit. At **Pontlevoy** an abbey was built in the eleventh century, almost destroyed during the Hundred Years War and partially rebuilt in the eighteenth century. Today it houses the Musée Municipal and the Musée du Poids Loirds. The first includes a collection of early advertising material of the Poulain chocolate factory in Blois. Auguste Poulain who founded the factory was a Pontlevoy man. There is also a superb collection of photographs of the village taken in the period 1902-1960. The second museum is devoted to the history of road transport, a collection of trucks and lorries being somewhat incongruously housed in the old stables.

The **Château de Gué Péan**, near the village of Monthou-sur-Cher, is beautifully positioned at the edge of the woodland, and there are good opportunities for picnics in the grounds. The château is roughly rectangular, with conical-roofed towers at three corners and with a

Montrichard as many unusual troglodyte houses

curious bell-shaped roof on the tower of the fourth corner. The main buildings are Renaissance in style and reached by a stone bridge over a dry moat. The rooms are furnished in Louis XV and Louis XVI style. It was here that Henry VIII's sister, Mary of York, married the Duke of Suffolk after the death of her husband Louis XII.

To the north, near the village of Cellettes, is the **Château de Beauregard**. Beauregard is set in wonderful parkland at the edge of the very fine Forêt de Russy, and looks extremely impressive when approached. But despite its elegant lines — particularly of the Renaissance entrance courtyard — it is the interior that holds the attention. The first floor gallery has over 300 portraits, while the Cabinet des Grelots, on the same floor, has some remarkable wood-carving by the Italian artist Scibec de Carpi who also worked at Fontainebleu. The name of the room derives from the three gold bells (*grelots*) that formed part of the coat of arms of the Beauregard family.

Between these two châteaux there is a third at **Fougères-sur-Bièvre**, a near perfect medieval castle saved from 'restoration' by the indignity of having been used as a spinning mill and allowed to fall into disrepair. From the village take the D7 towards Fresnes to find the Château de Roujoux, a theme park with picnic sites, children's play and games area, a *créperie* and a museum where puppets act out the history of the castle.

Romorantin-Lanthenay, a town which thankfully reduces its name to Romorantin most of the time, is the largest town of the Sologne, an area of country that will be explored in the Orléanais section of this chapter. In the town the visitor can learn about the Sologne at the museum devoted to it in the Hôtel de Ville and also follow the history of Matra racing cars at the Musée Municipal de la Course Automobile. Included in the museum are Matra's Formula One cars, including the one in which Jackie Steward won the 1969 World Championship.

The town has a pretty old quarter — in the area to the west of the Hôtel de Ville — and a splendid park, Square Ferdinal Buisson, which includes several islands in the River Sauldre, interconnected by footbridges. The old building on the smallest, southernmost, island was once a fulling mill.

On a completely different front, Romorantin was the setting for the introduction of beards into the French court, the story going that in 1521 François I was hit on the head by a carelessly thrown lump of wood during the Epiphany celebrations. His head was shaved to attend the wound and the king grew a beard to compensate, though it is not obvious why this should be seen as compensation. Everyone else followed suit, of course, and beards became *de rigeur*. Another royal connection is that the *Reine Claude* was born here, a plum named after François' wife, Claude who was born in the town. The plum was later introduced to England by Sir William Gage, and called the greengage. Another culinary story tells of the sisters Tatin who owned a hotel in town and who produced the first upside down fruit pie, the *Tatin*. It is still possible to buy tarts to the 'original' recipe in the town.

Going east from Romorantin along the D724 the visitor soon passes through **Selles-St-Denis** where the church has fourteenth-century frescoes depicting the life of St Genoulph, to whom it is dedicated. Since *genou* is 'knee' in French, the saint is claimed to have the power to heel leg problems, and sufferers still travel to the village to seek his help. Beyond the village is **Salbris**, of little interest except as a centre for trips into the Sologne forest, and as a terminus for the private railway that runs to Romorantin, a railway that is worth riding just for the views of the forest.

To the north of Blois the country is a little uninspiring, but there are a couple of places worth seeking out. **Talcy**, on the D15 north of Mer, is a quiet little village with a sixteenth-century château set on the street. It is a pleasant, if plain, building with a superb sixteenth-century circular dovecote topped by a conical roof with gabled entrances. When in use it held 1500 pigeons. There is also a superb sixteenth-century wine press that is still in working order.

To the west is **Vendôme**, a small industrial town. Here the novelist Balzac went to school: he hated it. The town's Holy Trinity Abbey, one of the finest Gothic buildings in the Loire Valley, was built after the Anjou Count Geoffrey Martel saw three fiery swords plunge into a fountain one night. The small museum in the abbey is mostly of religious art, but includes Marie-Antoinette's harp, an oddly poignant memento. The view of the abbey from the ruinous old castle is excellent, as are the walks on the wooded hillside beside the castle.

From Vendôme the Loir valley can be followed westward, passing through **Rochambeau**, a village with troglodyte houses, **Lavardin** which has beautiful old houses, a fine church and the interesting ruins of an eleventh-century castle, and **Montoire-sur-le-Loire** where the chapel of St Gilles has some superb twelfth-century frescoes.

Finally, travel to the north of the *département*, to **Mondoubleau** a village dominated by the ruins of a castle built in local red sandstone. There are some very old (fifteenth century) and pretty houses in the village, but the real delight is to walk along the Grand Mail, an avenue of trees reached from the public gardens. From this delightful walk there are superb views of the valley of the River Grenne.

Orléanais: The Département Of Loiret

There are more than thirty cities in France that are bigger than **Orléans**. Joan is encountered so often in the area around Orléans that it is easy to assume that her story is well-known, but apart from the fact that she lead an army against the English and the appalling way in which she died she is relatively unknown. As Orléans was the scene of her greatest triumph it is a good place to search out the real Joan.

Orléans was besieged by the English in the summer of 1428, after they had subdued the Loire valley downstream, and cut off the town from supply by river or land. By April 1429 the situation was desperate, the town's garrison close to surrender. It was at this time that Joan left her Domrémy home and went to see the Dauphin at Chinon. She was given a suit of armour, but no official position, and when she crept into Orléans on 29 April she was met with scepticism by the commanders even though the townsfolk were overjoyed. Friction between herself and the Orléans commanders continued, but despite it Joan was able to defeat the English force in the fortress of Les Tourelles and to lead an army that pushed them out of the Loire Valley. Joan then forced the Dauphin to accept the crown of

France — he was crowned on 17 July 1429 — and attacked Paris. Here myth and reality part company again, because the attack failed, Joan being wounded, and a further series of defeats left the army disillusioned with her. Soon she had been captured by the Burgundians, allies of the English, handed over to the English and been tried as a witch. She was burnt at the stake on 30 May 1431, barely 2 years after the start of her campaign, and having spent many months in captivity. It could be argued, and frequently is, that despite her limited success the very fact of her success was sufficient to goad the French into forcing the English from their country, although it was nearly 25 years before the Hundred Years War ended. Joan was a strong political symbol and has remained one ever since, the fact that she operated without official approval conveniently forgotten. She is now also a religious symbol, though she was, in fact, only sanctified in 1920. Unquestionably she was a remarkable woman.

Joan's Orléans was a much smaller place than today's city, occupying the north bank of the Loire around Pont George, which has replaced the bridge which once led to Les Tourelles. Within the city there is a superb stained glass window to Joan at the cathedral, showing her final minutes at the stake, a statue of her praying at the Town Hall, a fine equestrian statue in the Place du Martroi and a plaque near to the spot where the Les Tourelles fort stood. Within the old town are Maison Jeanne d'Arc (which, appropriately enough, stands in a square named for that other French political icon, General de Gaulle) and the Centre Jeanne d'Arc which is actually in Rue Jeanne d'Arc. Joan's house is well worth visiting: though not original it is a faithful reconstruction of the house of Jacques Boucher in which Joan stayed in 1429. History is reproduced by way of excellent dioramas. The centre is more for the serious historian, with a library of books and microfilms and other historical records.

To round off this short trip to Orléans use Pont George to cross the Loire. Before doing so, take a look at the cathedral of Ste Croix. Marcel Proust called it the ugliest church in France: others see elegance in the intricately fluted twin towers and elaborate west front.

Beyond Pont George is the wealthy suburb of Olivet and the superb park of La Source. This beautiful park covers about 30 hectares (75 acres) and has something for everyone: there are formal terraced gardens, rock gardens and 'wild' woodlands, all alive with flowers. There is also a fine lake and a rose garden with over 400 varieties. To complete the park the Loiret springs within it, and flamingoes and deer roam free.

South of Orléans is the **Sologne**, an area neglected not only by foreign visitors to the Loire valley, but also by French visitors. The area's name is thought to derive from the Latin for rye, the land having been drained and cultivated in Roman times. However, the underlying clay holds water extremely well and if the land is not actively drained it tends to revert to its marshy state. It was prosperous when the Loire was the royal playground, but a series of tax revolts in the late seventeenth century led to brutal suppressions and the Sologne became an impoverished area again. Today it is a mix of pleasant arable land, marshland, with some fine lakes, and forest. The area is rich in wildlife with otters and beavers among the animals, black woodpeckers, bitterns, golden orioles, black terns and whiskered terns among the birds and an abundance of flowers and butterflies. Access to the countryside was once extremely limited, walkers being liable to abuse from landowners or frought meetings with hunters. But things are improving, with numerous waymarked paths giving reasonable access. If you are venturing into the woods or marshes please keep to the paths. The history of the Sologne is well illustrated in the Sologne museum at Romorantin-Lanthenay.

Within the Sologne there are few specific highlights — apart from these offered by quiet exploration on foot. The **Etang du Puits** between Argent-sur-Sauldre and Cerdon-du-Loiret is a superb lake set among oak and pine woods and offering a range of water sports as well as a beach. For children there are pedaloes and a good playground. At **La Ferté-St-Aubin** there is a beautiful moated château comprising two parts, a small sixteenth-century building linked to a larger seventeenth century one. The château is furnished in eighteenth-century style and includes a small museum to horses and horse riding. Outside, the stables and saddlery can be visited and there is a children's zoo and model farm.

Another fine château is to be found at **Sully-sur-Loire**. The château stands at the confluence of the River Sange with the Loire, using the river as a natural moat, a fact that greatly enhances its beauty. It was at Sully that Joan of Arc persuaded the Dauphin to accept the crown of France after she had won the battle of Patay. Another visitor here, but three centuries later, was the writer Voltaire who spent many summers as the guest of the Duke of Sully. Within the château the upper hall of the keep is claimed to have the finest medieval wooden roof in France.

Upriver from Sully is **Gien** whose leather fair is thought to date from the sixth century. Gien is a pleasant town, dominated by the belfry of the church and château. The latter houses the International Hunting Museum, an environmentally unsound collection in these

A colourful tram in the superb La Source park at Orléans

green days, but one which does have the merit of looking at hunting from prehistoric times and including such items as paintings of hunting scenes and medieval weaponry. Sadly the obligatory trophy room is also present. Of more general interest is Gien's Pottery and Pottery Museum. Technically the Gien factory manufactures faience, earthenware with a white tin glaze that is hand painted. Faience has been made in the town since 1820, Gien having been ideally suited to the trade because of local deposits of clay and sand. During the latter years of the nineteenth century Gien-ware became popular because of a new technique which produced a deep blue colour. The museum on the site displays pieces in *bleu de Gien* as well as other items from the factory's production since 1820.

Close to Gien, at **Briare**, is the Pont-Canal, an aqueduct has Eiffel's touch, however: note the elegant lines and the use of wrought iron. The aqueduct is still in use and visitors can take the *bâteau mouche* which is both a delightful way of seeing the Pont-Canal and the local countryside and a very fine floating restaurant.

Heading north from Gien, the D44 skirts the Forêt d'Orléans to reach **Lorris** where there is a beautiful sixteenth-century oak-roofed market hall. Beyond, and still on the D44, is **Bellegarde** where the château is worth visiting for the views across the moat, now a fine pond, and the rose garden. North again is **Pithiviers** a town with a pretty, old centre and a museum of railway transport housed in an old station. The old line carried passengers and sugar beet to the local refinery. The museum includes old rolling stock and other railway memorabilia.

Finally, head back towards Orléans, passing through **Patay**, which lies to the north-west of the city. Here Joan of Arc fought, and won, her most decisive battle against the English. Southward from here the D3 can be followed to **Meung-sur-Loire** and a final Loire château. The château is a mix of styles having started life as a twelfth-century fortress and ended it as an eighteenth-century mansion. For many years it was the residence of the Bishops of Orléans, and after a tour of the above-ground buildings the visitor can proceed underground to see how those venerable gentlemen dealt with religious prisoners. There are dungeons and, worst of all, the *oubliette*. This is a cone-shaped well, prisoners being lowered on to a shelf half-way down and left there. Every day bread and water were lowered by rope, the quantity never changing so that if there were many prisoners starvation or thirst accounted for some: the food ration then went further. Any prisoner who fell off the platform was unable to climb up the sloping wall, even if he survived the fall. Only death came to the rescue of the occupants of the *oubliette*.

The tour of Loiret by wandering through the picturesque streets of old Meung. The old market is a delight and from it narrow lanes follow Les Mauvas, a series of streams that run down to the Loire. Following one of the streams is a good way to end a visit.

Further Information
— Touraine-Blésois-Orléanais —

Museum and other Places of Interest

Amboise
Le Clos-Lucé Manor/Leonardo Exhibition
Open: January to March daily 9am-6pm. April to mid-October daily 9am-7pm. Mid-Oct to December daily 9am-6pm.
☎ 47 57 62 88

Avoine-Chinon Nuclear Power Station
Station: Open: all year, Monday-Friday, guided tours at 9.15am and 2pm. Book in advance, take passport or other proof of identity.

Museum
Open: all year, Mon-Fri 9-10.30am, 2-3.30pm. Saturdays (May-October) 9-10.30am, 2.45-4.15pm. Saturdays (Nov-April) 2-3.30pm. Apply in advance ☎ 47 98 97 07

Chinon

Wine and Barrel Making Museum
12 Rue Voltaire
Open: April to September daily except
Thursday 10am-12noon, 2-6pm. October
daily except Sunday 10.30am-12noon.
☎ 47 93 25 63

Château
Open: January to mid-March daily
9am-12noon, 2-5pm. Mid-March to
June daily 9am-6pm. July and August
daily 9am-7pm. September daily 9am-
6pm. October daily 9am-5pm. November and December daily 9am-12noon,
2-5pm.
☎ 47 93 13 45

Château de Beauregard

Open: January to March daily except
Wednesday 9.30-11.45am, 2-4.45pm.
April to June daily 9.30-11.45am, 2-
6.15pm. July and August daily 9.30-
11.45am, 2-6pm. September and
October daily 9.30-11.45am, 2-6pm.
November and December daily except
Wednesday 9.30-11.45am, 2-4.45pm.
☎ 54 70 40 05

Château de Gué Péan

Open: Jan to March daily 10am-5pm.
April to September daily 9am-6.30pm.
Oct to Dec daily 10.30am-3.30pm.
☎ 54 71 43 01 or 54 71 46 09

Château de Meung-sur-Loire

Open: Jan to March, Sat, Sun 10-
11.30am, 2-5pm. April to June daily 10-
11.30am, 2-5.30pm. July to mid-Sept
daily 9am-5.30pm. Mid-Sept to mid-
October, Sat, Sun 10-11.30am, 2-5pm.
☎ 38 44 36 47

Château du Sully-sur-Loire

Open: March and April daily 10am-
12noon, 2-5pm. May to mid-June daily
10am-12noon, 2-6pm. Mid-June to mid-
September daily 10am-6pm. Mid-
September to October daily 10am-
12noon, 2-6pm. Nov daily 10am-
12noon, 2-5pm.
☎ 38 36 36 86 and 38 36 25 60

Descartes

Descartes Museum
29 Rue Descartes
Open: all year daily except Tues 2-6.30pm.
☎ 47 59 79 19

La Ferté-St-Aubin

Château/Musée de Cheval/Farm
Open: mid-March to mid-November
daily 10am-6.30pm.
☎ 38 96 52 72

Fougères-sur-Bièvre

Château de Roujoux/Theme Park
Open: April to August daily 11am-6pm.
☎ 54 79 53 55 and 54 79 53 39

Gien

Château/International Hunting Museum
Open: mid-February to April daily
except Monday 10am-12noon, 2-5pm.
May to September daily 9.30am-
6.30pm. October to December daily
except Monday 10am-12noon, 2-5pm.
☎ 38 67 69 69

Pottery/Pottery Museum
78 Place de la Vietaire
Open: January to June daily 9-11.45am,
1.45-5.45pm. July and August daily 9-
11.45am, 1.45-6pm. September to December daily 9-11.45am, 1.45-5.45pm.
☎ 38 67 00 05

Montpoupon

Château
Open: April to mid-June, Sat, Sun 10am-
12noon, 2-7pm. Mid-June to end June
daily 10am-12noon, 2-7pm. July and
August daily 10am-7pm. September daily
10am-12noon, 2-7pm. October, Sat and
Sun 10am-12noon, 2-7pm.
☎ 47 94 23 62 or 47 94 30 72

Orléans

Joan of Arc's House
Place du Général de Gaulle
Open: January to April daily except
Monday 2-5pm. May to September
daily except Monday 10-11am, 2-6pm.
October to December daily except
Monday 2-5pm.
☎ 38 42 22 69

Joan of Arc Centre
Rue Jeanne d'Arc
Open: all year Monday to Friday 9am-
12noon, 2-5.30pm.
☎ 38422269

La Source Park
Open: April to mid-November daily
9am-6pm. Mid-November to March
daily 2-5pm.
☎ 38 63 33 17

Pithiviers
Railway Museum
First Sunday in May-last Sunday in
October Sunday 2.30-6pm.
☎ 38 30 50 02

Pontlevoy
Old Abbey, Municipal Museum, Museum
of Road Transport
Open: April to June daily except
Monday 10am-12noon, 2.30-6.30pm.
July and August daily 9.30am-7pm.
September and October daily except
Monday 10.30am-12noon, 2.30-6.30pm.
☎ 54 32 60 80

Richelieu
Town Hall Museum
Open: Jan to June, Monday, Wednes-
day to Friday 10am-12noon, 2-4pm.
July, August daily except Tuesday
10am-12noon, 2-6pm. September to
November, Monday, Wednesday to
Friday 10am-12noon, 2-4pm.
☎ 47 58 10 13

Romorantin-Lanthenay
Sologne Museum
Hôtel de Ville
The museum is under refurbishment at
the time of writing and will open again
in 1994.
☎ 54 76 07 06 for details of opening times.

Matra Racing Car Museum
29-31 Fbg d'Orléans
Open: mid-June to mid-October daily
except Tuesday 10-11.30am, 2-5.30pm.
☎ 54 76 07 06

Savonnières
Grottes Petrifiantes
Open: Feb, March daily 9am-12noon, 2-
6.30pm; April to Sept daily 9am-7pm; Oct
to mid-Dec daily 9am-12noon, 2-6pm.

Château de Talcy
Open: January to March daily except
Tuesday 10am-12noon, 2-4.30pm. April
to September daily 9.30am-12noon, 2-
6pm. October to December daily except
Tuesday 10am-12noon, 2-4.30pm.
☎ 54 81 03 01

Tours
Gemmail Museum
7 Rue du Murier
Open: mid-March to mid-October,
Tuesday to Sunday 10-11.30am, 2-6pm.
☎ 47 61 01 19

Avoine-Chinon Nuclear Industry Museum
Open: all year Monday to Saturday 9-
10.30am, 1.45-3.15pm.
☎ 47 98 77 77

Vendôme
Abbey Museum
Open: all year daily except Tuesday
10am-12noon, 2-6pm.
☎ 54 77 26 13

Tourist Information Offices

Indre-et-Loire
Rue de Bouffon
37032 Tours
☎ 47 31 48 05

Loir-et-Cher
11 Place du Château
41000 Blois
☎ 54 78 55 50

Loiret
8 Rue d'Escares
45000 Orléans
☎ 43 54 83 83

10 • Berry-Bourbonnais

To the south of the Loire the land changes character again, Berry being a very specific part of the region of Centre-Val de Loire. In this chapter Berry is covered, taking in the *départements* of Indre and Cher. To these are added the Bourbon *département* of Allier. Technically Allier belongs to the Massif Central, the regions of the Auvergne, the Cévennes and Lanquedoc-Roussillon, but it is quite different from that land of high hills and raised plateaux. In character it is similar to Berry, the three *départements* forming the unique whole of Berry-Bourbonnais.

Geologically Berry is the transitional area between the Paris Basin and the Massif Central, a land of limestone overlaid by later clay deposits, a land where grain growing areas are interspersed with pockets of more ancient forests and wetland. To the south-east the Bourbonnais continues the trend, though here the fields are given over to more general agriculture. Here, too, there are fine patches of woodland, though there are fewer lakes and nothing to compare with the wetlands of the Brenne Regional Park.

This chapter we start in the west, south of Tours, heading east to the border of Burgundy before turning southward to visit the birthplace of the Bourbons.

Indre

Visitors heading south from Blois on the D956 cross into Berry beyond Selles-sur-Cher, the road soon cutting through the eastern edge of the fine Forêt de Gâtine to reach the town of **Valençay**. As the town is approached its superb château is glimpsed through the trees. Though well-known, the château demands inclusion as an off-the-beaten track site because it rarely appears on the itinerary of the Loire châteaux visitor, being too far to the south for most visitors.

The château was started in the mid-sixteenth century on the site of a former house, by a family whose sons had the happy knack of marrying heiresses and, in consequence, could afford to use the

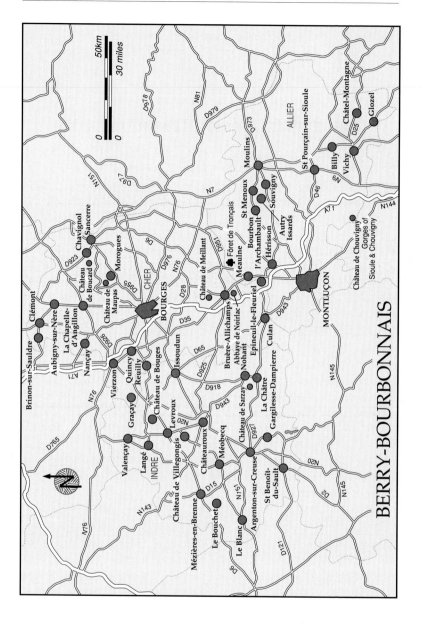

grand French Renaissance style. The château was never finished, even though work continued for a further two centuries, but despite that it is very beautiful. In the early nineteenth century Valençay passed to Talleyrand, Napoléon's Foreign Minister. Napoléon was

The grand château at Valençay

anxious that the new Republic should have a 'hotel' for visiting foreign dignitaries that would flatter both them and France, and instructed Talleyrand to find one. The then-owner of the château, an aristocrat who had missed the guillotine by a hair's breadth and was still living in fear, was offered official acceptance in exchange for a modest price and leapt at the chance.

Inside, the château's rooms are spacious and elegant, particularly the Duchess Room with its wall-to-wall mirrors and doors. One pleasing aspect is the way in which the windows offer delightful views out over the surrounding parkland. Once this was a deer park: today it is home for a somewhat incongruous collection of llamas, zebras and other animals. There are also black swans, and the gardens close to the building are patrolled by docile, elegant cranes, and a number of malevolent peafowl.

In addition to its llamas, the château's park is also home to a motor museum — the Musée de l'Automobile du Centre — with a collection of about seventy cars, the earliest dating from the late nineteenth century, and some very early Michelin maps and guides. Another interesting, and altogether more unusual, museum can be found about 10km (6 miles) south-west of Valençay, in the village of **Luçay-le-Mâle**. Here the history of the local gunflint industry is explored. From the time of the first guns, in the seventeenth century, to the invention of the percussion cap two centuries later, Luçay was one of the main centres for the extraction and preparation of flint for flintlock firearms.

From Valençay, the D956 heads south across a plain of wheatfields interspersed with clumps of trees. To the west of the road is **Langé**, a village that is actually easier to reach directly from Valençay. Langé is a typical Berry village, pleasant and unpretentious, but has a very interesting museum, housed in one room of the Mairie, which covers the areas's geology and includes a collection of fossils that have been found locally.

Equally interesting is the rarely visited **Château de Bouges**, which lies to the east of the D956 — take the turn to the left about 5km (3 miles) north of Levroux. The château was built in Italian style in the eighteenth century and has a fine collection of furniture from the Louis XV and Louis XVI periods. Surrounding the château is a huge park, well-planted with trees, a lake and formal flower gardens.

The next place of note is **Levroux** itself, at one time an important town with Royal connections. Several French kings stayed locally as a retreat from the Loire, and the town was also on the pilgrimage route to Santiago de Compostella. As a pilgrim town Levroux had hospices for the sick and being prosperous also tended poor folk from the local area. As the town's prosperity was based, in part, on the leather and parchment paper industries which drew cheap labour from the hostels for the unfortunate system — while wholly immoral — seemed to benefit both sides. The history of the two industries is explored in the Musée du Cuir et du Parchemin (Museum of Leather and Parchment).

Levroux's prosperity came to an end when the kings and pilgrims went away, leaving it a little run-down, but the oldest part of the town, close to the collegiate church of St Sylvain, is well worth visiting. The church has some fine carvings, and near to it is the Porte de Champagne, a delightful fifteenth-century gate with round towers and a tiled roof. The name derives not from the famous name, but from the fields, the *champagne*, of northern Berry. Look too for the Maison de Bois built, in the sixteenth century, for Catherine de Medici. Finally, a visit to the shops is worthwhile to sample the local goat's cheese. Anciently there were more fields given over to animals than to crops, but now sheep and goats are something of a rarity. But enough goats remain to produce a cheese that has been famous locally for centuries.

Still driving south on the D956 the visitor soon reaches a turn, to the right, for the Château de Villegongis, another rarely visited château, but one in authentic French Renaissance style. The château was begun around 1530 and completed relatively quickly so that it was, stylistically, whole. Two wings were demolished in the eighteenth century, but what remains, beautifully reflected in the moat that was never more than a decoration, is superb. Inside, the grand staircase takes the eye, though the furnishings are also excellent. Note especially the fine tapestries.

South of the château is **Châteauroux**, the principal town of the *département*. The town, named somewhat unimaginatively for the castle built here by a Berry prince, the interestingly named Raoulx the Large, is now a centre for cigarette making. It has little to detain the visitor, though the Musée Bertrand has an interesting collection of artwork illustrating the traditional life of Berry. However, the town is a good centre for exploring the southern part of Berry, particularly the Brenne Regional Park and the forest to the south. This, the Forêt de Châteauroux is explored by minor roads, a waymarked route visiting the better viewpoints.

Until the thirteenth century the land now protected by the **Brenne Regional Park** was a huge area of swamp. At that time the monks of several abbeys that lay close to the marsh edge dug channels and pits, creating ponds where fish congregated and canals that could be used by fishermen. The monks were, of course, looking to their own needs, fish being an important part of their diet, but the work they started, work which was continued over the centuries and is still going on today, has created a unique wetland area. Here the lucky visitor will see the booted eagle and the purple heron, while most visitors will see numerous species of ducks, grebes and other water birds. The Brenne supports good populations of otters and mink, as well as wild boar and musk rats. The plant lover is also catered for, orchids, irises and lilies thriving in the damp margins. Best of all, perhaps, is the sound of the Brenne during the mating season of the vast population of frogs and toads, each one croaking out its presence.

At the northern end of the Brenne is **Mézières-en-Brenne**, still the most important village in the area, though with little left of a once enormous castle built at the marsh edge in the tenth century. George Sand and Chopin once stayed in the village, Sand complaining that she had been eaten alive by fleas. Fishing seems to be the favourite local pastime, and there is also commercial fishing of pike and carp.

From Mézières roads criss-cross the Brenne, making their way between the lakes and the curious hillocks that pepper the area. In local mythology these hillocks were formed when the giant Gargantua scraped the mud from his boots. The roads offer a view of the Brenne, but a better one is obtained from the **Château de Bouchet** built on a ridge of red rock above the Etang de la Mer Rouge, the largest of the Brenne's lakes. The château is medieval and was occupied by the English for many years during the Hundred Years' War. In addition to its furnishings and a hunting trophy room (hardly in keeping with the conservation aims of the Regional Park) there are terraces and a keep from which the Brenne can be seen. The view, particularly over the Étang, is superb. The lake itself was named by a local knight after he had returned from a Crusade during which he had seen the real Red Sea, having been held prisoner on its shores. On the southern side of the lake is the chapel of Notre-Dame de la Mer Rouge named for a statue of the Virgin reputedly found, in the thirteenth century, in a hollow oak tree close to the site. The statue was burnt during the Wars of Religion.

In the hamlet of **Le Bouchet** beside the château is the office of the Regional Park, set among a collection of interesting old buildings, while southward, at **Le Blanc**, are the Ecomusée de la Brenne and the Musée des Oiseaux. The former deals with the ecology of the Brenne and the traditions of the folk who live within the park, while the latter features specimens of the park's birdlife, together with other species from around the world.

Le Blanc lies on the River Creuse, and the N151 follows the river eastward. To the south of the road the Brenne Park continues, though in this area there are many fewer lakes, the land being more heavily worked and forested. Off to the left at St Gaultier is the village of **Méobecq**. Méobecq, the last village of the Brenne Park, stands at the edge of the beautiful Lancosme Forest and is as peaceful as it is beautiful. However it was not always so peaceful. In 1569 the Huguenots burnt down an abbey which had stood in the town since the eleventh century. The remains of sections of the abbey still survive with some excellent fifteenth-century frescoes still intact.

Argenton-sur-Creuse is a busy town which grew up around a defensive castle built, in the eighteenth century, by the Frankish king Pepin the Short. Today it is most memorable for two viewpoints. The first, on the east side of the Creuse beside the old bridge (at the south end of the town) offers a panorama of the river and the old quarter. The second, from below the chapel of Nôtre-Dame des Bancs, which also takes in the old town and the river, is equally good. The chapel is topped by a 6½m (21ft), 6 ton statue of the Virgin. The statue, suitably gilded, was placed in position in 1899 and has been a landmark ever since.

South of Argenton the Creuse flows in a beautiful valley, the visitor often getting a surprising, and exquisite, view of the river

Le Mans cathedral, Pays de la Loire

Segré, Pays de la Loire

A street café in Argenton-sur-Creuse

from the road. One of the finest views is of the tight meander (known locally as Le Boucle) close to the village of Le Pin. Also close by here is the village of **Gargilesse-Dampierre**, one of the prettiest of all Berry villages, set in the valley of one of the Creuse's tributary streams. The village is popular with artists, and was once the home of George Sand who lived here with her son Maurice. The writer's house is now a museum. Also worth a visit is the village church, the crypt of which was elaborately frescoed in medieval times.

To the south of Le Pin the Creuse can be followed to the border with Limoges, the border laying at the southern end of the ribbon-like **Lac de Chambon** a lake formed in 1926 by the building of the Eguzon dam. The dam, impressive but hardly elegant, makes an excellent vantage point. From the lake the Brenne Park can be regained by travelling westward, the journey along the D36 soon reaching the village of **St Benoît-du-Sault** set on a rocky plateau above the meandering stream of the River Portefeuille. A walk through the old fortified town is very worthwhile, the walk visiting the old gate and clock tower, following a section of old wall and reaching the church, once the site of a priory, the terrace of which offers a fine river view.

Eastward from Lac de Chambon the country is inextricably linked with the writer George Sand, many of her works being set in the farming communities close to the town of La Châtre. Sand was born Aurore Dupin in 1804, taking her *nom-de-plume* from Jean Sandeau an early lover. Although today she is most famously remembered as Chopin's mistress, George Sand was a writer of significance, as well as being an early feminist. For most of her life she lived in the château at **Nohant** a village a short distance north of La Châtre. The château is now a fine museum to the writer. Close by, the visitor can find other places mentioned in Sand's writing. **St Chartier**, north of Nohant, was the setting for one novel and is a very pretty village with a fine church. Also close by is the **Château de Sarzay** which Sand included in another book. With its close-set towers and conical roofs the castle now looks a little forlorn, but when it was first built, in the fourteenth century it was huge, its encircling moat crossed by two drawbridges. Finally in this quest for George Sand, go to **La Châtre** itself. This charming town, built around a central, still-used, market place has a collection of memorabilia of the writer housed in the keep of the Château de Chauvigny, all that now remains of the fifteenth-century castle. The memorabilia is collected together on the first floor sandwiched between a huge array of stuffed birds and an interesting collection of the work of local craftsmen, these latter items constituting the Musée de la Vallée Noire. The valley of the name is the local valley of the Indre, and was used by Sand in her work.

North of La Châtre the D918 leaves the Indre Valley, taking the visitor towards Issoudun. To the right of the road, turn off at the village of Ambrault, are the twin forests of Bommiers and Choeurs, an area of about 5,000 hectares (over 12,000 acres) chiefly of oak. Roads cross the forest, offering yet another superb drive and the chance of excellent walking. If the forest roads are taken, Issoudin is reached by way of St Aubin, a village at the heart of the forest.

Issoudun is a very attractive town, betraying few signs of the part it played in the conflict between King Philippe-Auguste of France and England's Richard Coeur de Lion. At that time it was besieged several times and once put to the torch. The White Tower, at the eastern end of a section of old wall was built by King Richard. The nearby Clock Tower was also once part of the old wall. Elsewhere, the old Hôtel-Dieu, standing by the river in the elegantly named Rue de l'Hospice St-Roch, has an interesting collection of items from early pharmacies and apothecary's shops, many of the items dating back to the seventeenth century.

Cher

From Issoudun the visitor taking the D918 crosses into the *département* of Cher close to **Reuilly** a village which, like the nearby **Quincy**, about 15km (9 miles) to the east, is establishing a reputation for its wines. The white, sometimes disparagingly referred to as the poor man's Sancerre, is actually much better than that, and has been given *appellation controlée*. Of the village itself, there is little to detain the visitor, though Reuilly is more pleasant than Quincy, a balance perhaps for its wine being considered the inferior of the two.

North again, along the D918, is **Vierzon** an untidy industrial town that the visitor could be easily forgiven for bypassing. However, a visit to the old quarter will repay the effort. Vierzon was built where the River Yévre met the Cher and was fortified in medieval times, a section of old walls and a belfry — in pure Gothic style and once the town prison — being all that now remain. Clustered below these relics are some fine half-timbered houses, the slight air of neglect adding to the atmosphere of the place. The town church was built in the twelfth century in Romanesque style and from the terraced garden close by there is a fine view of the Yévre/Cher Valley. To the west of the old town the Berry canal reaches Vierzon. A stroll along the towpath, beside the old locks is rewarding, especially if it includes a visit to the fine gardens laid out as a memorial to the dead of the two World Wars.

Those interested in atmospheric old places can visit another from Vierzon, the village of **Graçay** lying in an almost forgotten part of Cher to the south-west. Here the medieval walls and many of the old houses still stand. The village church is also interesting, having been built at the transition from Romanesque to Gothic styles and having features of each.

North-east from Vierzon is another superb area of woodland, the huge forests of Vierzon, Vouzeron and Allogny. Here the oaks are interspersed with stands of other broadleaf trees, and also with some surprising copses of Scots pine. The woodland is thick, giving a dive through it a dark, moody feel, which gets the visitor in the right mood for visits to **Nançay** and **La Chapelle-d'Angillon**.

On 5 October 1886 Henri Alban Fournier was born in La Chapelle-d'Angillon, his birthplace, a house about 100m (328ft) north of the village cross-roads, on the left side of the D940 to Aubigny-sur-Nère, still standing. Fournier was educated at Epineuil-le-Fleuriel in neighbouring Allier (see below) and became a schoolmaster at the village school of Nançay. In his mid-twenties under the pseudonym Alain-Fournier he wrote a novel, *Le Grand Meaulnes*, which was published

A well-preserved half-timbered building in Abigney-sur-Nère

in 1913. It was the only book Henri ever wrote as he was killed in action of the Meuse in 1914 at the age of 27. is now considered a masterpiece of French literature, though it is still little known in English. It is a poetic tale, set in a moody, mysterious landscape that brilliantly evokes the dream-like qualities of parts of Cher and Allier, especially when there is a light mist and the trees are tinged with autumnal brown.

Both Nançay and La Chapelle pay homage to Fournier. At La Chapelle a room of the château is devoted to him. The château has a twelfth-century keep softened by later work in Renaissance style and stands beside a lake. The view from the terrace above the lake is worth the trip in itself, but inside there is much of interest. Besides the Musée Alain-Fournier there is the Frasheri collection of eighteenth-century Albanian *objet d'art* and an array of furnished rooms.

At Nançay the Grenier de Villâtre offers the Musée Imaginaire du Grand Meaulnes, a small collection of memorabilia, as well as examples of local crafts. As a complete contrast to the France of yesterday, the visitor can view the hi-tech radio-astronomy observatory in the village. Here displays and recorded commentaries, in English, explain the principles of the system.

To the north of La Chapelle the D940 follows a dead straight course across the last section of the Sologne (see chapter 9, Touraine-

Blésois-Orléanais) to reach **Aubigny-sur-Nère**, a beautiful little town with a Scottish ancestry. This most unusual history derives from John Stuart, a Scottish ally of Charles VII against the English during the Hundred Years War, having been given the seigneury in 1423. Stuart was succeeded by other Scots, all of whom brought Scottish relations to the area. Some of the Scottish immigrants were skilled in the production and weaving of wool, and Aubigny grew prosperous on the trade, that prosperity reflected in the quality of the surviving half-timbered houses in the centre of the town. The château dates from the same period, having been built by Robert Stuart, a successor of John, who fought for France in Italy. Also worth visiting are the Grands Jardins, or Duchess of Portsmouth's Park, laid out in the seventeenth century and named for the mistress of the English king Charles II who had been given nearby **La Verrerie Château** by Louis XIV.

The Château is frequently missed by the visitor. It stands in the beautiful Forêt d'Ivoy to the south-east of Aubigny and has some fine Renaissance interior work. There is also an excellent collection of nineteenth-century dolls.

To the west of Aubigny are two more fine villages. **Clémont** has a collection of excellent half-timbered houses and an imposing stone church with an elegant spire. Close by, but actually over the border in the *département* of Loiret, is the Étang du Puits a fine lake which, with its beaches and pedaloes, will be popular with younger visitors. Just a short distance from Clémont is **Brinon-sur-Souldre** a village whose church has a *caquetoir* — literally a chatter — an open gallery where the village could congregate after church to discuss village issues, or hear proclamations. Just north of the village is the Sauldre Canal, a favourite with anglers and popular with walkers who use its towpath to explore this quiet part of the Sologne.

To the south-east of Aubigny lie the Collines de Sancerrois, a more hilly area than the Sologne, but one of equal interest. **Léré** is a medieval fortified village, part of the old walls still standing, with a superb fifteenth-century church and excellent walking beside the Loire canal. Closer to Sancerre is **Chavignol** another very pretty village famous for its goat's cheese which tastes much better than it smells, the latter quality having given it the unappetising name of *Crottin de Chavignol*, Chavignol goat's dung — and its wine, Côtes de Mont Dâmnés. **Sancerre** is also famous for its wine, and for its almond sweetmeats. *Croquets de Sancerre* are small almond biscuits while *Lichens de Sancerre* are almond cakes. Because of its position, on a hill above the Loire which here forms the border with Burgundy,

Sancerre was fought over for centuries, and the remnant of its castle, the Tour des Fiefs, makes a superb vantage point. From it the old town, with its turreted houses, the Loire, Burgundy and the Sancerrois are laid out for the visitor. Almost as good is the view from the Esplanade de la Porte César to the north of the tower.

To the west of Sancerre the D7 leaves the D923, passing several excellent viewpoints on the way to Sens-Beaujeu. North of here is the **Château de Boucard**. Although it began life as a fortress in the thirteenth century, the château was later softened by a Renaissance wing. It is still reached by drawbridge, but its pastoral setting gives it quite a different feel to the Loire châteaux. Inside, it is elegantly furnished in seventeenth-century style. Outside, there are collections of saddles and horse-drawn coaches.

Heading south towards Bourges the visitor can gain a last, and memorable, view of the Sancerrois from the summit of the **Motte d'Humbligny** which lies beside the D44, which links the D22 near the pottery village of La Berne to the D955. The view is wonderful, but the sometimes-quoted statistic that the Motte is the highest point of the Collines is belied by local maps which note another top — about 2km (1 mile) to the north-east — that is all of 3m (10ft) higher.

When the D955 is reached, go right towards Bourges, perhaps turning off to the right at Les Aix-d'Angillon to visit the pretty little village of **Morogues** and the Château de Maupas. The château was begun in the thirteenth century but was comprehensively rebuilt in the fifteenth century. Inside the furnishings are eighteenth century and, in keeping with the local area's history of excellent potteries, there is also a fine collection of china.

Bourges is hardly off-the-beaten-track, but demands a visit from anyone making a tour of northern Berry. It is renowned as the city of Jacques Coeur, one of the greatest of medieval French merchants, who became Minister of Finance under Charles VII, and his magnificent *palais* can be visited. The cathedral is also compulsory viewing, a superb building, its flying buttresses as elegant as those of Nôtre-Dame de Paris or Chartres, its stained glass some of the finest early thirteenth-century work in Europe. But elsewhere there is much of interest. Beside the cathedral is a fine medieval two-storey tithe barn, beyond which there is a section of very early town wall. On the other side of the cathedral are the Jardins de l'Archevêché from where there is the best view of the flying buttresses.

From close to the cathedral Rue Bourbonnoux, probably the city's most picturesque street, runs down to the Hôtel Lallement a beautiful Renaissance building which now houses the museum of decorative arts. Another fine mansion, the Hôtel Cujas, close to Palais

The magnificent cathedral at
Bourges

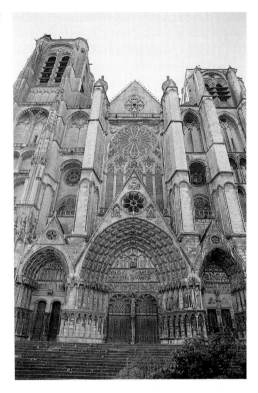

Jacques Coeur, houses the fascinating Musée du Berry, devoted to the history and folklore of the area.

Bourges is also a fine place for shopping — go to Rue Mayenne, to the west of the cathedral, and its continuation, Rue du Commerce — and for eating. If you are tempted to eat in the city it might be worth trying *truffiats*, a speciality potato cake.

Bourges lies on the Route Jacques Coeur, a journey through central France named for the great merchant even though most of the places on it have little or no connection with him. South of Bourges the Route passes close to a trio of fascinating places close to St Armand-Montrand, itself worth visiting for its fine Musée St Vic devoted to the history of the area from prehistoric to Renaissance times. Nearby are the Château de Meillant, a magnificent fifteenth-century building with remarkable external carvings and superb furnishings. The medieval Great Hall, with its wooden ceilings and carved knights is definitely the highlight. The Abbaye de Noirlac is the only Cistercian abbey to have survived in virtually complete form in France. It was begun in 1130, and is worth the visit just to walk the cool, shaded thirteenth-century cloister, of which three sides have survived. Finally, go to **Bruère-Allichamps,** on the banks of the Cher. This pretty village has a monument which claims that it is the geographical heart of France. That hardly sounds off-the-beaten-track for visitors, but it has to be said that two other local villages have similar monuments making similar claims!

To the west of the Cher one further château is worth visiting. The château at **Culan** was first raised in the late twelfth century as a fortress, but transformed in the fifteenth century. Admiral Culant, one of the staunchest supporters of Joan of Arc lived here and his room can be visited, as can the one occupied by George Sand during a flying visit. The château's church is also worth a visit.

Finally in the *département* of Cher head south from St Armand-Montrand, passing the magnificent château of Ainay-le-Vieil, a miniature Carcassone, to reach **Epineuil-le-Fleuriel**. As mentioned previously this was where Alain-Fournier went to school and where the story-teller of *Le Grand Meaulnes* was a pupil — though in the book the village's name is changed to St Agathe. The school is now a museum, both to Fournier and the old way of life.

Allier

Epineuil-le-Fleuriel is often claimed to be the last village of the Bourbonnais, though the official boundary of the area is the Cher which separates the *départements* of Cher and Allier. From Epineuil the first Allier village reached is **Meaulne** which gave its name to the hero in Fournier's book. The village stands at the edge of the Forêt de Tronçais one of the finest forests in France. About two-thirds of the trees in the forest are turkey oaks, tall, straight trees with long, slender leaves and acorns set in mossy cups. After years of abuse in the late medieval period the forest was in a poor state, but was rejuvenated by Colbert, Louis XIV's famous minister, who recognised the value of the oak-woods for ship building and the need to control cutting and to replant. Today the forest provides wood for high quality veneers, and is also a splendid place to walk with a system of marked tracks exploring the woods. The very lucky walker may see the rare wild boar and the elusive pine and beech martens. The forest lakes are also a haven for waterfowl.

To the east of the forest is **Bourbon l'Archambault,** named for the family who grew to be the most powerful in France, eventually providing the country with its final kings. The Bourbons, who once held a duchy that encompassed what is now the Bourbonnais, held estates close to this village and to nearby Souvigny at first. As their wealth and power grew they expanded their estates and were finally so powerful that they could challenge the throne of France, Bourbonnais at that time being an independent duchy. Though it is very pleasant, little remains in the town today to remind the visitor of past glories. Even the once great castle has been reduced to three towers, though the destruction was actually carried out during the Revolution rather than during any contest between the Bourbon dukes and the French monarchs. Unusually for France, entrance to the castle is free: there is an excellent view of the town and the Bourbonnais countryside from the tower tops.

Close to Bourbon is **St Menoux**, named after a seventh-century Celtic saint whose remains are held in a stone sarcophagus behind the altar. The sarcophagus has a hole in it and legend has it that stutterers can be cured of their affliction if they put their heads through the hole. The 'cure' was popular in medieval times when stutterers were brought in procession to the church, but if local rumours are to be believed many still come.

Souvigny, just a few miles south-east of Bourbon, beyond the pretty village of **Autry Issards**, is also a surprising place from which to envisage the growth of a race of kings. Nevertheless it is a pretty place, the priory church of St Pierre housing the tombs of the Bourbon dukes who were ancestors to the Sun King and the unfortunate Louis XVI. An altogether more intriguing object is found in the deconsecrated church of St Mark close to the priory church. Here there is an octagonal stone pillar, about 2m (7ft) high and weighing a ton, that was carved as a calendar in the twelfth century. The activities of the priory's monks during the seasons are carved on the faces, interspersed with the signs of the zodiac, flowers and mythical animals. It is a beautiful work, full of the joy of life.

East of Souvigny is **Moulins**, once the capital of the duchy of Bourbon, now capital of Allier. It is a delightful place worth visiting to see the cathedral with its tall nave, beautiful fifteenth-century stained glass and a Black Virgin that is a copy of the more famous one at Le-Puy-en-Velay to the south. Within the town there is a fine museum to the local folklore and the history of the town (the Musée de Folklore et du Vieux Moulins beside the cathedral), while in the suburb of Yzeure, east of the centre, is the Musée Historique du Bourbonnais which looks at the history of the Bourbon dukes.

South from Moulins is **St Pourçain-sur-Sioule** claimed to be at the heart of the oldest wine growing area in France, its first vineyards having been planted before the Romans arrived in this part of Gaul: Not surprisingly there is a museum in the town to viniculture and wine. The town makes a good centre for exploring the eastern edge of Alliers: all tours should include Billy a village at the edge of the Forêt de Marconat to the south-east of St Pourçain.

Billy grew up around a castle of the Bourbon dukes, built to hold the plain to the north of the Montagne Bourbonnais. With successive dukes adding to the fortifications, the village eventually became one of the most heavily defended sites in Bourbonnais. The fortress is still the central point of the village, its grey stone bulk rising above the neat red and grey tiled houses. Though the castle is now only a shell, a walk of its walls gives some idea of the way it once dominated the area. There are some fine medieval houses in Rue Chabotin.

South-east of Billy, only a short drive to the Montagne Bourbonnais, a hill range that could be termed the last of the Massif Central and one which is different in character to the rolling countryside of the real Bourbon. Here there are fine viewpoints, especially, the Puy du Roc, from where the Monts Dore and Monts Dômes in Auvergne are visible, and the Pierre Charbonnière on the D25 near **Châtel-Montagne**. Châtel is worth visiting for its church, once the church of a Benedictine Priory, which is beautiful throughout. Note especially the delightful Romanesque porch and the elegant lines, a mix of Romanesque Auvergne and Burdundian styles.

Southward from Châtel-Montagne on the D995, that links the mountains to Vichy, is **Glozel** a village infamous in archaeological circles, but virtually unknown to the non-specialist. Here, in 1926, a farmer unearthed a series of bones and pottery that were engraved with an unknown alphabet. Academia was, and to an extent is, divided on the find, some seeing the pieces as genuine and very early, others seeing them as fakes. Similar finds in Portugal and the dating of some of the pieces to around 700BC have suggested that they are indeed evidence of early writing. A museum in the village has an exhibition of the finds.

Vichy, to the north of Glozel, is notorious in French history, but is worth visiting to see its spa buildings and casino — the latter having the extraordinary claim to fame of being one of only two places where an opera singer has swallowed his false moustache during the course of a performance. The incident happened to Jan Verbeek during the second act of Boito's Mefistofele in 1955. On a somewhat less off-the-beaten-track note, Vichy is also a fine centre for water-sports since a dam on the Allier provided the town with a huge lake and a current-controllable river that is used by canoeists. Since there are also numerous facilities for other sports — facilities without number it sometimes seems — Vichy has become one of the leading sports centres in this part of France.

To the south of the Forêt de Tronçais the visitor approaching Montluçon on the D3 soon reaches **Hérisson** another Bourbonnais village of breathtaking beauty. For the best view of it walk up the hill topped by an old chapel. The village is set on a bank of the Aumance, on a hillock surmounted by the remains of a fourteenth-century Bourbon château, and is a delight to walk, its narrow alleys of ancient houses creating a web that is best enjoyed at a leisurely pace.

Montluçon is an industrial town and unlikely to trouble the visitor long, but the château, built as a fortress during the Hundred Years War, should be visited to see the collection of old instruments on the first floor of the town museum, which is housed there. The instruments include *vielles, bourrée*, cornemeuses and hurdy-gurdies, and also *cabrettes* (*musettes* in Bourbonnais), an early form of bag-pipes with a goatskin bellows.

Finally travel south-east from Montluçon, to the area close to the border with Auvergne. Here the River Sioule, flows in two beautiful gorges. The **Gorges de la Sioule**, with the dramatically sited Château Rocher is the best, but it lies just over the border, so go instead to the **Gorges de Chouvigny**. The gorge is extremely picturesque, and also has a beautifully positioned château. The **Château de Chouvigny** is an excellent example of medieval fortress architecture and offers a stunning view of the gorge and the Roc Armand, which almost blocks the gorge to the west of the castle.

Further Information
— Berry-Bourbonnais —

Museums and Other Places of Interest

Billy
Château
Open: June, Sat and Sun 2-5pm. July and August daily 9am-12noon, 2-5pm.
☎ 70 43 50 14

Le Blanc
Brenne Region Ecomuseum
Château Naillac
Open: Jan to May, Wed, Sat, Sun 2-6pm. June to Sept daily 10am-12noon, 2.30-6.30pm. Oct to Dec, Wed, Sat, Sun 2-6pm.

Bird Museum
Open: May to Sept daily 2-5pm. October to April, Saturday, Sunday 2-5pm.
☎ 54 37 36 24

Bourbon l'Archambault
Château of Duke Louis II Bourbon
Open: March to October, Mon to Sat 2-5pm. Sunday 9am-12noon, 2-5pm.
☎ 70 67 09 79

Bourges
Museum of Decorative Arts
Hôtel Lallement
Open: all year Tuesday to Saturday 10am-12noon, 2-6pm, Sunday 2-6pm.
☎ 48 57 81 15

Museum of Berry
Hôtel Cujas
4 Rue des Arènes
Open: all year Mon, Wed to Sat 10am-12noon, 2-6pm, Sunday 2-6pm.
☎ 48 57 81 17

La Chapelle-d'Angillon Château
Open: all year daily except Sunday
morning 9am-12noon, 2-7pm.
☎ 48 73 41 10

Châteauroux
Bertrand Museum
Open: June to September daily except
Monday 9am-12noon, 2-5pm. October
to May daily except Monday 2-5pm.
☎ 54 27 26 31

Château de Boucard
Open: March, Saturday, Sunday 2-
4.30pm. April to June daily except
Tuesday 10am-11.30am, 2-5.30pm. July,
August daily 10am-12.30pm, 2-6.30pm.
September, October daily except Tuesday
10-11.30am, 2-5.30pm. November,
Saturday, Sunday 2-4.30pm.
☎ 54 35 88 26

Château de Bouchet
Open: July, August daily except
Tuesday and Sunday mornings 10am-
12noon, 2-5pm. September to June
daily except Tuesday 2-5pm.
☎ 54 37 80 14

Château de Bouges
Open: July, Aug daily except Tuesday
10am-12noon, 2-7pm. April to June,
Sept and Oct daily except Tuesday
10am-12noon, 2-6pm. Nov, mid-Feb to
March, Saturday, Sunday 2-6pm.
☎ 54 35 88 26

Château de Sarzay
Open: January to March, Sat, Sun 10am-
12noon, 2-6pm. April to October daily
10am-12noon, 2-7pm. November and
December, Sat, Sun 10am-12noon, 2-6pm.
☎ 54 31 32 25

Château de Villegongis
Open: April to Sept by request only.
☎ 54 36 60 51

La Châtre
George Sand and Vallée Noire Museum
Château de Chauvigny
Open: February and March daily 9am-
12noon, 2-5pm. April to June daily

9am-12noon, 2-7pm. July and August
daily 9am-7pm. September to December daily 9am-12noon, 2-5pm.
☎ 54 48 36 79

Culan
Château
Open: March to June daily 9.30am-
12noon, 2-6.30pm. July, August daily
9.30am-7pm. September to November
daily 9.30am-12noon, 2-6.30pm.
☎ 48 56 64 18

Epineuil-le-Fleuriel
School Museum
The museum is closed at time of writing.
For more information ☎ 48 63 02 23

Gargilesse-Dampierre
Refuge de George Sand
Open: April to September daily 10am-
12noon, 2-5pm.
☎ 54 47 84 14

Glozel
Museum
Open: February to December daily
10am-12noon, 2-5pm.
☎ 70 41 12 96

Issoudun
Pharmacy/Apothecary Museum
23 Rue de l'Hospice St Roch
Open: mid-Feb to mid-April, Mon, Wed,
Thurs 2-6pm. Fri, Sat, Sun 10am-12noon,
2-7pm. Mid-April to mid-Oct, daily except Tues 10am-12noon, 2-7pm. Mid-Oct
to Dec Mon, Wed, Thurs 2-6pm. Fri, Sat,
Sun 10am-12noon, 2-7pm.
☎ 54 21 01 76

Langé
*Musée Geoligique et Paleontologique
(Geology and Fossil Museum)*
Open: all year daily 2-5pm.
☎ 54 40 86 37 or 54 40 84 16

Levroux
Museum of Leather and Parchment
Open: July, August daily 10am-12noon,
2-5pm. At all other times by request.
Ask at the Tourist Office, 3 Rue
Gambetta.

Luçay-le-Mâle
Museum of Gunflint
Open: all year daily 2-5pm.
☎ 54 40 43 97

Montluçon
Town Museum, Vieux Château
Open: mid-March to mid-October daily
except Tues 9am-12noon, 2-5pm. Mid-Oct
to mid-March, Wed to Sun 2-5pm.
☎ 70 05 00 16

Moroques
Château de Maupas
Open: April to June, Mon, Sat 2-7pm,
Sun 10am-12noon, 2-7pm. July to mid-
Sept daily 10am-12noon, 2-7pm. Mid-
Sept to mid-Oct, Monday to Saturday
2-7pm, Sunday 10am-12noon, 2-6pm.
☎ 48 64 41 71

Moulins
Folklore and Old Moulins Museum
Open: April to September daily 9am-12noon,
2-5pm. October to March, Mon to Wed, Fri,
Sat 9am-12noon, 2-5pm, Sun 2-5pm.
☎ 70 44 39 03

Nançay
Grenier de Villâtre
Open: April to December, Sat, Sun 10am-
12noon, 2-5pm. At other times by request.
☎ 48 51 80 22

Radio-astronomy Observatory
Open: September to June second
Saturday of each month at 2.30pm.
Guided tour with English commentary.
☎ 48 51 82 41

Nohant
Château
Open: Jan to March daily 10-11.15am, 2-
3.30pm. April to June daily 9-11.15am, 2-
5.30pm. July and Aug daily 9-11.30am,
1.30-6pm. September to mid-October
daily 9-11.15am, 2-5.30pm. Mid-October
to December daily 10-11.15am, 2-3.30pm.
☎ 54 31 32 25

Parc Naturel Régional de la Brenne
Main Office:
Maison du Parc
Hameau du Bouchet

36300 Rosnay
☎ 54 37 75 84

St Armand-Montrand
Museum St Vic
Cours Manuel
Open: all year Mon, Wed to Sat 10am-
12noon, 2-6pm, Sunday 2-6pm.
☎ 48 96 55 20 and 48 96 17 32

St Pourçain-sur-Sioule
Museum of Wine and Viniculture
Open: mid-June to mid-Sept daily 2-5pm.
☎ 70 45 38 25

Valençay
Château and Motor Museum
Open: mid-March to mid-June daily
9am-12noon, 2-7pm or dusk. Mid-June
to mid-September daily 9am-7pm.
Mid-September to mid-November
daily 9am-12noon, 2-7pm or dusk.

Animal Park
Open: January to mid-June daily 9am-
12noon, 2pm-dusk. Mid-June to mid-
Sept daily 9am-7pm. Mid-Sept to Dec
daily 9am-12noon, 2pm-dusk.
☎ 54 00 10 66

La Verrerie
Château
Open: mid-February to mid-November
daily 10am-12noon, 2-9pm.
☎ 48 58 06 91

Yzeure
Museum of Bourbonnais History
Open: all year Monday to Friday 10am-
12noon, 2-5pm.
☎ 70 20 01 40

Tourist Information Offices

Allier
Place de l'Hôtel-de-Ville
03000 Moulins ☎ 70 44 14 14

Cher
5 Rue de Séricourt
18000 Bourges ☎ 48 67 00 18

Indre
36 Rue Bourdillon
36000 Châteauroux ☎ 54 22 91 20

11 • Burgundy

It may at first sight seem difficult to get 'off the beaten track' in Burgundy. This large area of east-central France has been a crossroads of Europe since records began. Many travellers pass through it on their way from north to south, or east to west; some linger a few days, others hurry through, and only the occasional discerning visitor decides to make the region his holiday base. Those who do stay, however, can easily find many lesser-known but rewarding places to visit, and while doing so can enjoy some of France's greatest riches.

The very word has a rich sound. 'Burgundy' is a word in common use either as a description of velvety red wine or the deep warm colour associated with it. In fact both red and white wines of exceptional quality are produced in Burgundy, the whites including such famous names as Chablis, Meursault, Montrachet and Pouilly-Fuissé, the reds some of the finest and most expensive *Grands Crus* in the world. But to the French, the word *bourgogne* also suggests a renowned cuisine, including some of their great classic dishes such as *boeuf bourguignonne, coq au vin, quenelles de brochet* (pike dumplings with a white wine and mushroom sauce), *escargots* (snails) and frogs' legs. This is gourmet country, with a full-flavoured hearty cuisine containing red wine, cream, bacon, onions and mushrooms as common ingredients. The quality of food products is usually first-class and renowned, especially the ham (either served jellied with parsley or in a cream and white wine sauce known as a *saupiquet*), the Charollais beef, the corn-fed chickens from Bresse, cheeses such as Chaource and Epoisses, Dijon mustard and *Cassis*, a liqueur made from Burgundy's favourite fruit, the blackcurrant.

Burgundy is a region rich in history. It takes its name from a tall, blond-haired tribe of vandals from the Baltic in northern Germany, the *Burgondes*, who were said to dye and grease their hair with rancid butter! They settled peacefully in the area and merged with the more civilised local Gauls in the fifth-century AD, ruling alongside their

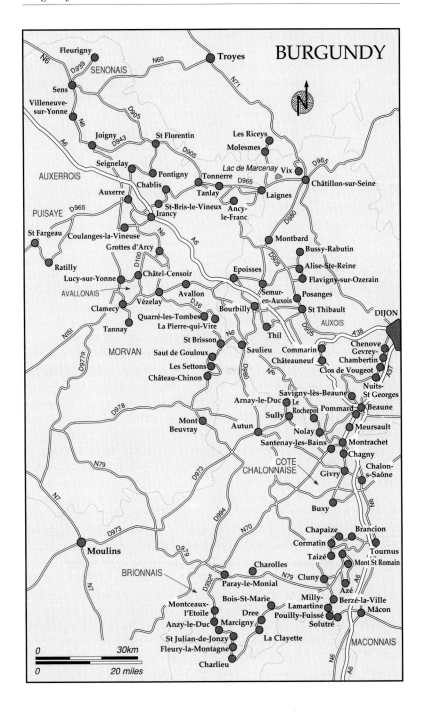

Germanic rivals the Franks and allying with them to beat back Attila and his Huns. Their rivalry with the Franks continued into the Middle Ages, when they sided with the English to defeat France in the Hundred Years' War. By the fifteenth-century, when Duke Philip 'the Good' ruled over Europe's wealthiest court at Dijon (his sash alone was worth a hundred thousand pounds!), Burgundy had become a powerful independent state, and its realm extended from Flanders in the north to Provence in the south. In the sixteenth century it lost its independence and was attached to the French crown.

Today the region comprises four departments, the Yonne, Nièvre, Côte-d'Or and Saône-et-Loire; it is bordered to the north by the Île-de-France, to the south by the Lyonnais, to the west by the Loire and to the east by Lorraine. It is a land of lush green fields crossed by canals, extensive forests, including the rugged wooded hills of the Morvan, vineyards (mainly on south-facing slopes, for example the sunny slopes of the Côte-d'Or) and broad river valleys. Its buildings have a distinctive style: large and solid, with warm yellow stone walls and red or multi-coloured roofs. Above all, it is a land of splendid châteaux, churches and other religious buildings.

Burgundy was the birthplace of medieval monasticism, from the founding at Cluny of the first Benedictine abbey in AD910. In the early Middle Ages this was the leading European abbey, controlling and ordering monastic life. Many beautiful Romanesque churches were built, including the 'greatest in Christendom' at Cluny. Though this was largely destroyed in the Revolution, many other examples remain to delight the visitor, with their wealth of realistic carvings on capitals and doorways. Fine examples can also be seen of churches and abbeys built in the more severe style of the later Cistercian order.

Apart from eating, drinking and looking at art and architecture, there is much in Burgundy to occupy the active traveller. The Morvan is an attractive and uncrowded area for walking, cycling and horse-riding, and for sailing, swimming and fishing in its many lakes and rivers. Boating on rivers such as the Yonne and canal-cruising down the broad *Canal de Bourgogne* are popular, and the region is well provided with *gîtes*, camp-sites and swimming pools — and an excellent road system. The French Grand Prix motor race is held each July at Magny-Cours, near Nevers; and there are many colourful local fêtes and festivals, including those attached to the church or the wine trade. Above all, Burgundians are down-to-earth, friendly and practical, with a sense of humour, and will readily welcome you to share their love of the good things in life.

Château at St Chartier,
Berry-Bourbonnais

The Wine and Barrel Making
Museum at Chinon, Touraine-
Blésois-Orléanais

A peaceful setting at La Rochepot, Burgundy

Northern Burgundy

Coming from the north, the first important town in Burgundy is **Sens**. This historic town still has a look of the Île-de-France about it, with its wide flowery boulevards replacing the ancient ramparts. Its crowning glory is the magnificent St Etienne cathedral, with its associations with Thomas à Becket — the story of his murder is depicted in one of the twelfth-century stained glass windows. The church, begun in 1140, is the oldest of the great French Gothic cathedrals, and has fine stained glass, flamboyant Gothic transepts and a rich treasury. The town has some impressive old buildings, especially the thirteenth-century Synod Palace.

The country round Sens is known as the **Senonais**, named after one of the most powerful Gallic tribes. To the east is the vast Othe Forest, known for its cider-producing apple orchards, which stretches over into Champagne. Fifteen kilometres (9 miles) north-east is **Fleurigny**, with its charming Renaissance château of patterned stone and brick set in a moat with swans and flanked by pepperpot towers. Inside in the guard room is a fine monumental fireplace by Jean Cousin, a local sculptor, and there are some good carved wooden ceilings. South of Sens the N6 follows the Yonne Valley, bypassing **Villeneuve-sur-Yonne** — but do not miss this gem of a medieval small town built in one piece as a residence for Louis VII. It has two handsome town gates, the Porte de Sens and the Porte de Joigny, and between them a wide main street flanked by old houses including one with seven carved heads. The Notre-Dame church in the centre, though mainly Gothic with a huge high nave, has a superb Renaissance façade.

South of Villeneuve and straddling the Yonne is **Joigny**, its old half-timbered houses and round towers giving it a more typically Burgundian appearance than Sens. Joigny has a sunny, holiday air about it, with cafés lining the river banks, stylish shops and fine *haute cuisine* restaurants. From here take the D943 along the north bank of the Yonne to Migennes, then the Armançon to **St Florentin**. This busy town is famous for two fine Burgundy cheeses — St Florentin and Soumaintrain — and is popular with fishermen. Its attractive but curiously unfinished church has some fine Renaissance stained glass. Ten kilometres (6 miles) south is **Pontigny**, a village famous as the home of the second Cistercian abbey, built in 1114, and containing its earliest intact church. The abbey has a long and chequered history: in its early days it was a refuge for three English archbishops of Canterbury, including Thomas à Becket, who retired here for 6 years after his quarrel with Henry II in 1164. Later, after sackings by

Huguenots and Revolutionaries, it became a secular retreat for European writers and intellectuals. Today the restored buildings are closed to the public and only the church may be visited; but its austere majesty, its huge size and solidity and its superb carved choir stalls make a visit well worth while.

Take the D5 west to **Seignelay**, a village with a picturesque seventeenth-century wooden covered market in its attractive main square. Ten kilometres (6 miles) south is **Auxerre**, capital of Lower (ie Northern) Burgundy and a charming town on a beautiful site. The best view of this is to the south, from the Yonne bridge, where the Ste Etienne Cathedral rears majestically above the river surrounded by warm Burgundian rooftops. Though bustling and commercial, Auxerre has a lovely old centre of narrow cobbled streets and timbered houses under its famous Gothic clock tower. There is much to see, including four fine churches and three museums; but you should not miss the crypts in the cathedral and St Germain abbey church. The former is early Romanesque (1023-30), the latter Carolingian (begun in AD858), and both contain superb early frescos — those in St Germain are the oldest in France. St Germain's upper church is now a museum of Burgundian art.

The celebrated vineyards of Northern Burgundy lie just to the south and east of Auxerre. The southern area, an *appellation régionale*, is the one for good free tastings, with its four main villages — **St Bris-le-Vineux**, **Irancy**, **Vincelotte**, and **Coulanges-la-Vineuse** — producing mainly white wines, though there is some fruity if rather sharp red at Irancy and Coulanges. The *Sauvignon de St Bris* is an excellent crisp dry white, the local *Bourgogne Aligoté* of high quality, and they make a *Chardonnay* which is a good cheaper alternative to *Chablis*. The area east of Auxerre is the *appellation communale* region of Chablis, whose world-famous *Chardonnay* wines are delicious, though expensive. The *Grands Crus* are superb, while the more affordable *Petits Chablis* are still deliciously crisp, fruity and bone-dry. **Chablis** itself is a small, quiet Burgundy town set amidst rolling, vine-covered hills, and nearby Chitry has a fortified church.

To the west of Auxerre is a little-known region called the **Puisaye**, a flat plateau of open cornfields, small lakes (*étangs*), marsh and forest. This was the home of the writer Colette, who called it a poor country of superstition and wolves! Its chief town is **St Fargeau**, whose imposing château was once the home of the fiery niece of Louis XIII, Mademoiselle de Montpensier, known as the 'Grande Mademoiselle'. It is surrounded by a large, attractive park. Sixteen kilometres (10 miles) south is another château at **Ratilly**, even older and more imposing (thirteenth century), though with a more welcoming interior. It now houses a pottery school, where courses in the local Puisaye industry can be followed. There is a beautiful flamboyant Gothic church at nearby Treigny, known as the 'cathedral of La Puisaye'.

The Châtillonais

This area of north-east Burgundy is less well-known than most of the region, but is worth a detour, partly for some of the gems to be found en route. East of Chablis on the D965 is **Tonnerre**, a pleasant market town on the Burgundy canal. Its proud possession is the Hospital Notre-Dame des Fontenilles (founded 1293), whose founder, Marguerite de Bourgogne, has a tomb in the chapel. Its great hall is 80m (262ft) long, and has a superb carved oak roof and wood panelling, and also in the chapel is a beautiful fifteenth-century sculpture, the *Entombment of Christ*. Another fine building in Tonnerre is the Renaissance façade of the Hôtel d'Uzès, now the savings bank. On a plateau above the town is a curious Gallo-Roman pool, the *Fosse Dionne* (meaning 'Divine Hole'), a pool of blue-green water 15m (49ft) wide, enclosed by a wall and encircled by a covered gallery decked with flowers. This charming spring was the only source of water for the town in Gallo-Roman times.

Two of the finest châteaux of Burgundy now lie across your route. The first, at **Tanlay**, is a beautiful sight when approached down a mile-long double avenue of limes. A decorous moat flanked by elegant pavilions leads to a Court of Honour and then the château itself, with its round towers and bell-shaped domes. Inside are some good frescos, *trompe-l'oeil* paintings and furniture.

The other château, **Ancy-le-Franc**, lies 14km (9 miles) south on the Burgundy canal. Its setting and exterior are less charming than Tanlay, and, being uninhabited, it is in need of restoration; but its interior is sumptuous, with magnificent furniture and decoration, including murals in the Sacrifice and Pharsala galleries, and a hall of the Roman emperors with a curious acoustic. It is a charming example of Italian Renaissance architecture, its inner closed courtyard richly decorated with pilasters, alcoves and dormer windows.

East of Tanlay is the pretty village of **Laignes**, with a large pool graced by swans at the side of the main square. Just beyond, to the left, is the **Marcenay Lake**, a popular spot for water-sports with a good restaurant. Thirteen kilometres (8 miles) north of here is **Molesmes**, with its ruined abbey and Romanesque church; and from here you can cross the border to the charming, sleepy enclave of **Les**

The pleasant market town of Tonnerre on the Burgundy canal

Riceys, in Champagne, where the pink champagne is excellent and cheap, and the local *vin rosé*, if they have any left, is superb.

Châtillon-sur-Seine, 17km (11 miles) east of Laignes, is an animated small town on the busy N71 Troyes-Dijon road. Here the Seine is a pretty stream, not far from its source, and in the centre of town it is fed by a vauclusian spring, the Douix, which emerges at the foot of a bank of rock in a charming setting of lawns, grottoes, flower-beds and trees. The town museum, housed in a Renaissance mansion, holds amongst other archaeological finds one of the greatest treasures of Gallo-Roman France, the Vase of Vix or krater, a huge sixth-century BC Greek bronze vase with a superb frieze of chariots and hoplites, and heads of Gorgons on the handles. It is 1.64m (5.37ft) high, 208kg in weight, and could have held 1,100 litres. It was found with other treasures at the nearby village of Vix when a Gallic princess's grave was excavated there. You can visit the village and site 7km (4 miles) north of Châtillon, under Mont Lassois.

South of Châtillon stretches the vast Châtillon Forest, and beyond that the sources of the Seine and Coquille, though there is little to see. Instead turn south-west on the D980 for Montbard, and after 28km (17 miles) turn left through the forest to **Fontenay Abbey**. This Cistercian monastery, founded in the twelfth century by St Bernard of Clairvaux, is one of the major tourist attractions of Burgundy, and visits are guided and strictly controlled. The site, in a peaceful wooded valley, is beautiful; and the buildings and gardens make a harmonious whole. The buildings are elegant but severely plain, in true Cistercian style, the gardens trim and formal, with a fine carp-pool. Though the church, cloisters and statue of the Virgin of Fontenay are particularly striking, the beauty of the buildings lies in their overall design and materials, and the strong impression you receive from them of the purity of the monastic life.

Nearby **Montbard** is a small town in an attractive setting flanking a hill and sandwiched between the river Brenne and the Burgundy canal. An industrial centre since the eighteenth century, it specialises in the manufacture of steel tubes. A former home of the Dukes of Burgundy (John the Bold spent his youth here), it is chiefly known as the birthplace of the famous eighteenth-century naturalist Buffon (1707-1788), and you can visit the Buffon Park which he designed and where he wrote his *Histoire Naturelle*. It provides pleasant walks, and contains the Aubespin tower, which gives a fine view over the town and valley from the top, the St Louis Tower, with an exhibition of his possessions, his study, the chapel where he is buried and the Buffon hotel, where he lived. Six kilometres (4 miles) from Montbard are the Buffon Forges, an eighteenth-century industrial centre with steel-making exhibits.

The Auxois

Take the D980 south from Montbard, and in 18km (11 miles) a fairy-tale sight will be spread before you. The profile of conical towers, spires and multi-coloured roofs, set on a pink-granite spur above the river Armançon, is a picture-book image of Burgundy and provides your first view of **Semur-en-Auxois**. One of its most attractive towns, Semur is the capital of the Auxois, an area between the Châtillonais and the Morvan which is rich in both culture and produce. This is quintessential Burgundy — enter the town by the fourteenth-century Sauvigny gate into a maze of narrow cobbled streets lined with old half-timbered houses and shops selling regional delicacies (try a blackcurrant ice-cream). In the town centre is the fine thirteenth-century Gothic Notre-Dame church, which has an unusually narrow nave and some good stained glass. Note the Burgundian snails carved on the façade. Nearby, a former Dominican convent houses an interesting museum and a library. The old ramparts, dominated by four circular fourteenth-century towers with pointed red-tiled roofs, provide a pleasant shaded walk with splendid views. There are some good restaurants in the town.

Semur is a good centre for exploring the fertile Auxois. Twelve kilometres (7 miles) west on the D954 is **Epoisses**, home of Burgundy's most delicious cheese (try it soaked in *Marc de Bourgogne*, a local *eau-de-vie* made from grape-skins). Epoisses' imposing feudal château has a long history dating back to the sixth century, and has associations with King Henri IV, the great Condé, Madame de Sévigné, and other famous figures. It is in a horseshoe shape, set a little apart from the village, with two sets of defensive walls, the outer one sheltering a cluster of houses round the twelfth-century church. You can only visit the outer part, which has formal gardens designed by Le Nôtre, four pointed square towers, a Renaissance well-head, a Louis XIV façade and a mansard roof; and in the grounds a massive sixteenth-century dovecote with 3,000 pigeon-holes. The walls of the vestibule are covered with portraits of the eminent personalities who stayed in the château.

South on the D36 is another château, **Bourbilly**. This restored fourteenth-century building was the ancestral home of Madame de Sévigné, and contains many souvenirs of her grandmother, St Jeanne de Chantal (1572-1641), founder of a religious order. Her relics are preserved in the chapel. A little further south, to the east of Précy-sous-Thil, near the village of **Thil**, are the ruins of a fourteenth-century church and ninth-century castle. These can only be reached on foot, a strenuous half-hour walk to the top of the Thil plateau; and you cannot enter the castle ruins without a guide. But both sets of ruins are imposing, and there are magnificent views from the top over the Auxois and the Morvan heights.

Take the D70 and D970 east to **St Thibault**, which has an elegant if rather neglected late Gothic church. Its portal, with lively, expressive sculptures of St Thibault, the Blessed Trinity, the twelve Virgins and local heroes, can claim to be one of the finest in Burgundy; and inside are some fine statuary and wood carvings in the choir and on reredos and altar screens. Nearby, to the north-east, is the restored fifteenth-century château of Posanges, with a splendid fortified entrance gate and three of its four round towers surviving. Further south there are two other impressive châteaux, both in ruins: one at **Commarin**, with an elegant façade, is surrounded by a moat in a pretty park; the other, at **Châteauneuf**, is a massive fortress in a picturesque site, surrounded by a lovely walled village with well-preserved old houses and narrow streets.

Before leaving the Auxois, three more sites east of Semur merit a visit. The first is **Flavigny-sur-Ozerain**, a medieval fortified town perched on a rocky promontory above its river and two tributaries.

Viewed from a distance it is striking, and as you enter through one of the machicolated gates into the narrow streets you are transported back to the Middle Ages. Built round an ancient (eighth century) abbey, Flavigny was then an important Burgundy town; later it fell into decay, but many of the old buildings are now being restored, and antique and curio shops abound. St Genest church has a beautiful statue of the Angel of the Annunciation and some lovely comic carvings on the choir stalls, and the abbey ruins in the south-west corner of the town are worth seeing. But the main interest is in strolling round the narrow streets or touring the ramparts, admiring as you go the Renaissance houses and sampling Flavigny's well-known aniseed sweets, still made in a section of the abbey buildings.

To the north of Flavigny, near the village of **Alise-Ste-Reine**, is the Gallo-Roman site of *Alésia*, which gives its name to the whole region. Alise is built on the side of Mont Auxois, which is topped by Millet's famous large bronze statue of Vercingétorix, overlooking an area that could be called the 'graveyard of Celtic Gaul'. This is thought to be the site of the last stand of the Gallic leader against Julius Caesar in 52BC, when Caesar with 40,000 men beseiged Vercingétorix' strongly-defended fort and, after 6 weeks, forced him and his large pan-Gallic army to surrender. The excavations, begun last century, are still going on, and you can see the remains of the Gallo-Roman town and, in a small museum, many of the objects found there. The second part of the village's name refers to a shepherdess saint who was decapitated in the third-century AD for refusing to marry a Roman centurion. A miraculous fountain with health-giving water appeared here and the chapel containing it is still a popular place of pilgrimage. An open-air theatre (seating 4,000), the *Théâtre des Roches*, has recently been built here on the slopes of Mont Auxois, where an annual performance of the Mystery of Ste Reine is performed each September.

Just north of Alise on the D954 is **Bussy-Rabutin**, whose château is one of the most original in France. This does not apply to its exterior which, though attractive, resembles many other châteaux of the *grand siècle* (seventeenth century), but to the lavishly-decorated interior, the work of its famous, or notorious, owner. Roger de Bussy-Rabutin (1618-93) was one of the great 'characters' of history: a writer, soldier and adventurer of dubious character (he has been variously called 'vain', 'indiscreet' and 'treacherous'), whose pen eventually made him fall foul of Louis XIV when he wrote verses ridiculing the young king's sad love affair with Marie Mancini. He was consigned to the Bastille in 1665, and later sequestered to his

Burgundy château and told to stay there; whereupon he wrote his scandalous memoirs and embellished his home with portraits, often satirical and sarcastically captioned, of many characters of history or the society of his day, including some of his own ex-mistresses. You can enjoy this entertaining décor, which amounts to Roger's autobiography, on a guided visit, the high point of which is the circular *Tour Dorée*, covered from floor to ceiling with lively paintings and inscriptions.

The Morvan and Avallonais

Return to Semur and continue west on the D954, then the N6, to **Avallon**. Most people speed through this town on the edge of the Morvan Regional Nature Park, but it is well worth a visit, especially on market day. It has a bloodthirsty past as a strategic gateway to Burgundy, and was sacked many times in spite of its strong defences (it is sited on a granite rock between two ravines, with stout ramparts). Today its attractive old centre is still guarded by weathered watchtowers and enclosed by ivy-covered ramparts, which provide a pleasant promenade round the town. Its church of St Lazare, once a place of pilgrimage as a centre for the cure of leprosy (it claimed to have a healing relic of St Lazarus), has beautiful, though damaged, carved twelfth-century portals and an ancient crypt, probably fourth-century AD. Nearby is a pretty fifteenth-century clock tower with archway, turret and campanile, a small museum and some fine old houses.

Perhaps the high spot of Burgundy, especially for those who love Romanesque art and architecture, is **Vézelay**, 13km (8 miles) west of Avallon on the D957. This picturesque hilltop village is crowned by the Basilica of Ste Madeleine, one of the jewels of Christendom and now designated by UNESCO as a world treasure. Its abbey, founded in AD878, was believed to hold the remains of St Mary Magdalene, and became a leading pilgrimage centre and starting point for pilgrim roads to Jerusalem and Compostela in the Middle Ages. The abbey was later destroyed by Huguenots and Revolutionaries, and the derelict church restored in the nineteenth century by Viollet-le-Duc. A 'pilgrim trail' leads up the hill from the car park in the *Champ-de-Foire*, through the lovely old village, to the front façade of the basilica. This is impressive, but its relief sculptures are surpassed by those of the inner doorways, which are magnificent in their detail and vivid realism. On the tympanum is Christ in glory with his apostles, surrounded by fabulous creatures, signs of the Zodiac and labours of the months. Inside the church, the nave is high and

Eating snails (escargots);
a renowned classic French dish

luminous, its arches attractively striped with bands of light and dark stone. But its capitals are its greatest treasures: 100 in all, in different styles and with a variety of subjects, they are a source of endless fascination, as they must have been to the medieval pilgrims whose instruction and entertainment they were designed to provide. A detailed guide would be useful to explain them; and beware — Vézelay is not off the beaten track for coach parties, so go early or late to avoid them.

For a contrast with Vézelay, the nearby church of **St Père-sous-Vézelay** is a splendid Gothic building (twelfth to fifteenth century). Its exterior is stylishly ornate while its interior is simple and pure, though with some interesting sculpture. Adjoining the church is an archaeological museum, exhibiting the finds from the site at **Les Fontaines Salées**, 2km (1 mile) away. This ancient site has a long, complex history, from its mesolithic beginnings (10,000-3,000BC) and its later use as an urn burial necropolis (1,200-800BC), to its Gallo-Roman development as a spa whose sacred saline springs had healing properties. The Gauls built a circular open-air sanctuary here in the second-century BC, with temple and sacred pool, and in the second-century AD the Romans replaced it with a thermal station. A combined visit may be made to the site and museum.

The Cure valley north of Vézelay becomes narrow, with limestone cliffs, and in 18km (11 miles) the N6 passes through a cliff tunnel, revealing the entrance to the caves of **Arcy-sur-Cure**. These are Burgundy's best-known caves, with 2km (1½ miles) of galleries and rooms (950m/3,116ft) on the visit) containing stalactites and stalagmites in fantastic shapes, and a little vivid green lake. Other nearby caves may be explored, and near the St More fountain is a medieval quarry for sarcophagi. From here, west on the D950, cross to the Yonne Valley, which has a similar series of cliffs and caves near le Saussois, a popular haunt of rock-climbers. Follow the Yonne southwards on the D100, through Châtel-Censoir and Lucy-sur-Yonne (both of which have fine Romanesque churches), to **Clamecy**. This charming old town, perched on a spur overlooking the Yonne, Beuvron and canal de Nivernais at the north-west corner of the Morvan, was the birthplace of the writer Romain Rolland, who described it as a 'town of beautiful reflections and supple hills'. At one time it was the centre of the Morvan wood industry, its rivers famous for their floating logs; now it is an important wood-processing and chemical centre. But its old town is still a maze of narrow, winding streets, with the splendid flamboyant Gothic church of St Martin in the centre. The 'Bethléem quarter' has an old chapel that belonged to the Bishops of Bethlehem, and you can visit the birthplace and museum of Romain Rolland. **Tannay**, 12km (7 miles) south, produces an excellent but little-known white wine.

South of Avallon, the Cousin Valley marks the northern edge of the **Morvan Massif**. Burgundy is mainly limestone country, but this is its granite heartland — a wild and underpopulated region of lakes, hills and forests, about 80km (50 miles) by 50km (31 miles) in size. Its people are still thought of as poor, backward and superstitious, with a strong accent (they roll their 'r's), and Morvan girls were often sent into service as wet-nurses. It is an attractive area, its dense pinewoods providing France with most of its Christmas trees, but it can be wet. It is now being developed as a holiday centre, with water-sports on its many lakes and reservoirs, canoeing on the Cure and Cousin, walking (the GR13 runs through it) and horse-riding — there are marked rides and equestrian centres.

The prettiest and most popular lake is the **Lac des Settons**, with swimming, boating and fishing facilities and some small resorts. Just north of this is an attractive waterfall, the *Saut de Gouloux*, and beyond at **St Brisson** is the office of the Regional Nature Park, with a floral garden and small museum of the World War II Resistance in the Morvan. Further north still, **Quarré-les-Tombes** is a quiet town named after the mysterious sarcophagi that surround the church, the work of primitive stone-masons; nearby St Léger-Vauban is the birthplace of the famous marshal and fortress-builder; and there is an abbey at La Pierre-qui-Vire (the 'Stone that Rocks') where the monks make and sell cream cheeses. South of Settons, the region becomes more hilly, with its highest point in the extreme south at **Mont Beuvray** (821m/2,693ft — good views from the chapel at the top). **Château-Chinon** is the largest resort, with an interesting Morvan Costume and Folklore Museum and good views from the Calvary above the town.

The best base for exploring the Morvan is **Saulieu**, on its eastern edge. This attractive town has an enviable reputation for gastronomy, being popular with travellers and pilgrims through the ages for its fine restaurants (Rabelais and Madame de Sévigné both praised the quality of its food and wine). It has a fine Romanesque church, the twelfth-century Basilica of St Andoche (an early local martyr), whose treasure is its figured capitals, with their charming mixture of sacred and secular themes. The church square has a lovely fountain, and the small museum next door combines archaeology with local history, folklore and crafts. In the pleasant old streets are some good food shops selling local delicacies.

South of Saulieu, the D980 takes you on a pleasant 41km (25 miles) run through the south-eastern corner of the Morvan to **Autun**, the old Roman capital of Burgundy. This was a chief Gallic city and stronghold, destroyed and then rebuilt by the Roman Emperor Augustus, who renamed it *Augustodunum*. Of the four original Roman city gates, two remain, the Arroux and St André gates, and only fragments remain of the old Roman theatre, once the largest in Gaul. Of the medieval town, part of the ramparts remain, and the Romanesque cathedral of St Lazare, famed for its amazing tympanum of the Last Judgement in the doorway. This is signed by one of the few medieval sculptors known by name, Gislebertus (twelfth century), who was renowned throughout Europe; and it is one of the most dramatic representations of the medieval world-view ever drawn — one of the masterpieces of Romanesque art. Inside the church are some fine carved capitals, mostly in the chapterhouse. In the superb Rolin Museum across the square is another Gislebertus masterpiece, a recumbent Eve, with a fifteenth-century *Virgin of Autun* in polychrome stone and a *Nativity* by the Master of Moulins.

The Côte-d'Or

Take the D973 east from Autun, and in 10km bear left on the D326 for **Sully** and its magnificent château, called by Madame de Sévigné 'the Fontainebleau of Burgundy'. Though you can only visit its exterior grounds and servants' quarters, the detour is well worth making. You approach it down an avenue of flat-topped bushes, then you cross the wide moat by a five-arched bridge. The Renaissance château, built in 1515, mixes fantasy and sobriety into a harmonious whole, its great monumental staircase leading from the centre of the north wing to a semicircular terrace overlooking an ornamental lake. The best view of it is from the north side, across the lake. North of Sully, **Arnay-le-Duc** is an attractive town with some good restaurants and an old almshouse staging an exhibition of regional crafts; while **Nolay**, 15km (9 miles) east, nestles prettily in a basin near a rocky, wooded *cirque*, with caves and waterfall, known as 'the End of the World'. Nolay's wooden covered market hall, surrounded by old shops, has superb timber work and a heavy roof of limestone slabs.

East of Nolay, cross the N6 to the château of **La Rochepot**, dramatically-sited on a rocky spur with its village clustered below, and clearly visible to travellers passing on the N6. This is a feudal castle refashioned in the fifteenth century, with six massive but elegant pepper-pot towers and a drawbridge leading to a courtyard bordered by a Renaissance wing with a Burgundian multi-coloured tiled roof. Inside, the visit includes the guardroom, with its massive chimney, dining room, kitchen, Chinese room and Gothic chapel. From the terrace by the right-hand tower is a fine view over the circle of surrounding hills which form the southern end of the Côte-d'Or. To the north of La Rochepot, the village of Orches produces a pleasant rosé wine, while to the south, across the Mont de Sène, **Santenay-les-Bains** is famous for its red wine, one of the great Burgundies. Santenay has a modern spa with a hot spring on the site of a Roman baths, and nearby, a Roman amphitheatre and a small twelfth-century Templar church.

Santenay is at the southern edge of the Côte-d'Or, the golden heartland of Burgundy where its most famous wines are produced. This south-east-facing scarp slope, known to the French simply as La Côte, starts just south of Burgundy's great capital, Dijon, runs down through its fabled wine capital, Beaune, and ends just north of Chagny. For most of its length it is skirted by three roads: the E17 motorway, the N74 trunk road and a local road. South of Beaune, where the slopes are known as the Côte de Beaune, the local road (D113) takes you from Santenay through the famous white wine

The famous Hôtel-Dieu at Beaune

villages of Chassagne-Montrachet, Puligny-Montrachet and Meursault, then via the renowned red-wine villages of Monthélie, Volnay and Pommard, to Beaune. This is a lovely area, but it is hardly 'off the beaten track'! Here is some of the most expensive land in the world: the rare and highly-prized *Le Montrachet*, 'the world's best white wine', is produced here. Less well-known is the charming village of **St Romain**, hidden in the Haute Côte, which produces good red and rosé and offers fine views over the area from a plateau above the village.

Beaune and its surrounding wine villages are seductive, and you will no doubt be tempted to join the crowds visiting the famous Hôtel-Dieu, or sampling the local product at the Marché aux Vins or one of the great wine houses. North of Beaune is the Côte de Nuits, where the terrain becomes even more exclusive and the wine dearer; but this should not deter you from following the Route des Grands Crus (D122) through villages with hallowed names: Aloxe-Corton, Nuits-St Georges, Vosne-Romanée, Vougeot, Chambolle-Musigny and Gevrey-Chambertin. This is where the fabled red wines are produced, some of the rarest and most expensive in the world, whose names themselves are sheer poetry — Le Musigny, Le Chambertin (Napoleon's favourite wine), Romanée-Conti, Richebourg, La Tache, Grands-Echézaux. But the Route des Grands Crus is a well-trodden road, and tastings of these precious wines are rare. To explore the region more fully, it is wiser to select one or two more rewarding sites to visit.

At Vougeot, you should not miss the **Château du Clos-Vougeot**. One of the most picturesque châteaux on the Côte, it stands proudly within its walled *clos*, its rust-coloured tiles gleaming among a sea of surrounding vines. Built by Cistercian monks in 1551, it is now the headquarters of the brotherhood of the Chevaliers du Tastevin, the famous confraternity of Burgundy wine producers which has existed since 1934, with three aims: to celebrate the region's long and glorious past; to promote Burgundy and its wines; and to enjoy an annual beano amid much colourful pomp and ceremony. Three sumptuous banquets, known as the Trois Glorieuses, are held in November each year, at Clos de Vougeot, Meursault and Beaune. Other feasts are held in the Vougeot château during the year for the vignerons and their guests, and you can learn about these on your visit. You can also see the vast twelfth-century cellars and the thirteenth-century *cuverie* (fermenting room) with its four huge wine presses.

South-west of Beaune, the Château de Pommard offers an interesting and informative visit, with some wine-tasting; and at **Chenôve**, at the very northern end of the wine-route, you can visit two ancient enclosed vineyards once belonging to the two main powers in the land. The *Clos du Chapitre* was once owned by the canons of Autun, the *Clos du Roi* by the Dukes of Burgundy; in the *cuverie* of the latter you can see two huge and magnificent thirteenth-century wine presses. At nearby **Fixin** is a fine statue of Napoleon by a local artist and friend, set in a pleasant park with a small museum of Bonaparte souvenirs. At **Nuits-St-Georges**, a small town based on an old Gallo-Roman settlement, there is an archaeological museum in the seventeenth-century clock-tower. **Savigny-lès-Beaune**, 4km (2 miles) north of Beaune, has a château housing a motorcycle museum; and from here a pleasant round tour can be made to Nuits-St Georges via the *Combe Pertuis*, a deep and narrow gorge. At Beaune itself, you should not miss the Musée du Vin de Bourgogne, housed in the old *hôtel* or mansion of the Dukes of Burgundy.

Whether you visit Burgundy's capital, **Dijon**, depends on your taste for large, bustling industrial towns; but if you do, the old centre, with its splendid and sumptuously-decorated Grand Dukes' Palace, is not to be missed. Dijon also has three fine churches, a good archaeological museum, and some exquisite old houses in the medieval streets behind and around the palace. Outside the city centre on the western side is the old Champmol Charterhouse, now a psychiatric hospital, and housing two fine groups of sculptures. Just beyond is the Kir lake (named, like the aperitif, after the much-loved mayor), a popular spot for city-dwellers, with a beach, leisure centre and sailing club. As befits its reputation as a gastronomic centre, Dijon has some excellent restaurants.

Southern Burgundy — The Brionnais and Mâconnais

South of Chagny and the Côte-d'Or is a less-explored region called the Côte Chalonnaise, after its chief town, Chalon-sur-Saône. It is undulating land but not so hilly as the Côte, and produces some fine wine (as at Mercurey, Rully and Givry) and a lot of drinkable wine under the *Bourgogne Rouge* label. It is a good area for liberal wine tastings — try the large Cave Co-operative at **Buxy**. **Givry** is a pleasant, quiet little town with an eighteenth-century-air and a church covered in cupolas; and the nearby Vallée des Vaux has some typical rustic farmhouses with adjoining cellars. **Chalon-sur-Saône** itself is a not-too-attractive river port and industrial town, but it has a good museum explaining the life and work of Nicéphore Niepce, a local man who (the French claim) invented photography.

South of Chalon the N6 leads to **Tournus**. This small town, squeezed between road and river on a busy highway, is hardly off the beaten track, yet it is often by-passed without a glance by travellers rushing south. To do so is to miss one of the finest and most unusual Romanesque churches in France, the Basilica of St Philibert. Founded by fugitive monks from the north-west, the abbey church has a northern simplicity of style, giving the impression of a powerful fortress. Its remarkable nave has tall, sturdy pillars and unusual transverse barrel vaulting, its stark effect softened by the delicate pinkish colour of the stone. The nave has been called a 'structural symphony', and is best appreciated from the eleventh-century St Michael's chapel on the first floor of the narthex. Those abbey buildings that remain are grouped round the cloister at the side of the church, and house exhibitions in summer. Tournus has two museums, one devoted to Bresse folk-lore, the other to a local painter, Greuze.

To the west and south-west of Tournus are two regions that together form one of the most attractive, and relatively little-known, parts of Burgundy. To the south-west is the hilly, wooded and vine-covered Mâconnais, to the west the gentler, undulating farmland of the Brionnais. Both regions are dotted with châteaux and pretty villages; and both are dominated by the influence of Cluny, whose legacy is a huge number of Romanesque churches and ruined abbeys. The D14 takes you first into the Mâconnais, over the Col de Beaufer and past the châteaux of Ozenay and Martailly to **Brancion**. This picturesque medieval village, dramatically perched on a rocky spur between two ravines, is encased in ramparts and only entered through a once-portcullised entrance gate. Once inside, you are back in the Middle Ages, with a fifteenth-century market, a communal bakehouse, a gibbet, a sanctuary stone and a well-restored tenth-fifteenth-century château. There are earth streets and houses overgrown with vegetation, but some of the houses have been beautifully restored, as has the twelfth-century Romanesque church, which has remarkable fourteenth-century frescoes. The hamlet of **La Chapelle**, at the foot of the hill, has a workshop for the restoration of frescoes.

The power and simplicity of early Romanesque can be seen a few miles west at **Chapaize**. Its eleventh-century church of St Martin, all that remains of a Benedictine priory, has a splendid 35m (115ft) high, slightly tapered Lombard bell-tower, visible for miles. Its interior is stark and impressive, with unusually thick pillars. The ruins of an eleventh-century convent can be seen at nearby **Lancharre**; and, further along the D14 at **Cormatin**, is a charming Renaissance château (1600) with exceptionally rich decor and sumptuous furnishings. South on the D981, both **Ameugny** and Taizé have Romanesque churches, and **Taizé** is well-known for its ecumenical religious community, founded in 1940 and involving Christians of many denominations from all over the world, many of them young people. This active community invites visitors to join their services and meetings or to share their hospitality. Nearby **Chissey-lès-Mâcon** has a thirteenth-century church with interesting capitals, and from here you can drive to the summit of **Mont St Romain** (579m/1,899ft), the high point of the Mâconnais, with fine views. Its eastern slopes are covered with vines which produce the fine white wines of **Mâcon-Lugny**; and its southern slopes are riddled with an extensive series of grottoes near **Fougnières** and at **Azé**, where there is a prehistoric site near a grotto with an underground river running through it, and a small museum. There are other interesting early churches at **Blanot** and **Donzy-le-Pertuis**.

Cluny lies at the heart of the Mâconnais, reflecting quietly on its past glory as home of the greatest and most powerful abbey in Christendom. Now, sadly, of the huge Romanesque church (nearly 200m/656ft long) that once dominated monastic life throughout Europe, only one transept tower, with two transepts and five naves, remains. The Benedictine monastery founded in AD910 and most of

The abbey church at Cluny

the church were destroyed after the Revolution in 1798, and some of its area has since been built over; but enough remains to give you an idea of its original massive beauty. In the surviving buildings are displays, models and unearthed fragments, including a fine set of figured capitals in the thirteenth-century flour store. In the town is a small museum, and a Romanesque church (1159) with a fine tower.

Two villages south of Cluny merit a visit; and a third evokes the memory of one of France's leading literary figures. **Berzé-le-Chatel** has a massive, triple-walled feudal château, visible from the main road, from the terrace of which you have a magnificent view over the surrounding Mâcon-Viré vineyards. But its sister village, **Berzé-la-Ville**, holds one of the treasures of France. In a small chapel that was once a summer retreat for Cluniac monks is a series of superb twelfth-century frescoes, miraculously preserved behind whitewash until uncovered in 1887. Byzantine frescoes are rare in France, but these, particularly the *Christ in Majesty* in the apse, rival in their startling colour and design anything that Italy or Greece can offer. The village of **Milly-Lamartine**, across the valley, was the childhood home of the Romantic poet. His family house may be visited, as may the Lamartine museum in his native **Mâcon**.

From here, two roads will take you west into the Brionnais: the N79/E62 is a rapid trunk road, while the more scenic D17 (bear right at Ste Cécile) takes you near the 592m/1,492ft-high Butte de Suin, which gives a fine view of the area. In 28km (17 miles) is **Charolles**, the town which gives its name to the famous white Charollais cattle of the region. This is lush, cattle-breeding country, and the pleasant town, dominated by its ruined château, has an important cattle market. Continue on the N79 to **Paray-le-Monial**, a charming market town on the River Bourbince and the Canal du Centre with a welcoming air and an architectural jewel — its magnificent Basilica du Sacré-Coeur. Paray may be said to have taken over the role of Cluny: since the seventeenth century it has been an important centre of Roman Catholicism, with annual pilgrimages to the Shrine of Ste Marguerite-Marie Alcoque and her cult of the Sacred Heart. The basilica is built on a plan that resembles Cluny, with three pointed towers and a beautiful eastern end with an array of fine chapels — its sober elegance striking when the church is lit up at night. Paray, with its museum of religious art, a fine town hall, and good restaurants and camping, is an ideal centre for touring the Brionnais.

To start this tour, take the D191 south for 12km (7 miles) to **Montceaux-l'Etoile**, whose church has a fine tympanum. South on the D174 is **Anzy-le-Duc**, whose beautiful Romanesque church is thought to have been the model for Vézelay. It has a lovely three-storied Lombard tower, and wonderful carvings on the tympanum and capitals. **Marcigny**, 6km (4 miles) south, has some fine old wooden houses and a good museum in the fifteenth-century Mill Tower. Nearby **Semur-en-Brionnais** has an attractive old centre, with a lovely Romanesque church at one end of the square and the ruins of a ninth-century château at the other. Continuing south, two other villages, **St Julian-de-Jonzy** and **Fleury-la-Montagne**, have churches with finely-carved tympana.

At the southernmost point of your tour, **Charlieu**, though just over the border from Burgundy, is not to be missed. It once had one of the most important Benedictine abbeys in the region, described as 'the most embellished of all the daughters of Cluny'. This is now in ruins, but important excavation work has helped to reconstruct its origins and history, and enough remains to give an impression of its past splendour. Its most glorious remnant today is the sculpture on the north face of the Narthex (which you can see from the road outside the abbey) — a ravishing display of medieval art with an oriental flavour brought back from the Crusades. Charlieu also has some fine Gothic houses in the town, and a splendid Gothic cloister in the Cordeliers' Convent just outside. Turning north-east on the D987, **La Clayette** has a moated château with a Motor Museum in the outbuildings; while nearby **Dree** has a pretty seventeenth-century château (both are closed for interior visits). **Bois-Ste-Marie**, 4km (2 miles) east, has an eleventh-century church, said to be the oldest in the Brionnais, with curious capitals.

From here a scenic route past the Montagne de St Cyr on the D41 leads to Dompierre-les-Ormes and the **Pezanin Arboretum**, a collection of exotic trees in an attractive setting. Rejoin the E62/N79 and return towards Mâcon, making a final detour at Prissé to visit the famed wine villages of **Pouilly-Fuissé**. This *appellation* combines five communes (Pouilly, Fuissé, Solutré, Vergisson and Chaintré) to produce a dry, fruity white wine to rival those of the Côte d'Or. One of these villages, **Solutré**, is famed for more than its wine: it has become a centre of prehistory after 100,000 skeletons of prehistoric animals were found under its distinctive rock (driven off the cliff by hunters) together with human skeletons and Bronze Age artefacts. The period 15,000-1,200BC is now known as the 'Solutrean Era'. There is a small museum in the village.

Pouilly-Fuissé and other more affordable white Chardonnay wines of the Mâconnais, and its pleasant red wines, can be sampled in the area or in the excellent *Maison des Vins* in Mâcon itself (north, off the N6). Though not a tourist centre, **Mâcon** is colourful and lively, with pleasant parks and some good restaurants. Its Municipal Museum, housed in an old Ursulines convent, includes finds from nearby **Solutré**. The fifteenth-century *Maison de Bois*, with comic carvings, and the Lamartine Museum, are also worth seeing. Afterwards, why not end your tour with a glass of good *Mâcon blanc* in a café beside the Saône?

Further Information
— Burgundy —

Museums and Other Places of Interest

NORTHERN BURGUNDY

Auxerre
Musée Leblanc-Duvernoy
9b Rue d'Eqleny
Open: 15 June to 30 September 2-6pm.
Rest of year 2-5pm. Except Mondays
and holidays.

Musée Lapidoire
In ancient chapel.
Open: 10am-12noon and 2-5pm
(summer only).

Musée Municipal
Pl. Maréchal Lederc (inc. Musée Eckmühl).

Fleurigny
Château
Open: daily August, Saturday, Sunday
and holidays April to October 2.30-
6pm; closed Monday.

St Fargeau Puisaye
Château
Open: daily 10am-12noon and 2-6pm
(2-5pm Nov to April); closed Tuesday.
Son et lumière.

CHATILLONAIS
Ancy-le-Franc
Château
Open: March to November 9.30am-
6.30pm. Guided visits on the hour.

Châtillon-sur-Seine
Musée du Maison Philandrier
Open: daily 9am-12noon and 2-6pm,
except Monday, March to October;
winter weekends only 10am-12noon
and 2-5pm.

Fontenay
Ancienne Abbaye
Open: daily 9am-12noon and 2 or 2.30-
6.30pm; guided tours every hour, or
½ hour July and August.

Montbard
Parc Buffon
Open: 8.30am-12noon and 2-5pm
except Tuesday April to October. For
Tour St Louis apply to caretaker.

La Grande Forge at Buffon
Open: 2.30-6pm except Tuesday, June
to September.

Tanlay
Château de Tanlay
Open: 9.15-11.30am and 2.15-5.15pm
Palm Sunday to 1 November; closed
Tuesday.

Tonnerre
Hôpital Notre-Dame des Fontenilles
Open: 10-11.30am and 2-5.30pm June
to September; closed Tuesday.

THE AUXOIS
Alise-Ste-Reine
Fouilles et Musée d'Alésia
Open: 9-7pm July to September; 10am-
6pm April to October.

Bussy-Rabutin
Château
Open: 9am-12noon and 2-6pm April to
November; 10-11am and 2-3pm
December to March; closed Tuesday
and Wednesday.

Commarin
Château
Open: (guided visits only) 2-6pm
except Tuesday, Easter to October.

Epoisses
Château
Open: (exterior only) 10am-12noon and
2-6pm April to September. Guided visits.

Semur-en-Auxois
Musée et Bibliothèque
Open: Museum Wednesday and Friday
2.30-6.30pm, June to September;
Library Wednesday 2-6pm all year.

MORVAN AND AVALLONAIS

Arcy-sur-Cure
Le Grande Grotte
Open: 9am-12noon and 2-6pm March
to November.

Autun
Musée Rolin
Open: 9.30am-12noon and 2-6.30pm 15
March to September; 10am-12noon and
2-4pm October to 14 March; closed
Tuesday/Sunday am.

Château-Chinon
*Musée du Folklore et du Costume en
Morvan*
Open: 2.30-6pm Wednesday, Saturday
and Sunday only June to September.

Clamecy
*Hôtel-Musée du Duc de Bellegarde et
Maison Romain Rolland*
Open: June to September 10am-12noon
and 2.30-5.30pm except Tuesday;
otherwise on request.

Saulieu
Musée
Open: 10am-12noon and 2-7pm except
Tuesday; September to May 10am-
12noon and 2-6pm except Tuesday.

St Père-sous-Vézelay
*Musée Archéologique Régional et Fouilles
des Fontaines Salées*
Open: 9am-12noon and 2-7pm. Closed
December to February and Wednes-
days, September to March.

THE COTE-D'OR

Beaune
Hôtel-Dieu et Musée
Open: daily 9am-6.45pm, 9am-5.30pm
in winter. Guided visits only.

Musée du Vin de Bourgogne
Open: 10am-12.30pm and 2-6.15pm.
Guided visits.

Dijon
*Palais des Ducs et des Etats de Bourgogne
- Musée des Beaux-Arts*
Open: 10am-6pm except Tuesday.

Musée Archéologique
Open: 9.30am-6pm except Tuesday
9am-12noon and 2-6pm in winter.

Nuits-St-Georges
Musée Archéologique
Open: daily July to September 2-6pm;
October to June, Sunday and holidays
only 2-6pm.

La Rochepot
Château
Open: 9.30-11.30am and 2.30-5.30pm
except Tuesday.

Savigny-lès-Beaune
Château-Musée du Moto
Open: 9am-12noon and 1-6.30pm.
Closed 15-31 December.

Sully
Château
Open: (exterior only) 10am-6pm Palm
Saturday to September.

Vougeot
Château du Clos-Vougeot
Open: 9-11.30am and 2.30-5.30pm;
closed 20 December-5 January.

SOUTHERN BURGUNDY — THE BRIONNAIS AND MACONNAIS

Azé
Site Préhistorique et Musée
Open: 9am-12noon and 2-7pm Palm
Sunday to 30 September.

Berzé-la-Ville
Chapelle des Moines
Open: 9.30am-12noon and 2-6pm, Palm
Sunday to 1 November.

Brancion
Château
Open: 9am-6pm Palm Sunday to
November (9.45am-6pm Sunday and
holidays); winter Sunday only 9.45am-
12noon and 2-6pm.

Chalon-sur-Saône
Musée Nicéphore Niepce and Musée Denon
Open: 9.30-11.30am and 2.30-5.30pm,
except Tuesday and holidays.

Charlieu
Ancienne Abbaye Bénédictine
Open: 9am-12noon and 2-7pm June to
September; April to May except
Tuesday; October to November and
February to March except Tuesday and
Wednesday. Guided visits.

Cluny
Musée Ochier
Open: 10am-12noon and 2-6.30pm in
summer, 9am-12noon and 2-4pm in winter; closed 20 December to 15 January.

Cormatin
Château
Open: 10am-12noon and 2.30-6.30pm
except Tuesday, Easter to October.
Guided visits.

Mâcon
Musée Municipal des Ursulines
Open: 10am-12noon and 2-6pm except
Tuesday, Sunday am and holidays.

Musée Lamartine
Open: 2-5pm except Tuesday May to
October.

Marcigny
Tour du Moulin
Open: 9.30am-12noon and 2.30-6pm
March to October.

Paray-le-Monial
Musée d'Art Sacré du Hiéron
Open: 9am-7pm 15 May to 8 September.

Tournus
*Musée Perrin-de-Puycousin and Musée
    Greuze*
Open: 9am-12noon and 2-6pm except
Tuesday; closed November to Easter.
Guided visits.

Tourist Information Centres

Autun
Office de Tourisme
3 Ave Ch de Gaulle ☎ 85 52 20 34

Auxerre
Office de Tourisme
1 & 2 quai République ☎ 86 52 06 19

Avallon
Office de Tourisme
6 rue Bocquillot ☎ 86 34 14 19

Beaune
Office de Tourisme
facing Hôtel-Dieu ☎ 80 22 24 51

Château-Chinon
Office de Tourisme
Rue Champlain ☎ 86 85 06 58

Châtillon-sur-Seine
Office de Tourisme
Pl Marmont ☎ 80 91 13 19

Dijon
Office de Tourisme
Place Darcy ☎ 80 43 42 12

Mâcon
Office de Tourisme
187 rue Carnot ☎ 85 39 71 37

Paray-le-Monial
Office de Tourisme
Ave Jean-Paul II ☎ 85 81 10 92

Semur-en-Auxois
Office de Tourisme
2 pl Gaveau ☎ 80 97 05 96

Sens
Office de Tourisme
Pl J. Jaurès ☎ 86 65 19 49

12 • The Jura

For a region that has given its name to a major geological period, the Jura is relatively unknown. The area of limestone laid down during the Jurassic period extends beyond what is known today as the Jura, but within the region all the characteristics of the period are present. During the Jurassic period, which began about 200 million years ago, what is now known as limestone was being formed at the bottom of a deep sea. This layer of limestone is recorded in certain parts of the Jura as being nearly 4,000m (13,000ft) deep.

About 50 million years ago the granite base on which the limestone lay began to move up. It broke through to become the Alps to the south of the region. This movement had the effect of pushing the more flexible limestone up and back, but movement to the north or west was prevented by the presence of older rock formations in the Vosges and the Massif Central. All this created an effect of compression and is responsible for the present shape of the Jura, a long line of mountains and hills running parallel on the south-eastern edge with wide large plateaux stretched out behind them dropping like a giant's stairway to the valley of the Saône. The Jura's original geological formation, despite the changes brought about by erosion in the intervening period, provides areas of great interest for those prepared to go off the beaten track. This formation is still evident whether seen as part of an overall view from, for example, the Pic de L'Aigle, a hill 1,000m (3,280ft) high in the centre of the region or observed in a particular characteristic such as the tortured rocks in the High Jura, known as Le Jura Plissé (The Folded Jura).

It is not easy to define precisely the limits of the area known as 'Le Jura', particularly as the geological outline of the Jura continues some way into present day Switzerland. There is a French *département* of this name, with its *Préfecture* at Lons-Le-Saunier, but this is relatively small and does not cover the whole of the area which the French would know as 'Le Jura'. They would undoubtedly include the *département* of Le Doubs to the north-east and part of the *département*

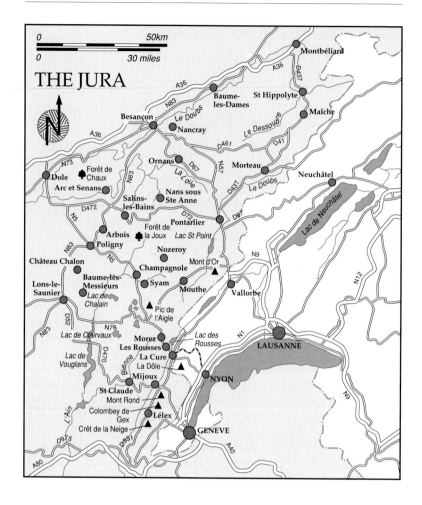

of L'Ain to the south-west because of their historical, geographical and economic links.

The Jura is the greater part of the region known as 'La Franche Comté', which only finally became part of France in 1678. The name goes back many centuries. Charlemagne's dream of a united Europe, created when he was crowned as Emperor in AD800, collapsed soon after his death. His empire was split into three, a western section, which was mainly modern France, a central part, and an eastern section. The area controlled locally by the Burgundians remained in the central part, although it was later split into two areas, the larger being ruled by the Duke and known as the Duchy, with the smaller being the County, ruled over by a Count. This was the age of feudalism and the Count paid homage direct to his German over-lord. This had the important effect of linking the Jura to the develop-ing Holy Roman Empire. However since it was so far removed from the centre of power, the area took on increasing independence. In the sixteenth century this was made a legal reality, when the county bought freedom from taxation for a payment of £200,000 every 3 years. The people of the region are very proud of this history of independence. Throughout the Middle Ages the French kings tried at various times to take over the Jura and the resistance to these attempts is part of the mythology of the region. Evidence of this can be seen in drama productions played out in various villages, in pictures and tapestries or even in caves used at one time by Resist-ance leaders.

The economy of the Jura is linked to its geology, its situation and its history. Within the rock have been found deposits not only of ore, but also of salt. The latter was important to the region and is seen in the names of such towns as Salins Les Bains and Lons-le-Saunier. The eroded edges of the lower plateau, as it meets the plain, are now particularly well positioned for growing vines from which many very good wines are made. The limestone base has always been good for trees and the whole area used to be completely covered by forests. Increasingly during the Middle Ages, particularly under the influ-ence of monastic houses, these forests were cleared. Although nowa-days large areas are open farmland, many farms were too small to be viable on their own. An example of this is in cheese making. A Comté cheese needs 600 litres of milk, but most isolated farms produce a maximum of 100 litres a day. For this reason a tradition of coopera-tion grew up, whereby farmers would deliver their milk to a local cheese-making centre, called a *fruitière*. These still function and a small *fruitière* in an out of the way village makes a very interesting and worthwhile visit.

The higher areas of the Jura are still largely covered by trees, and timber production continues to be an important staple industry, as any walk off the beaten track in these areas will show. Because of its situation, the Jura lent itself to the making of items, which used local raw materials, and needed a high degree of skill to manufacture, but were relatively small for ease of transport. Since wood was available in such quantities, a tradition grew up of manufacturing all sorts of wooden articles, from pipes and children's toys to cheese boxes. Minerals were mined locally and provided the raw material for manufacturing watches, mechanical parts and glasses. In addition to this skilled manufacture, the cutting and polishing of precious stones also continues to be an important local industry. These activities are still carried out in relatively small communities, and do not need large manufacturing sites. There is the additional benefit for those who prefer to stay off the beaten track that a visitor is nearly always welcome to see work in progress.

The most important towns in the region are undoubtedly Besançon and Dole, but they are hardly off the beaten track, situated as they are on the edge of the Saône Valley and so close to the A36 motorway, the line of which has always provided communication towards the East. However apart from these towns there are no great centres of population in the region. Lons-le-Saunier and Pontarlier have about 20,000 inhabitants, but the rest are half this size or considerably less.

The entire region, apart from the areas around Besançon and Dole is 'far from the madding crowd' and provides areas of interest for those prepared to leave busier parts and better known tourist haunts. As well as being a wonderful mixture of mountains, wooded hills, vast cliffs, vine-covered slopes, forests, upland farms and small towns and villages, the Jura is also a region of rivers and lakes. In addition, there are sites of historical, architectural and cultural interest throughout the region. The northern part is dominated by the presence of three rivers, La Loue, Le Dessoubre, and most important Le Doubs, which gives its name to the *département* which covers this part of the Jura. The central section of the Jura is the most varied with its vineyards, its forests, its lakes and its small market towns, while the southern section has the highest mountains and most deeply-cut valleys.

The Northern Jura

From Pontarlier to Besançon it is 56km (35 miles) in a direct line but the River Doubs takes 241km (150 miles), as it wends its way first north-east, then into Switzerland and finally back south-east towards its eventual destination, a meeting with the Saône. For this reason it was named by the Romans 'Dubius' the doubtful, the hesitant. The source of the Doubs is in central Jura and as it passes by and beyond Pontarlier it still has the look of a small river winding peacefully though fields and pleasant countryside, giving little evidence of either its later nature nor the nature of the terrain through which it has cut its way over the centuries.

Pontarlier is an unremarkable little town with an over-elaborate commemorative archway to mark the old entrance, the Porte St Pierre. However it has always been important as a centre of communication since it guards one of the main routes into Switzerland. If the

N57 is followed a little way in this direction the most perfect example of a cluse can be seen. This is a valley or gorge which cuts across a ridge or a line of hills. Since the hills of the Jura run from south-west to north-east, any cluse was used by travellers into and out of Switzerland to avoid the effort and danger of climbing over a 'col' or mountain pass. Inevitably the 'cluses' were heavily defended and such is the case with the Cluse de la Cluse-et-Mijoux, which has the Château de Joux on one side and a fort on the other. The Château, a museum of arms and military uniform, can be visited.

The Doubs then passes through **Morteau**, most famous for its *Jésus*. This is a cooked sausage and is a reminder that this part of the Jura is particularly well known for its cooked meats. They are usually smoked and this is done in a large wide chimney, known as a *tué* or *tuyé*. Wherever one of these is seen, a visitor will be welcome. In Morteau there is a delightful and little-known Clock Museum housed in a beautiful sixteenth-century house, the Château Pertusier which has murals in the salon relating to the Spanish occupation of the region.

Morteau's name comes from *Morte Eau* (Dead Water), describing the slow progress of the river at this point. This slow progress continues as it flows into the Lac de Chaillexon, beyond the village of Villiers-le-Lac. However beyond this lake it drops height in a most dramatic waterfall, the Saut du Doubs. This naturally attracts visitors who often take a boat along the lake. A way to see it but avoiding crowds is to drive or walk towards Le Pissoux and follow a sign to the hamlet of Les Vions. From here a road drops down to the river but the final very steep section must be walked. A corniche road in rather poor condition but with excellent views down to the lake below can be taken back to Villiers-le-Lac.

Beyond this point the Doubs enters a dramatic series of gorges and the road only approaches the river again near Goumois, where a corniche road gives superb views of the river below and Switzerland on the other bank. However before reaching the Goumois corniche it is worth turning right towards Switzerland after the village of Blancheroche. Just after the French border post where a passport will have to be shown on re-entry into France, there is a sharp little turn to the left into a minor road. This drops down into the gorge and after about 3km (2 miles) arrives at a small power station, set at the bottom of the gorge with towering cliffs all around. The Doubs has always marked the border with Switzerland and this point was part of a smugglers' route. To climb out of the gorge into France, the smugglers would use a series of ladders made of wood, which sometimes broke under the strain. The ladders became known as the Ladders of Death, *Les Echelles de la Mort*. They are now made of steel with solid handrails and can be reached after a five minute walk up through the trees. Above the ladders the pathway continues into France and after about 50 minutes a road is reached near a *fruitière* in the hamlet of Vaudey.

After Goumois, the Doubs, apparently doubtful as ever of its route, wanders off into Switzerland before coming back on itself into France where at the village of St Hyppolyte it is joined by the Dessoubre. This delightful river began life some 30 miles (48km) south-west and has been running parallel to the Doubs. Its starting point is in a large amphitheatre of cliffs, the **Cirque de Consolation**. Deep in this amphitheatre is a monastery, now used as a seminary. It cannot be visited, but it is possible to see the chapel and walk around the park. Also there are very large covered buildings, which can be used for picnics. All around, there are paths in the woods and a road leads tortuously out of the *cirque* to meet the main Besançon-Morteau road. Two miles (3km) south of this junction a left turn by a café leads to a viewing point from which can be seen the Cirque de Consolation with the Dessoubre flowing away north-east.

The region on either side of the Dessoubre and enclosed by the Doubs as it describes its large circle provides very good opportunities of getting well away from the 'beaten track'. It is wonderful undulating upland countryside with scattered farms and hamlets. Some farms keep horses, as in the village of Orchamps-Vennes near the Cirque de Consolation, where the Ecurie de Boussière organises excursions on horseback.

A little to the north of the valley of the Dessoubre near the village of Sancey-le-Long stands the Château de Belvoir high on a ridge. This dates from the twelfth century but was restored in the 1950s by the French artist, Pierre Jouffroy. There are many other places of interest nearby such as the cheese museum at Provenchère and a *fruitière* at Charmoille which make this rather isolated part of the Jura such a worthwhile area to visit.

Three other sites in the countryside between Belvoir and Besançon, which merit a visit, are the little town of Baume-les-Dames, the open-air museum at Nancray and the huge cavern, the 'Gouffre de Poudrey'. **Baume-les-Dames** is set in a beautiful valley in wooded hills near the River Doubs. The 'Dames' refers to the nuns in the local convent, who were only admitted if they were from sufficiently elevated aristocratic families! Two rivers flow into the Doubs near Baume-les-Dames, the Audeux and the Cusancin. Both pass through lovely country and provide delightful walks. South-east of Baume-les-Dames on the D484 in the village of **Nancray** is a museum devoted to regional life throughout the ages. It is an open-air museum with houses and farm buildings which have been saved from demolition or from falling into ruin and have been reconstructed on site. Trees, plants, shrubs and herbs are grown in the traditional manner. This small *écomusée* is not well known, but well worth a visit.

On the left of the N57 as it goes back towards Pontarlier is the **Gouffre de Poudrey**, the largest cavern in France with claims to be the largest in Europe. It has remarkable stalagmites and stalactites, some over 7m (23ft) in height.

As the N57 continues south it goes close to one of the most remarkable sites in this part of the Jura, the source of the River Loue. This is signposted at St Gorgon-Main and the road to it goes to the hamlet of **Ouhans**, where a right turn with the rather stylised chapel of Ste Marie des Anges on the hilltop above, leads to a car park. From this park it is quite a steep walk down to the source. However before taking this road, a better appreciation of the whole site and the course of the river can be gained by continuing on and turning right towards Révédale where there is a viewpoint and beyond that to the Belvédère du Moine de la Vallée.

The source of the River Loue, spoilt a little by the Eléctricité de France (EDF) plant and reservoir is nevertheless very interesting. The Loue comes out of the base of the cliffs a fully-fledged stream. It was always thought that its waters must come from the Doubs, 5 miles (8km) to the south, but there was no proof until 1901. In August 1901 there was an accident at the Pernod factory in Pontarlier and a million litres of absinthe flowed into the Doubs. Two days later the Loue smelled and tasted of absinthe. Proof indeed! The source of the Loue is celebrated in mythology as the lair of the Vouivre, a winged dragon, the French version of the Wyvern. According to legend this comes out of its cave once a year between the first and final strokes of midnight on Christmas Day, giving the brave just enough time to slip into his cave and steal the treasure which he guards.

From the source of the Loue there are very obvious paths leading downstream towards Mouthier-Haute-Pierre. One walk starts off on the left of the river and runs along but slightly above it, through the Gorges de Nouailles. After crossing the river by the power station, there are interesting caves to the right by the source of a small river, Le Pontet. One cave, accessible by ladders is the 'Grotte des Faux-Monnayeurs' — a base for counterfeiters at one time. The other walk from the source crosses the river and threads its way up the other side

The River Loue flowing through the village of Lods

and after many zigzags reaches the road to Mouthier-Haute-Pierre. Generally, although the source of the Loue might be crowded with tourists as one of the major sites of interest in the region, the walks through dramatic scenery and quite demanding at times are 'off the beaten track' for many.

Ornans; Le Pecheur statue sculptured by the artist Gustave Courbet

Mouthier-Haute-Pierre is renowned for its Kirsch and in spring-time the cherry trees on the hillsides are a sight to behold. The very dramatic scenery surrounding the source of the river is left behind, but it is still obvious that the Loue has cut a very deep valley as it descends. On the way there are interesting little villages, **Lods** being the most attractive with its bridge off to the left over the river and its little wine museum in a street on the right away from the river. The first town, **Ornans**, is famous as the birthplace of the artist Gustave Courbet, who found so much inspiration from the surrounding area. The house where he was born in 1819 is now a museum. It is on the opposite side of the river which has to be crossed by bridge from the main road. This, like the footbridge downstream, provides wonderful views of the backs of the riverside houses reflected in the water.

Downstream from Ornans is the Château de Cléron, built in the fourteenth century to protect the salt route from neighbouring Salins-les-Bains. It is a very good example of a fortified castle of this region with its square red-tiled central tower and its circular *donjons* (keep) It has a most picturesque exterior, seen to best advantage from the road bridge over the Loue or from the older unused bridge higher up to the left.

Central Jura

Salt is one of the products which over the years has given great wealth to the Jura, others being cheese, wine, timber and metal forging. Salt was of extreme importance for food preservation in the Middle Ages and the extraction of salt was a major industry in the region. The most productive seam of salt was discovered 300m (984ft) below the present-day town of Salins-les-Bains. It was not mined, but extracted in the form of brine after water was pumped down and then brought to the surface. The brine would be heated in large pans until the water had evaporated leaving the salt crystals behind. The salt works, *les Salines* in **Salins-les-Bains** is now a museum with its impressive underground galleries 400m (1,312ft) long. These were constructed in the thirteenth century to protect the original salt springs. Initially the local forests provided the enormous quantities of fuel needed for the process of heating and evaporation, which took from 12 to 18 hours to complete. Because of worries about the supply of wood there was a scheme in the eighteenth century to take the brine to the wood rather than the other way round. This led to the building of a most remarkable site, the royal salt works of **Arc et Senans**, 24km (15 miles) to the north of Salins-les-Bains, near the vast Forêt de Chaux.

Claude-Nicolas Ledoux, an inspector of salt works and a recognised architect, was given the task in 1793 of constructing the works. He had the notion of using this opportunity to create an entire new town according to the latest ideas of the time. The town was to be in concentric circles around the salt works and the Director's house. It would cater for every need with a church, a market place, public baths and a gymnasium. Unfortunately the works did not make as much money as had been predicted and although salt was produced for a number of years, Ledoux's scheme was never realised in full. The buildings which were created now house an International Centre for Studies of the Future as well as a salt museum and other temporary exhibitions.

The salt works in Salins-les-Bains were bought up in 1843 by a member of the de Grimaldi family, but his intention was to use the salt water in conjunction with the arrival of the railway in the town to satisfy the latest fashion for 'taking the waters'. Accordingly in 1854 he built the Thermal Baths, followed by the Grand Hôtel des Bains and the Casino. The baths still operate and they are run on friendly and informal lines so that they provide a good opportunity for the uninitiated to take their first *cure thermale*.

The town of Salins-les-Bains is nowadays dominated by the road running through it and not very attractive in places. However the countryside around with sites of interest such as Fort Belin and the Croix de Poupet provides very good walks. The Syndicat d'Initiative provides a series of excellent cards with all the various routes clearly marked on them.

Beyond Salins-les-Bains past Mont Poupet on the D492 lies the little village of **Nans-Sous-Ste-Anne**. Here there is a *taillanderie*, a small country forge where knives, sickles, scythe blades and other tools were manufactured. This is now a small museum, but a century ago the 25 workers who then worked there would turn out 20,000 scythe blades a year using the river as their power source. This is the only remaining *taillanderie* from over 50 in the region a century ago. A little to the south of the village is an amphitheatre of cliffs sheltering the source of the River Lison. This is a particularly beautiful spot, where the river already fully formed tumbles out of a cavern into a small lake before continuing its course downstream. The river can be seen in its early stages at the Cirque du Creux Billard, which like other walks, is well signposted and a little beyond the source. In the cliff face above the source is the 'Grotte Sarrazine'. The name derives from an episode during which a group of Spanish soldiers hid in the cave from the forces of Louis XIV in 1668. The cave is only a few feet deep for the casual visitor, but has been explored by experts to a depth of nearly 4,000m (13,120ft).

There are other places where it is possible for even the casual visitor to go deep into the hillside and the best of these is undoubtedly **Les Planches** near Arbois. The cave system at Les Planches is at the back of a *reculée*, a blind valley. This valley is in the form of a horse shoe and hence has been named 'Cirque du Fer à Cheval'. The edge of the lowest plateau has a number of these *reculées* as it joins the plain. It is thought that they were formed in the course of millions of years when the river cut a tunnel through the limestone, which enlarged to the point where the roof fell in and the resulting rock was slowly eroded and washed downstream.

A short path from the end of the road in the shadow of the immense slightly overhanging cliffs leads to the entrance of the cave system. The lower entrance of the cave was used by Bronze Age man as an emergency hide-out, but apparently not on a permanent basis. Deeper into the cave it is possible to see the varied effects of the water's erosion on the limestone as it creates strange shapes such as giants' pots, organ pipes and chimneys. These are formed from the bottom upwards by the pressure of the water. The whole system is imaginatively lit and has safe concrete walkways. In addition it has a short but clear guide book written in English.

The town of **Arbois** nearby is a centre of wine making with an important wine festival on the third Sunday in July. It is at the beginning of a long 'wine road' which skirts the edge of the plateau south-west for 80km (50 miles). The vineyards produce many types of wine. There are some red and rosé wines, but the region is particularly good for white wines made mainly from Chardonnay and Savagnin grapes. Arbois is known for its specialist wines, such as Le Vin Jaune and Le Vin de Paille. The former is made exclusively from Savagnin grapes and is matured in oak barrels for a minimum of 6 years. To make Le Vin de Paille grapes are first left to mature on a bed of straw for 2 or 3 months. The resulting wine is allowed to ferment slowly and is then matured in oak for 3 years. Five pounds (12 kilos) of grapes are needed to make 1 litre of Vin de Paille so it is neither abundant nor cheap. There is a very good little museum of wine at Arbois in the basement of the Hôtel de Ville, entered from round the back of the building.

A visit worth making in Arbois is to the house used throughout his life by Louis Pasteur. It is number 81 Rue de Courcelles just beside the River Cuisance. Pasteur was born in Dole, but his family brought him to Arbois at the age of 3. Although his work took him away, he constantly returned to his home, which is now a simple and rather lovely museum full of his everyday objects. It also has the laboratory and many of the test tubes and instruments which he actually used.

The 'wine road' south comes to the little town of **Poligny**, which is the cheese capital of the region with its cheese museum, La Maison

A typical Jura farm house in the wine making area near Arbois

du Comté, the headquarters of the CIGC (Comité Interprofessionel du Gruyère de Comté). Also in the town is a school of cheesemaking set up in 1988 and called nowadays the National Dairy Industry School. Poligny holds a number of events connected with its position as 'Capitale du Comté', such as the Regional Produce Fair in August. Other cheeses are made in the region, particularly in the mountain areas, but the plateaux are predominantly 'Comté' country. A Comté cheese is large and measures 70cm (25in) across. The rind has a light brown golden colour with the identifying symbol of bells printed around the edge. It is normally sliced with a two-handled knife. There are very strict rules about how it must be made, the only permitted variation being the amount of cream that can be taken from the milk before processing begins. The milk used to make Comté must be fresh and not pasteurised, it must be from pure-bred Montbéliard cows, fed only on grass or hay. If all the rules have been followed, the cheese earns an *Appellation d'Origine Controllée*, like a good wine.

South of Poligny the wine road continues towards Voiteur. On the left the vineyards can be seen stretched over the edge of the plateau as the little village of **Château-Chalon** is approached. The village is worth exploring on foot. It was orginally a fortified castle on the rocky spur overlooking the foothills and the plain. Although the present castle cannot be entered, the fortified eleventh-century church with its massive stone tiles makes a very interesting visit. An impression of the strategic importance of the village can be gained by looking down from the Belvédère de la Rochette near the church. Every summer there is an excellent *son et lumière* for thirteen nights depicting life in the village from 1630 to 1670 when La Franche Comté was resisting the armies of the King of France. There are many opportunities in the village to taste the local wines, which include its own Vin Jaune.

From Château-Chalon, a left turn at Voiteur leads along the D70 to one of the most dramatic sites in the Jura. This is **Baume-les-Messieurs**, a village set deep in a long *reculée*, centred round a monastery, which was established by the Irish monk St Colomba in the sixth century. It gained in social prestige to such an extent that it changed its name from Baume-les-Moines to Baume-les-Messieurs. Some of the monks were not as devout as one might imagine. One, Jean de Watteville, whose tomb is in the church, had a most colourful life, first as a mercenary throughout Europe and the Middle East, at one time embracing Islam, before becoming a monk and then abbot ruling the monks like a despot. The abbey was disbanded in 1792 but the church, the cloister and the monks' living area can be visited. There is also a good little folk museum. The end of the *reculée* where the River Dard issues from the cliff face is most attractive. A road from the village leads up to this point.

An alternative way to see the area, avoiding crowds is to drive round towards the village of Crançot on the D471, the Lons-Le-Saunier to Champagnole road. Near there beside a café called the 'Belvédère des Roches' in the hamlet of **Sur-Roche** there is a short walk to a look out point which gives a superb view along the valley below with its high limestone cliffs on either side and the village of Baume nestling at the end, a sight not to be missed. To the right of the viewpoint is a small sign to 'Grottes', which signifies the top of a steep pathway down into the valley, called L'Echelle de Crançot. The top section is a stairway cut into the rock. The steepest part is the first 20m (66ft). Once that is passed it is less daunting although still steep as it drops down through the wood to the valley bottom. The source of the Dard is up to the left and the cave from which it flows can be visited. A round trip on foot can be made by walking into the village and finding the GR59 pathway with its white and red markers off to the left just before the bridge. This climbs out of the valley by the Echelles de Sermu for a return to Sur-Roche along the plateau.

The plateaux rise in steps to the south and east of the 'wine road' until they meet the mountain area 40km (25 miles) away. They form an area of farmland, forests and lakes. The plateaux are drained by the River Ain which begins life by the town of Nozeroy. This is west of the thriving market town of **Champagnole** in the centre of the region which has a very good little Archaeological Museum above the Tourist Information Office. Early on, the River Ain becomes lost from sight as it plunges down into the limestone to emerge later. This is known as the 'Perte de l'Ain' which is not far from the 'Source de l'Ain'. Both these sites make interesting visits, and are well signposted.

The town of **Nozeroy** is on a ridge and overlooks the surrounding countryside. It was the home of the Chalons, the most powerful family in the Jura in the Middle Ages, who ruled the area in almost total independence, gaining the greater part of their wealth from the salt works at Salins-les-Bains. The most obvious point of interest is the Porte de l'Horloge, the imposing fortified gateway. The town was once encircled by ramparts and these can still be seen in many places. It is worth exploring on foot. The Grande Rue beyond the gateway still has a medieval feel and the Place des Annonciades at the other end gives an indication of the one-time importance of the town.

North of Nozeroy is the vast Forêt de la Joux. It is aptly named because like the name of the region, Jura, the word Joux comes from the Latin word *Juria* meaning a 'fir covered hill'. It is mainly a pine forest and to help visitors appreciate it, a special road has been marked out as 'La Route des Sapins'. This is about 50km (31 miles) long and it gives access to the most interesting and impressive sections. Within the forest at the Information Centre, 'La Maison Forestière du Chevreuil', an idea can be gained of the extent and importance of the forest. There are many roadside maps which are clear and indicate items of interest, such as La Glacière, the coldest spot in winter and Le Sapin Président, the King of the Forest, a fir tree which has grown to a height of 45m (148ft) and is thought to be over 200 years old.

Not far to the west of Nozeroy is the village of **Syam** which has a large foundry and rolling mill as well as a beautiful country house built for the owners of the foundry. This was constructed in 1818 in the style of the Italian Renaissance. Both the Forges de Syam and the villa can be visited.

As the River Ain, which passes close to Syam, proceeds west and south it skirts round a region of lakes, collecting waters from some of them before it flows into the largest lake in the region, the man-made **Lac de Vouglans**. This area has understandably become known as 'La Région des Lacs'. The largest of the natural lakes in this region, the Lac de Chalain, was formed by a lateral morraine blocking the western end of the valley. During a dry period the remains of a village dating back 5,000 years were found on the western side. The excavated discoveries are now in the museum in nearby **Lons-le-Saunier**, the birthplace of Rouget de l'Isle, the writer of the *Marseillaise*. The larger lakes, such as Chalain and Clairvaux have leisure facilities and are popular with tourists. The smaller ones further west are quieter. The Lac de Bonlieu is most picturesque and has a forestry road running up behind it, reaching quite a height and giving lovely views over the lake and the surrounding countryside.

Near Bonlieu is the hamlet of **Ilay** with the Auberge du Hérisson on the crossroads. This is named after the river which flows nearby, and which from this point drops 300m (984ft) in 3½km (2 miles) in a series of dramatic waterfalls. The river can be approached from Ilay where there is a car park. The pathway, well signposted, leads down past the upper falls to the lowest one. This is called L'Evantail, the Fan, where the water fans out over rocks in a most picturesque manner. Just above the Evantail Fall is the Grotte de Lacuzon, the nickname of Jean-Claude Prost, the most famous local Resistance leader, who used to stay there in the seventeenth century when planning his next move against the French. The Hérisson then continues on through the Lac de Chambly and the Lac du Val before joining the Ain. On a sunny summer's day the number of visitors might suggest that the Hérisson is not 'off the beaten track'. The road from Doucier up to the Evantail Falls most certainly is not! To avoid too many other walkers, it is possible to find paths down to the Hérisson to the left of the D39, the road from Ilay towards Doucier.

North of Ilay is a group of four little lakes, **Les Quatre Lacs**. They can best be observed from the 'Belvédère des Quatre Lacs', set in the wooded hills above. This is reached from Ilay by taking a left turn to La Boissière just before La Chaux-du-Dombief. Before reaching the forestry road that leads past the 'Belvédère', there is a small car park on the left at the foot of the 'Pic de l'Aigle'. This rises to 913m (2,995ft) and is a good point from which to see how the Jura is shaped with its valleys, its plateaux and to the south its mountains.

Southern Jura

In winter the mountains and the high ground of the Jura could hardly be said to be off the beaten track because it is precisely for the beaten tracks of the cross-country ski routes and the downhill 'pistes' that so many thousands flock there. It is regarded as the capital of cross-country skiing and every February more than 4,000 competitors take part in a 65km (40 mile) ski race, the Transjurassienne. More resorts are becoming equipped for downhill skiing, but cross-country skiers outnumber downhill skiers by two to one. However in the summer the cross-country ski tracks make delightful walks through the woods but the ski villages of this area look less than their best without a covering of snow.

There are two main mountain regions. One is around Mont d'Or to the south of Pontarlier and the other is in the area of the highest peak the Crêt de la Neige, 1,718m (5,635ft) high. This is one of the peaks on the long ridge which marks the southern extremity of the Jura as it stretches away from the Col de la Faucille, where the N5 begins the descent to Gex and on to Geneva.

The **Mont d'Or** at 1,463m (4,799ft) is quite easy to climb with a number of starting points south of the village of Métabief. To travel to the other mountain area, it is possible to go to Labergemont and turn left on the D437 to St Laurent en Grandvaux travelling along a long valley to the north of an extended mountain known as Mont Risoux. This would provide the opportunity of visiting the Source du Doubs, where the river comes out of a cliff in woods in the side of Mont Risoux about 5km (3 miles) from the village of Mouthe down a well signposted road. A more interesting route would be to pass into Switzerland and visit the long Lac de Joux on the southern side of Mont Risoux. This road leads to La Cure, a border village at the centre of the highest hills. This is the terminus for a little-known train which descends the steep Swiss slope of the Jura to Nyon on the northern shore of the Lake of Geneva (Lac Léman).

Before La Cure just inside the French border is an interesting museum in the village of **Bois d'Amont**. This is the 'Musée de la Boissellerie', dedicated to every kind of woodwork. This museum is well placed because evidence of the importance of the timber industry can be seen everywhere in the valley. This region was particularly well known for the manufacture of cheese boxes. Sadly one item no longer made is the *tavaillon*. This is the name given to the wooden slates attached to the western end of buildings as additional cladding against the rain and snow giving an attractive external appearance. Sadly this cladding is now made of metal and *tavaillons* are not much in evidence and, where they are, usually in a poor state of repair.

Just north of La Cure is the village of **Les Rousses**, the skiing capital of the region. The village seems dominated by car parks, but is an excellent base for many good walks both down to the Lac des Rousses and deep into the forests of Mont Risoux. Les Rousses is the

The impressive viaducts once used by trains at Morez

starting point for La Jurassienne, where the skiers set off along the Lac des Rousses, which in winter is covered with thick ice. Les Rousses is a watershed since water draining to the East will end up in the North Sea, but in every other direction will find its way into the Rhône and the Mediterranean.

From Les Rousses it is a short distance to drop down to **Morez**, the industrial centre of the area which is known for its metal working, spectacle making (at La Lunetterie) and clock making. There is an interesting museum on the Quai Jobez which highlights the development of these local industries. Morez is also the home of a cheese named after the nearby village of Morbier. This cheese has a layer of ash through the centre, thought to have been initially put there to convince customers that it was a Blue Cheese! A most memorable sight in Morez is the spectacular series of viaducts which were built to enable the railway to pass through such difficult terrain.

West of Les Rousses set in attractive hilly countryside is the village of Prémanon, which, besides facilities such as a synthetic ice rink, has two rather different attractions, a reindeer park and a Canadian village. From this village it is easy to return to La Cure, where a right turn along the N5 leads to the highest section of the Jura. On the left of this section of the N5 is **La Dôle**, the summit of which is in Switzerland and is only slightly lower than the Crêt de la Neige. It is a simple walk from the hamlet of Tobagno. The radio masts on the summit guide planes into Geneva Airport. The N5 continues on to the Col de la Faucille, but 10km (6 miles) before the Col a right turn drops down to the village of Mijoux. At the turn which is well signposted on an old-style square sign with a traditional hotel bearing the sign 'Bed and Breakfast' facing it, the Valserine Valley can be seen stretching away south. At this point a choice has to be made as to how to reach the highest points of the Jura. It is possible to continue on to the Col de la Faucille and to take a cable car up to the summit of the **Petit Mond Rond**. This is most people's choice. There is a café with a traditional 'tuyé' chimney on the summit and the terrace gives wonderful views of the Lake of Geneva (Lac Léman) with the city and the Alps to the south as well as the ridge of Jura peaks stretching away to the immediate south-west. Another way is to drive past the cable car station and take the Forestry Road which ends at the Châlets de la Morechaude. From this point it is a long (2 hour) but not too difficult walk up and along the ridge to the Crêt de la Neige.

If the choice not to continue on to Le Col de la Faucille is taken at the crossroads, it is possible to descend to Mijoux, drive on to Lélex 8km (5 miles) further down the valley of the Valserine, where there is a cable car, the Télécabine La Catheline. From the top cable car station it is a simple walk to the Col de Crozet for excellent views of Geneva and the Alps. Any one of these destinations also provides very good points from which to look back and see the varied, and attractive countryside of the Jura to the north.

Further Information
— The Jura —

Museums and Other Places of Interest

Arbois
Wine Museum
Open: June and September 3-7pm. July and August 10am-12noon and 3-7pm. Closed Tuesdays.

Home of Louis Pasteur
Closed Tuesdays and 2nd Sunday of month. Open from June until August 10-11.30am and 2-6.30pm.

Arc et Senans
Open: June, September and October 9am-12noon and 2-6pm. July and August 9am-7pm.

Baume-les-Messieurs
Abbey
Open: all year

Museum
Open: daily from July to September 10-11.30am and 2-6.30pm. Caves open from April to September 9am-6pm.

Bois d'Amont
Woodworking Museum and Workshop
Open: from Christmas to Easter on Wednesdays, Saturdays and Sundays 3-6pm. In June, July and August daily (except Tuesdays) 3-6pm.

Throughout the region there are numerous small workshops, cheese making *fruitières*, meat smoking *charcuteries* and wine cellars. These are often signposted as well as being advertised in local Tourist Information Offices. Visitors are always made welcome.

Champagnole
Archaeological Museum
Open: Wednesday to Sunday inclusive from mid-June to mid-September 2.30-7pm.

Château de Belvoir
Open: 1 July-30 August 10-11.30am and 2-6.30pm and on Sundays from Easter to July and September and October.

Château de Cléron
Open: 10 July to 18 August 2.30-6pm.

Château de Joux
Museum of Arms and Weapons
Open: from April to October 9am-12noon and 2-6pm.

Gouffre de Poudrey
Open: May to September 8.30am-12noon and 1.30-7pm. March, April, October, November 9am-12noon and 2-6pm.

Lods
Wine Museum
Open: 15 June to 15 September 9am-12noon and 2-6.30pm.

Lons-le-Saunier
Archaeological Museum
Open: daily except Tuesdays from Monday to Friday 10am-12noon and 2-6pm. Saturdays 4-5pm.

Morteau
Clock and Watch Museum
Open: daily except Tuesdays 10am-12noon and 2-6pm.

Nancray
Open-air Folk Museum
Open July and August 10am-6.30pm, April, May, June, September, October 2-6pm.

Nans-Sous-Ste-Anne
Taillanderre Small Forge
Open: daily from 1 May to 30 September 10am-12.30pm and 2-6.30pm. Sundays 2-6pm.

Ornans
Gustave Courbet's Birthplace
Open: daily except Tuesdays 9.30am-
12noon and 2-6.30pm.

Les Planches
Cave System
Open: 10 July to 25 August 9.30am-
6.30pm. April, May, June, September,
and Sundays until November 10am-
12noon and 2-6pm.

Salins-les-Bains
Salt Works
Visits from February to Easter at
10.30am, 2.30pm and 4pm. From Easter
to 15 September 9am, 10am, 11am,
2.30pm, 3.30pm, 4.30pm, 5.30pm.

Syam
Forge
Open: during July and August daily
(except Tuesday) 10am-6pm. Saturdays
and Sundays in May, June, September
10am-6pm.

Italian Style Château de Syam
Open: Saturdays, Sundays and
Mondays in July, August and Septem-
ber 2-6pm.

Tourist Information Offices

Arbois
Office de Tourisme
Place d l'Hôtel de ville
39600 Arbois
☎ 84 37 47 37

Besançon
Office de Tourisme
Place de la l'Armée
25000 Besançon
☎ 81 80 92 55

Comité Régional de Tourisme
de Franche-Comté
32 rue Charles Nodier
25000 Besançon

Dole
Office de Tourisme
Place Grévy
39108 Dole
☎ 84 72 11 22

Lons-le-Saunier
Maison de Tourisme
1 Rue Pasteur
39021 Lons-Le-Saunier
☎ 84 24 65 01

Maiche
Syndicat d'Initiative
25120 Maiche
☎ 81 64 11 88

Morez
Office de Tourisme
Place Jean-Jaurès
39400 Morez
☎ 84 33 08 73

Morteau
Office de Tourisme
Place de la Gare
25500 Morteau
☎ 81 67 18 53

Salins-les-Bains
Office de Tourisme
Place des Alliés
39110 Salins-Les-Bains
☎ 84 73 01 34

13 • Poitou-Charentes

As the A10 is the 'beaten track' which so many use, it is perhaps appropriate to use this as the starting point. The motorway drops down from Tours towards Poitiers following the Santiago de Compostela pilgrimage route. Leave the motorway at Châtellerault, a typical Loire Valley town, and start to work back in time. Take the N10 through and out of the town, and then turn left onto the D1 across the River Clain, turning right onto the small road that runs beside the river. A short drive brings you to some interesting Roman remains at **Vieux Poitiers**, with ruins of a theatre and kilns. Close by is the site of the eighth-century Battle of Poitiers, where the invading Moors were finally defeated; a defeat all the more psychologically crucial when one realises that Poitiers itself was the first major Christian centre in France.

A pleasant route towards Poitiers is to follow the River Vienne from Châtellerault as far as **Chauvigny** which boasts four *châteaux*, thus indicating its strategic position. There is no reason why you shouldn't continue along this very pretty river towards **Civaux**. There are a number of early churches at Civaux and St Pierre-les Eglises, where there are some interesting early wall paintings dating from the ninth or tenth century.

Of more interest, though perhaps the route to reach it is not quite as picturesque, is the small village of **St Savin**. Take the N151 from Chauvigny. The village is not really the object of this visit, rather the abbey church. Founded in the ninth century, the original abbey was ransacked by the Normans, and rebuilding didn't start until the late eleventh century. The abbey was subsequently fought over in the Hundred Years War and during the Wars of Religion, with the result that by the seventeenth century the place was almost in ruins. It is all the more surprising then, that the church contains the finest group of wall paintings from the eleventh century in the whole of France.

The church building itself is large if somewhat stark, with a long nave. There is some carving on the capitals, but the glory is the

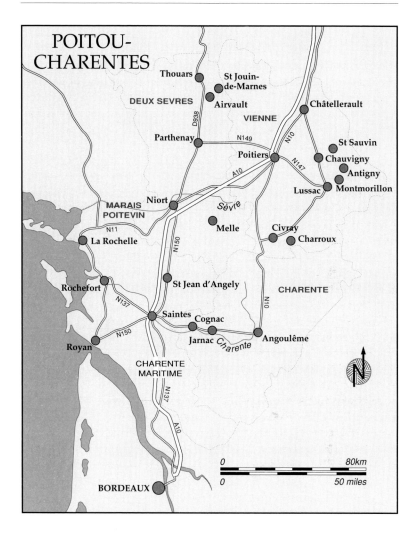

paintings. Some, inevitably, have disappeared or suffered the ravages of time, but the porch, and especially the nave and crypt have outstanding frescoes. In the porch are scenes from the Apocalypse, the lighter tones in the paintings compensating for the lack of light. The nave paintings depict the early part of the Old Testament, beginning at the Creation (left-hand side), then the Flood, the Exodus, and Moses. The right-hand side tells the stories of Abraham and of Joseph. The crypt paintings are more sombre, depicting primarily scenes from the lives of the church's patron saints — Savin and Cyprien.

St Savin lies on the River Gartempe, and now follow the river southwards taking the D11 through **Antigny** to **Jouhet**. Both of these villages have churches with further wall paintings. Antigny's are of the Passion, Jouhet's (dating from the fifteenth century) of the Old Testament, the Nativity, and the Final Judgement. From Jouhet continue along the D5 to **Montmorillon**, which again has wall paintings in the Ste Catherine crypt of the church (Notre Dame), depicting scenes from Saint Catherine's life. From here, take the D727 to Lussac, where it is possible to pick up the GR48 long distance footpath, and then the N147 to Poitiers.

Poitiers is well worth a visit to see its quite remarkable selection of historical monuments. It is a good touring base, with an excellent selection of hotels. Its importance as an historical centre of learning is not to be overlooked. In the Middle Ages control of the city passed from English to French and back again, notably after one of the fiercest battles of the Hundred Years War, won by the Black Prince. Poitiers' least known, but perhaps most important, claim to fame is that the road from the north, heading south-west through the gap between the higher ground, marked the change from the *langue d'oil* and the *langue d'oc*, the northern and southern versions of spoken French in earlier times.

At Poitiers the motorway, and the pilgrimage route, head southwest towards Saintes. It is possible to keep to one of the other pilgrimage routes heading due south to Angoulême, roughly following the N10, or much more preferable, the River Clain to Vivonne. This passes through some fine rolling countryside, and almost any side turning will take you into unspoilt villages.

A detour off this road takes you through the pleasant town of **Civray**, albeit restored, with a fine, twelfth-century church (St Nicholas) with an interesting façade of traditional theme. This road then leads to **Charroux** and the Abbey of St Sauveur. To look at the ruins today, partly hidden beneath present building, one could not imagine the importance of the abbey, whose holdings at its peak included land in England. The source of this importance were the relics that it possessed — parts of the True Cross, as well as flesh and blood of Christ. The abbey's luck ran out in the Wars of Religion in the eighteenth century, and much was demolished. Restoration and archaeological work has continued during this century, and the abbey makes an interesting visit, especially to see some of its treasure which includes some fine ivory. The abbey tower gives an inspiring impression of what the original building must have been like. The ground plan runs below many of the surrounding buildings.

Façade of the church at Angoulême

Heading south-west again towards **Angoulême**, one has no doubt of the importance that this town must have had in earlier times. The fortified centre rises up above the rest of the town and the surrounding countryside. The old quarter of the town presents a good feel of tiny streets and small, busy shops; and the long walk around the town walls is made more than worthwhile by the superb views across the Charente countryside. There is a reasonable amount of hotel accommodation. Much of Angoulême's wealth was built on paper mills (because of the quality of the water), but only a couple of mills are working now.

From Angoulême one of the prettiest trips in the whole area is to follow the valley of the Charente River downstream. In doing this one can travel a pleasant cross section from the hills that are now appearing in the south and east across to the Atlantic. The Charente, too, passes through important agricultural and wine-growing areas, before winding through the coastal plain and marshes, offering opportunities at the coast to see oyster beds.

It is possible to hire boats and cruisers on the Charente from a couple of locations, and this makes for an excellent way to explore this part of the countryside at a very slow speed. The river is slow moving, and the flatness of the land is borne out by just twenty-one locks along the hundred-mile length between Angoulême and Rochefort. The local or regional tourist offices can provide details, or the major boat companies in Britain usually book craft.

The River Charente (from which the *départements*, like so many, take their name) was described by Henri IV as the most beautiful river in his kingdom. Much of the surrounding landscape is dedicated to vineyards growing grapes for the production of Cognac. And whether you travel by car or boat (or, indeed, foot) Cognac is the town which acts as a focus for this area. The road follows the river along almost the whole of its length, with the more attractive lanes hugging the opposite banks, and the length of the valley can be explored by switching from one side to the other.

Almost all the villages are unspoilt and often quite charming, and many of the bridges, especially at St Simeux with its watermill, have superb views. There are regular appearances of *châteaux* or their remains either in the riverside towns, or close by. One of the prettiest is just inland from **Châteauneuf-sur-Charente** at Bouteville, where there are nice views both of the *château* and of the countryside. Returning through Châteauneuf, take the road back onto the north side of the river towards Jarnac. **St Simon** is a pleasant village, the houses overlooking the quiet quayside with shady trees. A little further is Bassac Abbey.

Originally founded in the eleventh century, the Benedictines built the abbey church, which has been added to, fortified, and restored across the years. The stark bell tower looks incongruous against the rest of the church, with four stories, each smaller than the previous, and topped by a spire. The interior of the church was completely altered at the start of the eighteenth century, with some wonderfully carved stalls, an eagle lectern, and the high altar, all the work of the monks and local artisans. Monks returned to the monastery after World War II.

The importance of Cognac (the brandy, not the town) is now well in evidence, with small producers offering their own wares, or most likely, Pineau; an interesting combination of brandy and wine. **Jarnac** is the next most important town to Cognac for production of brandy, and visits to many distilleries are available. It is easy to ignore the smaller producers in favour of the well-known, but the smaller ones are often the most interesting in terms of both the distillation process and the drink itself.

After Jarnac the river widens out, and the roads tend to keep just a little away from it. Keep to the north side, so you can visit the impressive dolmen at Garde-Epée, and then into **Cognac**. Brandy, of course, dominates this town, with most of the producers being close to the river, as this was the main method of transporting the brandy. There is also a Cognac museum. The town retains some of its old quarter, but the walls have gone, although the Porte St-Jacques overlooks the river. Many of the houses in the old quarter are blackened by the fungus which grows, encouraged by the evaporating alcohol. However, other than for the dedicated alcoholic, Cognac offers little else of interest.

After Cognac the river begins to meander down to Saintes. It is possible to hug the river, take a more direct route to Saintes, or head northwards a bit towards Burie and St Jean d'Angély to visit the ruined *château* of Richemont, in the quiet valley of the Antenne, and then the ruined **Fontdouce Abbey**, just off the D131 towards Saintes. Some buildings still stand, and the other ruins give an idea of the size and prosperity of the abbey.

The countryside remains quite calm and flat until one reaches the large and busy city of **Saintes**; large and busy since before the Romans invaded Gaul. Consequently the town retains bits and pieces of its history through the ages, including some impressive Roman ones. Saintes was also an important point on another of the Compostela pilgrimage routes, and has some impressive religious buildings. The motorway passes close to the city, but to escape one can follow the River Charente towards the sea. Saintes' importance as the regional capital and its position on the Compostela route, means that all around in the villages there are exquisite examples of Romanesque churches, often in the pale local stone. The simplicity of the design is often made up for by outstanding carving on the façades or other stonework.

Before heading north-west with the river, it is possible to make a loop down towards the Gironde, dipping (just) into the start of the Bordeaux wine region. A little way south-east of Saintes is **Pons**, situated on a hill, and once a most commanding fortress. The Lords of Pons were hugely influential in their corner of France, ruling over some sixty towns and over six hundred parishes. The *château* gives an impression of the power of the lords, being a solid stone keep, dating from the twelfth century, some 27m (90ft) high with three separate stories. The fanciful battlements were added at the turn of this century. There is a lovely view from the top of the keep.

Being on the Compostela route the church (St Vivien) is quite typical of the local style; and on the outskirts of the town is part of one of the hospices, where pilgrims could rest. The importance of this area during the twelfth century, and then later, during the Renaissance, means that there is a surfeit of churches and *châteaux*. Depending on one's interest it is possible to see one or two, or a dozen.

The Château d'Usson is a good example of a Renaissance *château*, but visiting is very limited, and only the exterior. Likewise, Plassac, further south. Between Usson and Plassac are some four churches worth looking at, Fléac (Renaissance), Avy, Marignac, and Chadenac (all twelfth century) which boasts a quite lavish façade with superb carving representing the struggle between Good and Evil.

Swing westwards, and head towards Royan, but call in at **Talmont**, which is a very pleasant seaside town with a lovely Romanesque church (Ste Radegonde) which sits on a rocky cliff overlooking the Gironde. After Royan, the countryside slips into sandy undulations, and the route heads northwards again towards Saintes.

From Saintes one can head up the coastal strip, or through the hinterland. The coastal strip is well trodden, with the two towns of Rochefort and La Rochelle acting as key points. Both are well covered elsewhere, and, unless you are visiting well out of season, are definitely on the beaten track. Even in the height of summer, the interior is remarkably quiet and uncrowded, with a pace of life that is far more heartening and relaxing.

Heading north-eastwards, towards Niort, one is tracing the main pilgrimage route to Santiago de Compostela which was followed briefly earlier. This heads through St Jean d'Angély and Aulnay to Poitiers, and the route offers opportunities to meander through the countryside as well as history. Indeed, **Taillebourg**, on the D114 is more famous for a battle which took place in 1242 between forces of Louis IX of France and Henry III of England for control of the bridge over the Charente. A result was only achieved two days later, closer to Saintes, with the routing of the English.

Close by is **Port d'Envaux**, again on the banks of the Charente, with two pleasant châteaux. The **Château de Panloy**, just to the north, is built on the remains of an earlier *château* but has the harmonious style of the Renaissance. The interior of the *château* contains some fine decoration including some tapestries. The **Château de Crazannes**, about 3km (2 miles) north, is again built on the base of an earlier *château*, has been added to since, and still retains some of the original fortifications.

If *châteaux* are your forté, then you should not miss **La Roche-Courbon** a few miles to the west. In launching his campaign to save the *château*, the writer Pierre Loti immortalised it as Sleeping Beauty's *château*, lost, as it was, in the heart of a forest. His campaign succeeded and the *château* and its superb gardens were restored during the 1920s. The *château* remains set in the woods, and you pass through the huge Lion Gate to reach it. Originally built in the fifteenth century, the *château* was remodelled in the seventeenth. Its formal gardens and terraces are a joy, and the view of the front, reflected in the little lake with the symmetrical formal gardens, is how you expect a French *château* to be.

From La Roche-Courbon one can cut back across country, over the Charente, to **Fenioux**, another stopping point on our now familiar pilgrimage route. Despite its twelfth-century façade, most of the church dates from the ninth century. The arches depict the seasons, the signs of the Zodiac, and the struggle between Good and Evil, all familiar to us from other churches in the region, and popular Saintonge themes. An interesting feature here is the graveyard *lanterne des morts*, a grouping of columns, and especially tall.

It is only a short run from Fenioux to **St Jean d'Angély**, set on a hill around which the River Boutonne curls. The centre of the town is a myriad of narrow streets and squares (known as '*cantons*') with several timber frame houses from the fifteenth and sixteenth centuries and some fine town houses of the seventeenth and eighteenth centuries. Ironically this town, once a major stopping point on the Compostela route, was a key centre during the religious reform of the sixteenth century.

The original abbey, of which some ruins remain, was destroyed by the Huguenots in the sixteenth century, but rebuilding was started in the eighteenth century. It was interrupted by the Revolution (when part of the new building was used as a prison), so that the abbey is unfinished. The façade however is impressive. Close by in the Canton du Pilori is a pretty well with an elaborate Renaissance cover which comes originally from a nearby *château*.

Heading northwards again on the historical route from Saintes to Angers the road arrives at **Aulnay**. Here the route moves from the Saintonge (the area influenced by Saintes) into Poitou and so the church reflects something of a change in style. The twelfth-century church of St Pierre stands alone, but its fine stonework and colour produces a rare harmony of style. There is some fine stone carving with traditional images, reflecting the traditional style of the building. Nearby churches also reflect the styles, and, moving further northwards, one notes a slight change. Not far from Aulnay is a pleasant *château* at **Dampierre-sur-Boutonne**. A Renaissance *château* built on an island in the middle of the River Boutonne, the main part remains, defended by two towers, and is divided into two galleries. The upper gallery has delicate carvings on the ceiling of emblems and proverbs, as well as the personal monograms of various worthies.

From Aulnay head straight for Niort, or back towards Poitiers. This latter route is worth holding to as far as Melle. En route pass the Forest of Chizé, some 5,000 hectares (12,500 acres), part of the Val de Sèvre Regional Park. There are lots of opportunities for walking and riding and it is possible to hire horse-drawn caravans from Aulnay. **Melle** is the last stop on the main Compostela pilgrimage route which comes from Poitiers, as afterwards the route heads northwards. It is best seen for the first time from the south, to appreciate its position in the narrow valley of the River Béronne, and owes its existence to the lead mines, and subsequently a mint. Its importance as a pilgrimage staging post is borne out by the number of churches in such a small area. St Hilaire's church is twelfth century, but in a pure Romanesque style, with a sober façade. Above the north doorway is carved a horseman, found on churches in this area, and the cause of great scholarly argument. A man sits on a horse which is trampling a sitting figure. This is supposed to represent Charlemagne or Christ overcoming the old ways, or Constantine defeating paganism. The interior has some lovely carvings, especially on the capitals. Two other churches in the town are worth visiting. Both are twelfth century, and both are in a simple Romanesque style, with decoration. These are St Pierre (on the northern side of the town) and St Savinien (just off the Avenue Bernier). St Savinien was used as a prison from the early nineteenth century, and is different in that the east door reflects the Limousin style rather than Poitou.

From Melle it is only a short hop to **Celles-sur-Belle**, which is dominated by the bell tower of the old abbey. The abbey is perhaps less famous than some of its abbots, which included Geoffrey d'Estissac, who is closely linked with Maillezais Abbey to the north-west of Niort in the Marais Poitevin; and Talleyrand, a famous French diplomat and politician of the late eighteenth century. It is possible to visit the refectory, the kitchens, and a part of the cloisters. The town church of Notre-Dame attracts a local pilgrimage on the first Sunday of September. The church was destroyed by the Huguenots in the sixteenth century and rebuilt in a fifteenth-century style. Part of the old church remains in the form of the large doorway — it is interesting in that its design reflects the oriental influences that returned up the Compostela route from Spain.

The countryside has changed during the drive inland into the higher ground, but the route turns back towards the sea, and the sea's influence, heading towards **Niort**. This is a good touring base, within reach of much of the southern part of this area of France. The change in the countryside towards the sea is reflected very much in that Niort has long been tied to the sea, as an important port for the area. As a result the place has a quiet bourgeois feeling to it. The town grew up on the banks of the Sèvre (known as the Sèvre Niortaise to distinguish it from the Sèvre Nantaise which flows further north to Nantes and the Loire) in Roman times, and of which nothing remains. In the Middle Ages great wealth came to the town, under the protection of Eleanor of Aquitaine. Jean de Berry, Count of Poitou, created the port, which quickly grew to export salt, cereals and wool throughout the Western European seaboard. In return, animal skins were imported and used in the extensive local leather industry, which still plays an important role today.

Niort retains several Middle Ages buildings, notably the castle, built on the edge of the river, and the sixteenth-century town hall (now a museum). The castle, started by Henry II (of England) and finished by Richard the Lionheart, was regularly fought over through the ages, ultimately ending up as a prison, and now an interesting regional museum. This contains traditional costumes and head-dresses, and the interior of a peasant home in the early nineteenth century — an excellent introduction to the local area.

The former town hall was built in a triangular shape in the sixteenth century and now houses the Musée du Pilori, a diverse series of collections, most with local interest. A short walk away is another museum — Beaux-Arts (fine arts) — with some interesting tapestries, and the church of Notre-Dame with a fine tower and steeple. The town offers a limited amount of accommodation, as well as train connections to Paris.

Before leaving the town, though, visit one area which, although it is partly in the Vendée and so in the Pays de la Loire, is best explored from Niort. This is the marshland area between Niort and the sea, lying either side of the Sèvre Niortaise and known as the Marais Poitevin (Poitevin Marshes). This strange and beautiful countryside has a character very much of its own.

In ancient times the coastline was much further inland and a huge bay extended from Jard-sur-Mer past Luçon, Maillezais, and Coulon, curving back round to Esnandes. In this bay were a number of islands. The action of the sea and of the various rivers led to the deposition of sands and alluvials, and the silting up of the whole bay, thus giving marshes.

From early on man sought to exploit this as the soil was extremely fertile, and the way was led in the eleventh century by monks from the abbeys in the marshes. They built fishponds, mills, and water control systems. These were elaborated in the thirteenth century when five abbeys cut a canal to drain the northern marshes. Bit by bit work continued, with more drainage canals until today, where the coastline is several miles away from where it once was. Today the marshes— which extend across some 60,000 hectares (150,000 acres) — divide into two parts. The 'wet' marsh lies inland, roughly between Niort and Damvix, and also goes under the name of the 'Venise Verte' or Green Venice. The 'dry' marsh, between Damvix and the sea is the largest area, primarily drained land turned over to pasture.

The 'Venise Verte' is the more attractive of the two, as the narrow canals criss-cross the area like a spider's web, beneath a canopy of trees. While one needs a car to explore, the best way to appreciate the area is to take to the water. A number of towns and villages offer boat trips around the year, notably Arçais, Damvix, Maillezais, Coulon and St Hilaire-la-Palud. Costs vary, but you need to allow about 1-2 hours for a trip, depending on your start point. Despite what you might see on postcards, you are unlikely to come across cattle being transported in the small punts. However, only by taking to the water can you appreciate the unspoilt nature of this corner of France.

From Niort then, head for Coulon, once a village of sailors, as the houses either side of the canalised river testify. **Coulon** is the main departure point for boat trips, but it is best to wait until you reach the **Abbey of Maillezais**. From Coulon follow the river to Arçais, then Damvix, both villages typical of the area. At Damvix take the D25 towards Vix, but turn off to the Abbey of Maillezais. The abbey is just a little further on than the village.

When the abbey was founded in the tenth century, it stood facing the sea, and has faced battles ever since. The beautiful buildings were sacked in the thirteenth century, and devastated during the Wars of Religion in the sixteenth century, when the bishop's seat was transferred to La Rochelle. Some substantial ruins remain — enough to give an idea of the size of the original abbey, and much of the ground plan is marked out. Building began in the eleventh century, with additions and alterations in the thirteenth, fifteenth and sixteenth. The monastery was largely completed in the fourteenth century, and one wing still stands, and can be visited. A little further down from the abbey you can take a trip on a punt through the canals for about 45 minutes. From Maillezais one can continue into the 'dry' marsh, or return to Niort.

From Niort the route now moves northwards again towards Parthenay. A little north of Niort, at **Echiré**, is the **Château de Coudray-Salbart**, a fine thirteenth-century fortress overlooking the Sèvre Niortaise, and dominating the countryside. The walls have six towers, and a passage for the defenders inside the walls has arrow slits facing inside and outwards so the castle could defend itself even if attackers reached the courtyard inside the walls.

A little further northwards, just before Champdeniers, a detour is called for to explore the pretty river valley of the Egray as far as St Ovenne. Here it is possible to take to byroads back towards Niort, otherwise, continue to **Parthenay**. Parthenay's location on a meander of the River Thouet and on a hillside meant it had great military value, as its fortress testifies. This is best appreciated from Pont-Neuf (on the N149 taking the main road north). You can see some of the ramparts and the old main entry gate of Porte St Jacques, with its narrow bridge, as well as the geographical location of the town. The town gate leads to Rue de la Vaux-St Jacques, once the main road, and lined with half-timbered houses. The fortress ramparts can again be seen in the small square at the top of the road, and the main entry to the fort is round the corner, through the Porte de l'Horloge (the Bell Gate) named after its bell and the fact that it was a belfry. The old quarter has a fascinating selection of shops, but there is limited hotel accommodation in the town, mostly in the newer parts.

At Parthenay the visit to Poitou-Charentes is nearly complete, but there is still quite a lot to see. From Parthenay head northwards, but bear westwards on the D19 towards La Chapelle St Laurent. This road runs through some very pretty countryside, especially between Clessé and La Chapelle. At La Chapelle, continue on the D19 to Moncoutant, and pick up the D38 north to Bressuire. Again, this is a very pretty road, going into the heart of the *bocage* countryside.

Bressuire is the first indication that this is further north, for the architecture is beginning to show other influences. In its church (Notre-Dame) the influence of the Loire Valley, or rather of the English can be seen! Although there are Romanesque aspects there are also Gothic and Renaissance features. Bressuire is important though, not for its church, but for the fact that it played an important role during the Vendée wars in the 1790s.

From Bressuire, head eastwards again, back down the N149, but then across country (and back into the hills) on the D725 to Airvault. **Airvault**, now a peaceful village, was an important centre of learning under the protection of the *château* of the Vicomtes of Thouars. The church (St Pierre), is an important regional monument, and again, as at Bressuire, there is a mixing of Romanesque and early Gothic styles. The fine porch leads into a delightful interior, with fine sculpture and carving. A little remains of the abbey itself — part of the cloister, and chapterhouse. A small museum of local folklore is also close by.

Not far from Airvault is **St Jouin-de-Marnes**, which has another abbey, of which only the church really remains. However, it is interesting to compare St Pierre at Airvault with St Jouin. Some elements are similar, such as the vaulting, but others have been affected by fortification and restoration. There is a fine façade outside, with another horseman, and traditional themes. The choir has some fine work.

From St Jouin head northwards again, taking a short diversion from the D37 to **Oiron**, whose *château* does strike memories (or foresights) of the Loire Valley. A fine building of sixteenth and seventeenth centuries, with a super gallery on one wing. The interior is beautifully decorated, with some superb ceilings, and a long gallery with fourteen frescoes based on the *Illiad* and the *Aeneid*.

Oiron is the last stop before reaching **Thouars**. The old part of Thouars juts out on a promontory, and its position is consequently well defended on three sides. The town's museum is a good introduction, as indeed, is a wander along the main road from the *château* to the church of St Médard. The *château* is of the seventeenth century whereas St Médard is twelfth century, and a fine example of the now familiar Poitou style. The façade has the familiar themes, and there is even a trace of Moorish influence, which no doubt came up the Compostela routes. Elements of the northern France influences can be seen in the town, as indeed can those of English rule at the Tour du Prince de Galles (Prince of Wales Tower). Thouars is a good place to end the tour, for from it you can head in any direction to find many more places of interest.

Further Information
— Poitou-Charentes —

Museums and Other Places of Interest

Angoulême
Town Museum
Open: daily except Tuesday, 10am-12noon, 2-6pm.

Archaeological Museum
Open: daily except Tuesday, 2-5pm.

Charroux
St Sauveur Abbey
Open: daily 10am-12noon, 2-6pm, except Tuesdays and holidays.

Châtellerault
Local History Museum
Open: afternoons daily except Sunday.

Science and Car Museum
Open: daily, 9am-12noon, 2-6pm.

Vieux Poitiers Roman remains south of town
Open: afternoons at weekends.

Cognac
Cognac Museum
Open: afternoons 2.30-6pm except Tuesdays and holidays.

Cognac Distilleries
Most offer visits between 9-11am and 2-5pm except weekends and, with very few exceptions, in July and August.

Coudray-Salbart
Château
Open: daily 10am-12noon, 2-5pm, except Tuesdays and holidays.

Crazannes
Château
Open: afternoons, 2.30-6.30pm, during French school holidays, and weekends.

Dampierre-sur-Boutonne
Château
Open: 10am-12noon, 2.30-5pm June to September, otherwise Sundays only.

Fontdouce Abbey
Open: daily except Friday, 10am-12noon, 2.30-5.30pm.

Maillezais Abbey
Open: daily 9am-12.30pm, 2-6pm. Boat trips available beside abbey — same times.

Niort
Castle Keep, Old Town Hall, Fine Arts Museum
Open: daily except Tuesday, 9am-12noon, 2-6pm, one ticket admits to all.

Oiron
Château
Open: daily except Tuesdays and Wednesdays, 10am-12noon, 2-4pm.

Panloy
Château
Open: Sundays and public holidays, 2.30-6pm.

Poitiers
Palace of Justice
Open: daily 9am-7pm.

Ste Croix Museum
Open: daily except Tuesday, 10am-12noon, 2-6pm.

La Roche-Courbon
Château
Open: daily except Wednesday, 10am-12noon, 2.30-5.30pm.

Saintes
Fine Arts Museum
Open: daily except Tuesday, 10am-12noon, 2-5pm.

Talmont
Interior of Ste Radegonde only open during July and August.

Tourist Information Offices

Angoulême
Place St Pierre
☎ 45 95 16 84
Open: daily (not Sunday) 9am-
12.30pm, 1.30-6.30pm.

Bressuire
Place de l'Hôtel de Ville
☎ 49 65 10 27
Open: Tue to Sat, 10am-12noon, 2-6pm.

Châtellerault
Boulevard Blossac
☎ 49 21 05 47
Open: daily (not Sunday), 8.45am-
12.15pm, 2.15-6.30pm.

Chauvigny
Hôtel de Ville
☎ 49 46 30 21
Open: daily (not Sunday), 9am-
12.30pm, 2-6pm.

Cognac
Place Monnet
☎ 45 82 10 71
Open: daily except Sunday, 8.30am-7pm.

Coulon
Place de l'Eglise
☎ 49 35 99 29
Open: June-Sept, 10am-12.30pm, 2-6.30pm.

Jarnac
Place du Château
☎ 45 81 09 30
Open: daily (not Sun), 9am-12noon, 2-6pm.

Montmorillon
Avenue Tribot
☎ 49 91 11 96
Open: daily (not Sunday) 10am-
12noon, 2-7pm.

Niort
Place de la Poste
☎ 49 24 18 79
Open: daily (not Sunday) 9.15am-
12noon, 1.30-6pm.

Parthenay
Palais des Congrès
☎ 49 64 24 24
Open: Tue-Sat, 9.15am-12noon, 1.30-6pm.

Poitiers
Rue Victor Hugo
☎ 49 41 58 22
Open: daily (not weekends) 9am-
12noon, 2-5.30pm.

Pons
Castle Keep
☎ 46 96 13 31
Open: June to September 10am-
12noon, 3-7pm.

St Jean d'Angély
Square de la Libération
☎ 46 32 04 72
Open: Tuesday-Saturday, 2-5.30pm.

Saintes
Esplanade Malraux
☎ 46 74 23 82
Open: daily (not Sunday or Monday)
9am-12noon, 1.30-7pm.

Thouars
Place St Medard
☎ 49 66 17 65
Open: daily (not Sun), 9am-12noon, 2-6pm.

Accommodation and Eating Out

A ll hotels are required to show their room rates, remember that the rate will be for the room, and not per person, and a menu if they have a restaurant, in their reception area. It is normal practice to visit the room before finally agreeing to take it, though this practice is not always followed, especially if you have booked your room from the local Tourist Information Centre and it is the last one in town. The Tourist Information Centre will usually charge you the price of the phone call to enquire/book the room, but that is a small price to pay. In most hotels breakfast will not be included in the price of the room. Check to make sure, and if it is not ask what breakfast will cost: you may well find that it will be cheaper to go to a local café or bar.

In advance of your stay it may also be worthwhile obtaining a copy of *Logis et Auberges de France*, from the French Government Tourist Office in your own country. This is an association of family-run hotels which offer good service and food at the lower end of the price spectrum.

Many other more modest, non-tourist, hotels exist in most towns and villages, as do furnished rooms and flats to let. Properly equipped country houses, villas, cottages and farms (or self-contained parts of them) can be rented as holiday homes (*gîtes*). *Gîtes* are usually rented by the week and are competitively priced, so much so that you will need to book early. All *gîtes* are inspected annually and are invariably in excellent condition. As they are usually in superb rural settings they offer a peaceful base, though having your own transport is likely to be a necessity.

When choosing a restaurant use a combination of three methods to ensure a good meal at the right price. The first is to consult the guide books, preferably in advance. The second is to ask, at hotel, camp-site, local Syndicat d'Initiative or bar, for a recommendation. The third is to study the menus which all restaurants must display, with their prices, outside their premises. These will show one or more menus, or fixed-price meals, as well as a list of *à-la-carte* dishes. Menus are always better value than going *à-la-carte* in French restaurants unless you want only one dish (the *plat du jour*) or a light snack. They offer three or more courses at a range of prices, from the cheaper *menu touristique* to the expensive and copious *menu gastronomique*. Gourmet restaurants may also offer a *menu dégustation*, which gives you a chance to taste smaller portions of a larger number of the chef's specialities.

The first course is usually a starter: often soup, pâté, cold meats or

332

crudités (raw salad vegetables). In a four-course meal the second course will usually be a fish dish, and the third course a meat dish. This may be lightly garnished with vegetables, or they may be served as a separate course. If you want a steak well-done, ask for it *bien cuit* or even *brulée* (burnt). *À point* is rare-to-medium, *saignant* (bloody) or *bleu* is hardly cooked at all. The fourth course with be either cheese or a sweet, or both if you are lucky. If so, the cheese will be served before the dessert. A choice of both cheeses and sweets is offered, with the *tarte maison*, or house fruit-flan, an alternative for dessert. Cheaper menus often include a drink in the price.

French restaurants are usually friendly and casual. Children are welcomed and accommodated, often with special menus. The French like to take their time over their meals, and there is sometimes a wait between courses. Lunch, often their main meal of the day, is taken early, at around 12noon, and is finished by 2pm — so get there in good time. Dinner starts at about 7.30pm, but you can go much later. Sunday lunch is the most popular eating-out time for the French, so you should book in advance for this. Sunday evening is very quiet and many restaurants are closed then.

At the other end of the scale, a good place for an *en-route* lunch is a transport café or *relais routier*. They are popular with the general public, and provide a simple but substantial meal at a reasonable price. You can easily recognise them by the distinctive blue and red circle displayed outside.

Currency and Credit Cards

All major credit cards (Access, Visa, American Express etc) are taken at most large restaurants, hotels, shops and garages. Eurocheques and traveller's cheques are also accepted. Banks are normally open from 8.30am-12noon, 1.30-4.30pm Monday to Friday only.

The French unit of currency is the French *franc*. There are no restrictions on the import of French or foreign currency. The export of currency valued at up to 5,000 French *francs* in any currency (including French francs) is permitted. Amounts worth in excess of 5,000 French *francs* may be exported, providing that the money has been declared on entry. The French *franc* (abbreviated for FF) is divided into 100 *centimes*. Current coins include 5, 10, 20 and 50 *centime* pieces as well as 1, 2, 5 and 10 *franc* pieces. Bank notes come in denominations of 20, 50, 100, 200 and 500 francs.

Telephone Services

Telephoning in France is very simple. There are only two regions, Paris and the Provinces. All subscribers have an 8-figure number, and to dial from province to province, or from Paris to Paris, you simply dial that number. From Paris to province you dial 16 then the 8-figure number; from province to Paris, dial 16 (1) then the 8 figures. All Paris numbers should begin with a 4, and in the outskirts a 3 or 6.

Telephoning France from the UK, you start with the international dialling code (010 33) then (1) plus the 8-figure number for Paris and its outskirts, or simply the 8-figure number for anywhere else in the country. The international dialling code for the USA and Canada is 011 33 and for Australia 0011 33.

Cheap rates give you 50 per cent extra time: on weekdays between 10.30pm and 8am, and at weekends starting 2pm on Saturdays.

Phonecards, called *télécarte*, operate in most booths. You can buy them from post offices, tobacconists, newsagents, and where advertised on telephone booths. Incoming calls can be received at phone boxes with a blue bell sign shown.

Tourist Offices

Larger resorts will have an Office de Tourisme, smaller ones a Syndicat d'Initiative, and their staff are usually only too willing to dispense local information, help and advice. Brochures are usually attractively produced, and often in English. Some of the major tourist offices now have an Accueil de France (Welcome to France) facility to help you with hotel bookings. For a small cover charge they will make hotel bookings for you throughout France on the same day you call or up to 8 days in advance. They are open from 9am to 8pm every day of the year except 25 December and 1 January. Tourist offices at main railway stations in Paris and a few other large towns are open daily except Sundays and Bank Holidays (8am-9pm Easter to October, 9am-8pm in winter).

The main French tourist offices are:

UK
178 Piccadily
London W1V 0AL
☎ 071 491 7622

USA
610 Fifth Avenue Suite 222
New York
NY 10020-2452
☎ 212 757 1683

Canada
1981 Avenue McGill College
Tour Esso Suite 490
Montreal
Quebec H3 A2 W9
☎ 514 288 4264

Australia
Kindersley House
33 Bligh Street
Sydney
NSW 2000
☎ (2) 231 5244

Tipping

Most restaurants make a service charge, either included in their prices or added on at the end. Cafés include it in the price of drinks if you sit at a table. Tips are customary to taxi-drivers and helpful hotel porters. When public toilets are guarded, an entrance charge will usually be made. When garage attendants clean your windscreen and check your oil, they will welcome, but not expect a tip.

Museums and Other Places of Interest
Wherever possible opening times have been checked, and are as accurate as possible. However, during the main holiday period they may be extended. Conversely, outside the main season, there may be additional restrictions, or shorter hours. Local tourist offices will always be able to advise you.

Generally all churches, and abbeys and monasteries still in use, are open every day from 9am-6pm, except during services. You should remember that these are places of worship as well as historical monuments, so dress and conduct should be appropriate.

Accommodation and Eating Out

*** Expensive
** Moderate
* Inexpensive

Chapter 1 • Paris: Gateway to France

Accommodation and Eating Out

There are around 68,000 hotel rooms in Paris, ranging from one to four stars. Hotels may be booked on arrival in Paris at the Tourist Information Offices: Charles de Gaulle airport, main-line railway stations (with the exception of Gare St Lazare) and the Office de Tourisme de Paris, 127 Avenue des Champs Elysées, Paris 75008.

Restaurants in Paris on or near the off-the-beaten-track routes

Ile de la Cité
Gourmets ***
26 Place Dauphine
☎ 43 26 72 92

La Lieutenance **
24 Rue Chanoinesse
☎ 43 54 91 36

Vert Galant ***
42 Quai des Orfèvres
☎ 43 26 83 68

Ile St Louis
Brasserie de l'Ile St Louis *
53 Quai de Bourbon
☎ 43 54 02 09

Au Franc Pinot *
1 Quai de Bourbon
☎ 43 29 46 98

Wally *
16 Rue le Regrattier
☎ 43 25 01 39

L'Ambroise **
65 Quai de la Tournelle
☎ 46 33 18 65

Auberges des Deux Signes **
46 Rue Galande
☎ 43 25 46 56

La Bûcherie **
41 Rue de la Bûcherie
☎ 43 54 78 06

Duquesnoy **
30 Rue des Bernardins
☎ 43 54 21 13

Le Petit Prince *
12 Rue de Lanneau
☎ 43 54 77 26

L'Odéon
Allard ***
41 Rue St André des Arts
☎ 43 26 48 23

Jacques Cagna ***
14 Rue des Grands Augustins
☎ 43 26 49 39

La Lozère **
4 Rue Hautefeuille
☎ 43 54 26 64

Relais Louis XIII ***
1 Rue du Pont de Lodi
☎ 43 26 75 96

Madeleine - Gare St Lazare
Cartouche Edouard VII ***
18 Rue Caumartin
☎ 47 42 08 82

Mövenpick **
12 Boulevard de la Madeleine
☎ 47 42 47 93

Le Roi du Pot au Feu **
34 Rue Vignon
☎ 47 42 37 10

North-West Marais
L'Ami Louis ***
32 Rue du Vertbois
☎ 40 87 77 48

Chez Jenny **
39 Boulevard du Temple
☎ 42 74 75 75

Brasserie Flo **
7 Cour des Petites Ecuries
☎ 47 70 13 59

Julien **
16 Rue du Faubourg St Denis
☎ 47 70 12 06

Montmartre
Charlot ler **
128bis Boulevard de Clichy
☎ 45 22 47 08

Chez Ginette *
101 Rue Caulaincourt
☎ 46 06 01 49

Wepler ✳✳
14 Place Clichy
☎ 45 22 53 24

Chapter 2 •
Pays du Nord

Accommodation and Eating Out

RESTAURANTS

Aire-sur-la-Lys
Host. Trois
Mousquetaires ✳✳
☎ 21 39 01 11
With accommodation.

Arras
La Faisanderie ✳✳✳
☎ 21 48 20 78

L'Univers ✳✳
☎ 21 71 34 01
With accommodation.

Beauvois-en-Cambrésis
Nr Cambrai
La Buissonnière ✳✳
☎ 27 85 29 97

Boulogne-sur-Mer
La Liègeoise ✳✳
☎ 21 31 61 15

Bar Hamiot ✳
☎ 21 31 45 06

Favières (Nr Rue)
La Clé des Champs ✳
☎ 22 27 88 00

Montreuil
Château de Montreuil ✳✳✳
☎ 21 81 53 04
With accommodation.

Picquigny
Somme
La Gourgardière ✳
☎ 22 51 48 56

Sains-du-Nord
Avesnois
Le Centre ✳
☎ 27 59 15 02
With accommodation.

Sars-Poteries (Avesnois)
L'Auberge Fleurie ✳✳✳
☎ 27 61 62 48

Téteghem
(Nr Dunkerque)
La Meunerie
☎ 28 26 01 80
With accommodation

Chapter 3 •
Normandy

Accommodation

L'Aigle
Dauphin ✳✳
Place de la Halle
☎ 33 24 43 12

Alençon
Le Grand St-Michel ✳
Rue du Temple 7
☎ 33 26 04 77

Le Grand Cerf ✳
Rue St-Blaise 21
☎ 33 26 00 51

Argentan
Hotel de France ✳
Boulevard Carnot 8
☎ 33 67 03 65

Avranches
La Croix d'Or ✳✳
Rue de la Constitution 83
☎ 33 58 04 88

Auberge St-Michel ✳
Place Général Patton 7
☎ 33 58 01 91

Bellême
Hotel du Golf ✳
Les Sablons
☎ 33 73 00 07

Bricquebec
Hotel du Vieux Château ✳
Cours du Château 4
☎ 33 52 24 49

Caudebec-en-Caux
Manoir de Rétival ✳✳
Rue St-Clair
☎ 35 96 11 22

Hotel de Normandie ✳
Quai Guilbaud 19
☎ 35 96 25 11

Coutances
Château de la Salle ✳✳✳
13km (8 miles) on the D7
and D27
☎ 33 46 95 19

Hotel Moderne ✳
Boulevard Alsace
Lorraine 25
☎ 33 45 13 77

Ducey
Le Moulin de Ducey ✳✳
Grande Rue 1
☎ 33 60 25 25

Auberge de la Sélune ✳
Rue St-Germain 2
☎ 33 48 53 62

Granville
La Mougine des Moulins à
Vent ✳✳
5km (3 miles) at Bréville-
sur-Mer
☎ 33 50 22 41
No restaurant.

Les Bains ✳
Rue Clémenceau 19
☎ 33 50 17 31

Michelet ✳
Rue Jules Michelet 5bis
☎ 33 50 06 55

Ste Mère-Eglise
Hotel le Sainte-Mère ✳
Rich Doux
☎ 33 21 00 30

St-Vaast-la-Hougue
Hotel de France et Des
Fuschias ✳
Rue Foch 18
☎ 33 54 42 26

Sees
Cheval Blanc ✳
Place St-Pierre 1
☎ 33 27 80 48

Tourouvre
Hotel de France ✳
Rue du 13 Aout 19
☎ 33 25 73 55

Eating Out

L'Aigle
Auberge de la Jardinière ✳
On the N26
☎ 33 24 26 65

Alençon
Petit Vatel ✳✳✳
Place Desmeulles 72
☎ 33 26 23 78

Argentan
Renaissance ✳✳
Avenue de 2e-Division-
Blindée 20
☎ 33 36 14 20
With accommodation.

Avranches
Gué du Holme ✳
5km (3 miles) on the D78
☎ 33 60 63 76

Bellême
Paix ✳
☎ 33 73 03 32

Carentan
Auberge Normande ✳✳✳
Boulevard Verdun
☎ 33 42 02 99

Granville
Normandy-Chaumière ✳
Rue Dr Paul-Poirier 20
☎ 33 50 01 71
With rooms.

Le Phare ✳
Rue Port 11
☎ 33 50 12 94

Villequier
Grand Sapin ✳
☎ 35 56 78 73

Chapter 4 •
Aisne

Accommodation

Ambleny
Le Millery ✳
2 rue des Fosses
☎ 23 74 29 64

Blérancourt
Hostellerie le Griffon ✳✳✳
25 Place du Général de
　Gaulle
☎ 23 39 60 11

Chamouille
Hotel Mercure Holigolf ✳✳✳
☎ 23 24 84 85

Château-Thierry
Ile de France ✳✳✳
Route de Soissons
☎ 23 69 10 12

Etréaupont
Le Clos du Montvinage ✳✳
8 rue Albert Ledent
☎ 23 97 40 18

Fère-en-Tardenois
Hostellerie du Château ✳✳✳
☎ 23 82 21 13

Guise
Champagne Picardie ✳✳
41 rue Godin
☎ 23 60 43 44

Laon
*Hotel de la Bannière de
　France* ✳✳
11 rue Franklyn Rooseveld
☎ 23 23 21 24

Hostellerie St-Vincent ✳✳
Avenue du Général de
　Gaulle
☎ 23 23 42 43

Landouzy-la-Ville
Domaine du Tilleul ✳✳✳
☎ 23 98 48 00

Le Nouvion-en-Thiérache
Hotel de la Paix ✳✳
37 rue Vimont Vicary
☎ 23 97 04 55

Longpont
Hotel de l'Abbaye ✳✳
8 rue des Tourelles
☎ 23 96 02 44

Marle
Le Central ✳✳
1 rue Desains
☎ 23 20 00 33

Monampteuil
Auberge du Lac ✳✳
☎ 23 21 63 87

Neuville-St-Amand
*Hostellerie Le Château de
　Neuville-St-Amand* ✳✳✳
☎ 23 68 41 82

Sinceny
*Auberge du Rond
　d'Orléans* ✳✳
☎ 23 52 26 51

Motel des Lions ✳✳
On route to Reims from
　Soissons
☎ 23 73 29 83

Ste Preuve
Château de Barive ✳✳✳
☎ 23 22 15 15
Motel des Lions ✳✳

St Quentin
Grand Hotel ✳✳✳
6 Rue Dachery
☎ 23 62 69 77

Vendeuil
Auberge de Vendeuil ✳✳
☎ 23 07 85 85

Vervins
La Tour du Roy ✳✳✳
45 Rue du Général Leclerc
☎ 23 98 00 11

Hotel du Cheval Noir ✳
33 rue de la Liberté
☎ 23 98 04 16

Eating Out

Château-Thierry
*Auberge Jean de la
　Fontaine* ✳✳✳
10 rue des Filoirs
☎ 23 83 63 39

Oigny-en-Valois
Le Château d'Oigny ✳✳✳
☎ 23 96 01 11

Samoussy
Relais Charlemagne ✳✳✳
☎ 23 22 21 50

St Quentin
Au Petit Chef ✳✳✳
31 rue Emile Zola
☎ 23 62 28 51

Chapter 5 •
Champagne-Ardenne

ARDENNES
Accommodation

Auvillers-les-Forges
Hostellerie Lenoir ✳✳✳
☎ 24 54 30 11

Bazeilles
Hotel du Château ✳✳
☎ 24 27 09 68

Charleville-Mézières
Hotel Restaurant Le Cleves ✳✳
43 rue de l'Arquebuse
☎ 24 33 10 75

Hotel Restaurant
  Le Pelican ✳✳
42 Avenue Leclerc
☎ 24 56 42 73

Haybes-sur-Meuse
Hotel Restaurant Le Jeanne
  d'Arc ✳
32 Grande Rue
☎ 24 41 11 44

Hotel Restaurant le Saint-
  Hubert ✳
47 Grande Rue
☎ 24 41 11 38

Monthermé
Hotel Restaurant Le
  Franco-Belge ✳✳
2 rue Pasteur
☎ 24 53 01 20

Hotel Restaurant de la
  Paix ✳
1 rue du Lieutenant-Barbaste
☎ 24 53 01 55

Mouzon
Hotel Restaurant Le Cheval
  Blanc ✳
Faubourg Sainte
Genevieve
☎ 24 26 10 45

La Neuville lez Beaulieu
Motel Restaurant Dubois ✳✳
☎ 24 54 32 55

Rethel
Hotel Restaurant Le
  Moderne ✳✳
2 Place de la Gare
☎ 24 38 44 54

Revin
Hotel Restaurant le
  Francois Ier ✳✳
Quai Camille-Desmoulin
☎ 24 40 15 88

Rocroi
Hotel Restaurant le
  Commerce ✳✳
Place Aristide-Briand
☎ 24 54 11 15

Sedan
Hotel Restaurant
  l'Europe ✳✳
5 Place de la Gare
☎ 24 27 18 71

Hotel Restaurant Le
  Strasbourg ✳✳
3 Place Goulden
☎ 24 29 14 12

Hotel Restaurant Le Saint
  Michel ✳
3 rue Saint Michel
☎ 24 29 04 61

Signy l'Abbaye
Auberge de l'Abbaye ✳
2 Place Aristide-Briand
☎ 24 52 81 27

Villers-Semeuse
(5km from Charleville-
  Mézières)
Hotel Restaurant
  Mercure ✳✳✳
Rue Louise Michel
☎ 24 37 55 29

Vouziers
Hotel Restaurant La Ville
  de Rennes ✳✳
18 rue Chanzy
☎ 24 71 84 03

Eating Out

Bazeilles
L'Orangerie ✳✳✳
In the Château de Bazeilles
☎ 24 27 52 11

Charleville-Mézières
Restaurant La Cigogne ✳✳
40 rue Dubois Crancé
☎ 24 33 25 39

Ecluse de Chooz
Restaurant Le Petit Chooz ✳✳
Les Trois Fontaines
☎ 24 42 72 48

Fumay
Hostellerie de la Vallée ✳✳
33 Place Aristide-Briand
☎ 24 41 15 61

Sedan
Restaurant au Bon Vieux
  Temps ✳✳
3 Place de la Halle
☎ 24 29 03 70

Signy l'Abbaye
Restaurant Le Gibergeon ✳
7 rue de l'Eglise
☎ 24 52 80 90

AUBE
Accommodation

Arcis-sur-Aube
Hôtel Restaurant du Pont
  de l'Aube ✳
12 rue de Châlons
☎ 25 37 84 81

Bar-sur-Aube
Hôtel Restaurant Le Relais
  des Gouverneurs ✳✳✳
38 rue Nationale
☎ 25 27 08 76

Bar-sur-Seine
Hôtel Restaurant Le
  Barsequanais ✳✳✳
Avenue du Général-Leclerc
☎ 25 29 82 75

Breviandes
(Near Troyes)
Le Pan de Bois ✳✳
35 Avenue Leclerc
☎ 25 75 02 31

Clairvaux
Hôtel Restaurant de l'Abbaye ✳
☎ 25 27 80 12

Dolancourt
Hôtel Restaurant Du
   Moulin du Landion ✳✳✳
☎ 25 27 92 17

Géraudot
Hôtel du Parc ✳
☎ 25 41 24 35

Maisons-les-Chaource
Hôtel Restaurant aux
   Maisons ✳✳
☎ 25 40 11 77

Mesnil-St-Père
Auberge du Lac ✳✳
☎ 25 41 27 16

Nogent-sur-Seine
Loisirotel ✳✳
19 rue des Fosses
☎ 25 39 71 46

Piney
Hôtel Restaurant le Tadorne ✳
3 Place de la Halle
☎ 25 46 30 35

Les Riceys
Hôtel Restaurant Le Magny ✳✳
38 rue du Général-Leclerc
☎ 25 29 38 39

Romilly-sur-Seine
Auberge de Nicey ✳✳✳
24 rue Carnot
☎ 25 24 10 07

La Rothiere
Auberge de la Plaine ✳✳
☎ 25 92 21 79

Ste-Savine
(Near Troyes)
Le Motel Savinien ✳✳
87 rue Lafontaine
☎ 25 79 24 90

Troyes
Hôtel de la Poste ✳✳✳
35 rue Emile Zola
☎ 25 73 05 05

Grand Hôtel ✳✳✳
4 Avenue Joffre
☎ 25 79 90 90

Villenauxe-la-Grande
Hôtel Restaurant du Château ✳
50 rue du Château
☎ 25 21 31 66

La Vove
½km (1 mile) from
Aix-en-Othe
Auberge de la Scierie ✳✳✳
☎ 25 46 71 26

Eating Out

Arcis-sur-Aube
St Hubert ✳
2 rue de la Marine
☎ 25 37 86 98

Lesmont
L'Auberge Munichoise ✳
☎ 25 92 45 33

Mussy-sur-Seine
Hôtel du Commerce ✳
90 rue Gambetta
☎ 25 38 40 37

Troyes
Restaurant le Bourgogne ✳✳✳
40 rue Général de Gaulle
☎ 25 73 02 67

Restaurant le Valentino ✳✳
Cour de la Rencontre
☎ 25 73 14 14

HAUTE MARNE
Accommodation and Eating Out

Andelot
Hotel Restaurant Le Cantarel ✳
Place Cantarel
☎ 25 01 31 13

Arc-en-Barrois
Hotel Restaurant du
   Château d'Arc ✳✳✳
Place Moreau
☎ 25 02 57 57

Bologne
Hôtel Restaurant Le
   Commerce ✳✳
4 rue du Chaumont
☎ 25 01 41 18

Bourbonne-les-Bains
Hôtel Restaurant Jeanne
   d'Arc ✳✳✳
12 rue Amiral Pierre
☎ 25 90 12 55

Hôtel Restaurant Herard ✳✳
29 Grande Rue
☎ 25 90 13 33

Chaumont
Hôtel Restaurant Terminus
   Reine ✳✳✳
Place du Général de Gaulle
☎ 25 03 66 66

Môtel-Restaurant l'Etoile
   d'Or ✳✳
Route de Langres
☎ 25 03 02 23

Hôtel le Relais ✳
Faubourg la Maladière
☎ 25 03 02 84

Colombey-les-Deux-Eglises
Môtel les Dhuits ✳✳✳
☎ 25 01 50 10

Auberge de la Montagne ✳✳
Rue d'Argentolles
☎ 25 01 51 69

Fayl-la-Forêt
Hôtel Restaurant du Cheval
   Blanc ✳
2 Place de la Barre
☎ 25 88 61 44

Joinville
Hôtel Restaurant du Soleil
   d'Or ✳✳
9 rue des Capucins
☎ 25 94 15 66

Langres
Grand Hôtel Restaurant de
   l'Europe ✳✳
23-25 rue Diderot
☎ 25 87 10 88

Hôtel Les Moulins ✳
5 Place des Etats-Unis
☎ 25 87 08 12

Montier-en-Der
Hôtel Restaurant au Petit
   Pont ✳
28 rue de l'Isle
☎ 25 04 20 18

Montigny-le-Roi
Hôtel Moderne ✳✳
Avenue de Lierneux
☎ 25 90 30 18

St Dizier
Hôtel Restaurant
Gambetta ✳✳✳
62 rue Gambetta
☎ 25 56 52 10

Hôtel Restaurant du Soleil
d'Or ✳✳✳
Route to Bar-le-Duc
2km from St Dizier
☎ 25 05 68 22

Ste Geosmes
(Near Langres)
Auberge des Trois Jumeaux ✳✳
☎ 25 87 03 36

Eating Out

Autigny-le-Grand
Hostellerie du Moulin de la
Planchotte ✳
Château de Planchotte
☎ 25 94 84 39

Chaumont
Restaurant du Buffet de la
Gare ✳
Place Général de Gaulle
☎ 25 03 15 49

Perthes
Relais Paris-Strasbourg ✳✳
☎ 25 56 40 64

St Dizier
Relais des Nations ✳✳
Route de Vitry
☎ 25 05 07 97

Vaux-sous-Aubigny
Restaurant Le Parc aux
Trois Provinces ✳
Route de Verdun
☎ 25 88 31 98

MARNE

Accommodation and Eating Out

Champillon
(6km/4 miles from Epernay)
Hotel-Restaurant Royal
Champagne ✳✳✳
☎ 26 52 87 11

Châlons-sur-Marne
Hotel d'Angleterre ✳✳✳
19 Place Monseigneur-
Tissier
☎ 26 68 21 51

Châlons-sur-Vesle
10km (6 miles) from Reims
Hotel Restaurant Assiette
Champenoise ✳✳✳
☎ 26 04 15 56

La Chaussée-sur-Marne
Hotel Restaurant du Midi ✳
☎ 26 72 94 77

Epernay
Hotel Restaurant Les
Berceaux ✳✳✳
13 rue des Berceaux
☎ 26 55 28 84

L'Epine
Hotel Restaurant Aux Armes
de Champagne ✳✳✳
☎ 26 66 96 79

Germaine
Relais de la Diligence ✳
☎ 26 52 88 46

Montmort-Lucy
Hotel Restaurant de la Place ✳✳
☎ 26 59 10 38

Reims
Hotel Altea ✳✳✳
31 Boulevard Paul Doumer
☎ 26 88 53 54

Hotel Restaurant
de la Paix ✳✳✳
9 rue Buirette
☎ 26 40 04 08

Grand Hotel Restaurant de
l'Univers ✳✳
41 Boulevard Foch
☎ 26 88 68 08

Hotel-Restaurant Boyer les
Crayeres ✳✳✳
64 Boulevard Henri Vasnier
☎ 26 82 80 80

Ste-Menehould
Hotel Restaurant Le Cheval
Rouge ✳✳
1 rue Chanzy
☎ 26 60 81 04

Sept-Saulx
Hotel Restaurant Le Cheval
Blanc ✳✳✳
3 rue du Moulin
☎ 26 03 90 27

Sézanne
Hotel Restaurant de la
Croix d'Or ✳✳
53 rue Notre Dame
☎ 26 80 61 10

Vertus
Hostellerie de la Reine
Blanche ✳✳✳
18 Avenue Louis Lenoir
☎ 26 52 20 76

Ville-en-Tardenois
Hotel Restaurant de la Paix ✳✳
Route d'Aulnay
☎ 26 61 81 45

Vinay
(6km/4 miles from Epernay)
Hostellerie de la
Briqueterie ✳✳✳
☎ 26 59 99 99

Vitry-le-François
Hotel Restaurant
de la Poste ✳✳✳
Place Royer Collard
☎ 26 74 03 84

Eating Out

Châlons-sur-Marne
Les Ardennes ✳✳
34 Place de la République
☎ 26 68 21 42

Châtillon-sur-Broue
Auberge du Pot Moret ✳
☎ 26 72 61 87

Reims
Le Chardonnay ✳✳✳
184 Avenue d'Epernay
☎ 26 06 08 60

Le Florence ✳✳✳
43 Boulevard Foch
☎ 26 47 12 70

Sézanne
Restaurant du Soleil ✳
17 rue de Paris
☎ 26 80 63 13

Thiéblemont-Farémont
10km (6 miles) from
Vitry-le-François
La Champenois ✳✳✳

Vitry-le-François
Le Gourmet des Halles ✳
11 rue des Soeurs
☎ 26 74 48 88

Chapter 6 •
Alsace et Lorraine

Accommodation

Colmar
Terminus-Bristol ✳✳
Place Gare 7
☎ 89 23 59 59

Auberge Père Floranc ✳✳✳
4½km (3 miles) to
Wettolsheim
☎ 89 80 79 14

Contrexeville
Cosmos ✳✳
Rue Metz
☎ 29 08 15 90

Souveraine ✳
In the park
☎ 29 08 09 59

Epinal
Campanile ✳
Bois Voivre
☎ 29 31 38 38
Caters for disabled guests.

Mercure ✳
Place E. Stein
☎ 29 35 18 68

Gerardmer
Grand Hotel Bragard ✳✳✳
Place Tilleul
☎ 29 63 06 31

Reserve ✳✳
Esplanade du Lac
☎ 29 63 21 60

Paix ✳
Avenue Ville-de-Vichy
☎ 29 63 38 78

Kaysersberg
Résidence Chambard ✳✳

Rue Général-de-Gaulle
☎ 89 47 10 17

Abbaye d'Alspach ✳
3km (2 miles) on the D28
☎ 89 47 16 00

Mulhouse
Parc ✳✳✳
Rue Sinne
☎ 89 66 12 22

Des Maréchaux ✳
Rue Lambert
☎ 89 66 44 77
No restaurant but caters
for handicapped guests.

Obernai
Parc ✳✳
Rue General Gouraud
☎ 88 95 50 08

Domaine Le Moulin ✳✳
Route Klingenthal
☎ 88 95 87 33
Caters for disabled guests.

Plombieres-les-Bains
Grand Hotel ✳✳
Avenue des Etats-Unis 2
☎ 29 66 00 03

Commerce ✳
Rue Hôtel de Ville
☎ 29 66 00 47

Ribeauville
Clos St-Vincent ✳✳✳
on the outskirts 1½km
(1 mile) north-east
☎ 89 73 67 65

La Pepiniere ✳✳
4km (2 miles) on D416
☎ 89 73 64 14

Rouffach
Château d'Isenbourg ✳✳✳
☎ 89 49 63 53

A la Ville de Lyon ✳
Rue Poincaré 1
☎ 89 49 65 51

Thann
Kleber ✳
Rue Kleber 39
☎ 89 37 13 66

Verdun
Coq Hardi ✳✳
Avenue Victoire 8
☎ 29 86 36 36

Orchidées ✳
2km (1 mile) along the N3
☎ 29 86 46 46

Wissembourg
Walck ✳
Rue Walk 2
☎ 88 94 06 44

Eating Out

Colmar
Schillinger ✳✳✳
Rue Stanislas 16
☎ 89 41 43 17

Maison des Tetes ✳✳
Rue des Tetes 19
☎ 89 24 43 43

Rapp ✳
Rue Molly 16
☎ 89 41 62 10
With accommodation.

Epinal
Les Abbesses ✳✳✳
Rue Louvière
☎ 29 82 53 69

Kaysersberg
Chambard ✳✳✳
Rue Général-de-Gaulle
☎ 89 47 10 17

Lion d'Or ✳
Rue de Gaulle
☎ 89 47 11 16

Mulhouse
Auberge de la Tonnelle ✳✳
Rue Maréchal-Joffre 61
☎ 89 54 25 77

*Aux Caves du Vieux
Couvent* ✳
Rue Couvent 23
☎ 89 46 28 79

Moulin du Kaegy ✳✳
9½km on D56
☎ 89 81 30 34

Marlenheim
Le Cerf ✳✳✳
☎ 88 87 73 73
With accommodation.

Ottrott-le-Haut
4km (2 miles) from Obernai
A L'Ami Fritz ✳
☎ 88 95 80 81

Ribeauville
Les Vosges ✳✳
Grand Rue 2
☎ 89 73 61 39
With accommodation.

Selestat
Edel ✳✳
Rue Serruriers 7
☎ 88 92 86 55

St-Avold
Le Neptune ✳✳
A la piscine
☎ 87 92 27 90

Vaucouleurs
Relais de la Poste ✳
☎ 29 89 40 41
With accommodation.

Wissembourg
L'Ange ✳
Rue République 2
☎ 88 94 12 11

Chapter 7 •
Brittany

Accommodation

Camaret-sur-Mer
Hôtel Thalassa ✳✳
29570 Camaret-sur-Mer
☎ 98 27 86 44 or 27 80 33

Carnac
Hôtel Les Rochers ✳✳
Boulevard Base Nautique
Carnac-Plage, 56342 Carnac
☎ 97 52 10 09

Dinan
Hôtel d'Avaugor ✳✳✳
1 Place du Champ-Clos
22100 Dinan
☎ 96 39 43 10

Fougères
Taverne du Cammerce ✳
3 Place de l'Europe
35300 Fougères
☎ 99 94 40 40

Ile de Brehat
Hôtel Bellevue ✳✳
Port Clos
22870 Ile de Brehat
☎ 96 20 00 05

Lannion
Hôtel de Bretagne ✳
32 Avenue du Général-
de-Gaulle
22300 Lannion
☎ 96 37 00 33

Morlaix
Hôtel des Halles ✳
23 Rue du Mur
29600 Morlaix
☎ 98 88 03 86

Plonévez-Porzay
Hôtel de la Plage ✳✳✳
Ste-Anne la Palud
29550 Plonévez-Porzay
☎ 98 92 50 12

Rennes
Hôtel Anne-de-Bretagne ✳✳
12 Rue Tronjoly
35000 Rennes
☎ 99 31 49 49

St Malo
Hôtel Central ✳✳
6 Grande-Rue
35400 St Malo
☎ 99 40 87 70

Tregastel
Hôtel le Golven ✳✳
Route de la Corniche
22370 Tregastel
☎ 96 23 87 77

Vannes
Hôtel Mascotte ✳✳
Rue Jean-Monnet
56000 Vannes
☎ 97 47 49 60

Eating Out

Campénéac
À L'Orée de la Foret ✳
Place de l'Eglise
56800 Campénéac
☎ 97 93 40 27

Carhaix-Plouguer
Le Jet d'Eau ✳✳
Bourg de St-Hernin
29270 Carhaix-Plouguer
☎ 98 99 57 11

Concarneau
La Coquille ✳✳✳
1 Rue de Moros
29900 Concarneau
☎ 98 97 08 52

Dinan
La Caravelle ✳✳✳
14 Place Duclos
22100 Dinan
☎ 96 39 00 11

Dol-de-Bretagne
Le Bresche Arthur ✳✳
36 Boulevard Deminiac
35120 Dol-de-Bretagne
☎ 99 48 01 44

Guingamp
Hôtel l'Escale ✳
26 Boulevard Clemencau
22200 Guingamp
☎ 96 43 72 19

La Roche-Bernard
Auberge Bretanne ✳✳✳
2 Place Duguesclin
56130 La Roche-Bernard
☎ 99 90 60 28

Lorient
L'Amphitryon ✳✳
127 Rue du Colonel Muller
56100 Lorient
☎ 97 83 34 04

Quimper
Crêperie Ty Krompouex ✳
32 Avenue de la France
Libre
29000 Quimper
☎ 98 95 62 09

Rennes
Le Piré ✳✳✳
23 Rue Maréchal Joffre
☎ 99 79 31 41

Trébeurden
Manoir de Lan Kerellec ✳✳
Allée Centrale
22560 Trébeurden
☎ 96 23 50 09

Vannes
Le Richemont ✵✵
Place de la Gare
56000 Vannes
☎ 97 42 61 41

Chapter 8 •
Pays de la Loire

Accommodation and Eating Out

All hotels have restaurants unless otherwise stated.

Angers
Hôtel St Julien ✵✵
Place Ralliement
☎ 41 88 41 62
(no hotel restaurant)
Friendly, traditional style hotel, centrally located for shops, sights, and restaurants.

Hôtel Ibis ✵/✵✵
Rue Poissonnerie
☎ 41 86 15 15
Modern, efficient city centre hotel.

Restaurant l'Entrecôte ✵✵
Avenue Joxé
☎ 41 43 71 77

La Baule
Hôtel Alexandra ✵✵/✵✵✵
depending on season
Boulevard R. Dubois
☎ 40 60 30 06
Pleasant hotel, with super views over the bay.

Châteauneuf-sur-Sarthe
Château des Briottières ✵✵✵
Champigné
☎ 41 42 00 02
Classic eighteenth-century château in pleasant grounds, close to Châteauneuf. Dinner is available on request.

Cheffes
Château de Teildras ✵✵✵
☎ 41 42 61 08

Fontevraud
Hôtel de la Croix Blanche ✵✵
Place Plantagenets
☎ 41 51 71 11
Welcoming hotel close to the famous abbey.

Laval
Grand Hôtel de Paris ✵
Rue Paix
☎ 43 53 76 20
Traditional provincial hotel, with popular restaurant.

Luçon
Hôtel Bordeaux/Restaurant Les Saisons ✵✵
Place Acacias
☎ 51 56 01 35
Friendly hotel with modern rooms, and fine restaurant.

Le Mans
Hotel Chantecler/Restaurant Feuillantine ✵✵/✵✵✵
Rue Pelouse
☎ 43 24 58 53

Hôtel Ibis ✵✵
Quai Ledru-Rollin
☎ 43 23 18 23
Modern city centre hotel, within walking distance of Le Mans old quarter, shops, and other restaurants.

Noirmoutier-en-l'Ile
Hôtel Fleur de Sel ✵✵✵
Rue des Saulniers
☎ 51 39 21 59
Pleasant, modern hotel, ideal for exploring the island of Noirmoutier.

La Roche sur Yon
Hôtel Ibis ✵
☎ 51 36 26 00
Located on edge of town, on the road to Sables d'Olonne.

Les Sables d'Olonne
Atlantic Hotel ✵✵/✵✵✵
depending on season

Promenade Godet
☎ 51 95 37 71
Modern hotel, overlooking the sea and bay.

Saumur
Hôtel Anne d'Anjou ✵✵/✵✵✵
Quai Mayaud
☎ 41 67 30 30
(no hotel restaurant)
Situated below the château, overlooking the River Loire, and within walking distance of the town centre's shops and restaurants.

Solesmes
Grand Hôtel ✵✵
☎ 43 95 45 10
Relaxing, friendly hotel, opposite the abbey.

In addition to the hotels listed above, the *Ibis* and *Campanile* chains offer inexpensive, and very good value, two-star hotels in, or on the edge of, many towns and cities in the Pays de la Loire. While they are modern, and perhaps lack individual character, they are clean, well managed, and welcoming. All have restaurants, and are well versed in dealing with children — family rooms are often available. Both chains are able to book forward accommodation at other hotels in their chain.

Chapter 9 •
Touraine-Blésois-Orléanais

Accommodation

Blois
Hôtel La Renaissance ✵
9 Rue du Pont du Gast

41000 Blois
☎ 54 78 02 63

Chinon
Hôtel Boule d'Or ✳✳
66 Quai Jeanne d'Arc
37500 Chinon
☎ 47 93 03 13

Descartes
Hôtel Moderne ✳✳
15 Rue Descartes
37160 Descartes
☎ 47 59 72 11

Gien
Hôtel Anne de Beaujeu ✳✳
10 Route de Bourges
45500 Gien
☎ 38 67 12 42

Meung-sur-Loire
Hôtel L'Auberge St Jacques ✳
60 Rue de Général de Gaulle
45130 Meung-sur-Loire
☎ 38 44 30 39

Mondoubleau
Hôtel Le Grand Monarque ✳
2 Rue Chrétien
41170 Mondoubleau
☎ 54 80 92 10

Montrichard
Hôtel La Croix Blanche ✳✳
62 Rue Nationale
41400 Montrichard
☎ 54 32 30 87

Orléans
*Hôtel Mercure Orléans
    Centre* ✳✳✳
44-46 Quai Barentin
45000 Orléans
☎ 38 62 17 39

Salbris
Hôtel du Midi ✳
12 Boulevard de la
    Rèpublique
41300 Salbris
☎ 54 97 18 34

Savonnières
Hôtel du Faisan ✳
Le Bourg
37510 Savonnières
☎ 47 50 00 17

Sully-sur-Loire
Hôtel La Post ✳✳
11 Rue du Fbg St Germain
45600 Sully-sur-Loire
☎ 38 36 26 22

Tours
*Hôtel Le Parc de
    Belmont* ✳✳✳
57 Rue Groison
37000 Tours
☎ 47 41 41 11

Eating Out

Amboise
Le Manoir St Thomas ✳✳✳
1 Mail St Thomas
37400 Amboise
☎ 47 57 22 52

Blois
L'Orangerie du Château ✳✳
1 Avenue Dr Jean Laigret
41000 Blois
☎ 54 78 05 36

Briare
Hostellerie Le Canal ✳✳
19 Rue du Pont Canal
45250 Briare
☎ 38 31 22 54

Cinq-Mars-la-Pile
Hôtel du Centre ✳
4 Rue de la Loire
37130 Cinq-Mars-la-Pile
☎ 47 96 40 33

Montrichard
Hôtel Du Courrier ✳
4 Route de Blois
41400 Montrichard
☎ 54 32 04 42

Orléans
Les Antiquaires ✳✳✳
2-4 Rue au Lin
45000 Orléans
☎ 38 53 52 35

L'Ambroise ✳
222 Rue de Bourgogne
45000 Orléans
☎ 38 68 13 33

Pithiviers
Hôtel La Chaumiere ✳✳
77 Avenue de la Rèpublique

45300 Pithiviers
☎ 38 30 03 61

Richelieu
Hôtel le Puits Dore ✳✳
24 Place du Marché
37120 Richelieu
☎ 47 58 10 59

Romorantin-Lanthenay
La Cabriere ✳
30 Avenue de Villefranche
41200 Romorantin-
    Lanthenay
☎ 54 76 38 94

Tours
Le Coq d'Or ✳✳
272 Avenue de Grammont
37000 Tours
☎ 47 20 39 51

Vendôme
Jardin du Loir ✳
6 Place de la Madeleine
41100 Vendôme
☎ 54 77 20 79

Chapter 10 •
Berry-Bourbonnais

Accommodation

Aubigny-sur-Nère
Hôtel Le Central ✳
6 Rue du Château
18700 Aubigny-sur-Nère
☎ 48 58 17 18

Bourbon l'Archimbault
Hôtel Sources ✳✳
Avenue Thermes
03160 Bourbon
    l'Archimbault
☎ 70 67 00 15

Bourges
Hôtel Le Christina ✳✳
5 Rue de la Halle
18000 Bourges
☎ 48 70 56 50

Bruère-Allichamps
Hôtel Les Tilleuls ✳
Route de Noirlac
18200 Bruère-Allichamps
☎ 48 61 02 75

Issoudun
Hôtel de France et
Commerce ✳✳
3 Rue Pierre Brossolette
36100 Issoudun
☎ 54 21 00 65

Levroux
Hôtel La Cloche ✳
3 Rue Nationale
36110 Levroux
☎ 54 35 70 43

Mézières-en-Brenne
Hôtel du Boeuf Couronne ✳
9 Place du Général de
Gaulle
36290 Mézières-en-Brenne
☎ 54 38 04 39

Montluçon
Hôtel Univers ✳✳
38 Avenue Marx Dormoy
03100 Montluçon
☎ 70 05 33 47

Moulins
Hôtel Parc ✳
31 Avenue Général Leclerc
03000 Moulins
☎ 70 44 12 25

Nançay
Hôtel Auberge les
Meaulnes ✳✳
Le Bourg
18330 Nançay
☎ 48 51 81 15

Valençay
Hôtel d'Espagne ✳✳✳
9 Rue du Château
36600 Valençay
☎ 54 00 00 02

Vichy
Hôtel Régina ✳✳✳
4 Avenue Thermale
03200 Vichy
☎ 70 98 20 95

Eating Out

Argenton-sur-Creuse
L'Hôtel de France ✳✳
8 Rue Jean Jacques Rousseau
36200 Argenton-sur-Creuse
☎ 54 24 03 31

Bourges
Ile d'Or ✳
39 Boulevard Juranville
18000 Bourges
☎ 48 24 29 15

Le Jacques Coeur ✳✳✳
3 Place Jacques Coeur
18000 Bourges
☎ 48 70 12 72

Châteauroux
L'Assiette ✳✳
Place de la Gare
36000 Châteauroux
☎ 54 34 01 18

Issoudun
Pile ou Face ✳
11 Rue Danièle Casanova
36100 Issoudun
☎ 54 03 14 91

La Châtre
L'Auberge du Moulin
Bureau ✳
53 Rue de Faubourg St Abdon
36400 La Châtre
☎ 54 48 04 20

Moulins
Des Cours ✳✳✳
36 Cours J. Jaurès
03000 Moulins
☎ 70 44 32 56

St Pourçain-sur-Sioule
Hostellerie des Cours ✳
Boulevard Ledru-Rollin
03500 St Pourçain-sur-
Sioule
☎ 70 45 31 92

Sancerre
De La Tour ✳✳
31 Place de la Halle
18300 Sancerre
☎ 48 54 00 81

Souvigny
Auberge des Tilleuls ✳
03210 Souvigny
☎ 70 43 60 70

Vichy
Brasserie du Casino ✳✳
4 Rue Casino
03200 Vichy
☎ 70 98 23 06

Vierzon
Hôtel le Berry Nord ✳✳
21 Rue du Dr Roux
18100 Vierzon
☎ 48 75 03 96

Chapter 11 •
Burgundy

Accommodation and
Eating Out

Arnay-le-Duc
Chez Camille ✳✳
☎ 80 90 01 38
With accommodation.

Joigny
A la Côte St-Jacques ✳✳✳
☎ 86 62 09 70
With accommodation.

Levernois
(Nr Beaune)
Host de Levernois ✳✳✳
☎ 80 24 73 58
With accommodation.

Mâcon
Rocher de Cancale ✳✳
☎ 85 38 07 50

Marcenay
(Nr Châtillon-sur-Seine)
Le Santenoy ✳
☎ 80 81 40 08
With accommodation.

Meursault
Relais de la Diligence ✳
☎ 80 21 21 32

Paray-le-Monial
Vendanges de
Bourgogne ✳✳
☎ 85 81 13 43
With accommodation.

Saulieu
Le Côte d'Or ✳✳✳
☎ 80 64 07 66
With accommodation.

Le Lion d'Or ✳
☎ 80 64 16 33
With accommodation.

Semur-en-Auxois
3km (2 miles) south
Le Lac ✳
☎ 80 97 11 11
With accommodation.

Tournus
Restaurant Greuze ✳✳✳
☎ 85 51 13 52

Vincelottes (Nr Auxerre)
Aub Les Tilleuls ✳✳
☎ 86 42 22 13
With accommodation.

Chapter 12 •
The Jura

Accommodation

Arbois
Les Messageries ✳✳
Promenade Pasteur
Arbois 39600
☎ 84 66 15 45

Arc-et-Senans
Le Relais ✳
Place de l'Eglise
Arc-et-Senans 25610
☎ 81 57 40 60

Bois D'Amont
Hôtel Club Risoux ✳✳
Bois D'Amont 39200
Swimming pool and sauna
☎ 84 60 94 24

Charquemont
Haut-Doubs Hotel ✳✳
Swimming pool
Charquemont 25140
☎ 81 44 01 82

Goumois
Hôtel Taillard ✳✳✳
Goumois 25470
☎ 81 44 20 75

Lajoux
Hôtel de la Haute Montagne ✳
Lajoux 39310
☎ 84 41 20 47

Maiche
Hôtel Des Combes ✳✳
Maiche 25120
☎ 81 64 09 36

Malbuisson
Le Lac ✳✳✳
Grande Rue
Malbuisson 25160
☎ 81 69 34 80

Morez
Hôtel de la Poste ✳✳
1 rue du Docteur Régad
Morez 39400
☎ 84 33 11 03

Poligny
*Hostellerie des Monts de
    Vaux* ✳✳✳
Poligny 39800
☎ 84 37 12 50

St Laurent en Grandvaux
*Hôtel Moulin des Truites
    Bleues* ✳✳✳
☎ 84 60 83 03

St Maurice
Au Bon Séjour ✳
Saint Maurice 39130
☎ 84 25 82 80

Eating Out

Arbois
Jean-Paul Jeunet ✳✳✳
Le Paris
Rue de l'Hôtel de Ville
Arbois 39600
☎ 84 66 05 67
Closed Tue and Wed
lunchtimes off season.

La Finette ✳✳
22 avenue Pasteur
Arbois 39600
☎ 84 66 06 78

Bonlieu
La Poutre ✳✳✳
Bonlieu 39130
☎ 84 25 57 77

Consolation
Restaurant de la Source ✳✳
Cirque de Consolation
Consolation 25390
☎ 81 43 55 38

Crançot
Le Belvédère ✳✳
Crançot 39570
☎ 84 48 22 18

Goumois
*Auberge le Moulin
du Plain* ✳✳
Goumois 25470
☎ 81 44 41 99

Les Rousses
*Restaurant de l'Hôtel de
    France* ✳✳✳
Les Rousses 39200
☎ 84 60 01 45

Maiche
Restaurant Ferme du Gey ✳
Maiche 25120
☎ 81 64 02 74

Nozeroy
Taverne des Remparts ✳
Nozeroy 39250
☎ 84 51 18 45

Poligny
La Vallée Heureuse ✳✳✳
Route de Genève
Poligny 39800
☎ 84 37 12 13
Closed Wednesday and
Thursday lunchtimes off
season.

St Laurent en Grandvaux
Auberge des Sapins ✳
Saint Laurent en
Grandvaux 39150
☎ 84 60 83 90

Salins-Les-Bains
Au Festin de Babette ✳
8 rue Liberté
Salins-Les-Bains 39110
☎ 84 37 90 79

Chapter 13 •
Poitou-Charentes

Accommodation and
Eating Out

All hotels have restau-
rants unless otherwise
stated.

Angoulême
Novotel ✳✳✳
Champniers
☎ 45 68 53 22

Comfortable, modern hotel, just north of the town, on the Poitiers road.

Celles-sur-Belle
Hostellerie de l'Abbaye ✳
Place Eglise
☎ 49 32 93 32

Cognac
Restaurant le Coq d'Or ✳✳
Place François I
☎ 45 82 02 56

Coulon
Hôtel le Central ✳
Rue d'Autremont
☎ 49 35 90 20

Auberge de l'Ecluse ✳✳
La Sotterie
☎ 49 35 90 42
Welcoming restaurant just outside Coulon.

Echiré
Motel des Rocs ✳✳
☎ 49 25 50 38
Very pleasant, quiet hotel in pretty grounds.

Parthenay
Hôtel St Jacques ✳
Avenue du 114e
☎ 49 64 33 33
(no hotel restaurant)
Well situated just outside old part of the town, but within walking distance of shops, sights, restaurants.

Poitiers
Hôtel Ibis-Beaulieu ✳
Quartier Beaulieu
☎ 49 61 11 02
Situated outside, but

within easy reach (and parking) of, the centre.

Auberge de la Cigogne ✳✳
Rue Planty
Buxerolles
☎ 49 45 61 47
Super restaurant, on opposite side of the river to, but within easy reach of, Poitiers city centre.

La Rochelle
Hôtel St Jean d'Acre/
Restaurant Au Vieux
Port ✳✳/✳✳✳
Place Chaine
☎ 46 41 73 33
Delightful hotel, with seafood restaurant, overlooking the Old Harbour.

Royan
Golf Hôtel ✳✳
Boulevard Garnier
☎ 46 05 14 66
(no hotel restaurant)
Opposite the beach, with views across the Gironde.

St Jean d'Angely
Hôtel de la Paix ✳
Allées d'Aussy
☎ 46 32 00 93

St Savin
Hôtel de France ✳✳
Place de la République
☎ 49 48 19 21

Saintes
Hôtel Avenue/Brasserie
Louis ✳
Avenue Gambetta
☎ 46 74 05 91
Modernised friendly hotel, with bustling brasserie, close to the abbey.

Thouars
Hôtel du Château ✳
Route de Parthenay
☎ 49 96 12 60
Some nice views, and a good value restaurant.

Château de la Roche ✳✳✳
Argenton l'Eglise
☎ 49 67 02 38
Delightful sixteenth-century Renaissance château, slightly north of Thouars at Argenton l'Eglise. Dinner available on request.

Vibrac
Hôtel des Ombrages ✳✳
☎ 45 97 32 33
Pleasant, quiet hotel, well placed for touring.

In addition to the hotels listed above, the *Ibis* and *Campanile* chains offer inexpensive, and very good value, two-star hotels in, or on the edge of, many towns and cities in the Poitou-Charentes. Whilst they are modern, and perhaps lack individual character, they are clean, well managed, and welcoming. All have restaurants, and are well versed in dealing with children — family rooms are often available. Both chains can book forward accommodation at other hotels in their chain.

Index

Page numbers in **bold** type indicate maps